German
Without the Fuss

BY

Helga Schier, Ph.D.

EDITED BY Zvjezdana Vrzić, Ph.D.

AUTHOR'S ACKNOWLEDGMENTS

I wish to thank my editor, Zvjezdana Vrzić, who kept me on my toes; my children, Sebastian and Gabriel,

who walked on theirs outside my office; and my husband, whose steady stride helped move us all along.

PUBLISHER'S ACKNOWLEDGMENTS

Thanks to the Living Language team: Tom Russell, Elizabeth Bennett, Christopher Warnasch,

Suzanne McQuade, Amelia Muqaddam, Denise De Gennaro, Linda Schmidt, John Whitman,

Alison Skrabek, Helen Kilcullen, Heather Lanigan, Fabrizio La Rocca, Guido Caroti, and Sophie Chin.

Special thanks to Annette Apitz who reviewed the manuscript.

Editor: Zvjezdana Vrzić
Production Editor: John Whitman
Production Managers: Helen Kilcullen and Heather Lanigan
Interior Design: Sophie Chin

First Edition
ISBN 1-4000-2083-2

Library of Congress Cataloging-in-Publication Data available upon request.

CONTENTS

WHAT'S GOING ON IN THE DIALOGUES	WHAT WORDS YOU'LL LEARN	WHAT STRUCTURES YOU'LL KNOW

WHAT'S GOING ON IN THE DIALOGUES	WHAT WORDS YOU'LL LEARN	WHAT STRUCTURES YOU'LL KNOW

WHAT'S GOING ON IN THE DIALOGUES	WHAT WORDS YOU'LL LEARN	WHAT STRUCTURES YOU'LL KNOW

Lesson 15: TO EACH HIS OWN • 259

WHAT'S GOING ON IN THE DIALOGUES	WHAT WORDS YOU'LL LEARN	WHAT STRUCTURES YOU'LL KNOW
Jedem Tierchen sein Pläsierchen The two people who met by accident enjoy a casual evening together	• **I won't take no for an answer:** How to convince and (not) be convinced • **You are so beautiful!** Paying compliments and accepting them gracefully	• **Coordinating conjunctions:** *aber, und,* and *oder* • **When you're ill, you've got an illness:** Word formation • **Alternatives to the passive voice**

GERMAN WITHOUT THE FUSS

ABBREVIATIONS

acc.	accusative
adj.	adjective
adv.	adverb
art.	article
coll.	colloquial
conj.	conjunction
dat.	dative
def.	definite
dir.	direct
fml.	formal
f.	feminine
gen.	genitive
infml.	informal
lit.	literal
m.	masculine
neut.	neuter
n.	noun
obj.	object
pl.	plural
prep.	preposition
pron.	pronoun
poss.	possessive
sg.	singular

WELCOME!

So you want to learn some *Deutsch?* But you don't want to do it by just memorizing long verb conjugation charts or ever-handy stock phrases like "Jeeves, please serve the mutton to the ambassador at eight." If that's the case, then you've come to the right place! *Herzlich Willkommen!* Welcome!

German Without the Fuss will help you learn as quickly and easily as possible, and the best part is, you'll have fun along the way. You'll have a chance to hear real talk, the kind you might actually hear on the street and not just read in textbooks. And you won't need a crash course in grammar jargon before you start. We've tried to make this book as accessible and user-friendly as possible. Of course, this doesn't mean you'll just wake up one morning fluent in German. The bad news is: You will have to do some studying, but the good news is: it won't be dry and boring. That you can count on.

So, what's *German Without the Fuss* all about? Well, you'll start off with an introduction to the sounds of the language. German is fairly easy that way; what you see is pretty much what you get, so you should be able to start speaking right off the bat. Then we really get down to business with 15 lessons, and an hour-long audio CD to give you plenty of listening and speaking practice. There are appendices, too, for quick reference if you get stuck, and a two-way glossary where you can look up any word in the book.

To make things easy, all the lessons have the same structure, and it's not just any structure—it's been scientifically designed to help you learn most effectively. Yes, we have the technology! Here's the basic layout of each lesson:

COMING UP . . .
Get a quick overview of what you'll learn in the lesson.

LOOKING AHEAD . . .
Get ready to listen to (and actually understand) the lesson's dialogues with some advanced info and tips to help you follow along.

LET'S WARM UP
Think ahead about the topic of the dialogue by doing a fun activity and learn a few new words so you can get more out of it.

HEAR . . . SAY
Listen to a dialogue, try to understand as much as you can, then read along and learn to speak by repeating the phrases from the audio CD.

HOW'S THAT AGAIN?
Check whether you got the gist of the dialogue.

WORKSHOP
Discover the secrets of the German language: **learn about its words and structure.**

WORDS TO LIVE BY
Stock up on new words and phrases and get to use them, too.

THE NITTY-GRITTY
Overcome your fear of grammar with simple explanations and plenty of practice.

TAKE IT FOR A SPIN
Practice makes perfect! Try out all the good stuff you've just learned.

LET'S PUT IT IN WRITING
Read all about it! Authentic texts help you learn to maneuver through the written word.

TAKE IT UP A NOTCH
Challenge yourself with additional practice that'll really make you think!

STRUT YOUR STUFF
Put it all together and review what you've learned with more practice, practice, practice.

CRIB SHEET
Get answers to all your questions, and check the translations of the dialogues.

But that's not all! You'll also get loads of good stuff that will spice up your learning, teach you how best to learn a new language, what pitfalls to avoid, and tell you about the culture and habits of the place. All at no extra cost!

TAKE A TIP FROM ME
Be smart and get the most out of your efforts—you'll **get tips on how to study,** shortcuts, and memory tricks.

HEADS UP!
Watch for the pitfalls and common mistakes typically made by new learners!

THE FINE PRINT
Get ambitious and **learn more about grammar or vocabulary.**

WORD ON THE STREET
Talk like a real German: learn common expressions, idioms, and even slang terms, so you won't sound like an out-of-date textbook.

DID YOU KNOW?
Get in the know by learning about Germany, Austria and Switzerland, their culture and the everyday life of the people. A great place to start not just talking like a German, or an Austrian or a Swiss, but feeling like one, too.

So, that's it! You're ready to start. Good luck, or as we say in German, *Viel Glück!*

GETTING STARTED IN GERMAN

BEFORE WE BEGIN

Let's talk a little bit about language learning in general. The first thing you need to know is: YOU KNOW MORE THAN YOU THINK! You don't believe me? Check out some of these words: *Alligator, Arm, Bank, blind, blond, Bus, Butter, elegant, Finger, Hamburger, Hand, Hotel, Idiot, Information, international, modern, Moment, Museum, Name, Nation, Orange, Problem, Radio, Religion, Restaurant, Rose, Service, Signal, Sport, Taxi, Tennis, Tunnel, wild, Wind.* So? What's the big deal, right? You already know English! Well, as it turns out, this means that you also already know some German because these words are spelled exactly the same and have the same meaning in both languages: They are perfect cognates, identical twins. The only difference is that in German they're pronounced a little differently, and that the nouns start with a capital letter. Well, that's easy enough, isn't it? And to make things REALLY easy, German has simply borrowed many words straight from English. Just look: *Babysitter, Boss, City, cool, Design, Dress Code, E-Mail, Fashion, Feeling, Fast Food, hip, Hit, Jet Set, Job, Jogging, Manager, Marketing, Party, Ranking, Shopping, Show, Steak, Thriller,* and the list goes on and on and on.

There are also many fraternal twins between English and German, or near cognates, words that are very similar but not exactly the same, but their meanings are easy to recognize. See for yourself:

Adresse	address	*Autor*	author
amerikanisch	American	*Bruder*	brother
Bluse	blouse	*Blut*	blood
Buch	book	*blau*	blue
Doktor	doctor	*Familie*	family
Elefant	elephant	*Kaffee*	coffee
Herz	heart	*Lampe*	lamp
gut	good	*Ding*	thing
kalt	cold	*lang*	long
Preis	price	*Medizin*	medicine
Musik	music	*Salat*	salad
Natur	nature	*Schuh*	shoe
Qualität	quality	*Salz*	salt
Tomate	tomato	*Schiff*	ship
Telefon	telephone	*Warnung*	warning
Zentrum	center	*populär*	popular
Wetter	weather	*Parfüm*	perfume
Konversation	conversation		

You get the idea. For the curious among you, the reason that so many English words look like German words, or so many German words look like English words, is that German and English have the same roots: they are both Germanic languages. That means that once upon a long long long time ago, German and English were almost like two dialects of the same language. The interesting part is that the similarities go even further. German and English don't only have word roots in common, they also have a few similar word endings. Take a look:

COMMON GERMAN WORD ENDINGS AND THEIR ENGLISH COUNTERPARTS

GERMAN	ENGLISH	EXAMPLE
-tät	-ty	*Realität* = reality
		Universität = university
		Formalität = formality
-ion	-ion	*Konversation* = conversation
		Information = information
		Diskussion = discussion
-ie	-y	*Harmonie* = harmony
		Symphonie = symphony
		Theorie = theory
-ell/-al	-al	*generell* = general
		universell = universal
		normal = normal
		ideal/ideell = ideal
-ent/-ant	-ent/-ant	*intelligent* = intelligent
		tolerant = tolerant
		elegant = elegant

And if you're feeling confident now, just wait! There's a lot more to *Kommunikation* (communication, of course) than just words and grammar. It's amazing how much you can glean from a *Konversation* (conversation) just by looking at facial expressions and body language. Try this sometime: watch a movie or a sitcom and mute the sound. You'll be surprised by how well you'll be in tune with what's going on without hearing a single word spoken.

And there's also *die Kultur* (You guessed it!). Communication happens in context, and the more you know about the context of daily life in German speaking countries and their rich history, the more easily you'll be able to read between the lines, get the point, and get your own message across. And don't worry, you're not on your own here either—there'll be plenty of cultural tidbits and information to help you impress (or fool!) even the most discerning locals.

Okay, so now that your head is probably bigger than your doorway and you're wondering why you need to study another language in the first place, let's get serious for a moment. The truth is (you might want to sit down for this) that despite how much you already know, you still have a lot to learn. (Do I sound like your parents, or what?) The good news is that I'll be there to help, not just by telling you WHAT you need to learn but by giving you some tips on HOW to do it easily and well.

Take a Tip from Me

Here comes my first tip: Pace yourself. Try to come up with a working schedule and set goals. Ideally, you will spend a little bit of time on your German every day—sometimes thirty minutes a day will go a lot further than two hours in one sitting. But if you can't manage to find time every day, don't despair: Just try to work regularly, and grab a free moment here and there to remind yourself of what you've learned. Take advantage of your free time—maybe you can rent a German movie on a movie night (subtitles are just fine!) or pop in some German music while you're cooking dinner. Many musicians, actors, filmmakers, painters, and writers from German-speaking countries are mentioned in this book. Check them out! Do anything you like, but do it *auf Deutsch!* The goal is to get as much and as varied an exposure to German as possible. Words and expressions have a way of creeping into your memory. You'll see, trust me. The most important thing is to have fun.

Genug geredet! Enough said! *Fertig?* Are you ready? *Los geht's!* Let's get started! Let's talk about German pronunciation.

SOUNDING IT OUT IN GERMAN

When it comes to pronunciation, you're in luck, because what you see is pretty much what you get. What I mean is that, unlike English, with its seemingly endless pronunciation rules which are forever being broken, German pronunciation rules are simple and straightforward. German words sound pretty much the way they look—their spelling is virtually phonetic. As long as you remember a few rules, you should sound like a German speaker in no time!

ABC'S

English and German share the same alphabet, even if the sound value of the letters, and their names, may be a little different sometimes.

THE GERMAN ALPHABET

a	[ah]	n	[ehn]
b	[beh]	o	[oh]
c	[tseh]	p	[peh]
d	[deh]	q	[koo]
e	[eh]	r	[er]
f	[ef]	s	[es]
g	[geh]	t	[teh]
h	[hah]	u	[oo]
i	[ee]	v	[fow]
j	[yot]	w	[veh]
k	[kah]	x	[eeks]
l	[el]	y	[üpseelon]
m	[em]	z	[tset]

Now that we have the alphabet out of the way, let's spend some time on individual sounds.

BASIC VOWEL SOUNDS

German vowels can be long or short. (In German, vowels are never silent.) As a simple rule, if the vowel is followed by two consonants, it is short. If, on the other hand, only a single consonant, another vowel or an "h" follows, it is long. If the vowel is at the end of the word, it is usually short but always pronounced.

BASIC VOWEL SOUNDS

LETTER	PRONOUNCED AS . . .	AS IN . . .
a	ah (short, as in "cup")	Mann, Stadt
	ah (long, as in "father")	W<u>a</u>hl, Wagen
e	eh (short, as in "bet")	Bett, schmecken
	eh (long, as in "hey," but without the ending "y")	M<u>ee</u>r, M<u>e</u>hl
i	ee (short, as in "winter")	Wind, Winter
	ee (long, as in "b<u>ee</u>t")	ihr, Tiger
o	oh (short, as in "hop")	Loch, kochen
	oh (long, as in "rose")	B<u>oo</u>t, Ohr
u	oo (short, as in "sh<u>oo</u>k")	Mutter, Butter
	oo (long, as in "st<u>oo</u>l")	Schuh, Fuß

THE *UMLAUTE*

The letters *a*, *o*, and *u* like to dress up with two little dots above them sometimes, as in *ä*, *ö*, and *ü*. Those two dots are called *der Umlaut* and show that the letters are to be pronounced differently.

UMLAUTED VOWELS		
LETTER	PRONOUNCED AS . . .	AS IN . . .
ä	very similar to the German letter "e," pronounced *eh* (short, as in "bet")	Männer
	very similar to the English letter "a" long, as in "bare,"	Mähne
ö	say *eh* with your lips very rounded (similar to "fur," but short)	möchte
	say *eh* with your lips very rounded (similar to "fur," but long)	mögen
ü	say a short *ee* with your lips very pouted and rounded	Glück
	say a long *ee* with your lips very pouted and rounded	Lüge

Take a Tip from Me

When you first begin to speak, do some warm-up exercises to loosen your mouth. Say all of the vowels in order (a-e-i-o-u), going from one vowel right into the next, and stretching your mouth as much as possible on each sound. Do this LOUDLY! Stand in front of a mirror and watch your mouth as you make each sound. When you're speaking, try to imitate a German speaker—try to feel the language, its melodic intonation. Exaggerate the sounds a little. Yes, it'll probably feel silly, but silly can be fun, too, and it will help you loosen up and get over the embarrassment of speaking—aaaaaaaah!—a foreign language! Also, try to get as much listening practice as you can. Hearing the sounds pronounced by a native speaker will help you develop an ear for the language, which will in turn improve the way you pronounce words. *Langsam aber sicher,* slowly but surely you'll be able to tell if something "just sounds right" or not, and that's your goal.

TWO-VOWEL COMBINATIONS

Okay, so now that we have the oohs and aahs in order, what happens when you have two vowels in a row? You get sounds, with the curious name "diphthongs," where the two vowels flow naturally one into the other, as when you say *Oy, vey!,* for instance. Here they are in German:

COMMON VOWEL COMBINATIONS		
LETTERS	PRONOUNCED AS . . .	AS IN . . .
ei, ai	*ay* (as in cry, e<u>ye</u>)	*klein, Mai*
au	*ow* (as in c<u>ow</u>)	*Haut, Sauerkraut*
eu, äu	*oy* (as in t<u>oy</u>)	*neu, Häute*

Heads Up!

Don't confuse the letter combination "ie," pronounced like the *ee* in "f<u>ee</u>t," with the diphthong "ei." "ie" is simply a long *ee,* whereas the vowel-combination "ei" sounds like the English word "e<u>ye</u>." Think *Bier* (beer) versus *Wein* (vayn).

Well then, that does it for vowels. Now let's take a look at the consonants.

PSSSST . . . !: CONSONANT SOUNDS

The good news about consonants is that most of them sound just like they do in English: a "b' is a *b*, and a "d" is a *d*. Other letters that are pronounced pretty much the same as in English are: "f," "g," "h," "k," "m," "n," "p," "q," "s," "t," and "x." *Kein Problem!* No problem.

But there are a few consonants that deserve a closer look.

"C" AND "Z": YOU'RE NUTS!

In German, the letter "c" is pronounced like *ts* in "nu<u>ts</u>" whenever it occurs before "ä," "e," "i," or "ö": *Ceylon* (tsey-lohn), *Celsius* (tsehl-see-yoos), *Cäsar* (tseh-zahr). Otherwise it is a *k* sound: *Computer* (kohm-pyoo-tehr), *Café* (kah-feh), or *Clown* (klown).

Like "c," the letter "z" sounds just like the *ts* in "nuts" as well: *Zug* (tsoog), *Zimmer* (tsee-mehr), *Zar* (tsahr).

"H": TO PRONOUNCE OR NOT TO PRONOUNCE

At the beginning of a word, "h" is pronounced just like its English equivalent: *Hotel.* In the middle of a word, the German "h" is always silent and only serves to make the preceding vowel longer—*Stuhl* (shtool).

"J": JA, I MEAN "YES"

The letter "j" in German has the sound of *y* in "yes." That's easy to remember, after all, *ja* means "yes."

Note that the "j" in *Jeans* is pronounced just like the English "j," and that is because the word has been taken from the English, complete with pronunciation and all. Other such words are: *John* and *Jumbo Jet.*

"L:" LIGHTEN UP!

Lighten up! The German letter "l" has a much lighter sound than its English counterpart; it is formed with the tip of the tongue just behind the upper front teeth.

"R": DON'T FORGET TO GARGLE!

In order to pronounce an "r" in German, you need to raise the back of your tongue towards your tonsils, as if you were gargling. Take a look at these German words and see how well you can gargle the German "r"s:

Radio	(rah-dee-oh)
rot	(roht)

| *Rose* | (roh-seh) |
| *Reis* | (rais) |

"ß": WHAT'S THAT SOUND?

The letter "ß" represents the *s* sound, as in *Straße* (shtrah-seh). This sound can also be represented by a double "ss," as in *nass* (nahs). As a rule, the "ß" appears after long vowels, whereas the "ss" is used after or between two short vowels. For example: *der Fuß* (foos) but *der Kuss* (koos).

VW BUGS: "V" VERSUS "W"

The German "v" is mostly pronounced like an *f*: *Vater* (fah-tehr), *viel* (feel). If however, the word has been borrowed from another language, such as French, the "v" is pronounced like the English "v": *Vase* (vah-seh).

The German "w," however, is always pronounced like the English "v": *Wasser* (vahsehr), *Wurst* (voorst). Just think of that classical German car, the *VW Käfer* (fow-veh kehfehr), and you won't ever mix up these two letters.

CONSONANT COMBINATIONS

There are a few consonant combinations in German you should know about.

"CH": THE SOUND OF GERMAN

"ch" is the letter combination that stands for a sound that makes German sound German. It is probably the most challenging German sound for an English speaker. Don't despair. To make the sound just imagine you are a hissing cat. For example, to say *ich* (I), simply pronounce a short *ee* and then make a hissing sound by pressing the middle of your tongue against the roof of your mouth and letting air escape through the narrow gap: *eeH*.

After the vowels *a*, *o* and *u*, "ch" is pronounced slightly differently: You get ready to "gargle" a German "r", but do not gargle, let air escape through the narrow gap far back in your throat: *ooH*.

Try the same thing with these words:

sicher	(see-Hehr)
manchmal	(mahnH-mahl)
wichtig	(veeH-teeH)

But:

Rache	(rah-Heh)
kochen	(koh-Hen)
Buch	(booH)

A common German ending *-ig* also ends in the sound *H*, as in:

richtig	(reeH-teeH)
wichtig	(weeH-teeH)

Heads Up!

When "ch" is at the beginning of a word, it is pronounced like a *k: Charakter* (kah-rahk-tehr).

And when "ch" is followed by the letter "s," the combination of letters, "chs," is simply pronounced like the English "x." Easy to remember, because "chs" shows up in the word *Fuchs*, which is a "fox."

"PF": PFFFFFFT—THE AIR IS OUT

"pf" is a rather common consonant combination in German and a bit hard to pronounce as well. Don't worry, just let your mind wander and imagine you are a balloon loosing air: pffffffff. Let's practice:

Pferd	(pfehrd)
Pforte	(pfohr-teh)
Pfarrer	(pfaah-rehr)

"SCH," "SP," "ST": SHHHHHHH!

All three letter combinations with "s" sound like the English letter combination "sh:" *Schule* (shoo-leh), *Sport* (shpohrt), *Stern* (shtehrn). When the letter "s" is followed by a vowel, it is pronounced as a *z*, just like in the English word "zoo:" *Sonne* (zoh-neh), *sieben* (zee-behn), *süß* (züs).

Take a Tip from Me

One of the best ways to improve your pronunciation is to hear yourself speak. University language classes require visits to the language lab where you can record yourself pronouncing assigned words or phrases and then compare your pronunciation to a native speaker's. Now, you don't have to invest thousands of dollars in a personal language lab, but you might want to consider spending a few bucks on a cassette voice recorder or a microphone for your computer. Then, as you work through the lessons, record yourself reading the dialogues in this book after you've listened to them on the CD. You can also record yourself reading individual words from this section, liner notes to a German music CD, a recipe from a German cookbook, a menu swiped from a German restaurant, or anything else you can get your hands on, as long as it's in German. Just listen to yourself speak. You'll be surprised by how easy it is for you to spot (and correct) your typical mistakes.

Okay, so now we've talked about the sounds that make up the German language. But how are these sounds combined into words?

Can You Handle Stress?

Sure you can! Word stress, that is. Word stress is the emphasis placed on one or more syllables of a word when you pronounce it. German words of one or more syllables are generally stressed on the first syllable, as in: *Farbe* (FAHR-beh), *Frage* (FRAH-geh), *Sprache* (SHPRAH-Heh), *Liebhaber* (LEEB-hah-behr). Foreign words such as *Hotel* (hoh-TEHL), *Musik* (moo-ZEEK), *Universität* (oo-nee-vehr-zee-TEHT) do not follow the German rules of stress, but they follow all other pronunciation rules.

Well, that's it on the sounds (and the stress!) of German. But before I let you go, one final word of advice: Never let the fear of saying something less than perfectly (whether it be due to a pronunciation or grammar or vocabulary problem) stop you from talking to someone. Even if you make a mistake, chances are that you will be understood, and that is your main goal in learning any language. Think of all the people you encounter who speak English with an accent, and yet you can do business with them, discuss politics with them, get to know them. The only way to learn to speak a foreign language is to actually speak it. Painfully obvious, I know, but you'd be surprised how many people seem to lose sight of this simple fact. Don't let that be you.

I've said my piece, so now we can move on and get down to business. *Los geht's!* Let's go! Lesson 1 awaits.

Viel Spaß! Have fun!

BIRDS OF A FEATHER FLOCK TOGETHER

Gleich und gleich gesellt sich gern
(Lit. Same likes to join with same)

COMING UP . . .

- *That's what I do:* Talking about professions

- *Hello, my name is . . . :* How to meet and greet people and say good-bye in German

- *Me, you, and my pet dog, too:* Personal pronouns

- *To be or not to be:* The verb *sein* in the present tense

- *Just say "no":* Negation with *nicht*

- *Is it a boy or a girl?* The gender of German nouns

- *(In)definitely so:* "The" and "a/an" in German

LOOKING AHEAD . . .

Hallo. Wie geht's? Hi, how's it going? Or if you like it a bit more formal, *Guten Tag! Wie geht es Ihnen?* Good day! How are you? *Gut,* I hope. In this first lesson you'll learn what to say in German when you meet people, and also . . . what not to say. It's happened to all of us. In an effort not to come across like an ignoramus, you say . . . the wrong thing. Relax! You are about to have a fun and exciting experience, the one of learning a new language and encountering a new *Kultur.* This task may seem a bit intimidating at first, but there's no need to go for perfection. Mistakes are a part of the learning process. I, your personal teacher, will lead you every step of the way. *Also, fertig?* So, are you ready? Let's get started. *Fangen wir an!*

ACTIVITY 1: LET'S WARM UP

I know you think you don't know any German. Think again, and I'm sure you'll figure out what these words and phrases mean. Match the German on the left with the correct English counterpart on the right.

1.	*Hallo.*	a.	That's a Porsche.
2.	*Gut.*	b.	How are you?
3.	*Danke.*	c.	Thanks.
4.	*Das ist ein Porsche.*	d.	Hello.
5.	*Wie geht's?*	e.	Good.

Take a Tip from Me!

The importance of listening to a new language as much as possible cannot be overstated. In the beginning, anewlanguagesoundslikeajumbleofsoundsandit'sveryhardtotelllonewordfromanother. Right? Listening trains your ear. At first all you'll notice will be the sounds and melody of the language. But before you know it, you'll be able to tell apart the different words. Practice makes perfect, so whenever possible, listen to the dialogues a few times before you read along or look at the translation provided at the end of the lesson. As you would in actual everyday conversations with Germans, listen, try to get the gist of what's being said rather than obsess over getting every single word.

So, let's do it: Pop in that CD and hit "play." *Los geht's!* Let's go.

In front of the *Kaffeehaus* »*Zur Krone*« in München Sebastian accidentally bumps into Gabriele. Gabriele drops her *Tasche* (bag) to the floor, and Sebastian bends to pick it up. They don't know each other. Or do they . . . ?

Sebastian: Oh, Entschuldigung. Hier.

Sebastian picks Gabriele's bag up and hands it to her.

Gabriele: Ach, das macht nichts. Und danke.

Gabriele wants to move on, but Sebastian, intrigued by her looks, doesn't let her go.

Sebastian: Bitte, gern geschehen. Kennen wir uns nicht?

Gabriele: Nein.

Sebastian: Doch. Sie sind aus Stuttgart, nicht wahr? Und Ihr Name ist Susanne Berger.

Gabriele: Ich heiße nicht Susanne Berger. Und ich bin auch nicht aus Stuttgart.

Gabriele is still trying to move on, but Sebastan just won't let go.

Sebastian: Ich heiße Sebastian. Sebastian Maier. Und Sie?

Gabriele: Gabriele.

Sebastian: Schön, Sie kennenzulernen. Gabriele ist ein schöner Name.

Gabriele can't believe her ears. This is probably the oldest come-on in history.

Gabriele: Danke. Nun entschuldigen Sie mich bitte. Ich bin in Eile.

Sebastian: Vielleicht später?

Gabriele: (rolling her eyes) Auf Wiedersehen.

Sebastian: Auf Wiedersehen.

Gabriele rushes off. Sebastian is about to turn the other way when he notices that something fell out of Gabriele's bag. He tries to run after her, but she has disappeared already.

Sebastian: Moment mal, Gabriele, ich. . . .

HOW'S THAT AGAIN?

Yes or no? *Ja oder nein?* Let's see how much of the dialogue you understood. You can answer in English or in German—a word will do.

1. Do Gabriele and Sebastian know each other? *(Kennen wir uns nicht?)*
2. Does Sebastian like Gabriele's first name? Do you? *(Ein schöner Name.)*
3. Does Sebastian ever find out Gabriele's last name? *(Wie heissen Sie?)*
4. Who is in a hurry? *(Ich bin in Eile.)*
5. Will Gabriele have time later? *(Vielleicht später?)*

The answers to these and other burning questions can be read in this week's *Enquirer*. Just kidding. But you CAN find them at the end of this lesson in the Crib Notes section.

WORKSHOP 1

WORD ON THE STREET

Doch is an emphatic way of saying "yes" in German when somebody contradicts you. So, when somebody says that you don't know a word of German, just say *doch* and they'll stand corrected.
Nein, wir kennen uns nicht.—Doch. Wir kennen uns aus Stuttgart.
No, we don't know each other.—Yes, we do. We know each other from Stuttgart.

THE NITTY GRITTY

ME, YOU, AND MY PET DOG, TOO: **PERSONAL PRONOUNS**

When you meet someone for the first time, you try to get to know each other, right? So, you end up talking about personal stuff a lot, and to do so you need personal pronouns, or words such as "I," "you," "he," "she," and so forth. Here are the German equivalents.

PERSONAL PRONOUNS			
SINGULAR		**PLURAL**	
ich	I	*wir*	we
du	you	*ihr*	you
Sie	you (sg., formal)	*Sie*	you (pl., formal)
er	he	*sie*	they
sie	she		
es	it		

Heads Up!

Note that the same form, *sie,* is used for "she," they," and the formal "you" (either singular or plural). The uppercase is used to distinguish in writing between the pronoun *sie* (she; they) and *Sie* (you, sg./pl., formal).

Did You Know?

USING THE RIGHT WORD

Germans can be a rather formal bunch. Adults, and kids when addressing adults, use the pronoun *Sie* if they don't know each other well, or if their relationship has a formal character. So, with your family and friends you'd use *du,* as you would with children and pets, but with your boss and strangers you'd use *Sie.* Of course, these rules have been loosening up over the past years. These days, teens and twens tend to simply use *du* right from the start among themselves. And whenever you're not sure which usage is correct, it is best to ask if it is OK to use *du* instead of *Sie,* even if everyone involved is a twen: *Darf ich "du" sagen?* May I use "du"? If you've started out with *Sie,* wait for the cue from the older person to make the switch to *du.* If everyone involved is the same age, wait for the cue from the person with the higher social status. In other words, if you just declare it to your boss that from now on you'll use *du* with him or her, I wouldn't count on a promotion.

ACTIVITY 3: TAKE IT FOR A SPIN

Did Gabriele and Sebastian use the formal *Sie* or the familiar *du* in the Hear . . . Say 1 section? Don't look just yet, answer based on your instincts and what you just learned about personal pronouns so far. Write down your answer. *Gut.* And now go back to their conversation for a search and rescue operation. Look for all personal pronouns used there including, but not only, *du* and *Sie,* and write them down. Was your answer correct?

ACTIVITY 4: TAKE IT FOR A SPIN

Would you use *du* or *Sie* with the following people?

1. With your mother?
2. With the cashier at the supermarket around the corner?
3. With a new colleague?
4. With your very best friend?
5. With your boss's eight-year-old daughter?
6. With your boss's wife?
7. With that new thirty-something neighbor?

8. With that annoying little dog down the street?
9. With the love of your life at the altar?
10. With the priest marrying you?

TO BE OR NOT TO BE: THE VERB *SEIN* (TO BE) IN THE PRESENT TENSE

When you meet someone for the first time, it's a good idea to make sure that they know who you are. Obviously you'll need the verb *sein* (to be) to say things about yourself. Just like in English, this pesky little verb changes depending on the personal pronoun you use with it. In other words, just like you say "I am" but "he is" in English, you need to say *ich bin* but *er ist* respectively in German. Here are all forms of *sein*.

THE PRESENT TENSE OF THE VERB *SEIN* (TO BE)			
SINGULAR		**PLURAL**	
ich bin	I am	*wir sind*	we are
du bist	you are	*ihr seid*	you are
Sie sind	you are (formal)	*Sie sind*	you are (formal)
er/sie/es ist	he/she/it is	*sie sind*	they are

Note that the same verb form is used with *sie* (they) and with *Sie* (you, sg./pl., formal).

You'll find that *sein* is extremely helpful when you're trying to make that good first impression.

You can say where you're from and what you do.

Ich bin aus Stuttgart.	I am from Stuttgart.
Ich bin Professor.	I am a professor.
Ich bin Amerikaner.	I am American.

Or, more modestly . . .

Ich bin ein Genie.	I am a genius.
Ich bin Millionär.	I am a millionaire.

You can introduce someone.

Das ist Peter.	That's Peter.
Sie sind Susanne Berger, nicht wahr?	You are Susan Berger, right?

You can pay compliments.

Gabriele ist ein schöner Name.	Gabriele is a beautiful name.

But make sure you don't overdo it, though . . .

Du bist aber sexy.	You are so sexy.

. . . or else you might hear the following.

Ich bin in Eile.	I am in a hurry.

Heads Up!

Please note that the verb form following the formal *Sie* is the same as the plural verb form, even if you're talking to only one person. Also note that, unlike in English, there is no indefinite article in German before words for professions or nationalities.

ACTIVITY 5: **TAKE IT FOR A SPIN**

Show off what you have learned and fill in the blanks with the correct form of *sein*.

1. *Ich* _____ *aus New York.*
2. *Er* _____ *Amerikaner.*
3. *Du* _____ *ein Genie.*
4. *Sie* (formal) _____ *Millionär.*
5. *Wir* _____ *in Eile.*
6. *Ich* _____ *sehr sexy.*

Heads Up!

Our helpful little word *sein* won't help if you'd like to ask how somebody is doing or to respond to the question yourself. Germans use the verb *gehen* (to go) in this context: *Wie geht's?* (How are you?, Lit. How's it going?) or *Wie geht es Ihnen?* (How are you? [formal]). The simplest and most common answer to the question is *Gut* (Fine) or *Danke, gut* (Fine, thanks).

THAT'S WHAT I DO: TALKING ABOUT PROFESSIONS

Let's take a closer look at *sein* used with the names of professions. In German, most professions have a masculine and a feminine form, just like *actor* and *actress* in English. In most cases, all you have to do is add *-in* to the masculine form of the noun to get the feminine form. Here are a few common examples.

TALKING ABOUT PROFESSIONS

	MASCULINE	FEMININE	MEANING	
Ich bin . . .	Professor	Professorin	professor	(von Beruf).
	Schauspieler	Schauspielerin	actor/actress	
	Lehrer	Lehrerin	teacher	
	Arzt	Ärztin	doctor	
	Zahnarzt	Zahnärztin	dentist	
	Student	Studentin	student	
	Frisör	Frisöse/ Frisörin	hairstylist	
	Apotheker	Apothekerin	pharmacist	
	Verkäufer	Verkäuferin	salesperson	
	Manager	Managerin	manager	
	Fahrer	Fahrerin	driver	

Heads Up!

Adding -*in* to the words denoting nationalities to get the female version works just as well. For example, the male term *Amerikaner* (American) becomes the female term *Amerkanerin,* or the male *Kanadier* (Canadian) becomes the female *Kanadierin.* There are exceptions, of course. A woman is a *Deutsche* (German) whereas a man is a *Deutscher* (German). Note that unlike in English, nouns denoting professions or nationalities are not preceded by an article.

ACTIVITY 6: TAKE IT FOR A SPIN

Fill in the blanks by inserting a word of profession in either masculine or feminine form.

1. *Frau Semmelrogge ist* (teacher) _____ *von Beruf.*
2. *Klaus ist* (doctor) _____ *von Beruf.*
3. *Andreas ist* (driver) _____ *von Beruf.*
4. *Susanne ist* (manager) _____ *von Beruf.*
5. *Herr Obermaier ist* (salesperson) _____ *von Beruf.*
6. *Erika ist* (hairstylist) _____ *von Beruf.*

JUST SAY "NO": NEGATION WITH *NICHT*

Great! Now you know how to say who you are and what you do. But what if you want to clear up that misunderstanding and make sure that the great person you just met knows that you are NOT a *Drogenhändler/in* (drug dealer) but an *Apotheker/in* (pharmacist)? Just use the word *nicht* (not) and place it right after the form of the verb *sein.* Here's how.

Ich bin Apotheker/in.	I am a pharmacist.
Ich bin nicht Drogenhändler/in.	I am not a drug dealer.
Ich bin aus Hamburg.	I am from Hamburg.
Ich bin nicht aus Buxtehude.	I am not from Buxtehude.
Ich bin Amerikanerin.	I am American.
Ich bin nicht Deutsche.	I am not German.

ACTIVITY 7: TAKE IT FOR A SPIN

Please negate the following sentences.

1. Ich bin Drogenhändler.
2. Er ist aus Freiburg.
3. Wir sind Kanadier.
4. Sie (formal) sind sexy.
5. Sie ist Studentin.

Take a Tip from Me

One of the best ways to learn new vocabulary is to use flash cards. Write the German word on one side and the English translation on the other. When you study from your flash cards, begin with the German first and always say the words out loud (or sound them out if you don't want to look like you are talking to yourself in public). Try to go through them as fast as you can. Ultimately you're aiming for instant recognition.

Once you have the German side down, start practicing with the English first. The great thing about flash cards is that they are portable and easy to use. Pop a few of them in your pocket and go through them as you're eating lunch, waiting for the bus, or even waiting in line in the supermarket.

Now here's some materials to put on those cards, if you haven't started yet.

WORDS TO LIVE BY

WHAT'S THE MAGIC WORD?

Germans really are a polite bunch, and their politeness shows in the many ways you can express the magic words.

PLEASE	THANK YOU	YOU'RE WELCOME	EXCUSE ME
Bitte.	Danke. (Thanks.)	Bitte. (You're welcome.)	Entschuldigung. (Excuse me.)
	Vielen Dank. (Thanks a lot.)	Bitte, gern geschehen. (My pleasure.)	'Tschuldigung. ('scuse me.)
			Entschuldigen Sie, bitte. (Excuse me. [formal])
	Herzlichen Dank. (Thank you very much.)	Keine Ursache. (Don't mention it.)	
			Entschuldige, bitte. (Excuse me. [informal])
		Ist doch selbstverständlich. (Why, of course.)	
	Besten Dank. (Thank you kindly.)		
	Tausend Dank. (Thanks a million.)		

You don't have to be able to use all these different phrases right away; a simple *bitte* and *danke* will do just fine most of the time, but be prepared to hear the different varieties.

HEAR . . . SAY 2

You remember that something fell out of Gabriele's purse when she rushed away, right? Well, it was her wallet, including her credit cards and her driver license. So the lucky Sebastian now knows where Gabriele lives, and a day later, make no mistake about it, he is at her door.

Sebastian: Guten Tag.

Gabriele: (surprised) Guten Tag!!!

Sebastian is suddenly very nervous.

Sebastian: Hier, der Geldbeutel . . . das ist doch Ihr Geldbeutel, nicht wahr?

Gabriele: Ja. Vielen Dank!

Sebastian: Gern geschehen. Es ist alles drin.

Gabriele, quite grateful that Sebastian has brought her wallet back to her, feels she should be nicer to Sebastian. She extends her hand to him.

Gabriele:	**Ich heiße . . .**
Sebastian:	**. . . Gabriele Kocher. Ich weiß.**

Gabriele has to laugh.

Gabriele:	**Natürlich. Und Sie?**
Sebastian:	**Ich heiße Sebastian Maier. Ich bin aus Hannover. Ich bin beruflich in München.**
Gabriele:	**Schön, Sie kennenzulernen.**
Sebastian:	**Gleichfalls.**
Gabriele:	**Was sind Sie denn von Beruf?**
Sebastian:	**Ich bin Zahnarzt.**
Gabriele:	**Oh.**

Now it is Sebastian's turn to laugh.

Sebastian:	**Ich weiß. Zahnarzt ist nicht gerade ein beliebter Beruf.**
Gabriele:	**Nein, das ist es nicht. Ich bin auch Zahnärztin.**
Sebastian:	**Das ist aber ein Zufall.**
Gabriele:	**Ja, das ist lustig.** (Gabriele laughs.) **Darf ich "du" sagen?**
Sebastian:	**Ja, das ist eine gute Idee. Ich heiße . . .**
Gabriele:	**. . . Sebastian. Ich weiß.**

ACTIVITY 8:   **HOW'S THAT AGAIN?**

Well, do you think Gabriele and Sebastian are off to a better start this time around? Feel free to give your answers in English for now.

1. Did Sebastian take something out of Gabriele's wallet?
2. Why is Sebastian in München?
3. What is Sebastian's profession?
4. What is Gabriele's profession?
5. What does Gabriele think is funny?

And remember, if you really need to, you can peek at the translation and the answers at the end of the chapter.

I SAY HELLO, YOU SAY GOOD-BYE: **HOW TO MEET, GREET, AND GET RID OF PEOPLE IN GERMAN**

The way you greet people in German depends very much on how familiar you are with them. With people you address with *du* you'd use more familiar words than if you address them with *Sie*. Here are a few examples.

HELLOS AND GOOD-BYES		
USE	WITH FRIENDS/ FAMILY OR CHILDREN	WITH PEOPLE YOU DON'T KNOW WELL AND WITH ELDERS
Hello.	*Hallo.*	*Guten Tag.*
	Tag.	*Guten Abend* (evening only)
	Grüß dich!	*Grüß Gott.*
How are you?	*Wie geht's?*	*Wie geht es Ihnen?*
Good.	*Gut.*	
Not bad.	*Nicht schlecht.*	
So so.	*Es geht.*	
My name is . . .	*Ich heiße . . .*	
	Mein Name ist . . .	
Meet . . . /This is . . .	*Das ist . . .*	
May I introduce (you to) . . .	*Darf ich (dir) . . . vorstellen?*	*Darf ich (Ihnen) . . . vorstellen?*
Nice to meet you.	*Schön, dich kennenzulernen.*	*Schön, Sie kennenzulernen.*
	Freut mich, dich kennenzulernen.	*Freut mich, Sie kennenzulernen.*
Nice to meet you, too.	*Gleichfalls.*	
Good-bye.	*Tschüs.*	*Auf Wiedersehen.*
	Ade.	
See you later.	*Bis später.*	
See you soon.	*Bis bald.*	
See you Monday.	*Bis Montag.*	

Did You Know?

Germans usually greet each other with a handshake, especially when they meet for the first time or if they are doing business with each other. The exception are children and teenagers, who don't generally shake hands when they meet each other, but may just wave a friendly "hello." Hugging and kissing are rare even among friends on an everyday basis, and completely unthinkable among business associates or acquaintances. Whether you hug and kiss within your family depends very much on your family's dynamic (and whether or not you like Aunt Klara's perfume). But, of course, you'd hug members of your immediate family if you haven't seen them for a while.

Ready to try some of this out?

TAKE IT FOR A SPIN

Gabriele is getting ready for a date with Sebastian. She wants to look good for her date, and decides to try out a new hair salon. Take Gabriele's role in the following dialogue and meet her fabulous new hairstylist, the *Frisör*.

Frisör:	*Guten Tag.*
Gabriele:	_____.
Frisör:	*Ah, Frau Kocher. Schön, Sie kennenzulernen.*
Gabriele:	_____.
Frisör:	*Wie geht es Ihnen?*
Gabriele:	_____. _____?
Frisör:	*Nicht schlecht.*

Did You Know?

When first meeting somebody, Americans usually have no trouble discussing their past and happily offer personal information about where they grew up or where they went to school. In fact that is what small talk is all about in this country. Germans, on the other hand, wouldn't quite know how to respond to questions about their personal life coming from relative strangers. Small talk of this kind is rather uncommon. At the same time, it is not uncommon at all for Germans to engage people they barely know in a heated political discussion. So don't be taken aback when somebody asks you whether you are a Democrat or a Republican (*Sind Sie Demokrat oder Republikaner?*) right off the bat, or if you find yourself in the middle of a political discussion right after. Germans, who love debate, will often take the opposing point of view just to keep the discussion alive.

WORKSHOP 2

THE NITTY GRITTY

IS IT A BOY OR A GIRL? THE GENDER OF GERMAN NOUNS

All German nouns are either masculine (*der/ein Mann* [the/a man]), feminine (*die/eine Frau* [the/a woman]) or neuter (*das/ein Kind* [the/a child]). Now this makes perfect sense with some nouns. *Frau* (woman) and *Tochter* (daughter) shouldn't be anything but feminine, *Mann* (man) and *Junge* (boy) and *Sohn* (son) shouldn't be anything but masculine, and even *Haus* (house) and *Auto* (car) shouldn't be anything but neuter, right? Remember that you've already learned that professions and nationalities have a masculine and a feminine form. So a man is *ein Lehrer* (male teacher), but a woman is *eine Lehrerin* (female teacher). That makes sense, too. But all other German nouns have a gender as well. Since there is no simple rule to predict which gender a noun will be, it is best to learn the gender along with the meaning of the word.

Here are a few examples.

THE GENDER OF NOUNS

MASCULINE	FEMININE	NEUTER
Mann (man)	*Frau* (woman)	*Kind* (child)
Hund (dog)	*Katze* (cat)	*Schwein* (pig)
Garten (garden)	*Blume* (flower)	*Gras* (grass)
Mond (moon)	*Sonne* (sun)	*Meer* (sea/ocean)

THE FINE PRINT

In writing, all German nouns start with a capital letter. Always. No exceptions. Nice, isn't it?

(IN)DEFINITELY SO: "THE" AND "A/AN" IN GERMAN

Just like English nouns, German nouns (words such as "*house*," "*tree*," "*woman*," or "*love*") are usually preceeded by little, but very important, words called articles. The tough part about these articles in German is that nouns have different genders (we just talked about that, right?), and that depending on the gender of the noun, the article is different. A masculine noun is preceded by the masculine articles *der* (the) or *ein* (a/an), a feminine noun is preceded by the feminine articles *die* (the) or *eine* (a/an), and a neuter noun is preceded by the neuter article *das* (the) or *ein* (a/an). The articles can be definite (*der, die, das*) or indefinite (*ein, eine, ein*)

THE GERMAN ARTICLES

	DEFINITE ARTICLES	INDEFINITE ARTICLES
MASCULINE SINGULAR	*der*	*ein*
FEMININE SINGULAR	*die*	*eine*
NEUTER SINGULAR	*das*	*ein*
PLURAL (m./f./neut.)	*die*	—

Please note that the definite article in the plural has only one form for all genders, *die*, and that the indefinite article has no plural at all.

Here are some examples:

der Mann	man
ein Mann	
der Freund	friend
ein Freund	

der Hund	dog
ein Hund	
der Mond	moon
ein Mond	
der Beruf	profession
ein Beruf	
der Geldbeutel	coin-purse
ein Geldbeutel	
die Frau	woman
eine Frau	
die Katze	cat
eine Katze	
die Blume	flower
eine Blume	
die Freundin	friend (female)
eine Freundin	
das Kind	child
ein Kind	
das Schwein	pig
ein Schwein	
das Meer	sea/ocean
ein Meer	
das Auto	car
ein Auto	

ACTIVITY 10: **TAKE IT FOR A SPIN**

Please go back to the two conversations in *Hear . . . Say 1* and *2* for a search and rescue operation. Write down all articles together with the nouns that follow them. Then write down these same nouns with the other article type. So, if a noun is preceeded by a definite article in the dialogue, write it down with an indefinite article as well, and vice versa. Then label them as to whether they are masculine, feminine or neuter.

ACTIVITY 11: **TAKE IT FOR A SPIN**

Masculine, feminine or neuter? Add the appropriate article.

1. _____ *Beruf*
2. _____ *Zahnarzt*

3. _____ *Lehrerin*
4. _____ *Idee*
5. _____ *Auto*
6. _____ *Frisör*
7. _____ *Kind*

TAKE IT UP A NOTCH

Translate the following dialogue into German. Ute Schneider and Erika Bauer meet in a classroom.

Ute Schneider:	Hello, how is it going?
Erika Bauer:	Good, thanks!
Ute Schneider:	My name is Ute Schneider. I am from Munich.
Erika Bauer:	Nice to meet you, Mrs. Schneider. My name is Erika, and I am a student.
Ute Schneider:	Nice to meet you, too. I am a teacher.

Klasse! Great job. I am so proud of you . . . And because you did so well, I'll let you in on a little secret. This was not a lesson on how to make a killing at the Frankfurt stock exchange. Noooo, it was about. . . . well, what was it about? If you still have any doubts about it, read the Crib Notes and you'll find out.

Take a Tip from Me
Once you've worked through the whole lesson, listen to the dialogues on your CD one more time, trying to repeat the phrases after the native speakers. After all the work you've done in this lesson, you will now listen to them in a very different way and notice and understand things you haven't before. This will be the very best reward for the hard work you've done so far. If you still have trouble understanding the dialogues, spend some time reviewing the lesson. But I'm willing to bet you are now ready to move on.

CRIB NOTES

Sebastian:	Oh, I'm sorry. Here.
Gabriele:	That's OK. And thanks.
Sebastian:	Don't mention it. Haven't we met before?
Gabriele:	No.
Sebastian:	Yes, we have. You are Susan Berger from Stuttgart, right?
Gabriele:	My name is not Susan Berger. And I am not from Stuttgart.
Sebastian:	My name is Sebastian. Sebastian Maier. And yours?
Gabriele:	Gabriele.
Sebastian:	Nice to meet you. Gabriele is a beautiful name.
Gabriele:	Thanks. I'm sorry, but I'm in a hurry.
Sebastian:	Maybe later?
Gabriele:	Bye.
Sebastian:	Bye.
Sebastian:	Wait a minute, Gabriele, I . . .

Sebastian:	Good day.
Gabriele:	Good day.
Sebastian:	Here, your wallet . . . This is your wallet, isn't it?
Gabriele:	Yes. Thanks a lot.
Sebastian:	Don't mention it. Everything is in there.
Gabriele:	My name is . . .
Sebastian:	. . . Gabriele Kocher. I know.
Gabriele:	Of course. And what is your name?
Sebastian:	My name is Sebastian Maier. I am from Hanover. I am in Munich on business.
Gabriele:	Nice to meet you.
Sebastian:	Nice to meet you, too.
Gabriele:	What do you do?
Sebastian:	I am a dentist.
Gabriele:	Oh.
Sebastian:	I know. A dentist is not a popular profession.
Gabriele:	No, it's not that. I am a dentist as well.
Sebastian:	What a coincidence.
Gabriele:	Yes, it's funny. May I say *du?*
Sebastian:	Yes, that's a good idea. My name is . . .
Gabriele:	. . . Sebastian. I know.

ACTIVITY 1

1. d
2. e
3. c
4. a
5. b

ACTIVITY 2

1. No, Gabriele and Sebastian don't know each other.
2. Yes, Sebastian likes her first name.
3. No, he never finds out Gabriele's last name.
4. Gabriele is in a hurry.
5. No, Gabriele says good-bye, rolling her eyes.

ACTIVITY 3

They used the formal *Sie*. The pronouns used were: *wir, Sie, ich, ich, ich, Sie, Sie, ich, ich.*

ACTIVITY 4

1. *du*
2. *Sie*
3. *Sie*
4. *du*
5. *du*
6. *Sie*
7. *Sie*
8. *du*
9. *du*
10. *Sie*

ACTIVITY 5

1. *bin*
2. *ist*
3. *bist*
4. *sind*
5. *sind*
6. *bin*

ACTIVITY 6

1. *Lehrerin*
2. *Arzt*
3. *Fahrer*
4. *Managerin*
5. *Verkäufer*
6. *Frisörin/Friseuse*

ACTIVITY 7

1. *Ich bin nicht Drogenhändler.*
2. *Er ist nicht aus Freiburg.*
3. *Wir sind nicht Kanadier.*
4. *Sie (formal) sind nicht sexy.*
5. *Sie ist nicht Studentin.*

ACTIVITY 8

1. *No, he didn't. Everything is still in there.*
2. *He is there on business.*
3. *He is a dentist.*
4. *She is a dentist, too.*
5. *That they are both dentists.*

ACTIVITY 9

Frisör:	*Guten Tag.*
Gabriele:	*Guten Tag. Ich heiße Gabriele Kocher./Mein Name ist Gabriele Kocher.*
Frisör:	*Ah, Frau Kocher. Schön, Sie kennenzulernen.*
Gabriele:	*Gleichfalls.*
Frisör:	*Wie geht es Ihnen?*
Gabriele:	*Gut, danke. Und Ihnen?*
Frisör:	*Nicht schlecht.*

ACTIVITY 10

Feminine: *eine Idee—die Idee*
Masculine: *ein Name—der Name, der Geldbeutel—ein Geldbeutel, ein Beruf—der Beruf, ein Zufall—der Zufall*

ACTIVITY 11

1. *der*
2. *der*
3. *die*
4. *die*
5. *das*
6. *der*
7. *das*

ACTIVITY 12

Ute Schneider:	Hallo, wie geht's?
Erika Bauer:	Gut, danke.
Ute Schneider:	Ich heiße Ute Schneider. Ich bin aus München.
Erika Bauer:	Schön, Sie kennenzulernen, Frau Schneider. Ich heiße Erika Bauer, und ich bin (eine) Studentin.
Ute Schneider:	Gleichfalls. Ich bin (eine) Lehrerin.

TOO MANY COOKS SPOIL THE BROTH

Viele Köche verderben den Brei

(Lit. Many cooks spoil the porridge)

LOOKING AHEAD . . .

Guten Tag. Hungrig? Hungry? Well, if you're not now, you will be as we'll talk a lot about food in this lesson. Now you're thinking all Germans like to drink beer and eat meat and potatoes, right? Wrong. I, for one, prefer a fine wine and pasta, or *Spätzle*, as we say *im Schwabenland*. Swabia is the area around Stuttgart in the state of Baden-Württemberg. That's where I'm from. We have a great variety of *Spezialitäten* (specialties), as do all other regions in Germany, Austria, and Switzerland. I bet you're getting *hungrig* now . . .

ACTIVITY 1: LET'S WARM UP

You can order *Speisen* (food) and *Getränke* (beverages) in a restaurant. Let's see if you can figure out which is which. Guess the meaning of each item on the list below and check off the appropriate column.

	SPEISEN	GETRÄNKE
1. eine Tasse Kaffee	_____	_____
2. eine Pizza	_____	_____
3. eine Brezel	_____	_____
4. ein Glas Milch	_____	_____
5. ein Mineralwasser	_____	_____
6. ein Eis	_____	_____

Having done so well on this activity, I think you are ready to listen to our next dialogue now. And again, concentrate on trying to understand the gist of it rather than every word.

Andreas, Britta and Petra are sitting in a restaurant trying to plan a *Festessen* (feast) this coming *Samstag* (Saturday) in honor of their friend Georg's *Geburtstag* (birthday). All four of them are from different regions, and so the menu for Georg's party is rather difficult to decide upon.

Petra:	Wann hat Georg denn Geburtstag?
Britta:	Am Samstag. Es gibt Kässpätzle und Salat.
Andreas:	Prima! Wie zu Hause, in der Schweiz.
Britta:	Nein. Es gibt schwäbische Kässpätzle, ohne Zwiebeln, wie in Süddeutschland.
Petra:	Na, ich weiß nicht. Kässpätzle, mit oder ohne Zwiebeln, sind nicht gerade festlich.
Britta:	(a little annoyed) Hast du vielleicht eine bessere Idee? Rheinischer Sauerbraten vielleicht?
Petra:	Warum nicht?
Britta:	Wir sind insgesamt zehn Personen. Sauerbraten für zehn Personen ist viel Arbeit.
Petra:	Schon, aber . . .

Just before Petra and Britta are about to get into an argument, the waiter arrives ready to take their order.

Kellner:	Guten Tag.
Andreas:	Gruezi.
Britta:	Grüß Gott.
Petra:	Hallo.
Kellner:	Was darf's sein?
Petra:	Ein Glas Weißwein, bitte.
Britta:	Für mich eine Apfelsaftschorle, bitte.
Kellner:	Und für Sie?
Andreas:	Ein Bier, bitte.
Kellner:	Und zu essen? Die Rindsrouladen sind heute besonders gut.
Petra:	(to her friends) Rindsrouladen! Das ist doch eine gute Idee für Georgs Geburtstag.
Andreas:	Und wir machen Kartoffelbrei und grüne Bohnen dazu. Und als Nachtisch Leckerli.
Petra:	Und als Vorspeise Krabbensalat.
Britta:	Und wer macht das alles?
Petra/Andreas:	Du natürlich.

Did You Know?

A quick word about birthdays, in case you happen to be in Germany on your own. Unlike in the United States, if you're the *Geburtstagskind* (birthday boy/girl) it's usually up to you to arrange the festivities, even though it is certainly common for family and friends to help you prepare your day. For children this may mean a party, but adults are not exempt. If you are going to the office that day, you are expected to provide some goodies such as cake, coffee, and perhaps even a bit of the bubbly. As a guest at an office birthday party you only need to offer congratulations, but a small gift is appropriate to give to friends. Don't give a birthday gift or congratulations in advance, as superstition regards this as tempting fate.*

ACTIVITY 2: **HOW'S THAT AGAIN?**

Let's see if you were able to read (or, rather, listen) between the lines. It's OK to answer the questions in English. But don't peek at the *Crib Notes* just yet!

1. Whose birthday are Britta, Petra and Andreas planning to celebrate? *(Wann hat Georg Geburtstag?)*
2. How many people will be at the party? *(Sauerbraten für zehn Personen ist viel Arbeit.)*
3. Where is Andreas from? *(Wie zu Hause, in der Schweiz.)*
4. Where is Britta from? *(Es gibt schwäbische Kässpätzle, wie in Süddeutschland.)*
5. And where is Petra from? *(Rheinischer Sauerbraten vielleicht?)*
6. Have Andreas, Britta and Petra decided upon a menu for the party? *(Rindsrouladen! Das ist doch eine gute Idee für Georgs Geburtstag.)*
7. Who will be cooking the food? *(Du, natürlich.)*

Did You Know?

Everybody likes to flip a few burgers and hot dogs on a grill in the summer, right? This beloved American summer tradition would be virtually unthinkable if it hadn't been for the influence of the German cuisine. The hot dog you are flipping this summer might be a wiener, which is short for *Wienerwurst* (Vienna sausage) from Vienna, or a frankfurter, which originated in Frankfurt, Germany. And that hamburger, you guessed it, is a *Bulette* from Hamburg, Germany. The influence of German immigrants and their cuisine goes even further: the sweet-and-sour mustard (*süß-saurer Senf*) you put on the hot dog, the potato salad (*Kartoffelsalat*) you eat with it, and the pickle (*saure Gurke*) that adorns your plate all originated in Germany as well.

---

* From: Phillips, Jennifer. In the Know in Germany. Living Language, New York, 2001.

WORDS TO LIVE BY

ALL ABOUT FOOD AND DRINKS

Among the greatest fun activities when traveling to a foreign country is tasting and learning about its cuisine. Germany, Austria and Switzerland offer some scrumptious specialties. And so you know what you are ordering, I've added a quick description.

	REGIONAL CUISINE		
	VORSPEISE (APPETIZERS)	*HAUPTSPEISE* (MAIN COURSE)	*NACHSPEISE* (DESSERT)
GERMAN	*Krabbensalat* (Northern German shrimp salad)	*Kässpätzle* (dumplings topped with cheese)	*Dresdner Stollen* (fruit cake, mostly served around Christmas)
		Wurstsalat (Southern German cold cut salad)	
		Spanferkel (Bavarian pig roast)	
		Buletten (Northern German meatballs)	
		Rheinischer Sauerbraten (Rhine Valley beef pot roast)	
AUSTRIAN		*Tafelspitz* (boiled beef)	*Käiserschmärren* (sugared pancakes with raisins)
		Wiener Schnitzel (boiled beef)	*Salzburger Nockerln* (Salzburg meringue served with vanilla sauce)
		Erdäpfel Salat (potato salad)	*Vanillekipferl* (crescent shaped vanilla cookies)
SWISS	*Engadiner Gerstensuppe* (Engadine barley soup)	*Schweizer Flan* (Swiss cheese pie)	*Leckerli* (spice cookies)
	Basler Mehlsuppe (Basel flour soup)		*Biberli* (cookies filled with almond paste)

Did You Know?

Das Mittagessen, lunch, is the main meal of the day for most people in Germany, Austria, and Switzerland. That's when people eat their *Kässpätzle* or their *Flan* or their *Schnitzel.* Many companies offer employees a warm mid-day meal at the company's cafeteria, and companies without a cafeteria offer meal tickets for local restaurants. School-age children who cannot go home for lunch eat a warm meal in the school cafeteria, which is usally staffed by volunteering parents. *Das Abendessen,* dinner, is usually just a light meal consisting of *belegte Brote* (open faced sandwiches), sampling the wide variety of *Wurst* (cold cuts) and *Käse* (cheese). *Das Frühstück,* breakfast, consists of *Brötchen* (fresh baked breakfast rolls) with *Marmelade* (jam), *Gelee* (jelly) or *Wurst* (cold cuts) and *Käse* (cheese), or the famous *Müesli* (granola and dried fruit mixed with either milk or yoghurt) which originated in Switzerland. Between lunch and dinner people enjoy *Kaffee und Kuchen* (coffee and cake), particularly on the weekends.

No meal would be complete without a drink to go with it. Sure, Germany is famous for its beer, but Germans also grow a variety of fine wines, just like Austrians: the Rhine valley in Germany is famous for its white wines, and the Burgenland is one of the major Austrian wine areas. Here are a few words to flow off your tongue.

GETRÄNKE			
ALKOHOLISCHE GETRÄNKE (ALCOHOLIC BEVERAGES)		**ALKOHOLFREIE GETRÄNKE** (NON-ALCOHOLIC BEVERAGES)	
das Bier	beer	*die Limonade*	lemonade
der Wein	wine	*das Mineralwasser*	mineral water
der Weißwein	white wine	*der Orangensaft*	orange juice
der Rotwein	red wine	*der Apfelsaft*	apple juice
die Weinschorle	wine cooler, spritzer (wine with mineral water)	*die Apfelsaftschorle*	apple juice with mineral water
der Sekt	sparkling wine	*die Milch*	milk
der Champagner	champagne	*der Kaffee*	coffee
die Spirituosen	hard drinks	*der Tee*	tea

Drinks come in glasses (wine, beer, sodas), or in cups (coffee, tea), or in pots (coffee, tea).

Was darf's sein?	What would you like? (Lit. What may it be?)
Ein Glas Weißwein, bitte.	A glass of white wine, please.
Ein Glas Mineralwasser bitte.	A glass of mineral water, please.
Eine Tasse Kaffee, bitte.	A cup of coffee, please.
Darf's auch ein Kännchen sein?	Would a pot be OK as well?

And then there's the beer, which comes in special measurements.

Eine Maß, bitte.	A big glass of beer, please.
Eine Halbe, bitte.	Half a liter (of beer), please. (Lit. A half, please.)

Heads Up!

The apostrophe in *Was darf's sein?* hides the little word *es* (it). The "e" is often dropped in the fast speech of colloquial German. You already know *Wie geht's?* (How are you?) and *Was gibt's Neues?* (What's new?). The two words, the verb and the pronoun that follows it, are pronounced as one: *darfs, gehts, gibts.*

And now let's look at a set table:

Der Tisch ist gedeckt!	The table is ready.
der Teller	plate
das Messer	knife

die Gabel	fork
der Löffel	spoon
die Karaffe	caraffe
das Glas Wein	glass of wine
das Glas Wasser	glass of water
die Tasse Kaffee	cup of coffee
der Nachtisch	dessert
die Rechnung	check

So now that we know WHAT to order, let's learn HOW to order in German.

WHAT CAN I GET YOU? ORDERING IN A RESTAURANT

When you order any of these delicious meals or thirst-quenching drinks in a restaurant, the *Kellner* (waiter) or *Kellnerin* (waitress) will most likely prompt you with a friendly . . .

Bitte?	Please?
Sie wünschen?	What would you like? (Lit. You wish?)
Möchten Sie bestellen?	Would you like to order?
Was darf ich Ihnen bringen?	What can I get you?
Was darf's zu trinken sein?	What would you like to drink? (Lit. What may it be to drink?)
Was darf's zu essen sein?	What would you like to eat. (Lit. What may it be to eat?)
Und für Sie?	And for you?
Noch etwas?	Anything else?

A good *Kellner* or *Kellnerin* will also make a few suggestions.

Ich empfehle . . .	I suggest . . .
Der Küchenchef empfiehlt . . .	The chef suggests . . .
Wie wär's mit . . . ?	How about . . . ?

Of course you could just as well point to the item you'd like on the *Speisekarte*, but why not get a bit more fancy? It's simpler than you think . . .

Haben Sie . . . ?	Do you have . . . ?
Für mich bitte . . .	For me . . .
Ich nehme . . .	I'll have . . . (Lit. I'll take . . .)

Let's play scrambled dialogues. Put together a dialogue by placing these sentences in the right order.

—*Ich nehme den Tafelspitz, bitte.*
—*Einen Orangensaft, bitte.*
—*Was darf's denn zu trinken sein?*
—*Und zu essen?*
—*Ein Glas Weißwein, bitte.*
—*Und für Sie?*
—*Kommt sofort.*
—*Das Wiener Schnitzel, bitte.*

Did You Know?

In most restaurants in Germany, Austria and Switzerland it is customary to seat yourself, and, once you are seated, it may take the *Kellner* (waiter) or *Kellnerin* (waitress) several minutes to greet you and/or to bring the menu to you. The idea is to allow the guest to settle in and chat a few minutes before ordering. Once you ordered, the food is usually served as it becomes ready rather than to all parties at the same time. Even though Germans are known as time-conscious people, when it comes to eating out, Germans like to take their time. After the main course, people tend to stay and chat, sometimes over dessert or coffee. It is not at all unusual to spend well over an hour for lunch. A *Kellner* or *Kellnerin* will not expect a large tip, as gratuity is automatically included in the price of the meal. While additional tipping is customary, you usually just add an euro or so, "rounding up" to the next five or ten euro amount. *Guten Appetit!* (Enjoy your meal!)

THE NITTY GRITTY

TO HAVE AND HAVE NOT: THE VERB *HABEN* (TO HAVE) IN THE PRESENT TENSE

The verb *haben* (to have), just like *sein* (to be) and in fact, all other German verbs, changes depending on the pronoun you use with it. Here are the present tense forms of *haben*.

THE PRESENT TENSE OF THE VERB *HABEN* (TO HAVE)			
SINGULAR		**PLURAL**	
ich habe	I have	*wir haben*	we have
du hast	you have	*ihr habt*	you have
Sie haben	you have (formal)	*Sie haben*	you have (formal)
er/sie/es hat	he/she/it has	*sie haben*	they have

The verb *haben* is a rather versatile little verb. You'll find it helpful, for example, when trying to drop a hint that you might like to be taken out for a drink or to dinner.

Ich habe Hunger.	I am hungry. (Lit. I have hunger.)
Ich habe Durst.	I am thirsty. (Lit. I have thirst.)

Heads Up!

Please note that in German, you say that you HAVE hunger and thirst: *Ich habe Hunger. Ich habe Durst.* **You can also use a structure more similar to the English:** *Ich bin hungrig* **(I am hungry) and** *Ich bin durstig* **(I am thirsty).**

Or maybe you'd prefer your friend to give you a party in honor of your birthday?

Ich habe bald Geburtstag.	My birthday is coming up soon. (Lit. I soon have [a] birthday.)

And if nothing helps, you might want to make a suggestion yourself.

Ich habe eine Idee.	I have an idea.

Once you're finally in the restaurant, *haben* helps to find out what's on the menu.

Haben Sie Kaiserschmarren?	Do you have Kaiserschmarren?

ACTIVITY 4: **TAKE IT FOR A SPIN**

Ready? Insert the correct present tense form of *haben* (to have).

1. *Ich* _____ *Durst.*
2. *Er* _____ *eine Idee.*
3. *Ja, wir* _____ *Flan.*
4. _____ *Sie* (formal) *am Samstag Geburtstag?*
5. *Du* _____ *Hunger.*
6. *Ich* _____ *Geld.*
7. *Ihr* _____ *Bier.*

THE WHAT? WHERE? AND WHEN? ESSENTIAL QUESTIONS

German has a few essential question pronouns that will help you find out everything you need to know about that great looking person who showed up at Georg's birthday dinner.

QUESTION PRONOUNS	
Wer?	Who?
Was?	What?
Wie?	How?
Wann?	When?
Wo?	Where?
Woher?	Where from?

Wenn =IF
WARUM = WHY

There is no such thing as a silly question. On the contrary, those who ask many questions learn a lot. Let's see what you can find out about the cute person you just met.

Wie heißen Sie?	What is your (formal) name?
Woher sind Sie?	Where are you (formal) from?

You can ask the same thing a little differently:

Woher kommen Sie?	Where do you come from?
Was sind Sie von Beruf?	What is your profession?

Or:

Was machen Sie beruflich?	What do you do professionally?

The following may not always be the polite thing to ask, so use your own judgement.

Wann haben Sie Geburtstag?	When is your birthday?

And finally, if you want to make sure that you are not invading someone else's territory, don't forget to ask:

Wer ist Ihr Mann/Ihre Frau?	Who is your husband/your wife?
Wo ist Ihr Freund/Ihre Freundin?	Where is your boyfriend/your girlfriend?

ACTIVITY 5: TAKE IT FOR A SPIN

Which question would you like to ask? Insert the correct question pronoun. The answers will give you a hint.

1. _WANN_ ist das Festessen?—Das Festessen ist am Samstag.
2. _WIE_ heißen Sie?—Ich heiße Peter.
3. _WAS_ ist Ihr Mann von Beruf?—Mein Mann ist Apotheker.
4. _WOHER_ sind Sie?—Ich bin aus Dresden.
5. _WER_ macht das alles?—Du natürlich.
6. _WAS_ darf's denn sein?—Das Wiener Schnitzel, bitte.

WHO'S ON FIRST: GERMAN WORD ORDER

The words in German statements follow the same order as they do in English. A statement starts with the subject followed by the verb followed by an object. Look at the following sentence, for example:

Ich habe Geld.	I have money.

Ich (I) is the subject, *habe* (have) is the verb, and *Geld* (money) is the object. Here are some more examples.

Ich esse die Spätzle.	I am eating *Spätzle.*
Susanne hat Hunger.	Susanne is hungry.

The word order changes if you ask a question: German simply switches the position of the subject and the verb.

Er trinkt. → *Trinkt er?*	He drinks. → Does he drink? (Lit. Drinks he?)

Here's another example:

Haben Sie Geld?	Do you have money? (Lit. Have you money?)

Subject and verb also switch position if you add question words into the mix.

Wo ist Ihre Frau?	Where is your wife?
Wann hat er Geburtstag?	When is his birthday?

ACTIVITY 6

You won't have much trouble unscrambling the following sentences, right? The punctuation tells you whether I'd like you to ask a question or make a statement.

1. *bist/aus München/du?*
2. *Ärztin/ist/Claudia.*
3. *sie/hat/Durst.*
4. *Geburtstag/er/wann/hat?*
5. *darf's/was/sein?* WAS DARF'S SEIN — WHAT WOULD YOU LIKE
6. *nehme/Wiener Schnitzel/ich/das.*
7. *macht/wer/das/alles?* WER MACHT DAS ALLES

And now, let's get back to our friends at the restaurant.

HEAR . . . SAY 2

Just as Britta was about to register her protest regarding the meal Petra and Andreas expect her to cook for Georg's birthday party, the waiter returns to take their food order.

Petra:	**Ich nehme den Rostbraten.**
Kellner:	**Mit Salat, Reis, Spätzle oder Bratkartoffeln?**
Petra:	**Bratkartoffeln, bitte.**
Andreas:	**Ich nehme die Rindsrouladen.**

Kellner:	**Und als Beilage?**
Andreas:	**Was empfehlen Sie?**
Kellner:	**Der Butterreis ist sehr lecker.**
Andreas:	**Gut, ich nehme den Reis.**
Britta:	**Ich nehme das Wiener Schnitzel mit Kartoffelsalat, bitte.**
Kellner:	**Sonst noch etwas?**
Britta:	**Nein, das ist alles.**
Petra:	**Also, zu Georgs Festessen machen wir Rindsrouladen, Kartoffelbrei und grüne Bohnen.**
Britta:	**Ich mache die Hauptspeise. Machst du den Nachtisch, Andreas? Leckerli sind schließlich aus der Schweiz.**
Andreas:	**Also gut.**
Britta:	**Krabbensalat ist nicht viel Arbeit. Machst du das, Petra?**
Petra:	**Na schön.**

Now that this has been taken care of, the friends enjoy a good dinner together. Just before they are ready to go, they ask for the bill.

Andreas:	**Ich bin satt.**
Britta:	**Ich auch.**
Petra:	(signaling to the waitress) **Die Rechnung, bitte.**
Kellner:	**Alles zusammen?**
Andreas:	**Zusammen.**
Britta:	**Wer zahlt?**
Petra/Andreas:	**Du natürlich.**

Heads Up!

Beware of false cognates! Even though German *also* looks like the English "also" (in addition, too), it is used more as an interjection, much like the English "well."

ACTIVITY 7: HOW'S THAT AGAIN?

Let's see if you are a gourmet and can remember the dishes mentioned in the dialogue.

1. Is Petra eating potatoes or rice? (*Die Bratkartoffeln, bitte.*)
2. What does the waiter suggest as a side dish? (*Der Butterreis ist sehr lecker.*)
3. What will be the main course at Georg's dinner? (*Also, zu Georgs Festessen machen wir Rindsrouladen, Kartoffelbrei und grüne Bohnen.*)
4. Who will prepare the dessert? (*Leckerli sind schließlich aus der Schweiz.*)
5. Why is Petra willing to make the shrimp salad? (*Krabbensalat ist nicht viel Arbeit.*)
6. Who will pay the bill? (*Wer zahlt?*)

Did You Know?

In most German restaurants the bill is paid directly to the waiter at the table. Often the waiter will add up the bill in front of the customers, asking first whether one person will settle the whole bill, or each customer will do it individually: *(Alles) zusammen?* ([All] together?) Among friends or among colleagues it is rather customary to split the bill. It is not even considered rude to split the bill on a date. If you want to treat somebody for a meal, you could say: *Darf ich Sie/dich einladen?* (May I treat you [formal/informal]?) If you want to make sure that you are the one who receives the entire bill, say, when you are out with that all important business associate, tell the waiter: *Geben Sie mir die Rechnung, bitte* (Please give me the bill). Remember to give an additional, small tip, even though gratuity is included. Round up to the next five or ten euro amount. Signal the waiter that you don't want any change back with a friendly *Stimmt so* (No change, please).

WORKSHOP 2

WORDS TO LIVE BY

PAY UP! ASKING FOR AND PAYING THE BILL IN A RESTAURANT

Once you're full and ready to settle your bill, you need to signal the waiter.

Zahlen, bitte.	(I'd like) to pay, please.
Die Rechnung, bitte.	The bill, please.

The waiter will respond with a polite . . .

Sofort.	Immediately.
Moment, bitte.	Just a moment, please.
Augenblick, bitte.	In an instant.

Once the waiter is at your table, you might want to ask.

Was macht das?	How much is it? (Lit. What does it make?)

The waiter will respond with a question.

(Alles) zusammen?	(All) together?
Zusammen oder getrennt?	One or separate bills?

It is rather customary to be sparse with words here and just respond with a friendly . . .

Zusammen.	Together.
Getrennt.	Separate.

Now you have to pay. Make no mistake about it. So when you hear the waiter say . . .

(Das macht) zweiund dreißig 32 Euro fürzig 40, bitte.	(That's) 32 euros 40, please.

You could give him 35 euros and say . . .

    Stimmt so.   No change, please. (Lit. That's correct.)

Or you could give him 40 euro and say . . .

    Fünfunddreißig (35).   Thirtyfive (35).
    Fünf (5) Euro zurück, bitte.   Five (5) euros in change, please.

ACTIVITY 8:   **LET'S TAKE IT FOR A SPIN**

Peter met Claudia at Georg's birthday dinner. Somehow he managed to get her to go to dinner with him. Now it's time to pay. Please take Peter's role in the following conversation.

Peter:	_____.
Kellnerin:	Einen Augenblick, bitte.
Peter:	_____, Claudia.
Claudia:	Ja. Das ist aber nett. Danke.
Kellnerin:	Alles zusammen?
Peter:	_____.
Kellnerin:	Das macht 37 Euro 30, bitte.
Peter (handing her two 20 euro bills):	_____.
Kellnerin:	Vielen Dank.

WORD ON THE STREET

When you agree with something, but only grudgingly so, throw in a little *Na schön* (Okay, then) or *Also gut* (All right, then). While by no means impolite, these expressions are only used among friends or co-workers you are friendly with. If hoping for a raise, German speakers will not use any of them to accept the task their superior has just assigned to them. An enthusiastic *Aber selbstverständlich* (Of course) or *Mit Vergnügen* (With pleasure) are better choices in that situation.

THE NITTY GRITTY

TALKING ABOUT THE PRESENT: **THE REGULAR VERB** *MACHEN* **(TO MAKE, TO DO)**

Machen (to make, to do) is a very common and versatile verb. Good news or bad news first? Alright. The bad news is that it changes depending on the personal pronoun you use, something you already encountered with the verbs *haben* and *sein*. The good news is that it is a regular verb you'll hear so often that you'll have its correct forms down in no time.

THE PRESENT TENSE OF THE VERB *MACHEN* (TO MAKE, TO DO)

SINGULAR		PLURAL	
ich mache	I make	*wir machen*	we make
du machst	you make	*ihr macht*	you make
Sie machen	you make (formal)	*Sie machen*	you make (formal)
er/sie/es macht	he/she/it makes	*sie machen*	they make

We said that *machen* is a regular verb. That means that only the endings you add to the verb stem change depending on the personal pronoun, not the verb stem itself. The verb stem of *machen* is *mach*-, and we get it by taking off the infinitive ending -*en*. Here are the endings used to form the present tense forms of all regular verbs.

PRESENT TENSE ENDINGS

SINGULAR		PLURAL	
-*e*	I	-*en*	we
-*st*	you	-*t*	you
-*en*	you (formal)	-*en*	you (formal)
-*t*	he/she/it	-*en*	they

Now let's look at some of the different meanings of *machen*.

THE MANY FACES OF *MACHEN*

TO PREPARE	*Ich mache den Kaiserschmarren.*	I'll prepare the *Kaiserschmarren.*
	Ich mache eine Party.	I'll have a party.
TO DO	*Was machst du am Samstag?*	What are you doing on Saturday?
TO COST	*Was macht das?*	How much is it? (Lit. What does it make?)
TO MATTER	*Das macht nichts.*	That's OK/It doesn't matter.

ACTIVITY 9: LET'S TAKE IT FOR A SPIN

Go ahead, make my day with *machen*. Insert the correct present tense form of the verb.

1. *Was _____ das zusammen?*
2. *Wir _____ den Kartoffelbrei und den Reis.*
3. *Was _____ ihr am Samstag?*
4. *_____ du den Salat?*
5. *Das _____ nichts.*
6. *Ich _____ am Samstag eine Party.*

LET'S TAKE IT FOR A SPIN

Now let's see if you can figure out what I am talking about. Please check off the correct meaning of the verb *machen*.

	"TO COST"	"TO MATTER"	"TO PREPARE"	"TO DO"
1. *Das macht Peter nichts.*	_____	_____	_____	_____
2. *Peter macht am Samstag nichts.*	_____	_____	_____	_____
3. *Das macht je 25 Euro.*	_____	_____	_____	_____
4. *Das macht doch nichts*	_____	_____	_____	_____
5. *Was macht das?*	_____	_____	_____	_____
6. *Wer macht das?*	_____	_____	_____	_____
7. *Wir machen ein Festessen.*	_____	_____	_____	_____

Did You Know?

Traditional eating habits in Germany have been changed under the influence of the various immigrant cuisines. The most popular foreign cuisines are Italian, Greek, Yugoslav, and Turkish, followed by Chinese and Indian. In larger cities you can also find Mexican and Japanese restaurants, and even restaurants offering cuisines from Africa. American fast food has found its way to Germany as well, and you'll find a MacDonalds or a Burger King just about everywhere. This culinary influence of the world can be also attested in every German household. Italian pasta dishes, Greek *gyros* (lamb roast), Yugoslav *cevapcici* (grilled meat rolls), and many other dishes are regularly on the menu in German households.

WORD ON THE STREET

Es gibt . . . is a phrase almost as common in German as the equivalent "there is/there are" is in English. The good news is that in German *Es gibt . . .* is used for both the singular (there is) and the plural (there are).

TAKE IT UP A NOTCH

When you complete this conversation by translating the English phrases into German, you'll be officially ready for a tour of German restaurants!

Gast: *Die Speisekarte, bitte.*

Waiter: There you go. What can I get you to drink?

Guest:	A glass of wine, please.
Kellner:	*Rot oder weiß?*
Guest:	Red, please. And a glass of mineral water.
Kellner:	*Und zu essen?*
Guest:	What do you suggest?
Kellner:	*Der Rostbraten ist heute besonders lecker.*
Guest:	OK. I'll take the Rostbraten.
Kellner:	*Und als Beilage?*
Guest:	Mashed potatoes and green beans
Kellner:	*Darf's noch etwas sein?*
Guest:	No, thanks.

CRIB NOTES

HEAR . . . SAY 1

Petra:	When is Georg's birthday?
Britta:	On Saturday. We'll have *Kässpätzle* and Salad.
Andreas:	Great! Just like at home, in Switzerland.
Britta:	No. We'll have Swabian *Kässpätzle,* without onions, just like in Southern Germany.
Petra:	Well, I don't know. Kässpätzle, with or without onions, are not really celebratory.
Britta:	Do you have a better idea? *Rheinischer Sauerbraten* perhaps?
Petra:	Why not?
Britta:	We are ten people altogether. *Sauerbraten* for ten people is a lot of work
Petra:	Yes, but . . .
Waiter:	Good day.
Andreas:	Good day.

Britta:	Good day.
Petra:	Hallo.
Waiter:	What would you like?
Petra:	A glass of white wine, please
Britta:	For me an apple juice with mineral water.
Waiter:	And for you?
Andreas:	A beer, please.
Waiter:	And to eat? The *Rindsrouladen* are particularly good today.
Petra:	*Rindsrouladen!* That's a good idea for Georg's birthday.
Andreas:	And we'll make mashed potatoes and green beans with it. And for dessert *Leckerli.*
Petra:	And as an appetizer shrimp salad.
Britta:	And who will prepare all this?
Petra/Andreas:	You, of course.

Petra:	I'll take the *Rostbraten*.		Britta:	I'll prepare the main dish. Will you make the dessert, Andreas? After all, *Leckerli* are from Switzerland.
Waiter:	With salad, rice, *Spätzle* or fried potatoes?			
Petra:	Fried potatoes, please.		Andreas:	OK.
Andreas:	I'll take the *Rindsrouladen*.		Britta:	Shrimp salad is not much work. Will you make that, Petra?
Waiter:	And as a side dish?		Petra:	Oh, all right.
Andreas:	What do you suggest?		Andreas:	I am full.
Waiter:	The butter rice is very scrumptious.		Britta:	I am, too.
Andreas:	Good. I'll have the rice.		Petra:	The bill, please.
Britta:	I'll have the *Wiener Schnitzel* with potato salad, please.		Waiter:	Together?
			Andreas:	Together.
Waiter:	Anything else?		Britta:	Who is paying?
Britta:	No, that's all.		Petra/Andreas:	You, of course.
Petra:	So, we'll prepare *Rindsrouladen*, mashed potatoes and green beans for Georg's birthday.			

ANSWER KEY

ACTIVITY 1

1. *Getränke* 2. *Speisen* 3. *Speisen*
4. *Getränke* 5. *Getränke* 6. *Speisen*

ACTIVITY 2

1. It is Georg's birthday.
2. There will be ten people at the party.
3. Andreas is from Switzerland.
4. Britta is from the South of Germany.
5. Petra is from the Rhine Valley.
6. Seems like it. They will have *Rindsrouladen,* mashed potatoes and grean beans.
7. Britta, most likely.

ACTIVITY 3

—*Was darf's denn zu trinken sein?*
—*Einen Orangensaft, bitte.*
—*Ein Glas Weißwein, bitte.*
—*Und zu essen?*
—*Ich nehme den Tafelspitz, bitte.*
—*Und für Sie?*
—*Das Wiener Schnitzel, bitte.*
—*Kommt sofort.*

ACTIVITY 4

1. *habe* 2. *hat* 3. *haben*
4. *Haben* 5. *hast* 6. *habe*
7. *habt*

ACTIVITY 5

1. *Wann* 2. *Wie* 3. *Was*
4. *Woher* 5. *Wer* 6. *Was*

ACTIVITY 6

1. *Bist du aus München?*
2. *Claudia ist (eine) Ärztin.*
3. *Sie hat Durst.*
4. *Wann hat er Geburtstag?*
5. *Was darf's sein?*
6. *Ich nehme das Wiener Schnitzel.*
7. *Wer macht das alles?*

ACTIVITY 7

1. Petra is eating potatoes.
2. The waiter suggests the rice.
3. The main course will be *Rindsrouladen,* mashed potatoes and green beans.
4. Andreas will prepare the desert.
5. Because it is not much work.
6. Britta, most likely.

ACTIVITY 8

Peter:	**Zahlen, bitte./Die Rechnung, bitte.**
Kellnerin:	*Einen Augenblick, bitte.*
Peter:	**Darf ich Dich einladen, Claudia?**
Claudia:	*Ja. Das ist aber nett. Danke.*
Kellnerin:	*Alles zusammen?*
Peter:	**Zusammen.**
Kellnerin:	*Das macht 37 Euro 30, bitte.*
Peter (handing her two 20 euro bills):	**Stimmt So.**
Kellnerin:	*Vielen Dank.*

ACTIVITY 9

1. *macht* 2. *machen* 3. *macht*
4. *Machst* 5. *macht* 6. *mache*

ACTIVITY 10

1. "to matter"
2. "to do"
3. "to cost"
4. "to matter"
5. "to cost"
6. "to prepare"
7. "to prepare"

ACTIVITY 11

Gast:	*Die Speisekarte, bitte.*
Kellner:	**Hier, bitte. Was darf's denn zu trinken sein?**
Gast:	**Ein Glas Wein, bitte.**
Kellner:	*Rot oder weiß?*
Gast:	**Rot, bitte. Und ein Glas Mineralwasser.**
Kellner:	*Und zu essen?*
Gast:	**Was empfehlen Sie?**
Kellner:	*Der Rostbraten ist heute besonders lecker.*
Gast:	**Gut. Ich nehme den Rostbraten.**
Kellner:	*Und als Beilage?*
Gast:	**Kartoffelbrei und grüne Bohnen, bitte.**
Kellner:	*Darf's noch etwas sein?*
Guest:	**Nein, danke.**

TIME IS MONEY

Zeit ist Geld

LOOKING AHEAD . . .

Wie spät ist es? (What time is it?) *So spät!* (That late!) Oops, we better hurry. Germans *sind gerne pünktlich* (like being on time). Actually, even if they didn't like it, they'd have to be, because trains and busses leave exactly at the time they are scheduled to leave, and every *Geschäft* (store) and *Restaurant* (restaurant) *schließt* (closes) promptly. So, let's learn how to ask for and tell the time in German. It'll help you fit right in.

ACTIVITY 1: LET'S WARM UP

Are you up for a *Frage* (question) and *Antwort* (answer) game? Figure out whether the person uttering the sentence below is asking a question or answering one, then check the appropriate box.

	FRAGE	ANTWORT
1. *Wie spät ist es*	_____	_____
2. *Der Supermarkt schließt um 19 Uhr*	_____	_____
3. *Ist es schon spät*	_____	_____
4. *Wann schließt der Supermarkt*	_____	_____
5. *Es ist 16 Uhr 30*	_____	_____
6. *Es ist schon sehr spät*	_____	_____

Find out how you fared in the *Crib notes*. Then armed with new confidence, listen to the dialogue. As always, try to understand the gist of it rather than worry about every single word.

It is *Freitag nachmittag* (Friday afternoon), almost *siebzehn Uhr* (5 o'clock in the afternoon). Ursula Heinrichs needs to get out of the office as soon as possible, so she'll have time to go *Lebensmittel einkaufen* (grocery shopping) before the *Supermarkt schließt*. But of course, that's exactly when her boss needs the *Verkaufszahlen* (sales figures). . . .

Renate Heller: **Frau Heinrichs, ich brauche die aktuellen Verkaufszahlen.**

Ursula Heinrichs: **Jetzt noch? Aber es ist doch schon fast siebzehn Uhr.**

Renate Heller: **Das dauert doch bestimmt nicht lange.**

Ursula Heinrichs: **Ich habe wirklich keine Zeit mehr. Ich brauche noch Lebensmittel für das Wochenende. Die Supermärkte schließen bald.**

Renate Heller: **Die Läden schließen erst um halb sieben. Sie haben also noch über eine Stunde Zeit.**

Ursula Heinrichs: (trying to protest) **Aber ich . . .**

Renate Heller: **Und Sie arbeiten doch immer so schnell und pünktlich.**

Ursula Heinrichs: **Ja, schon. Aber . . .**

Renate Heller: **Na also. Ich erwarte die Ergebnisse in zwanzig Minuten.**

Ursula Heinrichs: (resigned) **Wie Sie wünschen, Frau Heller.** (mumbling under her breath) **So was! Nicht einmal "danke" sagt sie.**

Renate Heller: (smiling) **Und vielen Dank auch, Frau Heinrichs.**

Ursula Heinrichs: (blushing) **Bitte, gern geschehen.**

WORD ON THE STREET

Na also! (Well then!) is an expression of approval used after an argument. Not a fight, mind you, but a friendly disagreement or discussion. The person who "won" the argument, the person who was able to convince the other party, seals the new "agreement" with *Na also*.

Let's see if you noticed how Frau Heller talked Frau Heinrichs into doing the assignment after all. Answer with true or false.

	TRUE	FALSE
1. Frau Heinrichs can't leave the office yet because Frau Heller needs her to get the current sales figures.	_____	_____
2. Frau Heinrichs has all the groceries she needs.	_____	_____
3. The supermarkets close in twenty minutes.	_____	_____
4. Frau Heinrichs has over one hour to complete the assignment.	_____	_____
5. Frau Heinrichs usually works promptly.	_____	_____
6. Frau Heinrichs is happy that her boss does not thank her.	_____	_____

WORD ON THE STREET

So was! is an expression of disbelief and annoyance similar to the English "I can't believe it!" Since it's used quite often, there are several different versions with the same meaning. *Also so was! Nein, so was!*

WORKSHOP 1

WORDS TO LIVE BY

THE COUNTDOWN: NUMBERS FROM 1 TO 24

One step at a time: If you want to tell time, you'll have to know the numbers first, right? In Germany, and much of the rest of Europe, people use the 24-hour clock system. So let's look at the numbers from 1 to 24.

NUMBERS FROM 1 TO 24

1	eins	11	elf	21	einundzwanzig
2	zwei	12	zwölf	22	zweiundzwanzig
3	drei	13	dreizehn	23	dreiundzwanzig
4	vier	14	vierzehn	24	vierundzwanzig
5	fünf	15	fünfzehn		
6	sechs	16	sechzehn		
7	sieben	17	siebzehn		
8	acht	18	achtzehn		
9	neun	19	neunzehn		
10	zehn	20	zwanzig		

And let's not forget the big fat 0 (zero), which in German is *null*.

Heads Up!

Sechs looses the *s* and *sieben* loses the *en* when combined with *zehn: sechzehn, siebzehn*. **Also note that numbers in the twenties first mention the number in the ones place and then the number in the tens place, just like in the English nursery rhyme "four and twenty blackbirds." Finally, *eins* becomes *ein* when combined with *zwanzig: einundzwanzig*.**

WORD ON THE STREET

Was für eine Null! (What a looser! [Lit. What a zero!]) is a heavy-duty insult, implying that the person referred to is a looser. This is not a phrase you'd want to use too often!

ACTIVITY 3: TAKE IT FOR A SPIN

Show me your mathematical genius! (Didn't expect this in a language course? Not to worry. We'll keep it to the most basic arithmetic.)

1. *zwei + zwei =*
2. *fünfzehn − neun =*
3. *einundzwanzig + drei =*
4. *vierundzwanzig − acht =*
5. *sieben + zehn =*
6. *vier − eins =*
7. *elf + zwölf =*
8. *neunzehn − dreizehn =*
9. *zwanzig + zwei =*
10. *elf + null =*

And now you're ready to talk time. There are two common ways of asking "What time is it?" in German.

Wieviel Uhr ist es?	(Lit. How many hours is it?)

and

Wie spät ist es?	(Lit. How late is it?)

The 12-hour clock essentially works as in English. Take a look.

THE 12-HOUR CLOCK		
ON THE HOUR	*Es ist acht Uhr.*	It is eight o'clock.
ON THE HALF HOUR	*Es ist halb zehn.*	It is half past nine. (Lit. It is half ten.)
ON THE QUARTER HOUR	*Es ist viertel vor sieben.*	It is a quarter to seven.
	Es ist viertel nach drei.	It is a quarter after three.
COUNTING THE MINUTES	*Es ist fünf (Minuten) vor zwölf.*	It is five (minutes) to twelve.
	Es ist zehn (Minuten) nach sechs.	It is ten (minutes) past six.

To make things more specific, follow with *morgens/vormittags* (in the morning), *nachmittags* (in the afternoon) and *abends* (in the evening), e.g., *Es ist halb zehn morgens.*

THE FINE PRINT

The only confusing thing about telling time German is the half hour. Unlike in English, where the half hour is added to the previous full hour, in German the half hour is subtracted from the next full hour. So, *Es ist halb sieben* (Lit. It is half [to] seven.) corresponds to the English "It is half past six."

Did You Know?

And to make it all even worse, in some areas, particularly in the south of Germany and Switzerland, people may tell the time in three-quarters rather than just quarters and halves. So, you may hear *Es ist dreiviertel sieben* (Lit. It is three quarters [on the way to] seven) instead of *Es ist viertel vor sieben* (It is quarter to seven).

And are you a bit uncertain about the 24-hour clock? Once you reach twelve P.M., or noon, keep on adding hours until you get to 24, or *vierundzwanzig*, or *Mitternacht* (midnight), which is also referred to as *null Uhr* (Lit. zero hour). When you use the 24-hour clock, don't use phrases like *halb* or *viertel* or *vor* or *nach*. Everything is expressed in terms of minutes after the hour. This system is always used in official announcements, in schedules of buses, trains, and planes, in school and work schedules. You will also hear people using the 24-hour clock in casual situations.

THE 24-HOUR CLOCK		
ON THE HOUR	Es ist 13 Uhr.	It is 1 PM.
	Es ist 1 Uhr.	It is 1 AM.
ON THE HALF HOUR	Es ist 16 Uhr 30.	It is 4:30 PM.
	Es ist 4 Uhr 30.	It is 4:30 AM.
ON THE QUARTER HOUR	Es ist 15 Uhr 15.	It is 3:15 PM.
	Es ist 3 Uhr 15.	It is 3:15 AM.
COUNTING THE MINUTES	Es ist 18 Uhr 13.	It is 6:13 PM.
	Es ist 6 Uhr 13.	It is 6:13 AM.

Heads Up!

Es dauert (it takes [Lit. it lasts]), similar to *es gibt* (there is/there are), which we discussed in Lesson 2, is an impersonal construction used to refer to how much time an action takes. Note that the verb *dauern* is always in the third person singular, *dauert,* regardless of the number of the noun that follows: *Es dauert eine Stunde* (It takes an hour) or *Es dauert drei Stunden* (It takes three hours).

TAKE IT FOR A SPIN

Let's see if you can handle the times. Look at the clocks and tell us what time it is.

1. 2. PM 3. 4.

5.  PM 6. AM 7. 8.

Did You Know?

Ever heard of *das akademische Viertel* (the academic quarter of an hour)? This expression refers to the unspoken rule that at German universities and colleges all classes start at a quarter AFTER the hour, even though they are scheduled to start ON the hour. This habit has become so popular that it is considered OK to be 15 minutes late for casual appointments or dates. BUT it is absolutely NOT OK to be late for a business meeting; and trains, planes and busses will definitely not wait around for anyone who is fashionably late. Finally, banging on the door of a grocery store 15 minutes after closing time won't help one bit either.

DAY BY DAY THE WEEK GOES BY: THE DAYS OF THE WEEK

Here is Frau Heinrichs *Kalender* (calendar) for next week:

MONTAG (Monday)	**FREITAG** (Friday)
12h Mittagessen mit Horst	*17h einkaufen*
DIENSTAG (Tuesday)	**SAMSTAG** (Saturday)
16h45 Frisör	*19h Georgs Geburtstag*
MITTWOCH (Wednesday)	
20h Restaurant Krone mit Hanna	**SONNTAG** (Sunday)
DONNERSTAG (Thursday)	*15h30 Kaffee bei Klaus*

And here's some more requisite vocabulary.

Let's look at a few common time expressions that might help you tell people about your plans.

der Tag	day
die Woche	week
nächste Woche	next week
heute	today
jetzt	now
sofort	immediately
immer	always
bald	soon
morgen	tomorrow
am Dienstag	on Tuesday
dienstags	Tuesdays, each Tuesday
nächstes Jahr	next year
*nächsten Samstag**	next Saturday
das Wochenende	weekend
am Wochenende	on the weekend

*In Northern and Eastern Germany, "Saturday" is *Sonnabend*.

LET'S TAKE IT FOR A SPIN

Answer the questions using the calendar above. Use the German words for the days and times.

1. When is Frau Heinrichs going to the hairdresser?
2. Is Frau Heinrichs going to a restaurant on Monday or on Wednesday?
3. When is she having coffee with Klaus?
4. At what time is she going to Georg's birthday?
5. When will she have lunch with Horst?
6. On what day is she completely free?

THE NITTY GRITTY

I'M COMING OVER: **TALKING ABOUT THE FUTURE USING THE PRESENT TENSE**

Let's quickly review: In Lesson 2 we looked at the present tense of the regular verb *machen* (to make, to do). There are many other regular verbs that form their present tense just like *machen*. For example: *arbeiten* (to work), *schließen* (to close, to lock), *warten* (to wait), *wünschen* (to wish), *brauchen* (to need), *sagen* (to say), *kaufen* (to buy), or *zahlen* (to pay). Just drop the final *-en* and add the present tense endings.

THE PRESENT TENSE OF REGULAR VERBS			
SINGULAR		**PLURAL**	
ich arbeit-e	I work	*wir schließ-en*	we close
du kauf-st	you buy	*ihr sag-t*	you say
Sie wünsch-en	you wish (formal)	*Sie wart-en*	you wait (formal)
er/sie/es brauch-t	he/she/it needs	*sie zahl-en*	they pay

THE FINE PRINT

If a verb stem ends in sounds/letters "m," "n," "d," or "t," e.g., *arbeit-en*, insert an -e before the endings -st and -t for ease of pronunciation. Compare: *du arbeitest* and *sie wartet*, but *du kaufst* and *du zahlst*.

And just like in English, the present tense can also be used to express events that are bound to happen in the near future.

> **Ich habe bald Geburtstag.** My birthday is (coming) soon.

The present tense is generally used to express future events that are scheduled, such as the departure or arrival of trains, buses and airplanes, or store hours.

> **Der Laden schließt heute um 18 Uhr.** The supermarket will close at 6 PM today.

LET'S TAKE IT FOR A SPIN

Frau Heinrichs is telling her boss about her weekend plans. Please insert the verbs in the correct form.

Renate Heller:	*Frau Heinrichs, Sie _____ heute aber schnell. (arbeiten)*
Ursula Heinrichs:	*Ich _____ Lebensmittel für das Wochenende. (brauchen)*
Ursula Heinrichs:	*Die Läden _____ um 18 Uhr. (schließen)*
Renate Heller:	*_____ Sie (formal) bald Geburtstag? (haben)*
Ursula Heinrichs:	*Ja, wir _____ am Samstag eine Party. (machen)*
Ursula Heinrichs:	*Ich _____ Sauerbraten. (machen)*
Renate Heller:	*Mmmm, Sauerbraten _____ sehr gut. (sein)*

Take a Tip from Me

As you surely know, German and English share common roots. Both are Germanic languages. Therefore many words in the two languages are "cognates" or words that share the same root and thus have the same or a similar meaning. Some of the days of the week, for example, *Montag* (Monday), *Freitag* (Friday) and *Sonntag* (Sunday) are virtually identical in English and German. So, if you encounter a German word that sounds or looks similar to an English word, you can assume that it also has the same meaning.

LET'S WARM UP

Can you figure out the meaning of these cognates? Please translate.

die Tomate, die Banane, das Brot, die Butter, der Salat, der Apfel, das Kilo, das Gramm

Now that you know how to figure out the meaning of German words, let's listen to the next dialogue. Let's see how Frau Heinrichs is doing.

Frau Heinrichs finished her last-minute assignment as quickly as she could and left the office at 5:55 PM. She raced into town at neck-breaking speed (rumor has it that she received a speeding ticket) to make it to the supermarket before closing. It is 6:17 PM as she enters the store.

Frau Heinrichs:	(crazed, mumbling to herself) **Was brauche ich denn alles? Brot, Butter, Eier und Marmelade fürs Frühstück. Aber zuerst gehe ich zum Obst und Gemüse und hole Äpfel, Bananen und Birnen. Ach ja, Kopfsalat, Tomaten und eine Salatgurke brauche ich auch noch. Wo ist denn die Waage? Ach, da ist sie ja. Mehr als zwei Kilo Äpfel und ein Kilo Birnen brauche ich nicht. . . . Entschuldigung, wo sind denn die Bananen?**
Verkäufer:	**Wir haben leider keine Bananen mehr. Es ist ja schon fast Ladenschluss.**
Frau Heinrichs:	**Wann bekommen Sie wieder Bananen?**
Verkäufer:	**Morgen haben wir bestimmt wieder Bananen.**
Frau Heinrichs:	**Danke.**

Frau Heinrichs proceeds to the deli section.

Verkäufer:	**Was darf's denn sein?**
Frau Heinrichs:	**Zweihundert Gramm Salami, bitte.**
Verkäufer:	**Geschnitten oder am Stück?**
Frau Heinrichs:	**Geschnitten, bitte. Und dann nehme ich auch noch zweihundert Gramm Schweizer Käse. Am Stück bitte.**
Verkäufer:	**Darf's ein bisschen mehr sein?**
Frau Heinrichs:	**Ja, natürlich.**

Frau Heinrichs finishes her shopping in a rush and hurries to the cashier.

Kasse 1:	**Beeilen Sie sich bitte.**
Frau Heinrichs:	**Ich weiß, es ist schon spät.**
Kasse 1:	**Ja, Sie haben Glück. Wir machen gleich zu.**

Heads Up!

The phrase *fürs Frühstück* hides the article *das,* and it is a contracted form of *für das Frühstück.* This is similar to the contraction of *es* to *'s* in *was gibt's* and *wie geht's* we discussed earlier, except that in the case of a contraction with *das,* as in *fürs,* no apostrophe is used.

Did you manage to keep up with Frau Heinrichs? Well, I trust you listened carefully, because this time, I'm raising the stakes, and I won't give you any more hints in parentheses. Answer the questions below by going over the dialogue and searching for sentences which answer them.

1. What does Frau Heinrichs intend to eat for breakfast?
2. Where will she get the apples, bananas and pears?
3. Why are they all sold out of bananas?
4. Which item is Frau Heinrichs *not* buying: *Tomaten, Kopfsalat, Birnen, Karotten, Salami,* or *Käse?*
5. Is Frau Heinrichs buying more cheese or more cold cuts?
6. Why does Frau Heinrichs have to hurry to the cashier?

Did You Know?

Make sure your watch is in working order, because except for the 24-hour convenience stores at the airports, at train stations or gas stations, set store hours are strictly enforced everywhere in Germany. Stores close at 6:30PM on weekdays, except Thursdays, when they are open until 8:30PM. On Saturdays most stores close at 4PM, or even earlier. On the first Saturday of the month, the *lange Samstag* (long Saturday), stores stay open until 6:30PM. On Sundays all stores are closed.

WORKSHOP 2

WORDS TO LIVE BY

SHOPPING FOR FOOD

As the last resource (or first?) you may just point at the item you'd like to buy, but I find it a bit more in your league to know the names of the things you eat. So here they are:

FOOD WORDS

Obst und Gemüse (Produce [Lit. fruit and vegetables])	*der Apfel*	apple
	die Birne	pear
	die Orange	orange
	die Pflaume	plum
	die Banane	banana
	die Ananas	pineapple
	die Kartoffel	potato
	die Zwiebel	onion
	die Tomate	tomato
	der Mais	corn
	der Spargel	asparagus
	der Salat	lettuce
	die Karotte	carrot
	der Paprika	pepper
	die/der Sellerie	celery
	die Gurke	cucumber
	der Spinat	spinach
Wurst (cold cuts)	*der Wurstaufschnitt*	cold cuts
	der Schinken	ham
	die Salami	salami
	die Lyoner	bologna
Fleisch (meat)	*das Rindfleisch*	beef
	das Kalbfleisch	veal
	das Schweinefleisch	pork
	das Lamm	lamb
	das Huhn	chicken
	das Brot	bread
	die Nudeln	pasta
	der Reis	rice
die Süßwaren (sweets)	*die Schokolade*	chocolate
	das Bonbon	candy
Gewürze (spices)	*der Zucker*	sugar
	das Salz	salt
	der Pfeffer	pepper
	der Paprika	paprika
Milchprodukte (dairy products)	*die Milch*	milk
	der Joghurt	yoghurt
	der Käse	cheese

Did You Know?

Weight is measured in *Gramm* (grams) and *Kilogramm* (kilograms) in all German-speaking and other European countries. One *Kilogramm* has 1,000 *Gramm*. (Please note that the German *Gramm* does not have an "s" at the end.) Half a *Kilogramm* is a *Pfund,* or 500 *Gramm,* which is about 50 *Gramm* more than the English *Pfund.* Liquids are measured in *Liter* (liters). These terms are usually abbreviated as: *das Gramm = g, das Kilogramm = kg, das Pfund = lb, der Liter = l.*

There are a few less exact measurements that Germans like to use. *Ein bisschen* refers to "a little," *ein bisschen mehr* is "a little more," and *ein bisschen weniger* is "a little less." *Ein paar* is "a few," and *viel* is "a lot."

In most grocery stores in Germany you have to *wiegen* (weigh) your produce yourself before you proceed to the cashier. There are several *Waagen* (scales) throughout the produce section, which calculate weight and price of your choice right on the spot and print out a label. There are no *Waagen* at the cashier. So, if you forget, you'll either have to leave without your produce or go back to the produce section to weigh them, and then return to the very end of a *Schlange* (checkout line).

ACTIVITY 9: TAKE IT FOR A SPIN

Shop 'til you drop. Go ahead and buy the items in parentheses.

1. *Wir haben kein Gemüse mehr.—Gut, ich kaufe ein Kilo _____.* (bananas)
2. *Was darf's denn sein?—Dreihundert g _____, bitte.* (ham)
3. *Was gibt's zum Frühstück?—Ich kaufe _____ und _____ und _____.* (bread, butter, jam)
4. *Das _____ ist heute sehr gut.—Gut, ich nehme ein _____.* (beef, pound)
5. *Zweihundert g Wurstaufschnitt, bitte.—Am Stück oder _____?* (sliced)

THE NITTY GRITTY

TWO'S COMPANY, THREE'S A CROWD: **THE PLURAL OF NOUNS**

One often isn't enough. If you need more than one, the English language simply adds an -s: *banana* → *bananas.* But even English has a few plurals that can make a language learner go gray. I mean "children" does not make much sense as the plural of "child," and "geese" is a rather silly plural for "goose." So don't be surprised that Germans have a few difficult plurals as well. Essentially there are five different groups of plurals in German.

GROUP I

The most common group adds an -*n* in the plural (if the noun ends on an -*e*, -*el*, or —*er*) or an -*en* (if the noun ends on a "g," "n," "r," or a "t"). Most female nouns belong to this group.

> *die Banane → die Bananen*
> *die Kartoffel → die Kartoffeln*
> *die Zeit → die Zeiten*

GROUP II

Another group of nouns adds an -*e* in the plural.

> *das Pfund → die Pfunde*
> *das Brot → die Brote*

If the noun ends in -*s*, that "s" is doubled in the plural.

> *das Ergebnis → die Ergebnisse*

GROUP III

Some nouns add -*er* in the plural. The vowels "a," "o," "u" turn into the Umlaute "ä," "ö," "ü."

> *der Mann → die Männer*
> *das Kind → die Kinder*

GROUP IV

Nouns ending in -*er*, -*en* and -*el* do not add an ending in the plural. They either do not change at all . . .

> *der Lehrer → die Lehrer*

. . . or their vowel turns into an Umlaut.

> *der Apfel → die Äpfel*
> *der Garten → die Gärten*

Words that originate in English usually add the English plural -s.

die Show → die Shows
das Ticket → die Tickets
das Auto → die Autos

Sound a little complicated? Don't worry, there is good news, too: The plural article for all nouns, no matter whether they are masculine, feminine or neuter, is always *die*.

Got it? Well, let's try it out.

ACTIVITY 10: TAKE IT FOR A SPIN

Aus eins mach zwei! Turn one into two—or more! Please rephrase the sentences using the numbers in parentheses.

1. *Ich habe ein Kind.* (2)
2. *Wir kaufen eine Orange.* (4)
3. *Er braucht eine Tomate für den Salat.* (3)
4. *Ich hole einen Apfel.* (5)
5. *Wir nehmen einen Salat.* (2)

Did You Know?

In Germany, Switzerland, and Austria, supermarkets normally do not offer free paper or plastic bags, but rather sell them to customers at their request. Most Germans bring their own shopping bags or baskets to the store, and not only because they want to save the money. Environmental awareness is in, and Germans try to live accordingly, using reusable cloth bags or shopping baskets rather than bags made of paper or plastic. The concern about environmental protection can be attributed to Germany's history as an industrial nation in the center of Europe. Over a century of industry in the 1900's has caused major pollution problems, and a 1994 addition to the *Grundgesetz* (Basic Law or Constitution) made it the state's duty to protect the environment. Strict governmental regulations require all companies to control the amount of pollution they emit and to pay for the environmental damage they cause. Individuals are required to combat pollution by using clean power and reducing car emissions. Recycling is required of everyone.

NO WAY, NO HOW: *NICHT* VERSUS *KEIN*

"No" is an important word in any language. German is no exception, except that German has two words for the same concept. Go figure. We've already talked a little about *nicht*, which is roughly the equivalent of the English "not:" *Nicht* is used to negate a whole sentence like . . .

> **Ich brauche die Ergebnisse.** → **Ich brauche die Ergebnisse nicht.**
> I need the results. → I don't need the results.
> **Es dauert lange.** → **Es dauert nicht lange.**
> It takes long. → It does not take long.

Kein, roughly equivalent to the English "no," on the other hand, is used to negate nouns with the indefinite article, such as *eine Banane* or no article at all, such as *Fleisch*.

> **Ich habe eine Banane.** → **Ich habe keine Banane.**
> I have a banana. → I don't have a banana. (Lit. I have no banana.)
> **Ich esse Fleisch.** → **Ich esse kein Fleisch.**
> I eat meat. → I don't eat meat. (Lit. I eat no meat.)

If a noun is preceded by a definite article, such as *das Fleisch* or *die Banane*, only *nicht* can be used.

> **Ich esse das Fleisch.** → **Ich esse das Fleisch nicht.**
> I eat the meat. → I don't eat the meat.
> **Ich habe die Banane.** → **Ich habe die Banane nicht.**
> I have the banana. → I don't have the banana.

Heads Up!

Note the word order: *Nicht* immediately follows the verb, e.g., *Es dauert nicht lange,* unless the verb has a direct object following it, e.g., *Ich esse das Fleisch nicht* or *Ich habe die Banane nicht.* In that case, *nicht* follows the verb + its object.

ACTIVITY 11: **TAKE IT FOR A SPIN**

Just say no!

1. *Haben Sie Zeit?*
2. *Arbeiten Sie nach 17 Uhr?*
3. *Schließen die Läden um 18 Uhr 30?*
4. *Kaufst du Bananen?*
5. *Sagt er 'danke'?*
6. *Haben Sie Wurst?*
7. *Haben Sie Obst?*

For some extra challenge, please answer the questions in German.

1. *Wieviel wiegen die Äpfel? (500 g.)*
2. *Wann schließt der Supermarkt? (20 Uhr 30)*
3. *Arbeitest du am Samstag? (nein)*
4. *Haben Sie Zeit? (nein)*
5. *Was brauchen wir fürs Frühstück? (Brot und Marmelade)*

Great job! Three lessons down, 12 more to go!

CRIB NOTES

HEAR . . . SAY 1

Renate Heller:	Frau Heinrichs, I need the current sales figures.
Ursula Heinrichs:	Now? But it is almost 5PM.
Renate Heller:	This won't take long.
Ursula Heinrichs:	I really don't have any time. I need groceries for the weekend. The supermarkets will close soon.
Renate Heller:	The stores close at half past six. So you still have more than an hour.
Ursula Heinrichs:	Yes, but . . .
Renate Heller:	And you always work fast and promptly.
Ursula Heinrichs:	Yes, of course. But. . . .
Renate Heller:	There you go. I expect the results in 20 minutes.
Ursula Heinrichs:	As you like it, Frau Heller. I can't believe it! She doesn't even say 'thank you.'
Renate Heller:	And thank you very much, Frau Heinrichs.
Ursula Heinrichs:	You're welcome.

HEAR . . . SAY 2

Frau Heinrichs:	What do I need? Bread, butter, eggs and jelly for breakfast. But first I'll go to the produce section and get apples, bananas and pears. Oh, right, I'll also need lettuce, tomatoes and a cucumber. Where is the scale? Ah, there it is. I won't need more than two kilos of apples and one kilo of pears. Excuse me, where are the bananas?
Sales Clerk:	We don't have any more bananas. It is almost closing time.
Frau Heinrichs:	When will you get bananas?
Sales Clerk:	We'll have bananas again tomorrow.
Frau Heinrichs:	Thanks.

Frau Heinrichs proceeds to the deli section.

Sales Clerk:	What can I get you?
Frau Heinrichs:	200 grams salami, please.
Sales Clerk:	Sliced up or in one piece?
Frau Heinrichs:	Sliced up, please. And I'll also have 200 grams of Swiss cheese. In one piece, please.
Sales Clerk:	Can it go over?
Frau Heinrichs:	Yes, sure.

Frau Heinrichs finishes her shopping in a rush and hurries to the cashier.

Cashier 1:	Please hurry up.
Frau Heinrichs:	I know, it's late.
Cashier 1:	Yes, you're in luck. We'll close promptly.

ACTIVITY 1
1. *Wie spät ist es?* (What time is it?)
2. *Der Supermarkt schließt um 19 Uhr.* (The supermarket closes at 7PM.)
3. *Ist es schon spät?* (Is it late already?)
4. *Wann schließt der Supermarkt?* (When does the supermarket close?)
5. *Es ist 16 Uhr 30.* (It is 4:30PM.)
6. *Es ist schon sehr spät.* (It is very late already.)

ACTIVITY 2
1. True,   2. False,   3. False,
4. True,   5. True,   6. False

ACTIVITY 3
1. *vier,*   2. *sechs,*
3. *vierundzwanzig,*   4. *sechzehn,*
5. *siebzehn,*   6. *drei,*
7. *dreiundzwanzig,*   8. *sechs,*
9. *zweiundzwanzig,*   10. *elf*

ACTIVITY 4
1. *Es ist halb vier.*
2. *Es ist 18 Uhr 30.*
3. *Es ist viertel nach zwölf.*
4. *Es ist zehn vor neun.*
5. *Es ist 13 Uhr 20.*
6. *Es ist 5 Uhr 15.*
7. *Es ist halb acht.*
8. *Es ist viertel vor eins.*

ACTIVITY 5
1. *Am Dienstag um 16 Uhr 45.* (On Tuesday at 4:45PM.)
2. *Am Mittwoch.* (On Wednesday.)
3. *Am Sonntag um 15 Uhr 30.* (On Sunday at 3:30PM.)
4. *Um 19 Uhr.* (At 7PM)
5. *Am Montag um 12 Uhr.* (On Monday at noon.)
6. *Am Donnerstag.* (On Thursday.)

ACTIVITY 6
arbeiten, brauche, schließen, Haben, machen, mache, ist

ACTIVITY 7
tomato, banana, bread, butter, salad, apple, kilo, gram

ACTIVITY 8
1. Bread, butter, eggs and jam. *(Brot, Butter, Eier und Marmelade.)*
2. In the produce section. *(Obst und Gemüse.)*
3. Because it is almost closing time. *(Es ist ja schon fast Ladenschluss.)*
4. She is not buying carrots. *(Karotten.)*
5. She is buying more cheese. *(Darf's auch ein bisschen mehr sein?)*
6. Because they are about to close. *(Wir machen gleich zu.)*

ACTIVITY 9
1. *Bananen,*   2. *Schinken,*
3. *Brot, Butter,*   4. *Rindfleisch, Pfund,*
   Marmelade,
5. *geschnitten*

ACTIVITY 10
1. *zwei Kinder,*   2. *vier Orangen,*
3. *drei Tomaten,*   4. *fünf Äpfel,*
5. *zwei Salate*

ACTIVITY 11
1. *Nein, ich habe keine Zeit.*
2. *Nein, ich arbeite nicht nach 17 Uhr.*
3. *Nein, die Läden schließen nicht um 18 Uhr 30.*
4. *Nein, ich kaufe keine Bananen.*
5. *Nein, er sagt nicht 'danke'.*
6. *Nein, wir haben keine Wurst.*
7. *Nein, wir haben kein Obst.*

ACTIVITY 12
1. *Die Äpfel wiegen 500 g.*
2. *Der Supermarkt schließt um 20 Uhr 30.*
3. *Nein, ich arbeite am Samstag nicht.*
4. *Nein, ich habe keine Zeit.*
5. *Wir brauchen Brot und Marmelade fürs Frühstück.*

4

WHERE THERE'S A WILL, THERE'S A WAY

Wo ein Wille ist, ist ein Weg

LOOKING AHEAD . . .

In most American cities taking the *Auto* (car) to town is most convenient. Well, not in Germany. Most German cities are so old that they were never designed with *Autos* (cars) in mind: So the roads are rather narrow and it is tough to find *Parkplätze* (parking) anywhere in or near downtown areas. So *öffentliche Verkehrsmittel* (public transportation), the *Bus* (bus), the *Straßenbahn* (street car) and the *Zug* (train), are becoming more and more popular. In this lesson we, too, will take a bus downtown.

ACTIVITY 1: **LET'S WARM UP**

But first, let's see how much about German transportation you can figure out intuitively. What belongs together?

1.	*der Zug*	a.	*der Parkplatz*
2.	*das Auto*	b.	*der Pilot*
3.	*das Taxi*	c.	*der Lokomotivführer*
4.	*der Bus*	d.	*der Taxistand*
5.	*das Flugzeug*	e.	*die Busfahrkarte*

HEAR . . . SAY 1

You know *wie wichtig* (how important) it is to be *pünktlich* in Germany, so it won't surprise you to hear Tristan hurrying along his wife, Isolde. Isn't it always the gals we have to wait for?

Tristan:	Isolde, bitte komm doch endlich. Es ist schon spät.
Isolde:	Ich finde den Mantel nicht.
Tristan:	Dann zieh doch eine Jacke an. Den Mantel suchen wir später.
Isolde:	Warum hast du es denn so eilig? Das Museum läuft doch nicht weg.
Tristan:	Nein, aber der Bus fährt bald ab. Ohne uns.
Isolde:	Wir nehmen den Bus? Ah, hier ist ja der Mantel. Gibt es denn einen Bus direkt zum Museum?
Tristan:	Nein. Zuerst nehmen wir den Bus, und dann die Straßenbahn. Beeil dich bitte, sonst verpassen wir den Bus.
Isolde:	Ich komme ja schon. Warum nehmen wir nicht das Auto?

Tristan:	**Der Bus ist doch sehr praktisch. Und billig.**
Isolde:	(in disbelief) **Du schlägst ja einen ganz neuen Ton an.**
Tristan:	(upon seeing Isolde in her coat) **Du siehst aber gut aus.**
Isolde:	(smiling) **Danke.** (Suddenly she is suspicious.) **Was ist los? Du fährst doch sonst so gern Auto.**
Tristan:	(hesitating) **Es ist kaputt.**

Heads Up!

Komm doch! (Come!), *Zieh . . . an!* (Put . . . on!) and *Beeil dich!* (Hurry up!) are imperative forms used to give commands and voice requests. Imperatives will be discussed at length in a later lesson.

HOW'S THAT AGAIN?

I bet you could tell that Tristan was hiding something . . . But what? Answer the questions below.

1. Isolde is looking for her . . .
   a. coat.
   b. money.
   c. keys.
   d. purse.
2. They are planning to go to . . .
   a. the movies.
   b. the theater.
   c. the museum.
   d. the beach.
3. Why is Tristan in such a hurry?
   a. Because they are late for an appointment.
   b. Because they will miss the train.
   c. Because he wants to catch a movie.
   d. Because the bus will leave without them.
4. They have to take . . . to get to the museum.
   a. a cab
   b. a bus and a streetcar
   c. a train
   d. all of the above

5. Tristan claims that public transportation is . . .
   a. too expensive.
   b. inconvenient.
   c. practical and cheap.
   d. uncomfortable.
6. Isolde is suspicious because . . .
   a. Tristan is usually not in favor of public transportation.
   b. Tristan is more complimentary than usual.
   c. Tristan usually likes to drive.
   d. all of the above.
7. Why are they not taking the car? I mean, why are they *really* not taking the car?
   a. Because Tristan can't drive.
   b. Because the car was stolen.
   c. Because the car broke down.
   d. Because Tristan lost his driver's license.

WORD ON THE STREET

The word *der Ton* (tune, tone) is often used in idiomatic expressions. Changing one's tune is *neue Töne anschlagen,* talking big translates as *große Töne spucken,* and if you don't like the way somebody talks to you, use *Ich verbitte mir diesen Ton* (Lit. I won't accept this tone).

Did You Know?
Germany would not be Germany without its *Autobahn.* Considering that there is no speed limit on the *Autobahn,* it is not surprising that some of the most formidable (sports) cars are 'Made in Germany': Porsche and Mercedes are from Stuttgart, BMW is from Munich, Audi and VW are from Wolfsburg. By the way, the Germans really love their cars, so much so that many a Saturday is spent washing and polishing them carefully in front of the house. If you wish to follow this custom as well while in Germany, make sure you do so on a private parking space. Washing cars on a public street is illegal.

WORKSHOP 1

WORDS TO LIVE BY

ON THE MOVE

There are countless ways to get from one place to another. Here are some of them.

MEANS OF TRANSPORTATION

VEHICLES		ACTIONS	
das Fahrrad	bicycle	*fahren*	to drive, to ride
das Auto	car	*fahren*	to drive, to ride
der Bus	bus	*fahren*	to drive, to ride
der Zug	train	*einsteigen/aussteigen*	to get on/off
die Straßenbahn	streetcar	*abfahren*	to leave
die U-Bahn	subway	*ankommen*	to arrive
das Flugzeug	plane	*fliegen*	to fly
der Hubschrauber	helicopter	*starten/landen*	to take off/to land
öffentliche Verkehrsmittel	public transportation	*nehmen*	to take

And then, there is simply *gehen* (to go).

You can catch a bus at the *Bushaltestelle*, a cab at the *Taxistand*, a train at the *Bahnhof*, and a plane at the *Flughafen*. Before you ever can get on a bus or a train, you have to buy *die Fahrkarte* (ticket); before you get on a plane, you have to buy *das Ticket* (ticket). *Der Fahrplan* (schedule) will tell you when the bus or the train leaves—*abfahren*—and arrives—*ankommen*. The plane, on the other hand, takes off—*starten*—and lands—*landen*. When it is time to board the train—*Alles einsteigen!* (All aboard!)—because the train will leave—*Der Zug fährt ab*—you better get to *das Gleis* (track). You need to get to the *Flugsteig* (gate) on time if you don't want to miss—*verpassen*—your flight—*der Flug*.

ACTIVITY 3: **TAKE IT FOR A SPIN**

Ready to go? Circle the word, which does not belong with the rest of them.

1. *das Taxi, der Bus, das Flugzeug, der Bahnhof, das Auto*
2. *das Ticket, einsteigen, die Fahrkarte, die Anzeigetafel, der Hubschrauber*
3. *der Pilot, der Busfahrer, die U-Bahn, der Autofahrer, der Radfahrer*
4. *einsteigen, abfahren, essen, fahren, fliegen*
5. *die Bushaltestelle, der Flughafen, das Flugzeug, der Bahnhof, der Taxistand*

Did You Know?

The trend in German cities, as all over Europe, actually, is to have *eine verkehrsfreie Innenstadt* (a traffic-free downtown area) functioning as *eine Fußgängerzone* (pedestrian zone). *Parken* (to park) is either impossible in or near downtown areas, or extremely expensive, because you have to park in the *Parkhaus* (parking garage). *Die Wohnviertel* (residential areas) are often in *Zone 30* (30 km zone), which means that you are not allowed to drive any faster than 30 km/hr, which is approximately 19 m/hr. You'll also find *die Spielstraßen* (play streets), where cars are required to drive *Schrittempo* (walking speed), roughly 15 km/hr or less than 10 m/hr, because children may be playing on the streets. Aside from these exceptions, the speed limit in German cities is 50 km/hr, or 31 m/hr, and the speed limit on the *Schnellstraße* (state highway) is 130 km/h, or 81 m/hr. There is no speed limit on the German *Autobahn* (interstate highway), unless you are driving near an airport, a city, or through construction sites. All of continental Europe measures distance and speed in kilometers. One mile is 1.61 kilometers.

THE NITTY GRITTY

AGENTS AND OBJECTS: THE SUBJECT AND THE DIRECT OBJECT IN GERMAN SENTENCES

Just like the English sentence, the German sentence consists of at least a subject and a verb.

> **Der Zug kommt.** The train is arriving.

The subject performs the action. The verb describes the action. If a noun is the subject, the form you use is the nominative case.

Now let's look at a more complicated sentence, one with a direct object:

> **Ich nehme den Zug.** I take the train.

The subject (*Ich*—I) performs the action, the verb (*nehme*—take) is the action, and the direct object (*den Zug*—the train) undergoes the action. To announce its role in the sentence the direct object takes on a special form in German, which is called the accusative case. But don't worry, this is not as difficult as it sounds. The only words that really change in the accusative are the masculine singular articles *der* and *ein*, and not the noun itself. Here are a few examples from the dialogue.

Subject in the nominative—*der Mantel:*

> **Wo ist der Mantel?** Where is the coat?

Object in the accusative—*den Mantel:*

> **Ich finde den Mantel nicht.** I can't find the coat.

Subject in the nominative—*der Bus:*

> **Der Bus fährt bald ab.** The bus is leaving soon.

Object in the accusative—*den Bus:*

> **Zuerst nehmen wir den Bus.** First we'll take the bus.

You'll be surprised how handy that accusative case can be. It lets you order a mouthwatering meal at a restaurant.

Ich nehme den Sauerbraten.	I'll take the Sauerbraten.
Ich trinke einen Rotwein.	I'll drink red wine.
Ich esse keinen Nachtisch.	I don't eat dessert.

Shopping is so much easier, too, now that you know the accusative case.

Ich kaufe den Käse.	I'll buy the cheese.

And remember, the feminine and neuter articles do NOT change in the accusative case.

Ich nehme die Tomate.	I'll take the tomato.
Ich zahle das Huhn.	I'll pay (for) the chicken.

Heads Up!

While German nouns normally do not take any accusative case endings, there is a group of nouns, the so-called *n*-nouns, which add an *-n* or *-en* (if needed for pronunciation) in the accusative. Unfortunately there is no easy way to recognize them, and so it is best to memorize the ones you encounter in this book. Examples of these nouns are *der Herr* (man, mister, sir), *der Name* (name) and *der Patient* (patient). For example: *Ich kenne den Herrn.* (I know the man.) *Ich kenne den Namen.* (I know the name.) *Ich kenne den Patienten.* (I know the patient.)

ACTIVITY 4: **TAKE IT FOR A SPIN**

Please insert the appropriate form of the definite or indefinite article. Use the cues in parentheses.

1. *Ich kaufe _____ Auto.* (indefinite)
2. *Wer zahlt _____ Taxi?* (definite)
3. *Nehmen Sie _____ Straßenbahn?* (definite)
4. *Ich finde _____ Jacke nicht.* (definite)
5. *Wir haben _____ Hubschrauber.* (indefinite)
6. *So verpasst du _____ Zug.* (definite)

Take a Tip from Me

If you are not quite sure whether a noun is the subject or the direct object of the sentence, ask yourself the following questions: *Wer macht das?* (Who is doing this?) This question goes for the subject. *Wen oder was?* (What is he doing?) These questions go for the direct object.

WATCH THAT VERB: IRREGULAR VERBS IN THE PRESENT TENSE

Regular German verbs change their endings to agree with the subject. Irregular verbs do that, too. The good news is that they use the same endings as the regular verbs. The bad news is that their stem also changes, albeit only in the *du* and *er/sie/es* forms. That's what makes them irregular. You already know some of these verbs: *nehmen* (to take), *geben* (to give), *essen* (to eat), and *fahren* (to drive). Here are their forms:

PRESENT TENSE OF IRREGULAR VERBS

NEHMEN (TO TAKE)		*GEBEN* (TO GIVE)		*ESSEN* (TO EAT)		*FAHREN* (TO DRIVE)	
ich	*wir*	*ich*	*wir*	*ich*	*wir*	*ich*	*wir*
nehm-e	nehm-en	geb-e	geb-en	ess-e	ess-en	fahr-e	fahr-en
du nimm-st	*ihr nehm-t*	*du gib-st*	*ihr geb-t*	*du iss-t*	*ihr ess-t*	*du fähr-st*	*ihr fahr-t*
Sie nehm-en	Sie nehm-en	Sie geb-en	Sie geb-en	Sie ess-en	Sie ess-en	Sie fahr-en	Sie fahr-en
er nimm-t	*sie nehm-en*	*er gib-t*	*sie geb-en*	*er iss-t*	*sie ess-en*	*er fähr-t*	*sie fahr-en*

Here are a few other stem-changing verbs. Now that you know how they work, we just have to list the way their stem changes, always in the *du* and *er/sie/es* forms.

- stem-change from *e* → *ie*
  sehen (to see): **seh-** → **sieh-**
  empfehlen (to suggest): **empfehl-** → **empfiehl-**

- stem-change from *a* → *ä*
  schlafen (to sleep): **schlaf-** → **schläf-**
  schlagen (to hit): **schlag-** → **schläg-**
  laufen (to run): **lauf-** → **läuf-**

ACTIVITY 5: TAKE IT FOR A SPIN

Let's take the edge off of these irregular verbs. Show what you've learned and rewrite the sentences using the cues in parentheses.

1. *Wir nehmen ein Taxi. (du)*
2. *Du isst gern Salat? (Sie [formal])*
3. *Fährt Herr Schneider Zug? (wir)*
4. *Empfehlen Sie den Reis oder die Nudeln? (er)*
5. *Ich schlage einen neuen Ton an. (sie)*

Take a closer look at these two sentences:

Ein̲steigen, bitte!	Boarding, please!
Steigen Sie bitte ein̲!	Please get in!

What's going on here? Simple: *Einsteigen* (to board, to get on) is a verb with a separable prefix. This means, quite literally, that the prefix *ein-* is separated from the verb *steigen* when it is used in one of those forms that show tense and person performing the action.

Ich steige in das Taxi ein.	I get in the cab.

The separation of prefix and verb is rather complete (divorce is imminent, so to speak), considering that the verb remains in its usual second position (one party keeps the house), yet the prefix goes all the way to the end of the sentence (the other party moves to the other side of town). The rest of the sentence follows the usual word order.

These separable prefixes are used to modify the meaning of the verb. For example, *fahren* (to drive) becomes *abfahren* (to leave). Here is the list of some common separable prefixes with examples.

- *ab: abfahren* (to leave), *abfliegen* (to take off), *abgeben* (to give up)
- *an: ankommen* (to arrive)
- *ein: einsteigen* (to get in), *einkaufen* (to buy)
- *aus: aussteigen* (to get out)
- *um: umsteigen* (to transfer)

Are you ready for a riddle full of separable verbs?

In Hamburg steigen 2 Männer und eine Frau in den Zug nach München ein.	In Hamburg two men and one woman board the train to Munich.
In Köln steigt ein Mann aus, eine Frau steigt in den Zug nach Berlin um, und drei Frauen steigen ein.	In Cologne one man gets off, one woman transfers to the train to Berlin, and three women board the train.
In Frankfurt steigt eine Mutter mit Kind ein.	In Frankfurt a woman and her child board the train.
In Stuttgart steigen vier Männer ein.	In Stuttgart four men board the train.
Wieviele Frauen kommen in München an?	How many women arrive in Munich?[2]

Still with me? Check the answer at the bottom of the page.

Did You Know?

Train travel in Germany, Austria and Switzerland is extremely fast, punctual and affordable. The *Deutsche Bundesbahn* (German Railroad), the *Schweizerische Bundesbahnen* (Swiss Federal Railroads) and the *Österreichische Bundesbahn* (Austrian Railroad) can take their passengers virtually anywhere in continental Europe. The ICE, short for Inter City Express, is the second fastest

---

* *Vier Frauen kommen in München an.* (Four women arrive in Munich.)

train in the world. The famous white German train with red stripes, which usually has an engine both in the front and the back to make maneuvering in and out of train stations easier, runs between all major cities within Germany, and even all over Europe. The fastest train in the world, by the way, is the French TGV. Third place is held by the *Shinkansen,* the Japanese bullet train.

TAKE IT FOR A SPIN

Please rephrase the sentences saying the opposite of what is stated in them.

1. *Der Zug kommt bald an.*
2. *Ich steige in Dresden aus.*
3. *Meine Kinder fahren morgen ab.*
4. *Wo fährt die Straßenbahn ab?*
5. *Komm, steig doch endlich ein!*

HEAR . . . SAY 2

As you remember, Tristan and Isolde have to take public transportation to town, because their car is broken. They took the bus downtown, and now they are waiting for their transfer to a street car.

Tristan:	Da kommt die Straßenbahn.
Isolde:	Na endlich. Moment mal, Tristan. Das ist die Nummer 6. Die fährt nicht in die Innenstadt.
Tristan:	Doch, hier steht's. Komm schon, steig bitte ein!
Isolde:	Na meinetwegen. (After a few minutes on the street car) **Tristan, die Straßenbahn fährt in die falsche Richtung.** (To the driver) **Entschuldigung, fahren Sie in die Innenstadt?**
Straßenbahnfahrer:	Nein, ich fahre auf die Burg.
Isolde:	Tristan, wir steigen aus. Das nächste Mal hörst du bitte auf mich.

They get off at the next best stop.

Tristan:	Wo sind wir denn eigentlich?
Isolde:	Keine Ahnung. Entschuldigung, wie komme ich in die Innenstadt?
Fußgänger:	(in disbelief) **Zu Fuß?**
Isolde:	Wie weit ist es denn?
Fußgänger:	Das sind etwa vier Kilometer. Das dauert bestimmt eine Stunde.

Tristan:	**Das ist zu viel für mich. Und außerdem fängt es gerade an zu regnen.**
Isolde:	**Das hört auch wieder auf. Solange es nicht schneit, laufen wir.**
Tristan:	**Ich laufe nur bei Sonnenschein. Wir nehmen die Straßenbahn.**
Fußgänger:	**Heute fährt keine Straßenbahn mehr. Es ist schließlich Sonntag. Warum fahren Sie nicht Auto?**
Isolde:	(annoyed) **Fragen Sie ihn doch!**

ACTIVITY 7: HOW'S THAT AGAIN?

1. Where do Tristan and Isolde want to go?
2. Where does the streetcar number 6 actually go?
3. Whom should Tristan listen to in the future?
4. How long does it take to walk downtown?
5. What are the two reasons for Tristan not to walk?
6. Why are there no more streetcars that day?

WORKSHOP 2

WORDS TO LIVE BY

HOW FAR IS IT? ASKING FOR DIRECTIONS, PART I

Taking public transportation can be confusing. And it doesn't get any easier if you have to do it in a foreign language. So let's look at a few ways to avoid getting lost like Tristan and Isolde.

First, you ask for directions when you realize that you are lost.

Entschuldigung, wie komme ich in die Innenstadt?	Excuse me, how do I get (Lit. come) downtown?
Entschuldigung, wo ist das Museum?	Excuse me, where is the museum?
Entschuldigung, wo fährt der Zug nach Freiburg ab?	Excuse me, where does the train to Freiburg leave from?

If you're not sure whether you should walk or drive you might want to ask about distances.

Wie weit ist es?	How far is it?
Wie lange dauert das?	How long will it take?

And this is what the *Einheimischen* (locals) might say.

Zu Fuß dauert das eine Stunde.	On foot that'll take one hour.
Nehmen Sie den Bus.	Take the bus.
Die Straßenbahn fährt auf die Burg.	The streetcar goes to the castle.

Still lost? Don't worry. Practice will make perfect.

TAKE IT FOR A SPIN

Please take part in this conversation.

Tourist: _____ *auf die Burg?*

Einheimischer: *Zu Fuß?*

Tourist: _____*?*

Einheimischer: *Das sind etwa drei Kilometer.*

Tourist: _____*?*

Einheimischer: *Das dauert etwa 45 Minuten. Nehmen Sie doch den Bus.*

Tourist: _____*?*

Einheimischer: *Der Bus fährt hier ab.*

Tourist: _____*.*

Einheimischer: *Bitte, nichts zu danken.*

RAIN OR SHINE: TALKING ABOUT THE WEATHER

Das Wetter (the weather) is hardly the reason for people to travel to Germany, Switzerland or Austria. Any season can be rather unpredictable, so it is best to be ready to handle all conditions. So, let's find out. The *Wetterbericht* (weather report) will tell us: *Wie ist das Wetter heute?* (What's the weather like today?).

Wetterbericht: Das Wetter diese Woche				
MONTAG	**DIENSTAG**	**MITTWOCH**	**DONNERSTAG**	**FREITAG**
Regen	teilweise bewölkt	sonnig	bewölkt	überwiegend sonnig
Höchsttemperatur 18°	Höchsttemperatur 19°	Höchsttemperatur 22°	Höchsttemperatur 18°	Höchsttemperatur 21°
Niedrigsttemperatur 8°	Niedrigsttemperatur 8°	Niedrigsttemperatur 9°	Niedrigsttemperatur 6°	Niedrigsttemperatur 10°

Did You Know?

In Europe the temperature is measured in *Celsius* (centigrade) rather than Fahrenheit. And if you are a mathematical genius, you'll even be able to convert between the two.

To Convert Centigrade/Celsius to Fahrenheit	To Convert Fahrenheit to Centigrade/Celsius
$(\frac{9}{5})\,C° + 32 = F°$	$(F° - 32)\,\frac{5}{9} = C°$
Divide by 5 Multiply by 9 Add 32	Subtract 32 Divide by 9 Multiply by 5

For the rest of us, here are a few guidelines: 61 degrees Fahrenheit are 16 degrees Celsius. And if you have a 40 degree Celsius fever, it's best to consult a doctor, because that is equivalent to a 104 degree Fahrenheit fever. And when the temperature at noon climbs to at least 30 degrees Celsius, German schools close their doors with *hitzefrei* (school's out due to heat) because it is in the high eighties in Fahrenheit, and that is indeed too hot to go to school!

Below are basic weather expressions.

WEATHER EXPRESSIONS			
der Regen	rain	*Es regnet.*	It is raining.
der Sonnenschein	sunshine	*Die Sonne scheint.*	The sun is shining.
der Schnee	snow	*Es schneit.*	It is snowing.
die Wolke	cloud	*Es ist bewölkt.*	It is cloudy.
der Nebel	fog	*Es ist neblig.*	It is foggy.
der Hagel	hail	*Es hagelt.*	Hail is falling.
die Kälte	cold	*Es ist kalt.*	It is cold.
die Wärme	warmth	*Es ist warm.*	It is warm.
die Hitze	heat	*Es ist heiß.*	It is hot.

Note that most weather expressions use the impersonal construction, e.g., *Es regnet/schneit/hagelt*, similar to *es gibt* and *es dauert* you learned earlier.

Heads Up!

If you want to express that you are hot or cold, be sure to use *Mir ist kalt* or *Mir ist warm* or *Mir ist heiß*. Be sure NOT to say *Ich bin heiß* (I am hot) or *Ich bin warm* (I am warm) or *Ich bin kalt* (I am cold). That would mean that you are hot and sexy or that you are gay or that you have a cold personality, respectively. In all likelihood, this is not what you are trying to say.

TAKE IT FOR A SPIN

Let's see if you can take the heat. Please answer the questions below using the *Wetterbericht* from above.

1. *Regnet es am Montag oder am Dienstag?*
2. *Wann scheint die Sonne?*
3. *Was ist die Höchsttemperatur am Freitag?*
4. *Und die Niedrigsttemperatur?*
5. *Wann ist es teilweise bewölkt?*

THE NITTY GRITTY

HE LIKES ME, HE LIKES ME NOT: THE ACCUSATIVE CASE OF PERSONAL PRONOUNS

Just like articles and some nouns, personal pronouns change their form depending on whether they function as subjects or as objects in the sentence.

Ich finde den Mantel nicht.	*Ich finde ihn nicht.*
I can't find the coat.	I can't find it.
Fragen Sie den Mann.	*Fragen Sie ihn.*
Ask the man.	Ask him.

In other words, the pronoun *ihn* (him; it), replacing the object nouns *den Mantel* and *den Mann,* takes the special accusative case form just like the object noun itself. Its corresponding subject form is *er* (he; it). Here are the nominative (subject) and the accusative (object) forms of all personal pronouns.

PERSONAL PRONOUNS			
SUBJECT PRONOUNS		**OBJECT PRONOUNS**	
ich	I	*mich*	me
du	you	*dich*	you
er	he	*ihn*	him
sie	she	*sie*	her
es	it	*es*	it
wir	we	*uns*	us
ihr	you	*euch*	you
sie	they	*ihnen*	them
Sie	you (formal)	*Ihnen*	you (formal)

The personal pronoun helps you avoid repeating yourself.

Instead of:

Da kommt der Bus. Siehst du den Bus?   There's the bus. Do you see the bus?

You say:

Da kommt der Bus. Siehst du ihn?   There's the bus. Do you see it?

Meine Frau weiß das bestimmt. Fragen   My wife surely knows that. Ask her.
Sie sie doch.

And a few pick-up lines will roll off your tongue a bit easier as well, now that you know you are using the personal pronoun in the accusative.

Kennen wir uns nicht?   Don't we know each other?

Darf ich Sie einladen?   May I invite you?

But don't make promises you don't intend to keep.

Ich rufe dich an.   I'll call you.

And once you are hitched, your relationship will remain romantic and loving with the following. (Note that in the next two sentences the pronoun in the accusative follows prepositions: *für* [for], *ohne* [without] and *auf* [to].)

Für dich mache ich alles.   For you, I'll do anything.

Ohne dich bin ich verloren.   I'm lost without you.

And of course, there's this one:

Bis der Tod uns scheidet.   Till death do us part.

ACTIVITY 10:   **TAKE IT FOR A SPIN**

Replace the underlined words with the appropriate object pronoun.

1. *Ich sehe den Hubschrauber.*
2. *Für meine Kinder mache ich alles.*
3. *Er zahlt den Zug.*
4. *Ohne meine Frau bin ich verloren.*
5. *Der Bus fährt ohne dich und mich los.*

ACTIVITY 11: TAKE IT UP A NOTCH

Let's help this tourist get to the bus stop. Can you say it in German?

Tourist:	Excuse me, how do I get downtown?
Local woman:	On foot?
Tourist:	How far is it?
Local woman:	I don't know. My husband knows. Ask him.
Local man:	It is far. Take the bus.
Tourist:	Where does it leave?
Local man:	The bus stop is not far.

CRIB NOTES

HEAR . . . SAY 1

Tristan:	Isolde, please come. It is late.
Isolde:	I can't find my coat.
Tristan:	Then put on your jacket. We'll look for the coat later.
Isolde:	Why are you in such a hurry? The museum won't run away.
Tristan:	No, but the bus will leave soon. Without us.
Isolde:	We're taking the bus? Ah, here's my coat. Is there a bus straight to the museum?
Tristan:	No. First we'll take the bus, then the street car. Hurry up, or we'll miss the bus.
Isolde:	I'm coming. Why are we not taking the car?
Tristan:	Public transportation is practical. And cheap.
Isolde:	You are changing your tune.
Tristan:	My, don't you look good.
Isolde:	Thanks. What's the matter? You usually like driving the car.
Tristan:	It broke down.

HEAR . . . SAY 2

Tristan:	There's the streetcar.
Isolde:	Well, finally. Wait a minute, Tristan. That's the number 6. That doesn't go to downtown.
Tristan:	Yes, it says so right here. Come on, get in, please!
Isolde:	OK. Tristan, the streetcar is going in the wrong direction. Excuse me, are you going downtown?
Bus Driver:	No, I'm going to the castle.
Isolde:	Tristan, we'll get off. Next time you listen to me, please.

They get off at the next best stop.

Tristan:	Where are we?
Isolde:	No idea. Excuse me, how do I get downtown?
Pedestrian:	On foot?
Isolde:	How far is it?
Pedestrian:	It's about 4 kilometers. That'll take an hour.
Tristan:	That's too much for me. And besides, it is starting to rain.
Isolde:	That'll stop. As long as it doesn't snow, we'll walk.
Tristan:	I'll only walk if the sun is shining. We'll take the streetcar.
Pedestrian:	There won't be another streetcar. It is Sunday, after all. Why don't you take the car?
Isolde:	Ask him!

ACTIVITY 1

1 c,   2 a,   3 d,
4 e,   5 b

ACTIVITY 2

1 a,   2 c,   3 d,
4 b,   5 c,   6 d,
7 c

ACTIVITY 3

1. *der Bahnhof,*   2. *einsteigen,*
3. *die U-Bahn,*   4. *essen,*
5. *das Flugzeug*

ACTIVITY 4

1. *ein,*   2. *das,*   3. *die,*
4. *die,*   5. *einen,*   6. *den*

ACTIVITY 5

1. *Du nimmst ein Taxi.*
2. *Sie essen gern Salat?*
3. *Wir fahren Zug?*
4. *Empfiehlt er den Reis oder die Nudeln?*
5. *Sie schlägt einen neuen Ton an.*

ACTIVITY 6

1. *Der Zug fährt bald ab.*
2. *Ich steige in Dresden ein.*
3. *Meine Kinder kommen morgen an.*
4. *Wo kommt die Straßenbahn an?*
5. *Komm, steig doch endlich aus!*

ACTIVITY 7

1. They want to go downtown.
2. It goes to the castle.
3. He should listen to his wife.
4. It probably takes an hour.
5. It is too much for him, and it is starting to rain.
6. It is Sunday.

ACTIVITY 8

Tourist:	*Wie komme ich auf die Burg?*
Local:	*Zu Fuß?*
Tourist:	*Wie weit ist es denn?*
Local:	*Das sind etwa drei Kilometer weit.*
Tourist:	*Wie lange dauert das?*
Local:	*Das dauert etwa 45 Minuten. Nehmen Sie doch den Bus.*
Tourist:	*Wo fährt der Bus ab?*
Local:	*Der Bus fährt hier ab.*
Tourist:	*Vielen Dank.*
Local:	*Bitte, nichts zu danken.*

ACTIVITY 9

1. *Es regnet am Montag.*
2. *Die Sonne scheint am Mittwoch.*
3. *Die Höchsttemperatur am Freitag ist 21 Grad Celsius.*
4. *Die Niedrigsttemperatur ist 10 Grad Celsius.*
5. *Am Dienstag ist es teilweise bewölkt.*

ACTIVITY 10

1. *Ich sehe <u>ihn</u>.*
2. *Für <u>sie</u> mache ich alles.*
3. *Er zahlt <u>ihn</u>.*
4. *Ohne <u>sie</u> bin ich verloren.*
5. *Der Bus fährt ohne <u>uns</u> los.*

ACTIVITY 11

Tourist:	*Entschuldigung, wie komme ich in die Innenstadt?*
Einheimische:	*Zu Fuß?*
Tourist:	*Wie weit ist es?*
Einheimische:	*Ich weiß nicht. Mein Mann weiß es. Fragen Sie ihn.*
Einheimischer:	*Es ist weit. Nehmen Sie den Bus.*
Tourist:	*Wo fährt er ab?*
Einheimischer:	*Die Bushaltestelle ist nicht weit.*

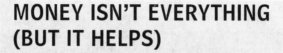
MONEY ISN'T EVERYTHING (BUT IT HELPS)

Geld allein macht nicht glücklich (aber es beruhigt)

(Lit. Money alone won't make you happy [but it'll calm you down])

COMING UP . . .

- *The countdown:* **Numbers above 24**

- *All about me:* **Asking for and giving out personal information**

- *Money isn't everything:* **Checks and balances**

- *I can do it!* **The present tense of modal verbs**

- *What's mine is yours:* **Possessive adjectives**

- *Give it to me!* **Indirect objects**

- *Who's on first:* **German word order in sentences with two objects**

- *Show me the money!* **The dative of personal pronouns**

Travelling to a foreign country can be a challenge because people don't speak English everywhere. But that is not your concern any more, because by the time you are ready to travel to a German-speaking country and you are done with this book, there will be no such thing as a language problem for you. Sometimes it is also the foreign *Währung* (currency) that may cause a few surprises. Granted, it is a bit easier now, because in January 2002 the euro was introduced in 12 participating member states of the European Union (Austria, Belgium, Finland, France, Germany, Greece, Ireland, Italy, Luxemburg, Netherlands, Portugal, and Spain). Note that *in der Schweiz* (in Switzerland), which is not part of the European Union, the *Schweizer Franken* (Swiss franc) is still in use and consists of 100 *Rappen*.

ACTIVITY 1: LET'S WARM UP

Before we go anywhere, make sure you know the answer to these questions.

1. *Ein Schweizer Franken* is . . .
    a. a man by the name of Frank born in Switzerland.
    b. the Swiss currency.
    c. a mountain range in Switzerland.
    d. a Swiss beer.
2. . . . is the best place to exchange money all over Europe.
    a. *Eine Gaststätte*
    b. *Ein Lokal*
    c. *Eine Bank*
    d. All of the above
3. *Eine Kreditkarte* is . . .
    a. an ID
    b. a menu
    c. a driver's license
    d. a credit card
4. Which one of these words translates into the English 'money'?
    a. *das Geld*
    b. *die Kohle*
    c. *die Moneten*
    d. All of the above

Brad Roth, a young American businessman, has just moved to Konstanz, Germany, for a year. When moving into his apartment, he met his charming neighbor, Helene Feuer. She helped him set up his apartment, and the two of them hit it off. About a week later, to thank Helene, Brad has invited her to lunch at a cozy village inn just across the *Schweizer Grenze* (Swiss border). Brad is rather smitten and really wants to impress her.

Helene Feuer: **Ein gemütliches Lokal ist das! Und so nahe an der Grenze. Woher kennen Sie es denn?**

Brad Roth: (trying to sound suave and cosmopolitan) **Ach, ich habe so meine Geheimnisse . . .** (to the waiter) **Zahlen, bitte.**

Kellner: **Zusammen?**

Brad Roth: **Ja, zusammen, bitte.**

Kellner: **Das macht 53 Franken 80.**

Brad is reaching for his wallet. Because he can't find it, he starts frantically looking through his jacket.

Brad Roth: (blushing) **Ich kann meinen Geldbeutel leider nicht finden.**

Kellner: (deadpan) **Tatsächlich.**

Brad Roth: **Mein ganzes Bargeld ist in meinem Geldbeutel.**

Kellner: (deadpan) **Ach wirklich?**

Helene Feuer: **Brad, darf ich die Rechnung begleichen?**

Brad Roth: **Das kommt überhaupt nicht in Frage.** (Brad hands over his credit card.) **Kann ich mit Kreditkarte bezahlen?**

Kellner: **Nein, wir nehmen hier nur Bargeld.**

Brad Roth: **Das kann doch nicht Ihr Ernst sein!**

Kellner: (deadpan) **Doch.**

Brad Roth: (embarrassed) **Das ist mir aber peinlich, Helene. Jetzt muss ich Sie doch um etwas Bargeld bitten.**

Helene Feuer: **Kein Problem. Ich übernehme die Rechnung gern.** (to the waiter) **Kann ich mit Euro bezahlen?**

Kellner: **Nein. Sie sind hier in der Schweiz.**

Helene Feuer: **Oh. Na, dann muss ich schnell auf die Bank gehen. Dort kann ich doch sicher Geld wechseln. Ist hier eine Bank in der Nähe?**

Kellner: **Ja schon, die Schweizer Nationalbank ist gleich gegenüber, aber . . .**

Brad Roth: (relieved) **Na also. Helene, ich . . .**

Kellner: **. . . Samstags haben die Banken hier geschlossen.**

Brad Roth/
Helene Feuer: **Oh . . .**

Let's see if you understood why Brad was turning a deep red. Go ahead, try to answer in German.

1. Does Frank live in Switzerland or in Germany? (use the verb *wohnen* [to live, to reside])
2. What is he unable to find? (use the verb *finden* [to find])
3. What is in his wallet? (use the noun *Geldbeutel* [wallet])
4. Can Brad pay with a credit card? (use the noun *Kreditkarte* [credit card])
5. Why can't Brad and Helene pay with euros? (use the verb *sein* [to be])
6. Why does Helene want to go to the bank? (use the verb *wechseln* [to exchange])
7. Why can't she go to the bank? (use the adjective *geschlossen* [closed])

Did You Know?

Even though *Kreditkarten* (credit cards) are fast becoming a major form of payment all over Europe, Europeans still use traditional forms of payment more than Americans. *Euroschecks* (European checks) and *Scheckkarten* (debit cards) issued from major European banks are accepted for virtually all purchases, whereas many restaurants and stores, particularly in smaller cities and towns do not accept credit cards. When service providers, such as doctors, lawyers or plumbers send a bill, they expect payment via *Überweisung* (automatic bank transfer) rather than via *Scheck* (check). In fact, many service providers do not accept *Scheck-* (debit) or *Kreditkarten* (credit cards) at all. Good old *Bargeld* (cash), of course, will open doors everywhere.

WORD ON THE STREET

Das kommt überhaupt nicht in Frage! (That is out of the question!) nicely expresses Brad's refusal to let Helene pay the bill. It also hints at the fact that their relationship is still rather formal. If they knew each other a little better, Brad would probably say something like *Das kann ich nicht zulassen* (I can't let you do that) or, if he is particularly adamant about it, even *Nur über meine Leiche* (Over my dead body).

WORKSHOP 1

WORDS TO LIVE BY

THE COUNTDOWN: **NUMBERS ABOVE 24**

Considering how much *Bargeld* (cash) is still used in Europe, you might want to have more than 24 *Franken* in your pocket when you travel to Switzerland. So let's play the number game above 24.

NUMBERS FROM 24 TO 100			
25	fünfundzwanzig		
26	sechsundzwanzig		
27	siebenundzwanzig		
28	achtundzwanzig	40	vierzig
29	neunundzwanzig	50	fünfzig
30	dreißig	60	sechzig
31	einunddreißig	70	siebzig
32	zweiunddreißig	80	achtzig
33	dreiundreißig	90	neunzig
34 . . .	vierunddreißig . . .	100	einhundert

And above 100 . . .

NUMBERS FROM 101 TO A BILLION			
101	einhundert(und)eins*	1000	eintausend
110	einhundert(und)zehn*	10 000	zehntausend
159	einhundert(und)neunundfünfzig*	a million	eine Million
200 . . .	zweihundert	a billion	eine Milliarde

Heads Up!

Remember that *sechs* looses the *-s* and *sieben* loses the *-en* when combined with *zehn,* and *eins* becomes *ein* when combined with the twenties and thirties, and so on, that is whenever it is followed by a number. *Dreißig* ends in *-ßig* instead of the otherwise usual *-zig*. Remember that all numbers in the twenties, thirties, and so on, are constructed in the way that follows the numbers in the nursery rhyme "four and twenty blackbirds." For example, when you say the number 36 in German, *sechsunddreißig,* you literally say "six and thirty," not "thirty-six."

ACTIVITY 3: TAKE IT FOR A SPIN

And just to make sure you're up on your feet, here are a few math problems to figure out.

1. *Brad isst den Rostbraten. Der Rostbraten kostet 29 Franken 80. Helene isst die Kässpätzle. Sie kosten 12 Franken 70. Beide trinken ein Glas Wein. Alles zusammen kostet 54 Franken 50. Wie teuer ist ein Glas Wein?*

2. *27 Gäste sind in dem Restaurant. 5 Gäste haben 15.000 Franken auf der Bank, 4 Gäste haben 549.000 Franken, 10 Gäste haben kein Geld. 3 Gäste haben 38.000 Franken, 3 Gäste haben 129.000 Franken, und 2 Gäste haben 5 Franken. Wieviele Franken haben die Gäste zusammen auf der Bank?*

3. *Und wieviele Franken haben die Gäste im Durchschnitt (average)?*

---

*The "und" after the *hundert* is often dropped.

Did You Know?

A euro consists of 100 cents and its value is roughly equivalent to one US dollar, with normal everyday fluctuations. Note that the German punctuation for numbers, and hence, currency amounts, may be a bit confusing: where Americans use a comma, the Germans use a period, and vice versa.

38.80 is	38,80
1,564.35 is	1.564,35

It is customary to write the currency after the amount:

35,80€	1.564,35€

"-" indicates no change (0 cents) as in 780,-€.

THE NITTY GRITTY

I CAN DO IT! THE PRESENT TENSE OF MODAL VERBS

Modal verbs express an attitude towards the action described by the verb. For example, modals express the difference between wanting to do something ("to want") or being forced to do it ("to have to"). Here are the modal verbs and their conjugated forms.

MODAL VERBS						
	KÖNNEN (TO BE ABLE TO)	**MÜSSEN** (TO HAVE TO)	**WOLLEN** (TO WANT)	**DÜRFEN** (TO BE ALLOWED TO)	**SOLLEN** (TO BE SUPPOSED TO)	**MÖCHTEN** (TO LIKE)
ICH	kann	muss	will	darf	soll	möchte
DU	kannst	musst	willst	darfst	sollst	möchtest
SIE	können	müssen	wollen	dürfen	sollen	möchten
ER/SIE/ES	kann	muss	will	darf	soll	möchte
WIR	können	müssen	wollen	dürfen	sollen	möchten
IHR	könnt	müsst	wollt	dürft	sollt	möchtet
SIE	können	müssen	wollen	dürfen	sollen	möchten
SIE	können	müssen	wollen	dürfen	sollen	möchten

Note that in a sentence with a modal verb and a main verb, the modal gets conjugated to express tense, e.g., "He wants to come." The main verb stays in the infinitive form, the neutral form without any tense endings, and stands at the end of the sentence.

Brad _möchte_ die Rechnung _zahlen_.   Brad would like to pay the bill.

Now it's your turn. Show that significant other what a great catch you are.

Ich will dich zum Essen einladen.	I want to take you to dinner.
Ich möchte immer bei dir sein.	I want to be with you, always.
Darf ich dich einladen?	May I treat you?

But don't move too quickly . . .

Darf ich um Ihre Hand bitten?	May I ask for your hand (in marriage)?

. . . or you might hear . . .

Das kann doch nicht dein Ernst sein!	You can't be serious!

WORD ON THE STREET

Das kann doch nicht Ihr Ernst sein! (You [formal] can't be serious! [Lit. This can't be your seriousness]) may have a complicated grammatical structure, but it is a rather popular colloquial expression. A less formal version is *Du machst wohl Witze* (You [informal] must be joking [Lit. You must be making jokes]).

Did You Know?

Switzerland is famous for its precision watches and its scenic beauty with rugged mountain ranges perfect for skiing and many lakes perfect for sailing. But it has been Switzerland's history of political neutrality and utter belief in privacy which has attracted many foreigners. During World War II, Switzerland became a safe haven for political refugees from Germany. Many famous Germans moved to Switzerland prior to World War II, among them the scientist Albert Einstein, the writers Thomas Mann and Hermann Hesse, the philosopher Friedrich Nietzsche, and the composer Richard Wagner. The American writer F. Scott Fitzgerald moved to Switzerland so his wife could undergo treatment in the relative privacy of Switzerland's well-known psychiatric clinics. And among today's foreign celebrities seeking privacy in Switzerland are the German tennis pro Boris Becker and the American musicians Yoko Ono and Tina Turner. What Switzerland is probably most famous for are its liberal banking laws, which allow anybody to open a *Nummernkonto*, a number account whose holder is known, even to bank officials, only by a number), affording the customer complete privacy.

ACTIVITY 4: **TAKE IT FOR A SPIN**

Qualify that sentence using the modal verb in parentheses in its correct form.

1. *Sie _____ mich wirklich zum Essen einladen?* (to want to)
2. *Ja, aber ich _____ leider nicht bezahlen.* (to be able to)
3. *Sie _____ hier nicht parken.* (to be allowed to)

4. *Aber wo _____ ich das Auto dann parken?* (to be supposed to)
5. *Warum _____ er zur Bank gehen?* (to have to)
6. *Er _____ Geld wechseln.* (to like)

WHAT'S MINE IS YOURS: POSSESSIVE ADJECTIVES

If you really want to score, why don't you share your possessions . . .

Meine Freunde sind deine Freunde.   My friends are your friends.

The little words that announce ownership (or a change thereof) are called possessive adjectives. Here are their basic forms:

THE POSSESSIVE ADJECTIVES			
mein	my	unser	our
dein	your	euer	your
Ihr	your (formal)	Ihr	your (formal)
sein	his	ihr (m./f./neut.)	their
ihr	her		
sein	its		

The tricky thing about sharing in German is that possessive pronouns change their endings depending on the gender, number, and case of the noun they precede. In a way, they work like the indefinite article, except that they do have a plural form. So, you'd say *mein Geld* (my money) but *meine Kreditkarte* (my credit card). Let's look at their nominative forms. Remember, the nominative is the case you use when the noun in question is the subject of the sentence.

NOMINATIVE FORMS OF *MEIN* (MY)		
	SINGULAR	**PLURAL**
MASCULINE	mein Geldbeutel	mein-e Geldbeutel
FEMININE	mein-e Kreditkarte	mein-e Kreditkarten
NEUTER	mein Auto	mein-e Autos

Ihre Rechnung kommt sofort.   Your bill will be there, shortly.
Ist das mein Freund oder dein Freund?   Is that my friend or is it your friend?
Ich bin euer Freund.   I am (both) your friend.

If the noun a possessive adjective precedes is a direct object, the possessive adjective changes as well. Let's look at the accusative forms of the possessive adjective *mein.*

ACCUSATIVE FORMS OF *MEIN* (MY)

	SINGULAR	PLURAL
MASCULINE	mein-en Geldbeutel	mein-e Geldbeutel
FEMININE	mein-e Kreditkarte	mein-e Kreditkarten
NEUTER	mein Auto	mein-e Autos

Ich sehe meinen Freund.	I see my friend.
Ohne meinen Geldbeutel kann ich nicht bezahlen.	I can't pay without my wallet.
Ich komme nicht ohne meinen Freund.	I won't come without my friend.

ACTIVITY 5: TAKE IT FOR A SPIN

Complete the following conversation by inserting the possessive pronoun in its correct form.

Kellner: *Darf ich _____ Rechnung bringen? (your, formal)*

Gast: *_____ Freund will die Rechnung begleichen. (my) Aber er kann*

_____ Geldbeutel nicht finden. (his) _____ Kreditkarte ist im Geldbeutel. (his) _____ Bargeld ist im Auto. (our)

Kellner: *Das kann doch nicht _____ Ernst sein. (your, formal)*

Did You Know?

Not only did Switzerland harbor famous foreigners, Switzerland also sent famous people out into the world. The linguist Ferdinand de Saussure (1857–1913), founder of modern study of language, linguistics, was born in Geneva, Switzerland. The writer Max Frisch (1911–1991), born in Zurich, whose plays and novels are widely read in schools in all German-speaking countries, is most well-known for his novel *Homo Faber,* made into a movie by Volker Schlöndorff in 1991. And Maximilian Bircher-Benner (1867–1939), a physician who propagated a healthy diet of vegetables and fruit in his sanatorium in Zürich, claims worldwide fame as the inventor of the *Muesli* cereal. Albert Schweitzer, the famous physician and philosopher, a Nobel Peace Prize winner, despite his name, was not Swiss. He was born a German in the Alsace in 1875, and became a French citizen in 1918, after World War I.

Just a few days after his embarrassing lunch date with Helene in Switzerland, Brad goes to the bank to open an account. He knows Helene Feuer works there, and obviously he hopes to see her again . . .

Brad Roth:	Ich möchte ein Konto eröffnen.
Bankangestellte:	Aber natürlich. Bitte folgen Sie mir.

The bank employee leads him to an office in the back to introduce him to . . .

Bankangestellte:	Meine Kollegin, Frau Feuer, wird Ihnen weiterhelfen.
Brad Roth:	(acting surprised) Helene! Das ist aber eine Überraschung.
Helene Feuer:	(genuinely surprised) Das kann man wohl sagen.
Brad Roth:	Schön, Sie wiederzusehen.
Helene Feuer:	Ja, gleichfalls. Sie wollen ein Konto eröffnen?
Brad Roth:	Ja, unter anderem.
Helene Feuer:	Ein Girokonto oder ein Sparkonto?
Brad Roth:	Was empfehlen Sie mir?
Helene Feuer:	Nun, bei einem Girokonto kann Ihr Arbeitgeber Ihr Gehalt direkt auf Ihr Konto überweisen. Und Sie können alle regelmäßigen Zahlungen, wie die Miete, zum Beispiel, direkt überweisen.
Brad Roth:	Das klingt sehr praktisch. Kann ich das gleich machen?
Helene Feuer:	Ja, selbstverständlich. Ich brauche nur ein paar persönliche Angaben wie Name, Geburtstag und Geburtsort. Zeigen Sie mir doch bitte Ihren Ausweis.
Brad Roth:	Ja, natürlich.

Brad reaches for his wallet to get his ID.

Helene Feuer:	(smiles) Ich sehe, Sie haben Ihren Geldbeutel heute dabei.
Brad Roth:	(embarrassed) Ja. Hier ist mein Ausweis.
Helene Feuer:	Danke. Oh. (Helene picks up a picture that fell out of Brad's wallet.) Das muss wohl Ihnen gehören.
Brad Roth:	(blushing) Ja, das ist meine Tochter.
Helene Feuer:	(surprised) Sie haben eine Tochter?
Brad Roth:	(hesitant) Ja.
Helene Feuer:	Sie sind also verheiratet?
Brad:	Ja. Das heißt nein. Ich bin geschieden.
Helene Feuer:	So ein Zufall. Ich auch.

Let's see what we (and Helene) learned about Brad in this conversation.

	TRUE	FALSE
1. Brad went to the bank only to open an account.	_____	_____
2. Brad knows that Helene works at the bank.	_____	_____
3. Brad has a son.	_____	_____
4. Brad has two daughters.	_____	_____
5. Brad is married.	_____	_____

Heads Up!

The two phrases *Schön, Sie wiederzusehen* (Nice to see you again) and *Schön, Sie kennenzulernen* (Nice to meet you) are, grammatically, infinitive constructions with *zu*. Even though this construction usually works much like its English equivalent, we are faced with a tricky spin here because both *wiedersehen* and *kennenlernen* are so-called separable verbs. These verbs come in two parts (*wieder* and *sehen, kennen* and *lernen*.) The *zu* which normally precedes the verb (e.g., *Schön, Sie zu sehen.* [Nice to see you]) stands between the two parts of the separable verbs.

WORD ON THE STREET

Wohl is often used to express emphasis and need not be translated: *Das kann man wohl sagen.* (That's for sure. [Lit. You can surely say that.]) *Das kann doch wohl nicht Ihr Ernst sein.* (You can't be serious. [Lit. This surely cannot be your seriousness.]) *Willst du das wohl lassen?* (Will you stop that?)

WORKSHOP 2

WORDS TO LIVE BY

ALL ABOUT ME: **ASKING FOR AND GIVING OUT PERSONAL INFORMATION**

Everybody loves to talk about him/herself. Right? Well, the trick is to ask the right questions to solicit the pertinent answers. Some of these questions and answers you already know..

Wie heißen Sie?   What's your name?
Ich heiße/Mein Name ist . . .   My name is . . .

| Was sind Sie von Beruf? | What is your profession? |
| Ich bin Lehrer von Beruf. | I am a teacher. |

Other questions, and their answers, are best used sparingly. . . .

Wie lautet Ihre Addresse?	What is your address?
Meine Adresse lautet Berliner Weg 25 in 1000 Berlin 20.	My address is 25 Berliner Weg in 1000 Berlin 20.
Wo wohnen Sie?	Where do you live?
Ich wohne im Berliner Weg.	I live in the Berliner Weg.

This is the most popular question these days . . .

| Wie ist Ihre Telefonnummer? | What's your phone number? |
| Meine Nummer ist 089/22334456. | My number is 089/22334456. |

Did You Know?

German addresses consist of the same elements as American addresses but are arranged a bit differently: Mommsenstraße 85, 509337 Köln. The street name (Mommsenstraße) is followed, not preceded, by the house number (85), yet the zip code (509337) precedes he name of the city (Köln). Telephone numbers consist of Vorwahl (area code) and Rufnummer (telephone number). Most area codes begin with a '0'. For example: 0711 (Stuttgart), 089 (Munich), 030 (Berlin). In writing, the area code is often noted in parentheses, or separated from the telephone number with a backslash. With variations depending on the size of the city, most telephone numbers consist of at least five numbers. They are arranged in pairs of two. In writing a space may be left between the pairs of two. For example: 31 78 79 or simply, 317879. A hyphen, backslash or period are not used to separate the pairs of numbers. In speech, you can either say numbers one by one, or in pairs of two. For example: drei eins sieben acht sieben neun or einunddreißig achtundsiebzig neunundsiebzig.

And here's one more question that may lead to very surprising answers.

Wie ist Ihr Geburtsdatum?	What is your date of birth?
Ich bin am 3. Mai 1980 geboren.	I was born on May 3, 1980.
Wo sind Sie geboren?	Where were you born?
Wann haben Sie Geburtstag?	When is your birthday?
Ich habe am 3. Mai Geburtstag.	My birthday is on May 3.

THE FINE PRINT

While in dates English states the month first, day second and year third, German starts with the day followed by the month and the year: 3. Mai 1980 (May 3rd 1980), 1. Januar 2005 (January 1st 2005). Ordinal numbers (numbers such as 1st, 2nd, 3rd) are used in dates. If not spelled out, ordinal numbers are marked by a period in German: 1. (erster), 2. (zweiter) 3. (dritter). More on ordinal numbers in Lesson 9.

And if you really need to have the details, you ask for *der Familienstand* (marital status)

Sind Sie verheiratet?	Are you married?
Nein, ich bin geschieden.	No, I am divorced.
Ich bin Witwer/Witwe.	I am a widower/widow.
Ich bin verlobt.	I am engaged.
Ich habe einen Freund/eine Freundin.	I have a boyfriend/girlfriend.
Ich bin ledig.	I am single.

ACTIVITY 7: TAKE IT FOR A SPIN

Please fill out this form with your own personal data. Check in the Crib Notes whether you answered correctly.

Name _____

Adresse _____

_____

Telefonnummer _____ (Privat) _____ (Büro) _____ (Handy)

Geburtstag _____

Geburtsort _____

Beruf _____

Familienstand ledig ☐   verheiratet ☐   geschieden ☐   verwitwet ☐

SHOW ME THE MONEY: CHECKS AND BALANCES

Banking in a foreign country is pretty much what it is at home—confusing. I mean, really, who can tell the difference between a savings and loan and a credit union? A credit union . . . well, this is not a course on banking, and so I won't go into detail. But I will dive into the relevant vocabulary.

die Bank (bank)	*die Sparkasse* (savings and loan)	*das Kreditinstitut* (credit union, bank)	
das Konto (account)	*das Girokonto* (checking account)	*das Sparkonto* (savings account)	*das Nummernkonto* (number account)
ein Konto einrichten (to open an account)	*ein Konto auflösen* (to close an account)	*Geld sparen* (to save money)	*Geld ausgeben* (to spend money)
die Einzahlung (credit)	*die Auszahlung* (debit)	*Geld einzahlen* (to credit one's account)	*Geld auszahlen* (to debit one's account)
die Kontonummer (account number)	*der Kontoauszug* (statement)		
der Kredit (credit)	*der Girokredit* (overdraft protection)		
der Scheck (check)	*die Scheckkarte* (debit card)	*die Kreditkarte* (credit card)	
der Dauerauftrag (regular automatic transfer)	*die Überweisung* (automatic transfer)	*Geld überweisen* (to transfer money)	
der Schalter (teller)	*der Geldautomat* (ATM machine)	*Geld abheben* (to take out money)	

ACTIVITY 8: TAKE IT FOR A SPIN

Please fill in the correct German term.

1. Most people pay their rent via _____.
2. If you want to check your balance, you need to check your _____.
3. After hours you can get money at the _____.
4. If you are short of money at the end of the month, you might need to use your _____.
5. If you are trying to save money, you'll need a _____.

Did You Know?

Most European banks offer an automatic *Girokredit* (overdraft protection) with a checking account. Since most regular payments such as rent, mortgage, telephone or utilities bills are due around the last of the month, and many customers receive their pay around the first of the month, the *Girokredit* is heavily used by many customers when paying their bills by *Dauerauftrag* (regular automatic transfer). The banks gladly allow such heavy usage and charge a hefty percentage. So, everybody wins, right? Most banks are open Monday through Friday from 8:30 or 9:00 to 4:00; many stay open until 5:30 on Thursdays. Smaller branches may be closed between 1:00 and 2:30 for lunch and on Wednesday afternoons.

THE NITTY GRITTY

GIVE IT TO ME! INDIRECT OBJECTS

We have learned that the subject (*Ich* in the sentence below) performs the action (*zeige* in the sentence below), and that the direct object (*den Ausweis* in the sentence below) undergoes the action. The indirect object (*ihr* in the sentence below) receives the action.

Ich zeige ihr den Ausweis.	I show her the ID. (or: I show the ID to her.)

Here's another example:

Brad gibt der Angestellten sein Geld.	Brad gives the employee his money. (or: Brad gives his money to the employee.)

To announce its role in the sentence, the indirect object takes on a particular form in German, the dative case, while in English it is usually preceded by a preposition. Here are all the forms.

THE DATIVE CASE OF ARTICLES		DEFINITE ARTICLE	INDEFINITE ARTICLE	PLURAL	
MASCULINE		*dem Mann*	*einem Mann*	*den Männern*	
FEMININE	*Ich gebe*	*der Frau*	*einer Frau*	*den Frauen*	*meine Nummer.*
NEUTER		*dem Kind*	*einem Kind*	*den Kindern*	

Note that the nouns only change in the plural with the addition of the ending *-n/-en*, that masculine and neuter forms of the article are both *dem*, and that the plural article is *den* for all three genders.

THE FINE PRINT

Note that *kein* (not any, no) and the singular possessive adjectives take the same case endings as the indefinite article: *Ich gebe einem/keinem/meinem Mann die Telefonnummer* (I give my number to a man/no man/my husband). In the plural, the possessive adjectives take the same case endings as the definite article: *Ich gebe den/meinen Kindern die Telefonnummer* (I give the number to the/my children).

Take a Tip from Me

If you're not sure if an object should take the dative or the accusative case in German, check if the preposition "to" fits in front of it in English. If so, you found the dative object.

Let's make sure that dative objects won't cramp your style. The next few sentences will help you appear in a good light.

Ich gebe dem Kellner immer viel Trinkgeld.	I always give a good tip to the waiter.
Ich überweise meinem Vermieter die Miete immer pünktlich.	I always transfer my rent to my landlord on time.

Some things you should always do yourself . . .

> **Bitte geben Sie meiner Sekretärin Ihre**   Please give your phone number to my assistant.
> **Telefonnummer.**

ACTIVITY 9:   **TAKE IT FOR A SPIN**

Please translate.

1. Can you (formal) help the man?
2. Can I give your mother my phone number?
3. I give the waiter a tip.
4. The waiter gives me the food.
5. We transfer the money to the landlord.

SHOW ME THE MONEY: THE DATIVE OF PERSONAL PRONOUNS

As you know, personal pronouns change their form depending on their function in the sentence just like do nouns, articles and adjectives. For example:

> **Ich zeige der Frau den Ausweis. → Ich zeige ihr den Ausweis.**
> I am showing the ID to the woman. → I'm showing her the ID.

Here are the dative forms of personal pronouns.

THE DATIVE CASE OF PERSONAL PRONOUNS			
NOMINATIVE OR SUBJECT		DATIVE OR INDIRECT OBJECT	
ich	I	mir	to me
du	you	dir	to you
Sie	you (formal)	Ihnen	to you (formal)
er	he	ihm	to him
sie	she	ihr	to her
es	it	ihm	to it
wir	we	uns	to us
ihr	you	euch	to you
sie	they	ihnen	to them

And now let's see these pronouns in action.

> **Geben Sie mir bitte Ihre Adresse.**   Please give me your address.
> **Können Sie ihm helfen?**   Can you help him?

And now, promises, promises . . .

Ich bleibe immer bei dir.	I'll always be with you.
Nichts kommt jemals zwischen uns.	Nothing will ever come between us.
Was mir gehört, gehört nun auch dir.	What belongs to me also belongs to you now.

WHO'S ON FIRST: GERMAN WORD ORDER IN SENTENCES WITH TWO OBJECTS

If a German sentence has both a direct and an indirect object, the indirect object always comes first, unless the direct object is a personal pronoun.

Brad gibt dem Kellner ein Trinkgeld.	Brad gives the waiter a tip.
Bitte zeigen Sie mir Ihren Ausweis.	Please show me your ID.
Bitte zeigen Sie ihn mir.	Please show it to me.

ACTIVITY 10:   TAKE IT FOR A SPIN

Please translate.

1. Please, can you help me?
2. I'll transfer the money to you (formal).
3. He shows her his ID.
4. She gives him his credit card.
5. This belongs to me.

ACTIVITY 11:   TAKE IT UP A NOTCH

Read the following story. Then replace the underlined words with the correct personal pronoun. But think first: Is it nominative, accusative or dative you want?

Meine Mutter möchte ein Sparkonto eröffnen. Ich möchte *meiner Mutter* helfen. Ich gehe mit *meiner Mutter* auf die Bank. *Meine Mutter und ich* sprechen dort mit *einer Angestellten*. *Die Angestellte* hilft *meiner Mutter und mir*. Ich zeige der Angestellten *den Ausweis*. Die Angestellte gibt *meiner Mutter* eine Kontonummer. *Meine Mutter* hat nun *ein Sparkonto*.

STRUT YOUR STUFF

This is a review section. We'll have one of these after Lesson 5, Lesson 10 and Lesson 15. Here you can put what you've learned so far together. So, are you ready? Go ahead. Impress yourself.

TAKE IT FOR A SPIN

Tell us about yourself. Please answer these questions.

1. *Wie heißen Sie?*
2. *Woher sind Sie?*
3. *Was sind Sie von Beruf?*
4. *Sind Sie verheiratet?*
5. *Haben Sie Kinder?*

TAKE IT FOR A SPIN

Now which question works with these answers?

1. *Das ist <u>meine Frau</u>.*
2. *Der Bus fährt <u>am Bahnhof</u> ab.*
3. *Es kostet <u>vier Euro</u>.*
4. *Ich empfehle <u>den Rostbraten</u>.*
5. *Mein Name ist <u>Rüdiger</u>.*

TAKE IT FOR A SPIN

Can you tell the story? Please put these sentences in their chronological order.

Ich nehme den Bus nach Hause. Ich bestelle den Rostbraten. Ich habe Hunger. Der Kellner bringt die Rechnung. Ich nehme den Bus zum Restaurant. Ich gebe viel Trinkgeld. Der Kellner bringt die Speisekarte. Ich bestelle Nachtisch. Der Rostbraten ist sehr gut.

TAKE IT FOR A SPIN

Who? Whom? To whom? That's the question. Nip those cases in the bud . . .

1. *Ich habe* (two children).
2. *Meine Kinder wollen* (a bicycle) *kaufen.*
3. *Mein Mann schenkt* (them) *ein Fahrrad.*
4. (My children) *fahren Fahrrad.*
5. *Meine Kinder nehmen* (the bus) *nicht mehr.*
6. *Ich habe* (no money) *mehr.*
7. (My husband and I) *müssen nun laufen.*

CRIB NOTES

Helene Feuer:	What a cozy restaurant/inn this is. And so close to the border. How come you know it?
Brad Roth:	Well, I have my secrets . . . The bill, please.
Waiter:	Together?
Brad Roth:	Yes, together, please.
Waiter:	That's 53 Francs 80.

Brad is reaching for his wallet. As he can't find it, he starts frantically looking through his jacket.

Brad Roth:	I can't find my wallet, unfortunately.
Waiter:	Really?
Brad Roth:	All my cash is in my wallet.
Waiter:	Indeed?
Helene Feuer:	Brad, may I take care of the bill?
Brad Roth:	That is out of the question! Can I pay with a credit card?
Waiter:	No, we only take cash here.
Brad Roth:	You can't be serious!
Waiter:	Indeed, I can.
Brad Roth:	That's so embarrassing, Helene. I have to ask you for some cash, after all.
Helene Feuer:	No problem. I'll gladly pay the bill. Can I pay with euro?
Waiter:	No. You're in Switzerland.
Helene Feuer:	Oh. Well, then I'll just have to go to the bank quickly. I'm sure I can exchange money there. Is there a bank close by?
Waiter:	Yes, of course, the Swiss National Bank is just across the street, but . . .
Brad Roth:	There you go. Helene, I . . .
Waiter:	. . . the banks are closed on Saturdays.
Brad Roth/ Helene Feuer:	Oh . . .

Brad Roth:	I'd like to open an account.
Bank Clerk:	Of course. Please follow me.

The bank employee leads him to an office in the back to introduce him to . . .

Bank Clerk:	My colleague, Frau Feuer, will help you.
Brad Roth:	Helene! That's a surprise.
Helene Feuer:	It certainly is.
Brad Roth:	Nice to see you again.
Helene Feuer:	Yes, indeed. You want to open an account?
Brad Roth:	Yes, among other things.
Helene Feuer:	Checking or savings account?
Brad Roth:	Which do you recommend?
Helene Feuer:	Well, with a checking account your employer can transfer your paycheck directly to your account. And you can transfer all regular payments, like your rent, directly.
Brad Roth:	That sounds very practical. Can I do this today?
Helene Feuer:	Yes, of course. I just need a few personal data like name, date of birth and place of birth. Please show me your ID.
Brad Roth:	Yes, of course.

Brad reaches for his wallet to get his ID.

Helene Feuer:	I see you have your wallet on you today.
Brad Roth:	Yes, here is my ID.
Helene Feuer:	Thanks. Oh. This must be yours.
Brad Roth:	Yes, that's my daughter.
Helene Feuer:	You have a daughter?
Brad Roth:	Yes.
Helene Feuer:	So you are married?
Brad Roth:	Yes. That means no. I am divorced.
Helene Feuer:	What a coincidence. I am too.

ACTIVITY 1
1. b   2. c   3. d
4. d

ACTIVITY 2
1. *Frank wohnt in Deutschland.*
2. *Er kann seinen Geldbeutel nicht finden.*
3. *Sein Bargeld ist im Geldbeutel.*
4. *Nein, er kann nicht mit der Kreditkarte bezahlen.*
5. *Sie sind in der Schweiz.*
6. *Sie kann dort Geld wechseln.*
7. *Die Banken sind geschlossen.*

ACTIVITY 3
1. *Ein Glas Wein kostet 6 Franken.*
2. *Die Gäste haben zusammen 2.772.010 Franken.*
3. *Im Durchschnitt haben die Gäste 102.667,03 Franken.*

ACTIVITY 4
1. *wollen,*   2. *kann,*   3. *können,*
4. *soll,*   5. *muss,*   6. *möchte*

ACTIVITY 5
Ihre, Mein, seinen, Seine, Unser, Ihr

ACTIVITY 6
1. False,   2. True,   3. False,
4. False,   5. False

ACTIVITY 7
Answers will vary. Here is the translation of the form items.
Name
Address
Phone number; (H); (O); (Cell)
Date of birth
Place of birth
Profession
Marital status; single; married; divorced; widowed

ACTIVITY 8
1. *Dauerauftrag,*
2. *Kontoauszug,*
3. *Geldautomat,*
4. *Girokredit,*
5. *Sparkonto*

ACTIVITY 9
1. *Können Sie dem Mann helfen?*
2. *Kann ich Ihrer/deiner Mutter meine Telefonnummer geben?*
3. *Ich gebe dem Kellner ein Trinkgeld.*
4. *Der Kellner gibt mir das Essen.*
5. *Wir überweisen dem Vermieter das Geld.*

ACTIVITY 10
1. *Bitte, können Sie mir helfen?*
2. *Ich überweise Ihnen das Geld.*
3. *Er zeigt ihr seinen Ausweis.*
4. *Sie gibt ihm seine Kreditkarte.*
5. *Das gehört mir.*

ACTIVITY 11
Sie, ihr, ihr, Wir, ihr, Sie, uns, ihn, ihr, Sie, es.

ACTIVITY 12
1. *Ich heiße . . . / Mein Name ist . . .*
2. *Ich bin aus . . .*
3. *Ich bin . . . von Beruf.*
4. *Nein, ich bin nicht verheiratet/Ja, ich bin verheiratet.*
5. *Ja, ich habe . . . Kind(er)./Nein, ich habe keine Kinder.*

ACTIVITY 13
1. *Wer ist das?*
2. *Wo fährt der Bus ab?*
3. *Wieviel macht/kostet das?*
4. *Was empfehlen Sie/empfiehlst du?*
5. *Wie heißen Sie?/Wie ist Ihr Name?*

ACTIVITY 14
Ich habe Hunger. Ich nehme den Bus zum Restaurant. Der Kellner bringt die Speisekarte. Ich bestelle den Rostbraten. Der Rostbraten ist sehr gut. Ich bestelle Nachtisch. Der Kellner bringt die Rechnung. Ich gebe viel Trinkgeld. Ich nehme den Bus nach Hause.

ACTIVITY 15
1. *Ich habe zwei Kinder.*
2. *Meine Kinder wollen ein Fahrrad kaufen.*
3. *Mein Mann schenkt ihnen ein Fahrrad.*
4. *Meine Kinder fahren Fahrrad.*
5. *Meine Kinder nehmen den Bus nicht mehr.*
6. *Ich habe kein Geld mehr.*
7. *Wir/Mein Mann und ich müssen nun laufen.*

HASTE MAKES WASTE!

Gut Ding will Weile haben
(Lit. Good things take their time)

Am Telefon (on the telephone) you'll really need to know your stuff around language. Talking to a person face-to-face can be tricky, but on the phone you don't have facial expressions and gesticulation to help interpret what is being said and express yourself. But don't worry, I'm right here with all the help you'll ever need *am Telefon* (on the phone). The most important tip right off the bat: *Immer zurückrufen!* Always call back! *Und zwar sofort!* And I mean, right away!

ACTIVITY 1: **LET'S WARM UP**

Before you make that first call in German, let's get a few basics straight.

1. *Eine Telefonzelle* is . . .
   a. a prison cell.
   b. a phone booth.
   c. a cell phone.
2. *Ein Handy* is . . .
   a. a cell phone
   b. a hand-held computer
   c. a handshake.
3. In Germany you answer the phone . . .
   a. with a friendly *"Hallo."*
   b. with a curious *"Wer ist denn am Apparat?"*
   c. by stating your name.
4. *Ein Anrufbeantworter* is
   a. a person taking a message
   b. an answering machine
   c. an operator

And now let's move on . . .

Claudia Kerner is trying to reach her friend Klaus Rosin. The two of them had arranged to have dinner and go see a movie tonight. Claudia is calling him now to discuss where to meet.

Anrufbeantworer:	Guten Tag. Sie haben den Anschluss von Klaus Rosin erreicht. Leider bin ich im Moment telefonisch nicht erreichbar. Bitte hinterlassen Sie mir eine Nachricht. Ich rufe Sie baldmöglichst zurück.
Claudia:	Hallo Klaus, ich bin's, Claudia. Wo steckst du denn? Hast du unsere Verabredung etwa vergessen? Ruf mich bitte zurück. Meine Nummer hast du ja. (She hangs up.) Das gibt's doch nicht. Er hat doch gesagt ich soll ihn heute um 18 Uhr anrufen. Na, ich versuch's mal im Büro. Vielleicht ist er länger dort geblieben. (She's looking through her purse.) Wo habe ich die Nummer nur aufgeschrieben. Ah, hier ist sie ja: 38 90 76.
Sekretärin:	Kohlmeier Schokoladen, Schneider am Apparat.
Claudia:	Ja, Kerner, guten Tag. Kann ich bitte Herrn Rosin sprechen?
Sekretärin:	Tut mir leid, Herr Rosin hat das Haus schon verlassen. Kann ich ihm etwas ausrichten?
Claudia:	Nein danke. Ich rufe einfach sein Handy an. Auf Wiederhören.
Sekretärin:	Auf Wiederhören.
Claudia:	(dialing) 0176 / 97 73 67 90. Besetzt! Jetzt gebe ich's auf. Soll er mich doch anrufen!

Meanwhile, across town, Klaus is trying to call Claudia on his cell phone. He is stuck in heavy traffic.

Klaus:	Besetzt! (He hangs up and dials another number.) Vielleicht hat sie mir ja eine Nachricht im Büro hinterlassen.
Sekretärin:	Kohlmeier Schokoladen, Schneider am Apparat.
Klaus:	Rosin. Frau Schneider, hat jemand für mich angerufen?
Sekretärin:	Ja, vor ewa 10 Minuten hat eine Frau Kerner angerufen. Sie hat aber keine Nachricht hinterlassen.
Klaus:	Danke. Und gehen Sie doch nach Hause. Es ist doch schon so spät.
Sekretärin:	Ja, ich bin schon auf dem Weg gewesen, da haben Sie angerufen.
Klaus:	Tut mir leid. Bis morgen dann. (He hangs up, and dials Claudia's number again.) Vielleicht ist jetzt nicht mehr besetzt.
Claudia:	Kerner.
Klaus:	Hallo, Claudia, ich bin's, Klaus. Ich bin . . .
Claudia:	Hallo? Wer ist denn da?
Klaus:	Claudia? Hallo?
Claudia:	Hallo? So was! Einfach aufgelegt!
Klaus:	Claudia? Ach, verflixt! Jetzt ist die Batterie leer!

Heads Up!

The apostrophe in *Ich bin's* (It's me) is hiding an "e" to show the contraction of the pronoun *es*, similarly to *Was gibt's* or *Was darf's sein*.

ACTIVITY 2: HOW'S THAT AGAIN?

Despite an answering machine, a secretary and a cell phone, Claudia and Klaus can't reach each other. What happened? Try to answer in German.

1. Who answers the phone at Klaus' apartment?
2. Does Claudia leave a message on his answering machine?
3. Who answers the phone at Klaus' office?
4. Is Klaus still at the office?
5. Where is Claudia calling after she called Klaus' office?
6. Why can't Klaus reach Claudia the first time he calls her?
7. Why can't he reach her the second time he calls her?

Did You Know?

There are several phone companies *in Deutschland* today, but this is a fairly recent development. *Die Deutsche Telekom,* which remains to be the major phone company, used to be part of the government-administered *Deutsche Bundespost,* which also administered the German postal service and had a complete monopoly over the communications industry until recently. But with privatization and the birth and success of the *Handy* (cell phone), pronounced as (hahn-dee), many more telephone companies came to life. The Germans fully embraced *Handys,* so much so that a greater percentage of the population now owns a *Handy* in Germany than in the USA. On the other hand, many private households in Germany may not yet have an answering machine, let alone an answering service, and even if they do, they may not use them on a daily basis. As a result, people may not be quite used to checking their messages or leaving them regularly. So, if it's urgent that you get your message across, it's a good idea to keep calling back until you talk to a live person.

WORDS TO LIVE BY

WILL YOU GET THAT PLEASE? TALKING ON THE TELEPHONE

Here are a few helpful phrases for your telephone relations:

ON THE PHONE		
WHAT YOU'D LIKE TO DO OR SAY	**HOW TO DO OR SAY IT IN GERMAN**	**THE ENGLISH EQUIVALENT**
BEFORE YOU EVER TALK ON THE PHONE	*ans Telefon gehen*	to answer the phone
ANSWERING THE PHONE	*(den Hörer) abheben*	to pick up the phone
	Rosin	Rosin.
	Kerner, guten Tag.	Kerner, good day.
	Firma Rubenstein & Co, Braunschmid am Apparat.	This is Rubenstein & Co, Braunschmid.
IDENTIFYING YOURSELF	*Kerner, guten Tag, . . .*	Kerner, good day, . . .
ASKING FOR SOMEONE	*. . . kann ich bitte mit Herrn Rosin sprechen?*	. . . can I speak with Mr. Rosin, please?
	. . . ist Herr Rosin im Hause?	. . . is Mr. Rosin in?
STALLING	*Augenblick, bitte.*	Just a moment, please.
	Bleiben Sie bitte am Apparat.	Please stay on the line.
	Warten Sie bitte einen Moment.	Hold on a moment.
EXPRESSING REGRET	*Nein, Herr Rosin ist leider nicht da.*	No, unfortunately, Mr. Rosin is not in.
	Es tut mir leid, Herr Rosin hat das Haus bereits verlassen.	I'm sorry, Mr. Rosin has already left the office.
CONNECTING SOMEONE	*Ich verbinde.*	I'll connect you.
TAKING/LEAVING MESSAGES	*Kann ich ihm etwas ausrichten?*	Can I tell him something?
	Kann ich ihm eine Nachricht hinterlassen?	May I leave a message?
	Kann er Sie zurückrufen?	Can he call you back?
	Kann ich später zurückrufen?	Can I call back later?
	Wann/Wo kann ich ihn erreichen?	When/Where can I reach him?
ENDING THE CONVERSATION	*Auf Wiederhören.*	Good bye.
AFTER THE CALL ENDED	*(den Hörer) auflegen*	to hang up (Lit. to put down the receiver)

And here are a few set phrases related to the telephone:

Kein Anschluss unter dieser Nummer.	This number has been disconnected. (Lit. No connection under this number.)
Die Leitung ist besetzt.	The line is busy.
Die Verbindung ist schlecht.	This is a bad connection. (Lit. The connection is bad.)
die Auskunft anrufen	calling information

Did You Know?

Let's talk *Telefon* for a moment. As always, it is extremely important to get off to a good start. In Germany it is considered rude to answer the phone with just a "*Hallo*" or "*Ja.*" Instead, answer the phone with your last name. An additional "*Guten Tag*" is optional. It is also a good idea to identify yourself when you are the one calling. Always mention your *Name* before asking to speak to someone or before requesting *Information*.

WORD ON THE STREET

Using an indefinite article in front of a personal name, as in <u>Eine</u> Frau Kerner hat angerufen, means that the person is not known to the person speaking. Equivalent usage exists in English, as in "A (certain) Frau Kerner called."

ACTIVITY 3: LET'S TAKE IT FOR A SPIN

Das Telefon klingelt (The phone is ringing). *Gehen Sie bitte an den Apparat* (Please answer the phone). Please participate in this conversation. Check the cues in parentheses.

Susanne Römer:	_____.
Andreas Kern:	*Kern, guten Tag. Kann ich bitte mit Ihrem Mann sprechen.*
Susanne Römer:	_____. (No, he's not there, unfortunately.)
Andreas Kern:	*Wann kommt er zurück?*
Susanne Römer:	_____. (I don't know. May I take a message?)
Andreas Kern:	*Nein, danke.*
Susanne Römer:	_____. (Can he call you back?)
Andreas Kern:	*Ja, bitte.*
Susanne Römer:	_____. (What's your number?)
Andreas Kern:	*089 / 56 78 93 0. Vielen Dank. Auf Wiederhören.*
Susanne Römer:	_____.

THE NITTY GRITTY

BEEN THERE, DONE THAT: **TALKING ABOUT THE PAST WITH THE PRESENT PERFECT**

The present perfect is the most commonly used past tense in German. It is a compound tense, which means that there are two pieces to it. Here are a few examples from the first dialogue.

Sie <u>haben</u> den Anschluss von Klaus Rosin <u>erreicht</u>.	You have reached Klaus Rosin.
<u>Hast</u> du unsere Verabredung etwa <u>vergessen</u>?	Did you forget our appointment?
Er <u>hat</u> doch <u>gesagt</u> ich soll ihn heute um 18 Uhr anrufen.	He said I should call him today at 6PM.
Wo <u>habe</u> ich die Nummer nur <u>aufgeschrieben</u>?	Where did I write down that number?

As you can see, the present perfect in German can translate into both, the English simple past or the English present perfect.

Let's see how to form this tense:

The present perfect in German consists of the conjugated form of *haben* or *sein* and the past participle of the main verb. So, the present perfect is easier than you think, because you already know the conjugations of *haben* and *sein*, right?

The main verb carries the meaning of the sentence, whereas the conjugated form of *haben* or *sein* shows that we're talking about the past. Let's first talk about the verbs that use *haben*.

The basic sentence structure using present perfect is:
> subject + *haben* in the present tense (+ object) + past participle.
> **Sie haben Klaus Rosin erreicht.**   You've reached Klaus Rosin.

Note that the past participle, *erreicht* (reached) in this case, moves to the end of the sentence and it is separated from *haben* by an object.

This is how you ask questions in the present perfect:
> *Haben* in the present tense + subject (+ object) + past participle?
> **Hast du unsere Verabredung etwa vergessen?** Did you forget our appointment?

Note that the form of *haben, hast* (you have) in the above sentence, is moved to the beginning of the sentence before the subject *du*.

And a negative sentence is put together as follows:
> subject + *haben* in the present tense (+ object) + *nicht* + past participle.
> **Sie haben Klaus Rosin nicht erreicht.**   You've not reached Klaus Rosin.

Most verbs use *haben* in the present perfect. Others use *sein*. Most of the latter verbs are those that indicate movement and a change of position, such as *fahren* (to drive), *fliegen* (to fly), *gehen* (to go), *kommen* (to come), *fallen* (to fall). Two others are the verb *sein* (to be, to exist) itself, used as a main verb, and *bleiben* (to stay). Note that these are so-called intransitive verbs, or verbs that do not take a direct object. The sentence structure and word order is the same as with the present perfect with *haben*.

Er ist im Büro geblieben.	He stayed in the office.
Ich bin gerade erst nach Hause gekommen.	I've just arrived home.

ACTIVITY 4: TAKE IT FOR A SPIN

Decide whether to use *haben* or *sein*, and insert the appropriate form of the verb.

1. *Wir _____ gestern abgefahren.*
2. *_____ du deinen Vater telefonisch erreicht?*
3. *Mein Mann _____ noch im Büro geblieben.*
4. *Ich _____ leider Ihren Namen vergessen.*
5. *Wer _____ denn angerufen?*
6. *Sie _____ eine Nachricht hinterlassen.*
7. *_____ Sie die Nummer aufgeschrieben?*

BEEN AND DONE: THE PAST PARTICIPLE

A past participle is a verb form used in the present perfect (and some other tenses) in German, equivalent to English "gone" or "worked" or "written." Past participles are formed differently in German, depending on the verb and what broad category it belongs to, weak or strong verbs. Unfortunately there is no simple rule to figure out which category a verb belongs to. Therefore you'll have to memorize the forms of the strong verbs as they come up.

WEAK VERBS

The past participle of regular weak verbs is formed with the prefix *ge-* + stem + *-t*. For example:

sagen* → *gesagt	(to say → said)
fragen* → *gefragt	(to ask → asked)
kaufen* → *gekauft	(to buy → bought)
zahlen* → *gezahlt	(to pay → paid)

Verbs with separable prefixes, such as *einzahlen* (to deposit money), do not separate in the present perfect. Instead they insert the *-ge-* between the prefix and the stem in the participle.

einzahlen* → *eingezahlt	(to deposit → deposited)
ausrichten* → *ausgerichtet	(to pass on → passed on)

But if the prefix is inseparable, as with the verb *erzählen* (to tell), weak verbs do not use *-ge-* at all.

erzählen* → *erzählt	(to tell → told)

Verbs that end in *-ieren* do not have a *ge-* prefix either.

telefonieren* → *telefoniert	(to phone → phoned)

THE FINE PRINT

Most regular weak verbs whose stem ends in *-d, -t,* or some combination of consonants, add *-et* to the stem to make pronunciation easier.

regnen* → *geregnet	(to rain → rained)
arbeiten* → *gearbeitet	(to work → worked)

STRONG VERBS

Strong verbs form their past participle with the prefix *ge-* + stem + *-en*. Many strong verbs also change their stem in the past participle. Again, there's no easy way to tell which ones change their stem, and so you'll have to memorize their forms as they come up. Examples of verbs with stem change are:

schreiben* → *geschrieben	(to write → written)
helfen* → *geholfen	(to help → helped)

Examples of verbs without stem change are:

laufen* → *gelaufen	(to run → run)
essen* → *gegessen	(to eat → eaten)
geben* → *gegeben	(to give → given)

Just like with weak verbs, strong verbs with separable prefixes, such as *aufschreiben*, insert *-ge-* between the prefix and the stem.

aufschreiben* → *aufgeschrieben	(to write down → written down)

If the prefix is inseparable, such as in *vergessen*, strong verbs do not use *ge-*.

vergessen* → *vergessen	(to forget → forgotten)

Heads Up!

The past participles of strong verbs are rather unpredictable. Therefore, they need to be memorized. Interestingly enough, many of the same verbs are irregular in English as well:

trinken → *getrunken*	(to drink → drunk)
fliegen → *geflogen*	(to fly → flown)
finden → *gefunden*	(to find → found)
schreiben → *geschrieben*	(to write → written)

ACTIVITY 5: TAKE IT FOR A SPIN

Imagine all this happened *gestern* (yesterday). Please rewrite the story using the present perfect.

1. *Ich rufe meinen Freund an.*
2. *Er ist nicht im Büro.*
3. *Er fährt schon nach Hause.*
4. *Ich erreiche ihn nicht.*
5. *Ich hinterlasse eine Nachricht.*
6. *Ich sage: "Ich gehe allein ins Kino".*

Did You Know?

The personal touch is so much more important in Europe than in the USA. People prefer to and will drop by to chat in person, rather than talk on the phone. Of course, this is facilitated by the fact that European cities are usually smaller, and people have far shorter distances to travel for a cup of coffee at a friend's house. Dropping in for a chat has retained its importance also because Europeans are far less likely to move away from their place of birth. Thus families and friends stay in close proximity, and there is no need, really, to have long long-distance calls or send e-mails to keep up relationships. Yet the personal touch is also vital in business relationships. While it is possible to make deals on the phone, Europeans appreciate face-to-face contact even during business negotiations. So, pick up that phone, or send that fax and e-mail, but also call to find out when it is best to drop by for a conversation and a cup of coffee.

HEAR . . . SAY 2

A few days ago, Ulrich put a personal ad on a website called *Hoffende Herzen* (Hoping Hearts). With trepidation he opens his *E-mail* (e-mail).

Ulrich:	Mal sehen, vielleicht hat ja jemand geantwortet . . .
Ulrichs Computer:	Hurra, hurra, die Post ist da.
Ulrich:	Toll. Gleich fünf Briefe habe ich bekommen. Na, da bin ich mal gespannt.
Sonja:	Ich bin sexy Sonja. Ich habe eine Web-Seite. Willst du sie dir einmal anschauen?
Ulrich:	Nein, lieber nicht. Diesen Brief lösche ich doch gleich mal.
Sabine:	Lieber Ulrich. Ich habe deinen Brief gelesen. Du klingst sehr nett. Wie alt bist du denn?
Ulrich:	Na aber so was fragt man doch nicht . . .
Sabine:	Ich bin letzte Woche dreizehn geworden.
Ulrich:	Oh je. Sofort löschen! Und der Brief ist von einem Horst. Ein Mann hat mir geantwortet?
Horst:	Hallo Ulrich. Dein Brief hat mich sehr interessiert. Ich suche Freundschaft und Geborgenheit. Du auch?
Ulrich:	Löschen!
Ulrike:	Hallo Ulrich. Ich heiße Ulrike. Schon unsere Namen passen gut zusammen, nicht wahr? Spass beiseite. Ich bin in Magdeburg geboren, und habe in Dresden Musik studiert. Nach dem Studium bin ich nach Berlin umgezogen. Hier kann ich allen meinen Hobbies nachgehen: ins Kino gehen, tanzen und Musik machen. Vielleicht hast du ja Lust, mal mit mir ins Kino zu gehen?
Ulrich:	Hmmm, warum eigentlich nicht? Ich bin schon lange nicht mehr im Kino gewesen. Aber ich lese erst mal weiter.
Barbara:	Ich habe dich sofort erkannt.
Ulrich:	Na was ist das denn für eine Masche.
Barbara:	Deine Vorliebe für heiße Schokolade hat dich verraten. Eine Mutter vergisst so etwas nie. Ruf mich doch mal an. Ich habe schon lange nichts mehr von dir gehört. Ich mache mir Sorgen. Mama
Ulrich:	Ach du dickes Ei . . .

Ach du dickes Ei! (Oh, no! [Lit. Oh, you thick egg!]) is a common phrase expressing surprise, shock, and possibly even anguish. Similar expressions are *Ach du liebes bisschen!* (Oh, no! [Lit. Oh, you dear little bit!]) and a simple *Ach herrje!* (Oh, my!)

ACTIVITY 6: TAKE IT FOR A SPIN

Aren't the personals fun? Answer the following questions about them.

1. How many people answered Ulrich's ad?
2. What does Ulrich do with Sonja's letter?
3. How old is Sabine?
4. What did Ulrike do in Dresden?
5. What are her hobbies?
6. Does Ulrich go to the movies often?
7. Who wrote the last letter?
8. Why is Ulrich's mother worried?

Did You Know?

The largest German Internet provider is *t-online.de*. Therefore many German e-mail addresses end on *t-online.de*. However, many German private households have turned to American internet providers, like AOL. URLs are cited as they are in English. For example: www.duden.de or www.berlin.de. Most German Internet addresses end on *.de*, most Austrian Internet Addresses end in *.at*, and most Swiss Internet addresses end in *.ch*, rather than *.com* or *.org* or *.edu* as used in the United States.

WORDS TO LIVE BY

STAY CONNECTED: COMPUTER AND INTERNET VOCABULARY

Much of the terminology used around the Internet in German is borrowed from English. So you have a head start here, don't you? Here are the most important terms.

SURFING THE NET

Online	online
das Internet	Internet
die Web-Seite	Web page
die Homepage	homepage
die Internetadresse	URL
die E-Mail	e-mail
die E-Mail Adresse	e-mail address
der Anhang	attachment
die Links	links
der Chat-Room	chat room
das Internet-Café	Internet Café
eine E-Mail schicken	to send an e-mail
E-Mail abfragen	to check e-mail
E-Mail beantworten	to reply to e-mail
E-Mail weiterleiten	to forward e-mail
beifügen	to attach
löschen	to delete
herunterladen	to download
suchen	to search
anmelden	to log on
abmelden	to log off

Did You Know?

E-mail correspondence follows common German orthographic rules. Unlike in English, it is not appropriate to use only lower case or only upper case in an e-mail. In addition, e-mail correspondence, particularly business correspondence, follows the common etiquette of letter writing. Use the form of address you would in a letter, such as *Liebe Frau Meier* (Dear Mrs. Meier), *Lieber Herr Bauer, Sehr geehrte Frau Schneider* (Esteemed Mrs. Schneider), *Sehr geehrter Herr Sommer*. End the e-mail as you would a letter. For example: *Mit freundlichem Gruß* (With friendly greetings) or *Herzliche Grüsse* (Best regards). In business e-mails, please note your contact information below your signature at the end of the e-mail.

Here are a few sentences you might need:

Wie komme ich ins Internet?	How do I connect to the Internet?
Kann ich online buchen?	Can I book online?
Wie lautet Ihre Internet-Adresse?	What is your URL?
Wie lautet Ihre E-Mail-Adresse?	What is your e-mail address?
Gibt es in der Nähe ein Internet-Café?	Is there an Internet café nearby?
Wie lädt man diese Datei herunter?	How do I download this file?

TAKE IT FOR A SPIN

Fill in the correct words.

1. *Wie _____ Ihre Internet-Adresse?*
2. *Ich _____ meiner Freundin eine E-Mail.*
3. *Ob ich wohl Post habe? Ich muß meine E-Mail _____.*
4. *Kannst du mir die E-Mail noch einmal schicken? Ich habe sie _____.*
5. *Zuerst muss ich die Datei _____. Dann kann ich sie lesen.*

THOSE WERE THE DAYS: TIME EXPRESSIONS REFERRING TO THE PAST

Yesterday, all my troubles seemed so far away . . . And so you really won't have any trouble talking about yesterday, let's work on it.

Was hast du . . . gemacht?	What did you do . . .
*. . . **gestern** . . .*	. . . yesterday?
*. . . **letzte Woche** . . .*	. . . last week?
*. . . **letzten Monat** . . .*	. . . last month?
*. . . **letztes Jahr** . . .*	. . . last year?
*. . . **letzten Montag** . . .*	. . . last Monday?
*. . . **nach dem Studium** . . .*	. . . after college?
*. . . **früher** . . .*	. . . earlier/in earlier times?
*. . . **vor drei Jahren** . . .*	. . . three years ago?

TAKE IT FOR A SPIN

Please translate.

1. *Ich habe dir* (last week) *eine E-mail geschickt.*
2. *Haben Sie* (four years ago) *eine Web-Seite gehabt?*
3. *Er hat sie* (yesterday) *angerufen.*
4. *Wir haben* (last Tuesday) *eine Nachricht hinterlassen.*
5. *Ich bin* (after college) *nach Amerika gezogen.*

WHO'S ON FIRST: WORD ORDER WITH TIME EXPRESSIONS

In German, as said earlier, the typical word order is:
subject—(conjugated) verb—object—(participle)

Ich schreibe dir.	I am writing to you.
Ich habe dir geschrieben.	I wrote to you.

When time expressions are added to the mix, things get a bit more complicated. Time expressions follow the conjugated verb.

Ich habe gestern geschrieben.	I wrote yesterday.

If the sentence contains a time expression and an object, the time expression follows the object.

Ich schreibe Georg morgen.	I'll write to Georg tomorrow.
Ich habe dir gestern geschrieben.	I wrote to you yesterday.

If the sentence includes a direct object, the time expression precedes the direct object, unless, as in the sentences above, the object is a personal pronoun.

Ich habe gestern eine E-Mail geschrieben.	I wrote an e-mail yesterday.

If a sentence includes a direct and an indirect object, the time expression goes between the indirect and the direct object.

Ich habe meinem Bruder gestern eine E-Mail geschrieben.	I wrote an e-mail to my brother yesterday.

If there is both, a time expression and an expression of location, the time expression usually precedes the expression of location.

Wir studieren bald in München.	We'll study in Munich soon.
Wir haben früher in München studiert.	We studied in Munich earlier.

The time expression may be moved to the beginning of the sentence for emphasis. In that case the position of the subject and verb is reversed.

Heute schreibe ich dir.	Today, I'm writing to you.
Heute rufe ich dich an.	Today, I'll call you.
Gestern habe ich dir geschrieben.	Yesterday, I wrote to you.
Gestern habe ich dir eine E-Mail geschrieben.	Yesterday, I wrote you an e-mail.
Gestern habe ich dich angerufen.	Yesterday, I called you.
Gestern habe ich meinem Bruder einen Brief geschrieben.	Yesterday, I wrote a letter to my brother.
Früher haben wir in München studiert.	Earlier, we studied in Munich.

ACTIVITY 9: TAKE IT FOR A SPIN

Rephrase the sentences by emphasizing the time expression.

1. *Er hat mich letzten Monat angerufen.*
2. *Ich habe gestern meinem Bruder eine Nachricht hinterlassen.*

3. *Wir haben vor zwei Jahren studiert.*
4. *Mein Mann hat den Flug letzten Monat im Internet gebucht.*
5. *Horst ist um 18 Uhr nicht mehr im Büro gewesen.*

TAKE IT UP A NOTCH

Write your own personal ad, using the following cues.

in Stettin wohnen; in Berlin studieren; nach Zürich umziehen nach dem Studium; vor fünf Jahren in Zürich heiraten; geschieden sein; ein Haus mit Garten haben; Hobbies: lesen, ins Theater gehen, tanzen.

CRIB NOTES

HEAR . . . SAY 1

Answering Machine:	Hello. You've reached Klaus Rosin. Unfortunately, I can't come to the phone right now (Lit. Unfortunately, I can't be reached by phone right now). Please leave a message. I'll call you back as soon as possible.
Claudia:	Hi Klaus, it's me, Claudia. Where are you? Did you forget our date? Please call me back. You've got the number. Unbelievable! He said I should call him today at 6PM. Well, I'll try his office. Maybe he stayed longer. Where did I write down that number? Ah, here it is: 38 90 76.
Secretary:	Kohlmeier Schokoladen, Schneider speaking.
Claudia:	Yes, Kerner, good day. Can I speak to Mr. Rosin?
Secretary:	I'm sorry, but Mr. Rosin has already left for the day. May I take a message?
Claudia:	No, thanks. I'll call him on his cell phone. Good bye.
Secretary:	Good bye.
Claudia:	0176 / 97 73 67 90. Busy! I give up. Let him call me!

Meanwhile, across town, Klaus is trying to call Claudia on his cell phone. He is stuck in heavy traffic.

Klaus:	Busy! Maybe she left a message for me at my office.
Secretary:	Kohlmeier Schokoladen, Schneider speaking.
Klaus:	Rosin. Ms. Schneider, did somebody call for me?
Secretary:	Yes, about 10 minutes ago a Ms. Kerner called. But she didn't leave a message.
Klaus:	Thanks. And go home. It is so late already.
Secretary:	Yes, I was on my way already, and then you called.
Klaus:	Sorry. See you tomorrow, then. Maybe it's no longer busy.
Claudia:	Kerner.
Klaus:	Hello, Claudia, it's me, Klaus. I am . . .
Claudia:	Hello? Who is this?
Klaus:	Claudia? Hello?
Claudia:	Hello? What's that! Just hung up!
Klaus:	Claudia? Oh, darn! Now the battery is gone

Ulrich:	Let's see, maybe somebody actually answered.
Ulrichs Computer:	You've got mail
Ulrich:	Great! I got five letters. Well, I'm curious.
Sonja:	I am sexy Sonja. I have a website. Would you like to see it?
Ulrich:	No, I'd rather not. I'm deleting this letter right away.
Sabine:	Dear Ulrich, I have read your letter. You sound really nice. How old are you?
Ulrich:	Well, you don't ask questions like that . . .
Sabine:	I turned thirteen last week.
Ulrich:	Oh dear. Delete immediately! And this letter is from a certain Horst. A man answered me?
Horst:	Hello, Ulrich. Your letter interested me very much. I am looking for friendship and security. Are you, too?
Ulrich:	Delete!
Ulrike:	Hello, Ulrich. My name is Ulrike. Our names go well together, already, don't they? Joking aside. I was born in Magdeburg, and studied music in Dresden. After college, I moved to Berlin. I can enjoy all my hobbies here: going to movies, dancing and making music. Maybe you'd like to come to the movies with me some time?
Ulrich:	Hmmm, why not? I haven't been to the movies in a while. But first, I'll continue reading.
Barbara:	I recognized you immediately.
Ulrich:	Well, what kind of come-on is that?
Barbara:	Your preference for hot chocolate gave you away immediately. A mother will never forget that. Call me sometime. I haven't heard from you in a while. I am worried. Mama
Ulrich:	Oh, no!

ACTIVITY 1
1. b   2. a   3. c
4. b

ACTIVITY 2
1. *Sein Anrufbeantworter beantwortet das Telefon.*
2. *Ja, sie hinterlässt eine Nachricht.*
3. *Seine Sekretärin, Frau Schneider, beantwortet das Telefon.*
4. *Nein, er hat das Haus schon verlassen.*
5. *Sie ruft sein Handy an.*
6. *Es ist besetzt.*
7. *Die Batterie ist leer.*

ACTIVITY 3
Susanne Römer: Römer (, guten Tag).

Andreas Kern: Kern, guten Tag. Kann ich bitte mit Ihrem Mann sprechen.

Susanne Römer: Nein, er ist leider nicht da.

Andreas Kern: Wann kommt er zurück?

Susanne Römer: Ich weiß es nicht. Kann ich ihm etwas ausrichten?

Andreas Kern: Nein, danke.

Susanne Römer: Kann er Sie zurückrufen?

Andreas Kern: Ja, bitte.

Susanne Römer: Wie ist Ihre Telefonnummer?

Andreas Kern: 089 / 56 78 93 0. Vielen Dank. Auf Wiederhören.

Susanne Römer: Auf Wiederhören.

ACTIVITY 4
1. *sind,*   2. *Hast,*   3. *ist,*
4. *habe,*   5. *hat,*   6. *hat,*
7. *Haben*

ACTIVITY 5
1. *Ich habe meinen Freund angerufen.*
2. *Er ist nicht im Büro gewesen.*
3. *Er ist schon nach Hause gefahren.*
4. *Ich habe ihn nicht erreicht.*
5. *Ich habe eine Nachricht hinterlassen.*
6. *Ich habe gesagt: "Ich bin allein ins Kino gegangen."*

ACTIVITY 6
1. *Fünf haben seinen Brief beantwortet.*
2. *Er löscht ihn.*
3. *Sabine ist dreizehn.*
4. *Sie hat in Dresden Musik studiert.*
5. *Ihre Hobbies sind ins Kino gehen, tanzen und Musik machen.*
6. *Nein, er ist schon lange nicht mehr im Kino gewesen.*
7. *Ulrichs Mutter hat den Brief geschrieben.*
8. *Sie hat schon lange nichts mehr von Ulrich gehört.*

ACTIVITY 7
1. *lautet,*   2. *schicke,*
3. *abfragen,*   4. *gelöscht,*
5. *herunterladen*

ACTIVITY 8
1. *Ich habe dir letzte Woche eine E-Mail geschickt.*
2. *Haben Sie vor vier Jahren eine Web-Seite gehabt?*
3. *Er hat sie gestern angerufen.*
4. *Wir haben letzten Dienstag eine Nachricht hinterlassen.*
5. *Ich bin nach dem Studium nach Amerika gezogen.*

ACTIVITY 9
1. *Letzten Monat hat er mich angerufen.*
2. *Gestern habe ich meinem Bruder eine Nachricht hinterlassen.*
3. *Vor zwei Jahren haben wir studiert.*
4. *Letzten Monat hat mein Mann den Flug im Internet gebucht.*
5. *Um 18Uhr ist Horst nicht mehr im Büro gewesen.*

ACTIVITY 10
Ich habe in Stettin gewohnt. Ich habe in Berlin studiert. Nach dem Studium bin ich nach Zürich umgezogen. Ich habe vor fünf Jahren in Zürich geheiratet. Jetzt bin ich geschieden. Ich habe ein Haus mit Garten. Meine Hobbies sind: lesen, ins Theater gehen und tanzen.

HONESTY IS THE BEST POLICY

Ehrlich währt am längsten

(Lit. The honest one lasts the longest)

COMING UP . . .

- *If looks could kill:* **Descriptions**

- *That's what I like:* **Expressing likes and dislikes**

- *Getting around, part II*

- *Isn't she amazing?* **Adjectives**

- *From me to you:* **A look at prepositions**

- **Prepositions with the dative**

- **Prepositions with the accusative**

- **Two-way prepositions**

LOOKING AHEAD . . .

There's no doubt about it that *Fußball* (soccer) is the favorite *Zuschauersport* (spectator sport) in Germany, and it is clearly also among the most popular participatory sports. There are *Fußballclubs* (soccer clubs) in every single town and city, and at one point or another in their lives, most Germans, male and female alike, have played *Fußball*. Many a Saturday is spent at the *Fußballstadion* (soccer stadium) to watch *die Fußballmannschaft* (soccer team) play on the *Fußballfeld* (soccer field). And those who can't make it to the *Stadion* watch the most important games of the *Bundesliga* (federal league) on TV. So, if on a Saturday you are strolling through a residential area and you hear people screaming *Tooooooor* (gooooaaaal) behind the windows, you know that the home team has scored a goal. It seems to be a requirement for German citizenship to know all about soccer. But then again, there are a few of us, like myself and Rita in the following dialogue, who need somebody to *erklären* (explain) the *Fußballregeln* (soccer rules) to them.

ACTIVITY 1: **LET'S WARM UP**

Every soccer player knows how important it is to warm up your muscles before a game. So let's do the same. Try to figure out the meaning of the following words:

1. *Fußball* is identical to . . .
   a. rugby.
   b. football.
   c. soccer.
2. A person who is crazy about soccer is a
   a. . . . *Fußballfan.*
   b. . . . *Fußballspieler.*
   c. . . . *Torwart.*
3. A person watching the game is a . . .
   a. . . . *Spieler.*
   b. . . . *Zuschauer.*
   c. . . . *Torwart.*
4. A *Tor* is . . .
   a. . . . the ball used in soccer.
   b. . . . a goal.
   c. . . . a penalty.
5. *FC* is short for . . .
   a. . . . *Fanclub.*
   b. . . . *Fitnessclub.*
   c. . . . *Fußballclub.*

Rita is supposed to go to a *Fußballspiel* (soccer match) with her new *Freund* (boyfriend). Afraid to embarrass herself, she calls Ernst to brush up on the rules of the game—the rules of the soccer game, that is, not the dating game . . .

Rita:	**Hallo, großer Bruder. Du musst mir unbedingt helfen.**
Ernst:	**Wo brennt's denn, kleine Schwester?**
Rita:	**Kannst du mir die Fußballregeln erklären?**
Ernst:	(laughing) **Wieviel Zeit hast du denn?**
Rita:	**Fünf Minuten.**
Ernst:	(in mock seriousness) **Fußall ist ein sehr komplexes Spiel. Ich kann dir das nicht in . . .**
Rita:	(interrupts him) **Ernst, der Mann meines Lebens ist auf dem Weg zu mir. Er hat Tickets für das Spiel von FC Bayern München gegen Schalke 04. Das Spiel ist heute nachmittag. Ich will mich nicht blamieren. Also, der Torwart muss . . .**
Ernst:	**Ist er nett?**
Rita:	**Wer? Der Torwart?**
Ernst:	**Na, dein neuer Freund. Ist er ein netter Mensch?**
Rita:	**Ja, er ist sehr nett.**
Ernst:	**Und?**
Rita:	(irritated) **Und was?**
Ernst:	**Wie heißt er, hat er blaue oder braune Augen, einen dicken Geldbeutel oder . . .**
Rita:	(interrupts him) **Er heißt Wilfried, sieht sehr gut aus, ist Mitte dreißig und ein erfolgreicher Rechtsanwalt. Er hat ein schönes Haus und ein schnelles Auto.** (pause) **Und er ist ein großer Fußballfan. Also bitte, Ernst, kannst du mir endlich die Fußballregeln erklären?**
Ernst:	(teasing) **Du wirst aber ungeduldig. Bayern gegen Schalke hast du gesagt . . . hmmm . . . das ist bestimmt ein interessantes Spiel. Hat der nette Freund von dir vielleicht noch ein Ticket für mich?**
Rita:	**Ernst!**

The person asking *Wo brennt's denn?* (Where is the fire? [Lit. Where is it burning?]) is not necessarily a fireman. Among family and friends this expression is used to respond to a casual request for help. The phrase borders on irony, jokingly implying that the request can't be all that urgent or serious.

ACTIVITY 2: **HOW'S THAT AGAIN?**

Well, we may never find out if Ernst ever helped his sister Rita, but we already do know the answers to these questions. Try your German.

1. Are Rita and Ernst friends (*Freunde*) or siblings (*Geschwister*)?
2. Is soccer an easy game according to Ernst?
3. Which two teams are playing that afternoon?
4. What does Rita's boyfriend do for a living?
5. Is he a nice person?
6. Is Wilfried a soccer fan?
7. Does Ernst want to see the game as well?
8. Does Rita want him to come along?

WORKSHOP 1

WORDS TO LIVE BY

IF LOOKS COULD KILL: DESCRIPTIONS

Imagine you have just started a new relationship. Wouldn't you want to call all your friends and family to tell them about him or her? And wouldn't you want them to know exactly what he or she is like? Well, for this you'll need lots and lots of adjectives. These are the descriptive words that make all the difference in a sentence. Here's a list of adjectives to keep handy.

IF LOOKS COULD KILL	
schön	beautiful (usually reserved for women)
häßlich	ugly
gutaussehend	handsome (usually reserved for men)
hübsch	pretty (usually reserved for women)
groß	tall, big, large
klein	small

schlank	slender
kräftig	strong, big
dünn	thin, skinny

Let's put this to use . . .

Er ist gutaussehend.	He is good looking.
Sie ist sehr hübsch.	She is very pretty.

WHAT A COLOR!	
blond	blonde
dunkelhaarig	dark-haired
braun	brown
schwarz	black
blau	blue
grün	green
grau	grey
hell	light
dunkel	dark

Hat sie grüne Augen?	Does she have green eyes?

AGE DOESN'T MATTER	
alt	old
jung	young
neu	new
reif	mature
unreif	immature

Ich habe einen neuen Freund.	I have a new boyfriend.
Er ist so unreif.	He is so immature.

FOR RICHER OR POORER	
reich	rich
arm	poor
erfolgreich	successful
erfolglos	unsuccessful

Er ist ein erfolgreicher Rechtsanwalt.	He is a successful lawyer.

IT'S WHAT'S INSIDE THAT COUNTS	
nett	nice
ehrlich	honest
lustig	fun, amusing
ernst	serious

schüchtern	shy
gesellig	gregarious
langsam	slow
schnell	fast
geduldig	patient
ungeduldig	impatient
laut	loud
leise	soft
intelligent	intelligent
dumm	dumb

Mein Freund ist sehr nett.   My boyfriend is very nice.

WORD ON THE STREET

Exercise caution when describing somebody's physical features: Words like *dick* or *fett* (big, fat) and *dünn* (skinny) should not be used for a person's size or weight. *Kräftig* (strong, big) and *schlank* (slender) respectively will bring your point across without hurting anybody's feelings.

ACTIVITY 3: PUT IT IN WRITING

Write down the opposite of the following adjectives.

1. *schön*
2. *gesellig*
3. *arm*
4. *klein*
5. *dünn*
6. *langsam*
7. *ernst*
8. *reif*
9. *kräftig*
10. *geduldig*

Did You Know?

Of course, except for *König Fußball,* there are other sports that are quite popular in Germany, Austria and Switzerland. The most popular recreational winter sports are *Skifahren* (skiing) and *Snowboarding* (snowboarding), which is not very surprising, considering that all three countries border on the Alps. Popular summer sports are tennis and squash. The younger generation has taken up rollerblading and skateboarding. Jogging does not enjoy quite the popularity it does in the United States, and golf, which is very popular in the United States, is a rather expensive and less popular pastime in Europe. Joining a golf club may cost thousands of euros per year in membership fees.

THE NITTY GRITTY

ISN'T SHE AMAZING? ADJECTIVES

WHEN ADJECTIVES DO TAKE ENDINGS

When adjectives precede a noun, they have to agree with the gender, number and case of the noun.

Das ist mein neuer Freund.	That is my new boyfriend.
Das ist meine neue Freundin.	This is my new girlfriend.
Ich gehe mit meinem neuen Freund ins Stadion.	I go to the stadium with my new boyfriend.
Ich gehe mit meiner neuen Freundin ins Stadion.	I go to the stadium with my new girlfriend.

The endings of adjectives also depend on whether or not the adjectives are preceded by an indefinite article or *ein*-words such as *mein* or *kein*, a definite article or no article. Compare:

Mein neuer Freund ist immer nett.	My new boyfriend is always nice.
Der neue Freund ist immer nett.	The new boyfriend is always nice.

Here are the different forms of the adjectives.

ADJECTIVES PRECEDED BY *EIN*-WORDS				
	MASCULINE	**FEMININE**	**NEUTER**	**PLURAL**
NOM.	*ein neuer Freund*	*eine neue Freundin*	*ein neues Spiel*	*meine neuen Spiele*
ACC.	*einen neuen Freund*	*eine neue Freundin*	*ein neues Spiel*	*meine neuen Spiele*
DAT.	*einem neuen Freund*	*einer neuen Freundin*	*einem neuen Spiel*	*meinen neuen Spielen*

ADJECTIVES PRECEDED BY *DER*-WORDS				
	MASCULINE	**FEMININE**	**NEUTER**	**PLURAL**
NOM.	*der neue Freund*	*die neue Freundin*	*das neue Spiel*	*die neuen Spiele*
ACC.	*den neuen Freund*	*die neue Freundin*	*das neue Spiel*	*die neuen Spiele*
DAT.	*dem neuen Freund*	*der neuen Freundin*	*dem neuen Spiel*	*den neuen Spielen*

UN-PRECEDED ADJECTIVES				
	MASCULINE	**FEMININE**	**NEUTER**	**PLURAL**
NOM.	*neuer Freund*	*neue Freundin*	*neues Spiel*	*neue Spiele*
ACC.	*neuen Freund*	*neue Freundin*	*neues Spiel*	*neue Spiele*
DAT.	*neuem Freund*	*neuer Freundin*	*neuem Spiel*	*neuen Spielen*

Don't panic! This is much less complicated than it looks. Here are a few tips to sort through these charts: If the article shows the gender distinction, the adjective doesn't, yet if the article doesn't show the gender distinction, the adjective will. For example: *ein neuer Freund* versus *ein neues Spiel* but *der neue Freund* versus *das neue Spiel*.

TAKE IT FOR A SPIN

Here's your chance to talk about yourself. (Admit that you love it!) Fill in suitable descriptive words from the *If Looks Could Kill* section to draw a picture of yourself. Make sure the adjective agrees with the gender, number, and case of the noun. And watch those articles! I'm curious: Will you be *ehrlich?*

Ich habe _____ Haare. Ich habe _____ Augen. Ich bin _____ von Beruf. Ich habe ein _____ Haus. Ich habe ein _____ Auto. Ich habe _____ Kinder. Ich bin ein _____ Mensch. Ich suche eine _____ Frau/einen _____ Mann.

WHEN ADJECTIVES DON'T TAKE ENDINGS

Adjectives do not take gender endings when they do NOT stand next to a noun but rather follow the verb *sein* (to be) or the verb *werden* (to become). Compare the following:

Ich habe einen netten Freund.	I have a nice boyfriend.
Ist er nett?	Is he nice?
Viele Kinder haben ungeduldige Mütter.	Many children have impatient mothers.
Du wirst aber ungeduldig.	You are getting impatient.

Here are a few more example sentences. Actually, what follows is a description of Rita's dream date!

Er ist groß.	He is tall.
Seine Haare sind schwarz.	His hair is black.
Seine Augen sind blau.	His eyes are blue.
Er ist reich.	He is rich.
Seine Katze ist schön.	His cat is beautiful.
Und er liebt mich.	And he loves me.

Oops. That last example kind of sneaked in, as it contains no adjectives. But it is a rather important requirement for a long lasting relationship, isn't it?

TAKE IT FOR A SPIN

Please translate.

1. My father is old.
2. My mother is pretty.
3. My brother is shy.
4. My sister is tall.
5. My husband is rich.
6. My wife is slender.
7. My children are intelligent.

And here's a more challenging exercise.

TAKE IT UP A NOTCH

Describe your ideal partner! Fill in suitable descriptive words from the categories above. Decide where adjective agreement is necessary, and where it is not. Go ahead! Dream the dream!

Er/Sie ist _____. Er/Sie hat _____ Haare. Er/Sie hat_____ Augen. Er/Sie ist ein _____ Mann/eine Frau. Er/Sie hat _____ Kinder. Er/Sie fährt gern _____ Autos. Er/Sie hat ein _____ Haus. Das _____ Haus hat einen _____ Swimmingpool.

LET'S WARM UP

Now, if I was on one of my first dates with a new partner, I'd make sure I know exactly when to use which phrase. So you're prepared, try to match the following phrases with the right situation.

1. *Ich liebe dich.*
2. *Ich mag Spinat nicht!*
3. *Ich möchte gern ins Kino gehen.*
4. *Das Auto gefällt mir.*

a. A potential buyer to a car salesperson
b. Friends discussing evening plans
c. One lover to another
d. A child protesting a mother's dinner suggestion

Rita's *großer Bruder* decided to take pity on her after all and explained the *Fußball-regeln* to her. Armed with her newfound knowledge of *Fußball*, Rita chats away with her new boyfriend on their way to the *Fußballstadion*. As they got stuck in traffic around the stadium, Wilfried, who is new in town, is getting a little impatient.

Wilfried:	Ich stehe nicht gern im Stau. Es muss doch auch noch einen anderen Weg ins Fußballstadion geben.
Rita:	Ja, wir können an der nächsten Kreuzung rechts abbiegen und die Neben-straßen nehmen. Nach etwa einem Kilometer müssen wir dann wieder links abbiegen. Dann geht's noch etwa zwei Kilometer geradeaus. Das Sta-dion liegt dann auf der rechten Seite.
Wilfried:	Du kennst dich aber gut aus. Du bist wohl schon öfter im Stadion gewe-sen.
Rita:	(slightly hesitant) Ja, natürlich.
Wilfried:	Ein echter Fußballfan, also.
Rita:	Nicht unbedingt.
Wilfried:	Aber die Fußballregeln kennst du doch, nicht wahr?
Rita:	Eine Mannschaft hat elf Spieler auf dem Feld. Die Spieler schießen den Ball ins Tor. Der Torwart steht vor dem Tor. Ein guter Torwart hält den Ball, sogar bei einem Elfmeter. Ein Spieler ist im Abseits wenn . . . äh, jetzt weiß ich nicht mehr weiter.
Wilfried:	(laughing) Du hast wohl im Lexikon nachgelesen?
Rita:	(embarrassed) Nein, ich habe mit meinem Bruder telefoniert. Er ist der Fußballfan in der Familie.
Wilfried:	Und welcher Sport gefällt dir?
Rita:	Ich spiele gern Squash und . . . halt, du musst hier rechts in die Neben-straße abbiegen!
Wilfried:	Ich habe eine Idee. Lassen wir den Stau doch einfach hinter uns liegen und gehen Squash spielen.
Rita:	(surprised) Und was ist mit den Tickets für das Fußballspiel?
Wilfried:	Aber du interessierst dich doch gar nicht für das Fußballspiel.
Rita:	Nein, aber du interessierst dich dafür.
Wilfried:	Ich interessiere mich für dich. Sehr sogar.

HOW'S THAT AGAIN?

Wilfried sounds like quite a guy, doesn't he? Let's see if you noticed what was going on. *Auf Deutsch, bitte!*

1. *Warum nehmen Wilfried und Rita einen anderen Weg ins Fußballstadion?*
   a. *Wilfried kennt den anderen Weg.*
   b. *Wilfried steht nicht gern im Stau.*
   c. *Wilfried will nicht ins Stadion.*
2. *Warum kennt sich Rita gut aus?*
   a. *Sie war schon öfter im Stadion.*
   b. *Sie ist ein Fußballfan.*
   c. *Sie spielt gern Squash.*
3. *Ein guter Torwart . . .*
   a. *. . . steht vor dem Tor.*
   b. *. . . hält den Ball auch bei einem Elfmeter.*
   c. *. . . steht im Abseits.*
4. *Welcher Sport interessiert Rita?*
   a. *Fußball.*
   b. *Squash*
   c. *Rita interessiert sich nicht für Sport.*
5. *Warum will Wilfried Squash spielen gehen?*
   a. *Fußball interessiert ihn nicht.*
   b. *Wilfried hat keine Tickets für das Fußballspiel.*
   c. *Rita interessiert sich nicht für Fußball.*

Did You Know?

German *Fußballfans,* like other fans around the world, often behave in less than desirable ways. It certainly doesn't help that most European *Fußballstadien* (soccer stadiums) allow the sale and consumption of alcohol during games. In an attempt to avoid injuries, alcohol is no longer sold in containers that could turn into potential weapons, such as bottles, glasses or cans. All drinks are sold in plastic cups.

WORKSHOP 2

WORDS TO LIVE BY

THAT'S WHAT I LIKE: **EXPRESSING LIKES AND DISLIKES**

Where American English uses "love" and "hate," German distinguishes a whole host of verbs expressing shades of emotion.

- *gefallen* + dative (to like someone/something, Lit. to be pleasing to someone)
- *schmecken* + dative (to like [some food], Lit. to taste good to someone)

Gefallen and *schmecken* always take the dative case:

Du gefällst mir.	I like you. (Lit. You are pleasing to me.)
Sauerkraut schmeckt mir.	I like Sauerkraut. (Lit. Sauerkraut tastes good to me.)

Note that these verbs work exactly the opposite from the English "to like." The subject in the English sentence (I) becomes the object in the German sentence (*mir*). The object in the English sentence (you/Sauerkraut) is the subject in the German sentence (*du/Sauerkraut*).

WORD ON THE STREET

The phrase *Die Sache schmeckt mir nicht* is meant to express anxiety about a situation rather than distaste of a food, a bit like the English "Something seems fishy here."

Welcher Sport gefällt dir?	Which sport do you like? (Lit. Which sport is pleasing to you?)
Du gefällst mir.	I like you. (Lit. You are pleasing to me.)

Gefallen can be used with people and things. Preferences for food are expressed with *schmecken*.

Sauerkraut schmeckt mir.	I like sauerkraut. (Lit. Sauerkraut tastes good to me.)

WORD ON THE STREET

The phrase *Du gefällst mir heute aber gar nicht* is meant to express that a person does not look good and may be sick or tired or sad. It is not at all meant to express that the person is not liked. If you wish to say that, you might want to say *Ich mag dich nicht.*

- *sich interessieren* (*für*) (to be interested [in])

Ich interessiere mich nicht für Fußball.	I'm not interested in soccer.
Ich interessiere mich für dich.	I'm interested in you.
Ich interessiere mich für Squash.	I am interested in squash.

Sich interessieren für can be used with people, activities and things.

THE FINE PRINT

Sich interessieren (*für*) (to be interested [in]) is a reflexive verb. We will deal with these verbs in a later lesson. Now just this: Reflexive verbs always refer back to the subject of the sentence with a reflexive pronoun *sich*. The English equivalent of *sich* would be "oneself" as in "to wash oneself." For example: *Ich wasche mich* (I wash myself).

- **gern** + verb (to enjoy, to like)

Ich spiele gern Squash.	I enjoy playing Squash.
Ich stehe nicht gern im Stau.	I don't like being in traffic.

Gern is always used in conjunction with a verb expressing the action that is liked by the subject.

- **mögen** (to like)

Ich mag dich.	I like you.
Ich mag Sauerkraut.	I like Sauerkraut.

Mögen can be used to express likes and dislikes for people, things, and food or drinks.

- **lieb haben** (to like)

Ich habe dich lieb.	I like you.

Lieb haben is usually used among family members or with romantic overtones.

- **lieben** (to love)

Ich liebe dich.	I love you.

Lieben is usually reserved for people, especially love among family members, and for romantic love. German rarely uses this word to express enjoyment of a sport, food or activity.

WORD ON THE STREET

Here's the full scope of emotions toward people in ascending order of intensity. *Er interessiert mich.* (I'm interested in him.) This usually has a romantic overtone. *Sie gefällt mir.* (I like her.) This does not necessarily have any romantic connotations. *Ich habe ihn gern.* (I like him./I'm fond of him.) This might be used towards a friend or a distant relative. *Ich mag dich.* (I like you.) This has usually romantic overtones, or expresses deep devotion to a friend. *Ich habe dich lieb.* (I like you.) This has usually romantic connotations, or expresses love among family members. *Ich liebe dich.* (I love you.) This is reserved for lovers and close family members.

ACTIVITY 9: TAKE IT FOR A SPIN

Who do you think is saying this?

1. *Die Sache schmeckt mir nicht.*
2. *Ich liebe dich.*

a. A mother to a son.
b. A celebrity interviewed for a newspaper about her hobbies.

3. *Der Junge gefällt mir aber gar nicht.*

   c. A person anxious about a certain situation awaiting him.

4. *Ich habe dich sehr lieb.*

   d. A friend inquiring about another's love life.

5. *Ich spiele gern Golf.*

   e. A doctor about a patient.

6. *Interessierst du dich für sie?*

   f. A bride to the groom.

THE NITTY GRITTY

FROM ME TO YOU: A LOOK AT PREPOSITIONS

Prepositions are the little words like "on," "to," "from," or "against," used to express the location and direction of the action, or relations among objects described in the sentence. In German, the noun that follows a preposition must be in a given case. In this lesson, we'll look at prepositions that always take the dative case, those that always take the accusative case, and those that can take both.

PREPOSITIONS WITH THE DATIVE CASE

The prepositions followed by the dative case are:

PREPOSITIONS WITH THE DATIVE		
MIT (WITH)	*Ich habe mit meinem Bruder telefoniert.*	I was on the phone with my brother.
NACH (AFTER)	*Nach einem Kilometer müssen wir abbiegen.*	After a kilometer we need to turn.
BEI (WITH, BY)	*Ein guter Torwart hält den Ball bei einem Elfmeter.*	A good goalie stops the ball even with a penalty kick.
ZU (TO)	*Der Mann meines Lebens ist auf dem Weg zu mir.*	The man of my life is on his way to me.
AUS (FROM)	*Er steigt aus dem Auto aus.*	He's getting out of the car.
VON (FROM, OF)	*Er kommt von einem Tennisspiel.*	He is coming from a tennis match.
SEIT (SINCE, FOR)	*Ich warte seit einer Stunde.*	I've been waiting for an hour.
AUßER (EXCEPT FOR)	*Außer dem Torwart steht niemand vor dem Tor.*	Except for the goalie nobody is in front of the goal.
GEGENÜBER (ACROSS)	*Das Restaurant ist gegenüber der Bank.*	The restaurant is across from the bank.

TAKE IT FOR A SPIN

Please complete the sentences using the cues. Watch for the preposition and the case it takes.

1. *Ich habe _____ meiner Schwester telefoniert.* (with)
2. *Außer _____ weiß niemand wo sie ist.* (me)
3. *Sie ist _____ Ihrem neuen Freund.* (with)
4. *Er hat ein Haus gegenüber _____.* (the tennis courts)
5. *Ich gehe jetzt _____ _____.* (to her)

PREPOSITIONS WITH THE ACCUSATIVE

The prepositions taking the accusative case are:

PREPOSITIONS WITH THE ACCUSATIVE		
FÜR (FOR)	Ich interessiere mich für dich.	I'm interested in you.
OHNE (WITHOUT)	Der Bus fährt ohne uns ab.	The bus is leaving without us.
GEGEN (AGAINST)	Eine Fußballmannschaft spielt gegen eine andere Mannschaft.	One soccer team plays against another team.
DURCH (THROUGH)	Wir müssen durch die Stadt fahren.	We have to drive through town.
UM (AROUND)	Die Zuschauer stehen um den Tennisplatz.	The spectators are standing around the tennis courts.

TAKE IT FOR A SPIN

Please complete the sentences using the cues. Watch for the preposition and the case it takes.

1. *Zum Fußballstadion müssen wir durch _____ fahren.* (the town)
2. *Nein, wir können auch _____ die Stadt fahren.* (around)
3. *Das Spiel fängt _____ uns an.* (without)
4. *Aber das Spiel kann nicht ohne _____ anfangen.* (the goalie)
5. *Ich interessiere mich nicht _____ ihn.* (for)

TWO-WAY PREPOSITIONS

There are nine two-way prepositions; all are listed with examples in the table below.

All two-way prepositions indicate location.

The noun that follows such a preposition is in the dative case when the preposition indicates a position in space.

Der Ball ist im Tor. The ball is in the goal.

Curiously enough, the noun that follows such a preposition is in the accusative case when the preposition indicates a change of location or movement.

> **Der Spieler schießt den Ball ins Tor.**   The player shoots the ball into the goal.

To find out which case to use ask either *wo?* (where, in what place?) or *wohin?* (to where, to what place?).

TWO-WAY PREPOSITIONS				
PREPOSITION	ACCUSATIVE/DIRECTION		DATIVE/LOCATION	
IN (IN, INSIDE, INTO)	*Die Spieler schießen den Ball ins Tor.*	The players are kicking the ball into the goal.	*Nun ist der Ball im Tor.*	Now the ball is inside the goal.
AN (AT, AT THE SIDE OF, TO, ON),	*Ich fahre an die Kreuzung heran.*	I am approaching the intersection.	*Wir können an der nächsten Kreuzung rechts abbiegen.*	We can turn right at the next intersection.
AUF (ON, ON TOP OF, ONTO)	*Ich lege mich auf die rechte Seite.*	I am turning onto my right side.	*Das Stadion liegt auf der rechten Seite.*	The stadium is located on the right.
ÜBER (ABOVE, OVER, ACROSS)	*Der Ball fliegt über das Tor.*	The ball is flying over the goal.	*Der Ball bleibt über dem Tor liegen.*	The ball stays over the goal.
UNTER (UNDER, BENEATH, AMONG)	*Der Torwart mischt sich unter die Zuschauer.*	The goalie joins the spectators.	*Der Torwart ist schon unter den Zuschauern.*	The goalie is among the spectators already.
VOR (IN FRONT OF, BEFORE, AGO)	*Der Spieler stellt sich vor das Tor.*	The player places himself in front of the goal.	*Der Torwart steht schon vor dem Tor.*	The goalie already stands in front of the goal.
HINTER (IN BACK OF, BEHIND)	*Die Zuschauer gehen hinter das Tor.*	The spectators are going behind the goal.	*Die Journalisten sind schon hinter dem Tor.*	The journalists are already behind the goal.
NEBEN (BESIDE, NEXT TO)	*Der Torwart stellt sich neben das Tor.*	The goalie places himself next to the goal.	*Der Torwart steht neben dem Tor.*	The goalie is standing next to the goal.
ZWISCHEN (BETWEEN)	*Der Schiedsrichter stellt sich zwischen DIE SPIELER.*	The umpire moves between the players.	*Der Schiedsrichter steht zwischen den Spielern.*	The umpire is standing between the players.

THE FINE PRINT

Please note that many prepositions followed by the definite article in the accusative form a contraction: *in das* contracts to *ins, an das* contracts to *ans* and *auf das* contracts to *aufs* . . . You get the idea. The same is true for many prepositions followed by the definite article in the dative case: *in dem* contracts to *im, an dem* contracts to *am,* and *zu dem* contracts to *zum.*

ACTIVITY 12: **TAKE IT FOR A SPIN**

Please complete the sentences. Make sure you are using the correct case.

1. *Ich fahre _____ Fußballstadion. Mein Freund ist schon _____ Fußballstadion.*
2. *Elf Spieler kommen _____ Spielfeld. Der Torwart ist schon _____ _____ Spielfeld.*
3. *Der Torwart schießt den Ball nicht _____ Tor, die Spieler schießen den Ball _____ Tor.*

GETTING AROUND, PART II

Let's put the two-way prepositions to use by looking at ways to get around town again.

If you are asking for directions, you are most likely looking for ways to get from one place to another. That indicates a change of location or movement, and thus the two-way prepositions will be followed by a noun in the accusative case.

Gibt es noch einen anderen Weg ins Fußballstadion?	Is there another way to the soccer stadium?
Wie komme ich in die Stadt?	How do I get to town?
Du musst hier rechts in die Nebenstraße abbiegen!	You have to turn right into the side street.

If you follow the directions, you'll arrive at the right location. The dative is used after the preposition to indicate a location.

Das Stadion liegt dann auf der rechten Seite.	The stadium is on the right-hand side.
Die Bushaltestelle ist an der Ecke, direkt neben dem Stadion.	The bus stop is at the corner, right next to the stadium.

When trying to get around town, there are a few words other than prepositions that might come in handy. Let's just take a closer look.

rechts	right-hand
links	left-hand
die Ecke	corner

die Kreuzung	intersection
die Straße	street
die Hauptstraße	main street
die Nebenstraße	side street
der Weg	way
lang	long
kurz	short
weit	far
nah	near
Ist das der Weg ins Fußballstadion?	Is that the way to the soccer stadium?
Wir müssen an der nächsten Kreuzung links abbiegen.	We have to turn left at the next intersection.

ACTIVITY 13: TAKE IT FOR A SPIN

Please translate.

My new friend and I are going to the soccer stadium. He bought the tickets at the corner across from the stadium. He is a big soccer fan. I am not interested in soccer. I am interested in him. I like him.

Did You Know?

Here's a bit of FYI: German soccer is divided into two federal leagues. Teams such as the Hamburger SV or the FC Bayern München play in the *1. Bundesliga* (1st Bundesliga). Currently playing in the *2. Bundesliga* (2nd Bundesliga) are teams such as the FC Köln and Eintracht Frankfurt. If a team moves up from the 2nd to the 1st Bundesliga it is called *aufsteigen,* and if a team moves down it is called *absteigen.* Soccer is an international game. There are championships within Europe and worldwide. The *Europameisterschaft* (European championship) and the *Weltmeisterschaft* (World championship) are competitions between the national teams of the participating countries. The UEFA cup, on the other hand, is played among local teams from around the world. Well-known European soccer teams are: FC Liverpool and Manchester United of Great Britain; FC Porto of Portugal; Juventus Turin and Inter Mailand of Italy; Real Madrid of Spain; and Ajax Amsterdam of the Netherlands. National teams to reckon with are: Germany, Italy, France, England, Spain, and the Netherlands in Europe, and Mexico, Brazil, and Argentina in the Americas.

CRIB NOTES

Rita: Hello, big brother. You have to help me.

Ernst: What's the matter, little sister?

Rita: Can you explain the soccer rules to me?

Ernst: How much time do you have?

Rita: 5 minutes.

Ernst: Soccer is a very serious game. I cannot explain it to you in . . .

Rita: Ernst, the man of my life is on his way to me. He has tickets for the game between the FC Bayern München and Schalke 04. The game is this afternoon. I don't want to embarrass myself. So, the goalie has to. . . .

Ernst: Is he nice?

Rita: Who? The goalie?

Ernst: Your new friend, of course. Is he a nice person?

Rita: Yes, he is very nice.

Ernst: And?

Rita: And what?

Ernst: What's his name, does he have blue or brown eyes, a heavy wallet or . . . ?

Rita: His name is Wilfried, he is handsome, in his mid-thirties and a successful lawyer. He has a beautiful house and a fast car. And he is a big soccer fan. So, Ernst, can you please explain the soccer rules to me.

Ernst: You are so impatient. Bayern against Schalke you said . . . hmmm . . . I'm sure that'll be an interesting game. Does this nice boyfriend of yours have an extra ticket for me?

Rita: Ernst!

Wilfried: I don't like being stuck in traffic. There must be another way to the soccer stadium.

Rita: Yes, we can turn right at the next intersection and take the side streets. After about one kilometer we have to turn left again. Then we'll have to go straight for about two kilometers. The stadium will be on the right-hand side.

Wilfried: You know your way around here. You have probably been in the stadium several times.

Rita: Yes, of course.

Wilfried: A real soccer fan, then.

Rita: Not necessarily.

Wilfried: But you do know the soccer rules, don't you?

Rita: A team has eleven players on the field. The players kick the ball into the goal. The goalie stands in front of the goal. A good goalie stops the ball, even with a penalty kick. A player is off-side if . . . ahhh, I don't really know any more.

Wilfried: You must have checked this in the encyclopedia?

Rita: No, I talked to my brother on the phone. He is the soccer fan in the family.

Wilfried: And which sports do you like?

Rita: I like to play squash and . . . stop, you have to turn into the side street here!

Wilfried: I have an idea. Why don't we leave the traffic jam behind us and play squash?

Rita: And what about the tickets for the soccer game?

Wilfried: You're not interested in the soccer game.

Rita: No, but you are.

Wilfried: I am interested in you. Very much.

ACTIVITY 1

1. c   2. a   3. b
4. b   5. c

ACTIVITY 2

1. *Rita und Ernst sind Geschwister.*
2. *Nein, Fußball ist ein komplexes Spiel.*
3. *FC Bayern München und Schalke 04.*
4. *Er ist Rechtsanwalt.*
5. *Ja, er ist ein netter Mensch.*
6. *Ja, Wilfried ist ein großer Fußballfan.*
7. *Ja, er will das Spiel auch sehen.*
8. *Nein.*

ACTIVITY 3

1. *häßlich*
2. *schüchtern*
3. *reich*
4. *groß*
5. *dick*
6. *schnell*
7. *lustig*
8. *unreif*
9. *schlank*
10. *ungeduldig*

ACTIVITY 4

Answer will vary according to the adjectives used.
Ich habe _____ Haare. Ich habe _____ Augen. Ich bin _____ von Beruf. Ich habe ein _____ Haus. Ich habe ein _____ Auto. Ich habe _____ Kinder. Ich bin ein _____ Mensch. Ich suche eine _____ Frau/einen _____ Mann.

ACTIVITY 5

1. *Mein Vater ist alt.*
2. *Meine Mutter ist hübsch.*
3. *Mein Bruder ist schüchtern.*
4. *Meine Schwester ist groß.*
5. *Mein Mann ist reich.*
6. *Meine Frau ist schlank.*
7. *Meine Kinder sind intelligent.*

ACTIVITY 6

Answer will vary according to the adjectives used.
Er/Sie ist _____. Er/Sie hat _____ Haare. Er/Sie hat _____ Augen. Er/Sie ist ein _____ Mann/eine Frau. Er/Sie hat _____ Kinder. Er/Sie fährt gern _____ Autos. Er/Sie hat ein _____ Haus. Das _____ Haus hat einen _____ Swimmingpool.

ACTIVITY 7

1. c   2. d   3. b
4. a

ACTIVITY 8

1. b   2. a   3. b
4. b   5. c

ACTIVITY 9

1. c   2. f   3. e
4. a   5. b   6. d

ACTIVITY 10

1. *mit*   2. *mir*   3. *mit*
4. *den Tennisplätzen*   5. *zu ihr*

ACTIVITY 11

1. *die Stadt*   2. *um*   3. *ohne*
4. *den Torwart*   5. *für*

ACTIVITY 12

1. *ins/zum im*   2. *aufs, auf dem*
3. *ins, ins*

ACTIVITY 13

Mein neuer Freund und ich gehen ins/zum Fußballstadion. Er hat die Tickets an der Ecke gekauft, gegenüber vom Stadion. Er ist ein großer Fußballfan. Ich interessiere mich nicht für Fußball. Ich interessiere mich für ihn. Ich mag ihn./Er gefällt mir./Ich habe ihn gern.

BLOOD IS THICKER THAN WATER

Blut ist dicker als Wasser

Die Familie (the family) in Europe is often much more than just *Mutter* (mother), *Vater* (father), *Brüder* (brothers), *Schwestern* (sisters) and *Kinder* (children). *Opa* (Grandpa) and *Oma* (Grandma), *Enkel* (grandchildren), *Tanten* (aunts) and *Onkel* (uncles), *Vettern* (male cousins) and *Kusinen* (female cousins), as well as *Urgroßvater* (greatgrandfather) and *Urgroßmutter* (greatgrandmother), *Großtante* (great aunt) und *Großonkel* (great uncle), are an essential part of it. Due to the fact that many Europeans live their entire lives in the same general area where they were born, many people are quite close to their families.

ACTIVITY 1: LET'S WARM UP

As if family relations weren't confusing in your own language . . . Match the term with the correct description.

1. *mein Onkel*
2. *mein Sohn*
3. *meine Schwester*
4. *meine Oma*
5. *meine Kusine*

a. *die Mutter meines Vaters*
b. *die Tochter meines Vaters*
c. *der Bruder meiner Mutter*
d. *die Tochter meines Onkels*
e. *der Enkel meiner Mutter*

HEAR . . . SAY 1

The scene: A wedding reception. The players: The wedding guests, including bride and groom and their respective families and friends. The plot: Gossiping, and even some backstabbing. May the newlyweds live happily ever after.

Kerstin Johannsen:	Sagen Sie mal, wer ist denn die Frau im grünen Kleid?
Ruth Piffel:	Das ist die Schwester der Braut. Sie ist geschieden.
Kerstin Johannsen:	Ach, natürlich. Ich habe sie gar nicht erkannt.
Ruth Piffel:	Ihr Mann hat sie wegen einer anderen Frau verlassen. Kurz nach der Hochzeit.
Kerstin Johannsen:	Ach ja?
Ruth Piffel:	Der Mann neben ihr ist ihr neuer Freund. Er ist auch geschieden. Er hat seine Frau während der Schwangerschaft verlassen.
Kerstin Johannsen:	Also so was!

Ruth Piffel:	Und das Mädchen mit den langen Haaren ist die Kusine der Braut. Sie hat trotz aller Warnungen ihrer Eltern die Schule nicht abgeschlossen. Sie ist Ende dreißig und lebt immer noch zu Hause.
Kerstin Johannsen:	Das ist ja unglaublich!
Ruth Piffel:	Ja ja, die Familie der Braut ist ganz verkorkst. Und über die Freunde und Freundinnen will ich erst gar nicht reden . . .
Kerstin Johannsen:	Warum denn nicht?
Ruth Piffel:	(whispering) Ich habe gehört . . . die Brautjungfer und der Vater der Braut . . . Sie wissen schon . . . Aber darf ich mich vorstellen: Ruth Piffel. Ich bin die Tante des Bräutigams.
Kerstin Johannsen:	Angenehm. Kerstin Johannsen. Ich bin die Brautjungfer.
Ruth Piffel:	Oh, wie peinlich!

Did You Know?

There are many different traditions and customs for the night before the wedding. One of the more popular ones brings the friends of both bride and groom together at a party where they watch bride and groom perform games together to show that they make a good team. One of the games has the party guests bring objects of glass or porcelain, which are shattered as they arrive at the party. Bride and groom must sweep up the broken pieces together using only one single mop, thus showing that together they can make sure that theirs will be a clean and safe household.

ACTIVITY 2: HOW'S THAT AGAIN?

I guess not all families are *glückliche Familien* (happy families). *Familienkrach kommt wohl in den besten Familien vor* (Family conflicts happen in the best families). Let's review what is going on in the bride's family.

1. *Ist die Frau im grünen Kleid verheiratet?*
2. *Hat die Schwester der Braut einen Freund?*
3. *Wer hat lange Haare?*
4. *Wo wohnt die Kusine der Braut?*
5. *Wer ist Frau Piffel?*
6. *Wie heißt die Brautjungfer?*

WORKSHOP 1

WORDS TO LIVE BY

HOW OLD ARE YOU? TALKING ABOUT AGE

For many of us this is a sore subject, particularly considering that certain ages seem to come with certain expectations.

Sie ist Ende dreißig und lebt noch immer zu Hause.	She is in her late thirties (Lit. she is [at] the end [of] thirty) and still lives at home.

Anyway, here's the way to talk about age.

Wie alt sind Sie?	How old are you?
Ich bin 26 Jahre alt.	I am 26 years old.
Mein Sohn ist schon fast 10 (Jahre alt).	My son is almost 10 (years old).
Sie ist Mitte zwanzig.	She is in her mid-twenties.
Er ist in seinen fünfzigern.	He is in his fifties.
Er ist in seinen besten Jahren.	He is in his best years.
Er ist über sechzig.	He is over sixty.
Das ist ein reifes Alter.	That is a mature age.

Did You Know?

In Germany, children start school when they are 6 years old. As soon as young people hit 16 they are allowed to consume alcohol, drive a moped, and get married, but the latter only if their parents agree. The consumption of hard liquor is a privilege for 18-year-olds, as is driving a car or getting married without their parents' consent. In short, once you hit 18, you are considered an adult. If you are a man, this means you are subject to a universal draft and are required to serve in the military or the civil service for a period of 15 to 18 months. Retirement awaits you at age 62. And in Swabia (a part of Baden Württemberg), people believe that you become extra smart on the day you turn 40. So there's still hope for some of us . . .

ACTIVITY 3: TAKE IT FOR A SPIN

Tell us about your family. Please insert the proper ages using the cues provided . . .
Mein Vater ist _____ *(? years old). Meine Mutter ist* _____ *(in her ?s). Meine Schwester/Mein Bruder ist* _____ *(over ?). Meine Schwester/Mein Bruder ist* _____ *(almost ?). Und ich bin* _____ *(early/mid/late ?ies).*

Did You Know?

In Germany, many younger people choose a *standesamtliche Trauung* (civil wedding) at the *Standesamt* (Registrar's Office) over a *kirchliche Trauung* (church wedding) in a *Kirche* (church). Compared to the United States, religion plays a lesser role in family life, and the number of church-goers has declined steadily in recent years. Many younger people even choose to live together, out of wedlock. As this is a rather popular trend, the law had to follow suit and guarantee such common-law couples the same legal rights and protections as married couples.

THE NITTY GRITTY

THE BRIDE'S FAMILY: EXPRESSING POSSESSION USING THE GENITIVE

German uses the possessive or the genitive case to show possession or close relationship. The noun that expresses the possessor takes a special form and follows the noun that expresses the possessed.

*Das ist die Schwester **der Braut**.*	That is the bride's sister. (Lit. That is the sister [of] the bride.)

"*Der Braut*" is in the genitive case and translates as "the bride's" or "of the bride." Here are two more examples.

Ich bin die Tante des Bräutigams.	I am the groom's aunt. (Lit. I am the aunt [of] the groom.)
Er ist der Mann meines Lebens.	He is the man of my life.

Here are all the forms of nouns in the genitive case.

THE GENITIVE CASE OF ARTICLES, NOUNS AND ADJECTIVES			
	MASCULINE	FEMININE	NEUTER	PLURAL ALL GENDERS
Das ist die Schwester . . .	*des Vaters*	*der Mutter*	*des Kindes*	*der Väter* *der Mütter* *der Kinder*
	eines Vaters	*einer Mutter*	*eines Kindes*	—
	meines Vaters	*meiner Mutter*	*meines Kindes*	*meiner Väter* *meiner Mütter* *meiner Kinder*
	keines Vaters	*keiner Mutter*	*keines Kindes*	*keiner Kinder*
	des netten Vaters	*der netten Mutter*	*des netten Kindes*	*der netten Väter* *der netten Mütter* *der netten Kinder*

And more examples . . .

Ich mag den Bruder der Braut.	I like the bride's brother.
Der Sohn meiner Kusine ist Mitte zwanzig.	My cousin's son is in his mid-twenties.
Ihr Mann ist nicht der Vater ihres Kindes.	Her husband is not the father of her child.

To ask the question use *Wessen?* (Whose?)

Wessen Braut ist sie jetzt?	Whose bride is she now?
Sie ist die Braut des Rechtsanwaltes.	She is the lawyer's bride.

Heads Up!

Most masculine and neuter nouns simply add an *-s* ending in the genitive, whereas most female nouns do NOT add an ending at all. For example: *der Vater → des Vaters*, but: *die Braut → der Braut*. Masculine and neuter monosyllabic nouns and those ending in -s, -ß, -z, -tz, -st, -zt, -sch add an *-e-* before the *-s* to facilitate pronunciation. For example: *der Mann → des Mannes, das Haus → des Hauses*.

PETER'S OR TOM'S? THE POSSESSIVE "S"

German, similar to English, can also express possession by adding an "s" to a noun that precedes another one. Unlike English, German can add an "s" only to proper names. Note that in German the possessive "s" is NOT preceded by an apostrophe.

Das ist <u>Peters</u> Freundin.	This is Peter's girlfriend.
Das is <u>Petras</u> Freundin.	This is Petra's girlfriend.
Das ist <u>Herrn Schneiders</u> Frau.	That is Mr. Schneider's wife.

Heads Up!

So called *n*-nouns, such as *der Herr* (man, mister, sir) or *der Patient* (patient) add an *-n* or *-en* ending in all cases, including the genitive. For example: *der Herr → des Herrn, der Patient → des Patienten.*

ACTIVITY 4: TAKE IT FOR A SPIN

Please complete the sentences.

1. *Ein Enkel ist* _____ (the son of a son).
2. *Meine Mutter ist* _____ (my father's wife).
3. *Seine Schwester ist* _____ (his mother's daughter).
4. *Die Brautjungfer ist* _____ (the girlfriend of the bride).
5. *Sabine ist* _____ (Horst's aunt, not Caroline's sister).
6. *Der amerikanische Präsident ist* _____ (the son of a president).

Did You Know?

While most are not fervently religious, most Germans are baptized and either nominally and/or traditionally Protestant (38%) or Catholic (34%). Generally speaking, the southern regions and the Rhineland have a Catholic majority while the northern and eastern regions are mainly protestant. The first and foremost Protestant was Martin Luther (1483–1546), who found the Catholic Church (not the religion!) to be corrupt and initiated reforms. His Reformation broadened, and the Protestant movement swelled following his excommunication from the Catholic Church in 1521. Today, Catholicism and Protestantism coexist peacefully with each other and with Judaism, Islam and smaller Christian denominations, such as Mormons or Jehovah's witnesses. Religion is considered a deeply private matter in Germany and usually not an appropriate subject matter for a conversation. Germany has no strict division of church and state, many public holidays celebrate Christian feast days, and churches receive tax money. Yet churches and their officials do not have a great deal of political clout nor are political figures likely to embrace religious platforms.

A SECOND LOOK AT PREPOSITIONS: PREPOSITIONS WITH THE GENITIVE

There are four prepositions that are followed by the genitive case in the German language.

PREPOSITIONS WITH GENITIVE		
WEGEN (BECAUSE)	*Er hat sie wegen einer anderen Frau verlassen.*	He left her for (Lit. because of) another woman.
WÄHREND (DURING)	*Er hat sie während der Schwangerschaft verlassen.*	He left her during her pregnancy.
(AN)STATT (INSTEAD OF)	*Sie hat einen alten Mann statt eines jungen Mannes geheiratet.*	She married an old man instead of a young man.
TROTZ (DESPITE)	*Sie hat ihn trotz seines Alters geheiratet.*	She married him despite his age.

Heads Up!

You will notice that in spoken German these prepositions are often followed by the dative case. So you may also hear *Sie hat ihn trotz seinem Alter geheiratet.*

ACTIVITY 5: TAKE IT FOR A SPIN

Please complete the following story with the correct translation of the cues in parentheses. Watch that case!

Während _____ (the wedding) meiner Schwester habe ich eine Frau kennengelernt. Sie ist etwas zu alt _____ (for me). Ich habe trotz _____ (her age) _____ (with her) gesprochen. Sie hat mich _____ (her son) vorgestellt. Aber sie hat _____ (with me) statt _____ (her son) getanzt.

A wedding reception wouldn't be complete without the speeches . . .

Vater der Braut:	(gently tapping his wine glass) **Meine Damen und Herren. Darf ich um Ihre Aufmerksamkeit bitten.**

1. Hochzeitsgast:	**Ruhe bitte! Der Vater der Braut will eine Rede halten.**
Vater der Braut:	**Liebes Brautpaar, sehr verehrte Gäste. Ich will mich kurz fassen.**

2. Hochzeitsgast:	**Von wegen kurz. Der schwingt immer große Reden.**
3. Hochzeitsgast:	**Und du klopfst immer große Sprüche!**
Vater der Braut:	**Mit nur 10 Monaten machte meine Tochter ihre ersten Schritte. Mit nur 16 Monaten sagte sie ihre ersten Worte. Mit nur 18 Jahren kaufte sie ihr erstes Auto. Mit nur 20 Jahren studierte sie. Und heute, mit nur 23 Jahren, heiratete sie ihren ersten Mann. Kaum zu glauben.** (pause) **Diese Hochzeit kostete mich ein Vermögen. Ich hoffe, ihr erster Mann ist der Mann ihres Lebens.** (laughter) **Meine Tochter lernte ihren Mann vor zwei Jahren kennen. In meinem Büro. Kai arbeitete damals für mich. Er war damals so jung und hatte kein Geld. Heute habe ich kein Geld und arbeite für ihn.** (laughter) **Und für die Zukunft meiner beiden Kinder . . . und vieler Enkelkinder. Die beiden sind ein gutes Team! Ich möchte das Glas auf das Wohl meiner Tochter und meines Schwiegersohnes heben. Ich wünsche euch in eurem gemeinsamen Leben Gesundheit, Geborgenheit und Glück! Für die Liebe müsst ihr schon selbst sorgen . . . Zum Wohl!**

1. Hochzeitsgast:	**Zum Wohl!**
2. Hochzeitsgast:	**Auf das Brautpaar!**
3. Hochzeitsgast:	**Alles Gute!**

ACTIVITY 6: HOW'S THAT AGAIN?

Did you cry? I'm sure the bride's mother did . . .

1. *Wer hält die Rede?*
2. *Wer machte die ersten Schritte mit 10 Monaten?*
3. *Was sagte sie mit 16 Monaten?*
4. *Was kaufte sie mit 18 Jahren?*

5. *Wo lernte sie ihren Mann kennen?*
6. *Was machte er im Büro ihres Vaters?*
7. *Für wessen Zukunft arbeitet der Vater der Braut jetzt?*
8. *Wem wünscht der Vater der Braut Gesundheit, Geborgenheit und Glück?*

Did You Know?

Traditionally, it is the father of the bride who pays for the *Hochzeit* and the *Hochzeitsreise* (honeymoon). In addition, the family of the bride used to give a more or less generous *Mitgift* (dowry) to help the new family get started. Many fathers today will still be happy to pay for the wedding and the honeymoon, yet the *Mitgift* has become a *Hochzeitsgeschenk* (wedding present) among many others. Many women getting married today are rather educated, and many are gainfully employed. The *Mitgift,* as a way to help earn their keep, is no longer necessary.

WORKSHOP 2

WORDS TO LIVE BY

LADIES AND GENTLEMEN: MAY I HAVE YOUR ATTENTION?

Most *Festreden* (speeches at parties) begin with the *Redner* (speaker) asking for attention (*um Aufmerksamkeit bitten*):

Ruhe, bitte!	Silence, please!
Ich bitte um Ruhe.	May I ask for silence, please?
Darf ich um Ihre Aufmerksamkeit bitten?	May I ask for your attention?

Then the *Redner* continues addressing the audience with the *Begrüßung* (greeting):

Meine Damen und Herren . . .	Ladies and gentlemen . . .
Sehr geehrte Gäste . . .	Esteemed guests . . .
Meine sehr verehrten Gäste . . .	My esteemed guests . . .
Liebe Gäste . . .	Dear guests . . .

The *Redner* may address the specific person the *Rede* is for:

Liebes Brautpaar . . .	Dear couple . . .
Liebes Geburtstagskind . . .	Dear birthday boy/girl . . .
Lieber Ehrengast . . .	Dear honorary guest . . .
Liebe Preisträgerin . . .	Dear prize recipient . . .

The *Redner* may announce that his speech is coming to a close.

Abschließend will ich noch sagen . . .	In closing, I'd like to say . . .
Zum Schluß darf ich noch bemerken . . .	In the end I'd like to remark . . .

Most *Festreden* end on well wishes for the person lauded.

Ich erhebe nun das Glas auf . . .	I lift the glass to . . .
Erheben wir das Glas nun auf . . .	Let's lift the glasses to . . .
Prost!	Cheers!
Zum Wohl!	Cheers!
Auf Ihr Wohl!	Cheers!
Auf Ihre Gesundheit!	To your health!
Alles Gute!	All the best!

LET'S PUT IT IN WRITING

This is the flash card the bride's father used to stay focused during his speech.

---

1. Um Aufmerksamkeit bitten: *Ich bitte um Ihre Aufmerksamkeit!*

2. Gäste begrüßen: _____

3. Brautpaar begrüßen: _____

4. das Brautpaar beschreiben: *Sie kennen sich seit zwei Jahren. Kai hat bei mir gearbeitet. Meine Tochter war so jung.*

5. Einen Witz machen über die Kosten der Hochzeit: _____

6. Rede beenden: _____

7. Dem Paar Glück wünschen: _____

8. Das Glas auf das Brautpaar erheben: _____

ACTIVITY 7: TAKE IT FOR A SPIN

The bride's father left parts of his cue card empty. Can you fill it in by looking back at the bride's father's speech?

Did You Know?

It is still a rather common custom in Germany to "steal the bride" during the wedding reception. The bride's friends and family take her to an undisclosed location, a location she liked or frequented a lot before being married. The groom and his friends and family have to find her as quickly as possible. If the groom is lucky, he'll know his new wife well enough, so he knows where to look for her. If he's not, he'll have to enlist the help of the members of her family and friends who stayed at the wedding reception to find out where she might have been taken. Of course, the tricky question is whether the groom gets along well enough with his in-laws to have them help him find his wife . . .

ONCE UPON A TIME: THE SIMPLE PAST OF REGULAR VERBS

When speaking about the past, German most often uses the present perfect.

Ich habe ihn vor zwei Jahren kennengelernt. I met him two years ago.
Ich bin gestern nach Hause gekommen. I came home yesterday.

Yet there are circumstances where the simple past is appropriate.

Ich lernte meinen Schwiegersohn vor zwei Jahren kennen. I met my son in law two years ago.

The simple past is preferred in writing, in speeches referring to the past, in stories and fairytales, and with a few common verbs such as *sein*, *haben* and *werden*.

Regular verbs form the simple past by adding a past tense marker *-t-* and the personal ending to their stem. Let's look at *machen* (to do, to make) as an example.

THE SIMPLE PAST TENSE OF *MACHEN* (TO DO, TO MAKE)	
ich mach + t + -e	I made, was making
du mach + t + -est	you made, were making
er mach + t + -e	he made, was making
wir mach + t + -en	we made, were making
ihr mach + t + -et	you made, were making
sie mach + t + -en	they made, were making
Sie mach + t + -en	you made, were making

Sie machte ihre ersten Schritte mit 10 Monaten. She made her first steps at 10 months.

Let's look at a few other regular verbs:

Sie sagte ihre ersten Worte mit 16 Monaten. She said her first words at 16 months.
Sie kaufte ihr erstes Auto mit 18 Jahren. She bought her first car at 18.
Die Hochzeitsfeier kostete ein Vermögen. The wedding reception cost a fortune.

There are many other regular verbs that are conjugated in the same manner, such as *fragen*, *telefonieren*, *studieren*, *heiraten*, *lernen*, *öffnen*, *reden*, *tanzen*, *zahlen*.

Heads Up!

If the verb's stem ends in -"*d*" or -"*t*" or in a consonant cluster, an -"*e*"- is inserted between the stem and the past tense marker -"*t*"-.

Er redete auf der Hochzeit seiner Tochter. He spoke at his daughter's wedding.

TAKE IT FOR A SPIN

Tell the bride's story in German.

> I met him three years ago. He worked for my father in Munich. I studied in Bremen. We talked on the phone. We spoke a lot. The bill was very high. My father paid the bill. Yesterday we got married. My father also paid the wedding reception. That made my husband very happy.

ONCE UPON A TIME, TOO: **THE SIMPLE PAST OF *SEIN, HABEN* AND *WERDEN***

Sein, haben and *werden* are usually used in the simple past, even in conversation. They are all highly irregular verbs. But not to worry, you'll use them so much you'll have their forms down in no time.

THE SIMPLE PAST TENSE OF *SEIN* (TO BE), *HABEN* (TO HAVE) AND *WERDEN* (TO BECOME)		
sein	haben	werden
ich war	ich hatte	ich wurde
du warst	du hattest	du wurdest
Sie waren (formal)	Sie hatten (formal)	Sie wurden (formal)
er war	er hatte	er wurde
wir waren	wir hatten	wir wurden
ihr wart	ihr hattet	ihr wurdet
sie waren	sie hatten	sie wurden

Er war damals so jung.	He was so young at the time.
Er hatte kein Geld.	He had no money.
Ich wurde letztes Jahr zwanzig.	I turned twenty last year.

TAKE IT FOR A SPIN

And now, tell the groom's story in German.

> I met her three years ago. She was so beautiful. She was a student in Bremen. I was an assistant for her father in Munich. We didn't have a car at the time. She became my girlfriend despite the distance (*die Entfernung*). And yesterday she became my wife. That made me very happy.

ONCE UPON A TIME, YET AGAIN: **A FEW TIME EXPRESSIONS IN THE PAST**

This should be easy, because we've dealt with many of these expressions in Lesson 6 already. Let's review.

- **vor** + dative

Ich habe sie vor einem Jahr kennengelernt.   I met her one year ago.

- **nach** + dative

Nach einem Jahr trennte sich das Paar.   The couple split after one year.

- **letzte** + noun

Letzte Woche war ich auf einer Hochzeit.   Last week I was at a wedding.

- **damals**

Ich war damals mit einer anderen Frau   At the time I was married to another woman.
verheiratet.

- **früher**

Früher war alles ganz anders.   In the past, everything was different.

- **später**

Ich lernte sie erst später kennen.   I didn't meet her until later.

And by the way, you know *gestern* (yesterday), but do you know *vorgestern* (the day before yesterday)? And you know *letzten Monat* (last month), but have you ever heard of *vorletzten Monat* (the month before last)? And you know *morgen* (tomorrow), but what about *übermorgen* (the day after tomorrow)?

ACTIVITY 10:   **TAKE IT FOR A SPIN**

Please answer the questions.

1. *Wann heirateten Ihre Eltern?* (30 years ago)
2. *Wann lernten Sie den Bräutigam kennen?* (last year)
3. *Wann waren Sie auf seiner Hochzeit?* (a week ago)
4. *Wann studierte die Braut in Bremen?* (in the past)
5. *Wann trennte sich die Frau von ihrem Mann?* (at the time)
6. *Wann wurde sie 30 Jahre alt?* (one year later)

Herr und Frau Bergmann
laden Sie hiermit herzlich dazu ein,
die Eheschließung ihrer Tochter
Anna Maria mit Max Stempfer
zu feiern.

**Die kirchliche Trauung findet am
16. Mai 2004 um 14 Uhr
in der St. Stephanskirche in Rostock statt.**

Anschließend bitten wir Sie zu einem
Sektempfang
in das Hotel zur Krone am Marktplatz.

CRIB NOTES

HEAR . . . SAY 1

Kerstin Johannsen:	Tell me, who is the woman in the green dress?
Ruth Piffel:	That is the sister of the bride. She is divorced.
Kerstin Johannsen:	Oh, of course. I didn't recognize her.
Ruth Piffel:	Her husband left her for another woman. Just after their wedding.
Kerstin Johannsen:	Oh, really?
Ruth Piffel:	The man standing next to her is her new boyfriend. He is divorced as well. He left his wife during her pregnancy.
Kerstin Johannsen:	Don't tell me!
Ruth Piffel:	And the girl with the long hair is the bride's cousin. She didn't finish school despite her parents' warnings. She is in her late thirties and still lives at home.
Kerstin Johannsen:	That is unbelievable!
Ruth Piffel:	Oh, yes, the bride's family is really messed up. I don't even want to begin talking about her friends.
Kerstin Johannsen:	Why not?
Ruth Piffel:	I heard . . . the bridesmaid and the bride's father . . . You know what I mean . . . But may I introduce myself: Ruth Piffel. I am the groom's aunt.
Kerstin Johannsen:	Nice to meet you. Kerstin Johannsen. I am the bridesmaid.
Ruth Piffel:	Oh, how embarrassing!

Father of the Bride:	Ladies and gentlemen. May I ask for your attention, please?
Wedding Guest 1:	Silence, please! The bride's father would like to give a speech.
Father of the Bride:	Dear bride and groom, honored guests! I will be brief.
Wedding Guest 2:	As if he'd really be brief. He always tells tall tales.
Wedding Guest 3:	And you keep talking big!
Father of the Bride:	At just 10 months my daughter took her first steps. At 16 months she spoke her first words. At age 18 she bought her first car. At age 18 she went to college. And today, at the age of only 23, she married her first husband. Hard to believe. This wedding cost a fortune. I hope her first man is the man of her life. My daughter met her husband two years ago, in my office. Kai worked for me at the time. He was so young, and he had no money. Today I have no money, and I work for him. And for the future of my two children . . . and many grandchildren! The two of them are a good team. I want to lift the glass to my daughter and my son-in-law. I wish both of you health, closeness and luck in your life together. You have to supply the love yourself. Cheers!
Wedding Guest 1:	Cheers!
Wedding Guest 2:	To the bride and groom!
Wedding Guest 3:	All the best!

ACTIVITY 1

1. c 2. e 3. b
4. a 5. d

ACTIVITY 2

1. *Nein, sie ist nicht verheiratet. Sie ist geschieden.*
2. *Ja, sie hat einen Freund.*
3. *Die Kusine der Braut hat lange Haare.*
4. *Sie wohnt zu Hause/bei ihren Eltern.*
5. *Frau Piffel ist die Tante des Bräutigams.*
6. *Die Brautjungfer heißt Kerstin Johannsen.*

ACTIVITY 3

Answers will vary depending on the ages.
*Mein Vater ist _____ Jahre alt. Meine Mutter ist
in den _____ gern. Meine Schwester/Mein
Bruder ist über _____. Meine Schwester/Mein
Bruder ist fast _____. Und ich bin
Anfang/Mitte/Ende _____.*

ACTIVITY 4

1. *Ein Enkel ist der Sohn eines Sohnes.*
2. *Meine Mutter ist die Frau meines Vaters.*
3. *Seine Schwester ist die Tochter seiner Mutter.*
4. *Die Brautjungfer ist die Freundin der Braut.*
5. *Sabine ist Horsts Tante, nicht Carolines Schwester.*
6. *Der amerikanische Präsident ist der Sohn eines Präsidenten.*

ACTIVITY 5

*der Hochzeit, für mich, ihres Alters, mit ihr, ihrem Sohn,
mit mir, ihres Sohnes.*

ACTIVITY 6

1. *Der Vater der Braut hält die Rede.*
2. *Die Braut machte die ersten Schritte mit 10 Monaten.*
3. *Sie sagte ihre ersten Worte mit 16 Monaten.*
4. *Sie kaufte ein Auto mit 18 Jahren.*
5. *Sie lernte ihren Mann im Büro ihres Vaters kennen.*
6. *Er arbeitete im Büro ihres Vaters.*
7. *Er arbeitet für die Zukunft seiner beiden Kinder und der Enkelkinder.*
8. *Der Vater der Braut wünscht seiner Tochter und seinem Schwiegersohn Gesundheit, Geborgenheit und Glück.*

ACTIVITY 7

1. *Um Aufmerksamkeit bitten:* Ich bitte um Ihre Aufmerksamkeit!
2. *Gäste begrüßen:* Liebe Gäste/Sehr geehrte Gäste . . .
3. *Brautpaar begrüßen:* Liebes Brautpaar . . .
4. *Das Brautpaar beschreiben:* Sie kennen sich seit zwei Jahren. Kai hat bei mir gearbeitet. Meine Tochter war so jung.
5. *Einen Witz machen über die Kosten der Hochzeit:* Die Hochzeit hat mich ein Vermögen gekostet.
6. *Rede beenden:* Abschließend will ich noch sagen/Zum Schluß will ich noch sagen . . .
7. *Dem Paar Glück wünschen:* Ich wünsche euch viel Glück.
8. *Das Glas auf das Brautpaar erheben:* Ich erhebe das Glas auf das Brautpaar.

ACTIVITY 8

*Ich lernte ihn vor drei Jahren kennen. Er arbeitete für
meinen Vater in München. Ich studierte in Bremen. Wir
telefonierten. Wir redeten viel. Die Rechnung war sehr
hoher. Mein Vater bezahlte die Rechnung. Gestern
heirateten wir. Mein Vater zahlte auch die Hochzeitsfeier. Das machte meinen Mann sehr glücklich.*

ACTIVITY 9

*Ich lernte sie vor drei Jahren kennen. Sie war so schön.
Sie war Studentin in Bremen. Ich war Sekretär bei ihrem
Vater in München. Wir hatten damals kein Auto. Sie
wurde trotz der Entfernung meine Freundin. Und gestern
wurde sie meine Frau. Das machte mich sehr glücklich.*

ACTIVITY 10

1. *Meine Eltern heirateten vor 30 Jahren.*
2. *Ich lernte den Bräutigam letztes Jahr kennen.*
3. *Ich war vor einer Woche auf seiner Hochzeit.*
4. *Die Braut studierte früher in Bremen.*
5. *Damals trennte sich die Frau von ihrem Mann.*
6. *Sie wurde ein Jahr später 30 Jahre alt.*

9

TO ERR IS HUMAN

Irren ist menschlich

- Making reservations

- Month by month the year goes by

- *First things first:* Ordinal numbers

- Dealing with problems and voicing complaints

- *Watch it!* How to issue commands and orders

- The simple past of modal verbs

- *What's done is done:* The simple past of strong verbs

Many older *Hotels* (hotels) in Germany, Austria and Switzerland have historical charm, but fewer amenities than newer hotels. When traveling in the area you may still find beautiful, tastefully decorated old hotels offering only one *Dusche* (shower) and *Badezimmer* (bath) for several *Zimmer* (rooms) to share. Often the flair of these hotels makes up for this many times over. You get the most important impression of a hotel in the *Empfangshalle* (entrance hall) and the *Rezeption* (Reception). Thus working at the reception of a hotel in Europe as an *Empfangschef* (hotel clerk) or *Empfangsdame* (female hotel clerk) carries some status. Traditionally, *Frühstück* (breakfast) is included in the price of an overnight stay in an *Einzelzimmer* (single room) or a *Doppelzimmer* (double room). In addition, *Zimmerservice* (room service) will offer lunches and dinners. Most hotels in German-speaking countries have a *Restaurant*, which serves traditional *Spezialitäten* (specialties) of the region.

ACTIVITY 1:   LET'S WARM UP

And now let's see how much you already know about the art of hotel booking . . .

1. If you booked your room beforehand you have a . . .
   a. . . . *Problem.*
   b. . . . *Reservierung.*
   c. . . . *Rezeption.*
2. A person traveling alone would most likely book a . . .
   a. . . . *Doppelzimmer.*
   b. . . . *Einzelzimmer.*
   c. . . . *Doppelzimmer mit Frühstück.*
3. The older hotels in Europe may not offer a . . . in every room.
   a. *Bad*
   b. *Telefon*
   c. *Frühstück*
4. If you wish to order breakfast or lunch or dinner in your room, you need to call . . .
   a. *Zimmerservice.*
   b. *Rezeption.*
   c. *Putzdienst.*
5. To get into your room you'll need a . . .
   a. *Telefon.*
   b. *Schlüssel.*
   c. *Kreditkarte.*

It is late. Alexander Müller is arriving at his hotel.

Empfangschef:	**Kann ich Ihnen behilflich sein?**
Alexander Müller:	**Guten Tag. Ich habe ein Zimmer auf den Namen Müller reserviert.**
Empfangschef:	**Müller. Ach ja, da haben wir's ja schon. Ein Doppelzimmer mit Bad für drei Nächte. Vom sechzehnten bis zum neunzehnten August.**
Alexander Müller:	**Ich wollte eigentlich bis zum einundzwanzigsten bleiben.**
Empfangschef:	**Das ist kein Problem. Ihr Zimmer ist im dritten Stock. Hier ist Ihr Schlüssel. Der Aufzug ist hier links. Ihre Frau Gemahlin erwartet sie schon auf . . .**
Alexander Müller:	**Bitte wer?**
Empfangschef:	**Ihre Gemahlin. Sie ist bereits auf Ihrem Zimmer.**
Alexander Müller:	**Ich bin nicht verheiratet.**
Empfangschef:	(smiling) **Nun, ob die Dame Ihre Gemahlin ist oder nicht ist wirklich ganz Ihre Sache . . . Ah, da kommt Ihre . . . äh . . . die Dame ja.**

At that very moment a female customer approaches the counter.

Alexandra Müller:	**Kann ich . . .**
Alexander Müller:	(talking to the hotel clerk, yet pointing at Frau Müller) **Ich kenne diese Frau nicht.**
Alexandra Müller:	**Unterbrechen Sie mich bitte nicht, mein Herr!**
Alexander Müller:	(to Frau Müller) **Tut mir leid.** (to the hotel clerk) **Ich kann nicht mit ihr auf einem Zimmer wohnen. Geben . . .**
Alexandra Müller:	**Wie bitte? Wie kommen Sie denn dazu . . .**
Alexander Müller:	(to Frau Müller) **Bitte unterbrechen Sie mich nicht.** (to the hotel clerk) **Geben Sie mir bitte ein anderes Zimmer!**
Empfangschef:	**Wir sind ausgebucht.**
Alexander Müller:	**Wie bitte?**
Empfangschef:	**Wir nahmen an . . . ich meine Sie haben denselben Namen und kommen aus derselben Stadt . . . es schien ganz logisch . . . Sie gehören also nicht zusammen?**
Alexander und Alexandra Müller:	(emphatic) **Nein.**

Gemahlin and *Gemahl* are somewhat oldfashioned words for *(Ehe)frau* (wife) and *(Ehe)mann* (husband). The terms are still common in circumstances where extremely polite speech is appropriate.

ACTIVITY 2: HOW'S THAT AGAIN?

What a mix-up! Maybe you can help find a solution to this *Problem* (problem) by answering these questions.

1. *Auf welchen Namen hat Alexander sein Zimmer bestellt?*
2. *Hat noch jemand anderes ein Zimmer auf den Namen Müller bestellt?*
3. *Wie lange will Alexander in Hannover bleiben?*
4. *Ist das ein Problem?*
5. *Wer soll bereits angekommen sein?*
6. *Warum kann er nicht mit Alexandra ein Zimmer teilen?*
7. *Warum kann Alexander kein anderes Zimmer haben?*
8. *Was ist passiert?*

WORD ON THE STREET

Wie kommen Sie denn dazu . . . ? (Lit. How do you get to . . . ?) is roughly equivalent to "How dare you . . . ?" The expression clearly expresses indignation at a suggestion or comment, and can be used in formal and informal settings

WORKSHOP 1

WORDS TO LIVE BY

MAKING RESERVATIONS

Making reservations is a ready skill to have if you are traveling to Europe.

Ich möchte ein Zimmer reservieren.	I would like to reserve a room.
Haben Sie noch Zimmer frei?	Do you still have rooms available?
Kann ich ein Zimmer für vier Nächte vorbestellen?	Can I reserve a room for four nights?
Ein Einzel- oder ein Doppelzimmer?	A single or a double room?
Mit Dusche oder Bad?	With a shower or with a bath?
Mit Balkon?	With a balcony?

Mit Blick aufs Meer/auf die Berge/auf den See?	With ocean/mountain/lake view?
Auf welchem Stock ist mein Zimmer?	What floor is my room on?
Ihr Zimmer liegt auf der dritten Etage.	Your room is on the fourth floor.
Wir sind leider ausgebucht.	Unfortunately, we are booked.
Ich habe ein Zimmer auf den Namen Müller bestellt.	I made reservations for a room for Müller. (Lit. I reserved a room in the name Müller.)

Heads Up!

German has two words for floor, *Stock* and *Etage* (pronounced as [eh-tah-zheh]). Both are rather common, with *Stock* possibly more typical in the south, and *Etage* more common in the north.

WORD ON THE STREET

Don't ask me how this came about, but German has some rather strange rules about when you can use the verbs *bestellen* (to order) and *reservieren* (to reserve). In a restaurant you either "reserve" a table—*einen Tisch reservieren*—or you "order" a table—*einen Tisch bestellen*. You also either "order" or "reserve" tickets for a movie or the theater—*Karten bestellen/reservieren*—or a room in a hotel—*ein Zimmer bestellen/reservieren*. Also, you can either "reserve" or "book" a hotel room or a flight—*ein Zimmer/einen Flug reservieren/buchen*. But when you "order" food, use only—*Essen bestellen*—and when you "reserve" a seat on a train, use *einen Platz reservieren*.

ACTIVITY 3: **TAKE IT FOR A SPIN**

Please take part in this conversation.

Empfangschef:	Kann ich Ihnen behilflich sein?
Guest:	_____.
Empfangschef:	Eine Reservierung für Schneider. Einen Augenblick, bitte. Ach ja, da haben wir's ja schon. Ein Doppelzimmer für drei Nächte.
Guest:	_____.
Empfangschef:	Vier Nächte sind kein Problem.
Guest:	_____.
Empfangschef:	Leider haben wir kein Zimmer mit Blick auf das Schloss mehr frei. Darf es auch Blick auf den Garten sein?
Guest:	_____.

Empfangschef:	Selbstverständlich. Ein Zimmer mit Blick auf den Garten und Badezimmer.
Guest:	_____.
Empfangschef:	Ja, natürlich haben wir Zimmerservice. Das Restaurant ist bis 23 Uhr geöffnet.

MONTH BY MONTH THE YEAR GOES BY

Let's take a quick look at the months of the year and seasons in German. Since most are English cognates, using the names of the months in German should be a piece of cake for you.

MONTHS AND SEASONS OF THE YEAR			
SEASON	MONTH	SEASON	MONTH
Winter	Januar	Sommer	Juli
	Februar		August
Frühling	März	Herbst	September
	April		Oktober
	Mai		November
Sommer	Juni	Winter	Dezember

Yet pay attention to their pronunciation: *Januar* is pronounced (yah-noo-ahr), and *Juni* is pronounced (yoo-nee).

Der Frühling fängt im März an.	Spring begins in March.
Im Sommer ist es sehr heiß.	It is very hot in the summer.
Im Herbst fallen die Blätter von den Bäumen.	In the fall, the leaves fall from the trees.
Im Winter ist es kalt.	It is cold in the winter.
Weihnachten ist im Dezember.	Christmas is in December.

FIRST THINGS FIRST: ORDINAL NUMBERS

You have learned the so-called "cardinal" numbers so far, like *eins, zwei, drei, vier* and so forth. Now it's time to learn the "ordinal" numbers, which indicate a position of an item in a series, such as the English "first," "second," "third" and so forth. In German the ordinal numbers are formed by adding -"*t*"- to the numbers from 2 to 19, e.g., *neunzehn-t-er* (19th), and by adding -"*s*"- to the numbers from 20 to 100, e.g., *zweiundzwanzig* → *zweiundzwanzig-st-er* (22nd). There are four irregular ordinal numbers: *eins* → *erster* (first), *drei* → *dritter* (third), *sieben* → *siebter* (seventh) and *acht* → *achter* (eighth).

Like other adjectives, ordinal numbers must agree with the noun in gender, number and object case.

THE ORDINAL NUMBERS

1st	*erster, -e, -es*	13th	*dreizehnter, -e, -es*
2nd	*zweiter, -e, -es*	14th	*vierzehnter, -e, -es*
3rd	*dritter, -e, -es*	15th	*fünfzehnter, -e, -es*
4th	*vierter, -e, -es*	16th	*sechzehnter, -e, -es*
5th	*fünfter, -e, -es*	17th	*siebzehnter, -e, -es*
6th	*sechster, -e, -es*	18th	*achtzehnter, -e, -es*
7th	*siebter, -e, -es*	19th	*neunzehnter, -e, -es*
8th	*achter, -e, -es*	20th	*zwanzigster, -e, -es*
9th	*neunter, -e, -es*	21st	*einundzwanzigster, -e, -es*
10th	*zehnter, -e, -es*	30th	*dreißigster, -e, -es*
11th	*elfter, -e, -es*	100th	*einhundertster, -e, -es*
12th	*zwölfter, -e, -es*	101st	*hunderterster, -e, -es*

Ordinal numbers are used in dates.

Vom sechzehnten bis zum neunzehnten August.	From the 16th to the 19th of August.
Eigentlich wollte ich bis zum einundzwanzigsten bleiben.	I actually wanted to stay until the 21st.
Am vierundzwanzigsten Dezember ist Heiligabend.	Christmas Eve is on December 24th.
Am ersten Januar ist Neujahr.	New Year is on January 1st.

The hotel clerk will use ordinal numbers to direct you to your floor.

Ihr Zimmer ist im dritten Stock.	Your room is on the fourth floor.
Der Aufzug fährt nur bis zur dreizehnten Etage.	The elevator will only go to the fourteenth floor.
Wer wohnt denn im fünften Stock?	Who lives on the sixth floor?

THE FINE PRINT

As mentioned before, if the number is not spelled out, a period is used to signify ordinal numbers in writing. Here are a few dates: *1. Januar 2005* or *Mein 30. Geburtstag war am 21.03.98.* (My 30th birthday was on 03/21/98.) Remember that in German, when dates are given, the day is mentioned first, and the month second. And if you want to say where you live, say: *Ich wohne im 5. Stock.*

Did You Know?

In Germany, Austria and Switzerland going in an *Aufzug* (elevator) can be somewhat confusing for Americans. The *Aufzug* will start from the *Erdgeschoss* (ground floor) and go to the *erster Stock* (second floor, Lit. first floor), then go on to the *zweiter Stock* (third floor, Lit. second floor) and so forth. While Germans, like Americans, have issues with the number thirteen and consider it unlucky, the thirteenth floor is never simply skipped.

Ready for a few riddles?

1. *Meine Tante wohnt in der neunten Etage. Ich wohne drei Etagen höher. Mein Bruder wohnt eine Etage unter ihr.*
   a. *Auf welcher Etage wohne ich?*
   b. *Auf welcher Etage wohnt mein Bruder?*
2. *Herr Schneider ist am 3. Mai geboren. Seine Frau hat genau neun Monate vor ihm Geburtstag. Sein Sohn hat zweiundzwanzig Tage nach ihm Geburtstag.*
   a. *Wann hat Herrn Schneiders Frau Geburtstag?*
   b. *Wann hat Herrn Schneiders Sohn Geburtstag?*
3. *Frau Müller kommt am 14. August in Hannover an. Sie will drei Tage in Hannover bleiben. Dann fährt sie für vier Tage nach Hamburg. Und dann fährt sie weiter nach München.*
   a. *Wann fährt sie nach Hamburg?*
   b. *Und wann fährt Frau Müller nach München?*

THE NITTY GRITTY

WATCH IT! HOW TO ISSUE COMMANDS AND ORDERS

The imperative forms are used to give commands, instructions, suggestions, and requests. English has only one imperative, because there is only one word for "you." But German has three words for "you"—*Sie, du,* and *ihr*—and therefore needs three imperative forms.

***du*-form:**	***Unterbrich mich nicht, Klaus!***
	Don't interrupt me, Klaus!
***ihr*-form:**	***Unterbrecht mich nicht, Kinder!***
	Don't interrupt me, children!
***Sie*-form:**	***Unterbrechen Sie mich nicht, mein Herr!***
	Don't interrupt me, sir!

If you want to soften the request, add *bitte.*

Bitte unterbrecht mich nicht, Kinder!   Please don't interrupt me, children.

DU-FORM

If you are ordering just one person around, and a friend no less, use the *du*-form. The *du*-form is basically the stem of the verb, which you get by taking off the infinitive ending—*en: sagen* minus *-en* becomes *sag.* Do NOT repeat the pronoun *du.*

Sag mir bitte deinen Namen.   Please tell me your name.

Heads Up!

Verbs, such as *unterbrechen* (to interrupt) or *geben* (to give), that take vowel changes in the second and third person singular in the present tense, take the same vowel change in the imperative:

Du unterbrichst mich. (You are interrupting me.) → **Unterbrich mich nicht, Klaus!** (Don't interrupt me, Klaus.)

However, verbs with vowel changes from *a* to *ä* in the second and third person singular present, such as *laufen* (to run) und *fahren* (to drive), do not add the *Umlaut* in the imperative.

Du fährst schnell (You are driving fast) → **Fahr nicht so schnell!** (Don't drive so fast!)

THE FINE PRINT

> Verbs with a stem ending on -*t*, -*d*, or -*ig*, such as *warten* or *antworten*, always add an -*e* in the imperative: *Warte auf mich!* (Wait for me!), *Antworte mir!* (Answer me!)

SIE-FORM

The *Sie*-form is used to command or make suggestions to those you refer to with the formal *Sie*. The imperative form is identical to the *Sie*-form of the present tense. It is necessary that you use the personal pronoun *Sie* when using this form. But notice that the subject (*Sie*) and the verb (e.g., *unterbrechen*) trade places.

Unterbrechen Sie mich nicht, meine Dame!	Don't interrupt me, madam!
Antworten Sie mir bitte! (sg./pl.)	Answer me.
Geben Sie mir bitte den Schlüssel zu meinem Zimmer.	Give me the key to my room.

IHR-FORM

When you are ordering around a group of people (*ihr*) simply use the regular present tense form for the second person plural. DO NOT use the pronoun.

Unterbrecht mich nicht, Kinder!	Don't interrupt me, children.
Wartet auf mich!	Wait for me.

THE FINE PRINT

> The verb *sein* (to be) is the only verb with an irregular imperative form. Take a look at the examples:
>
> | | |
> |---|---|
> | *Bitte seien Sie pünktlich, Herr Müller!* | Please be punctual, Mr. Müller! |
> | *Bitte sei leise, Klaus!* | Please be quiet, Klaus! |
> | *Seid nicht so laut, Kinder!* | Don't be so loud, children! |

Heads Up!

If you want to make suggestions and include yourself, German uses the verb *lassen* (to let) similarly to the way English uses "Let's" in *Laß uns das Zimer teilen* (Let's share the room). You can also simply use the *wir*-form of the verb and switch subject and verb: *Teilen wir uns das Zimmer* (Let's share the room).

TAKE IT FOR A SPIN

1. Take the hotel clerk's part in the conversation, answering the guest's questions with a suggestion formed as an imperative.

Gast:	*Haben Sie ein Einzelzimmer?*
Empfangschef:	_____. (Yes, we have a single room.)
Gast:	*Wie komme ich auf mein Zimmer?*
Empfangschef:	_____. (Please take the elevator to the third floor.)
Gast:	*Wo kann ich jetzt noch etwas essen?*
Empfangschef:	_____. (Please call room service.)

2. Take the mother's part in this conversation, answering the child's questions with a suggestion formed as an imperative.

Tochter:	*Soll ich mit Horst ins Theater oder mit Peter ins Kino gehen?*
Mutter:	_____. (Go to the movies with Peter.)
Tochter:	*Wie kann ich es Horst sagen?*
Mutter:	_____. (Just call him.)

3. Take the father's part in this conversation, answering the family's questions with a suggestion formed as an imperative.

Familie:	*Was machen wir am Wochenende?*
Vater:	_____. (Let's go to the museum.)
Familie:	*Fahren wir mit dem Bus oder mit dem Auto?*
Vater:	_____. (Let's take the car.)

THE FINE PRINT

The "Do not disturb" sign in a hotel, *Bitte nicht stören,* is actually a special command form used in public announcements, using *bitte* and the infinitive of the verb.

HEAR . . . SAY 2

Remember the unfortunate Alexander and Alexandra Müller? Could you imagine something like this happening to you . . . or even worse, your partner? Well, after a somewhat lengthy "discussion" with the *Empfangschef,* Alexander decided to give the guy a break and, with his help, moved into a hotel a few blocks down the road. As an apology for the mix-up, the hotel also offered to pay for a dinner for two at a restaurant well-known for its beautiful *Gartenterrasse.* The two Müllers decided they were hungry and could use some company, so Alexander made a *Reservierung* for *19 Uhr* that same evening.

Alexander Müller:	Guten Abend, ich habe einen Tisch auf den Namen Müller reserviert.
Kellnerin:	Ja, natürlich, Herr Müller. Ein Tisch für zwei. Folgen Sie mir bitte.

The waitress leads them to a table in a separate room inside the restaurant.

Alexander Müller:	Ich wollte eigentlich einen Tisch auf der Gartenterrasse.
Kellnerin:	Auf der Terrasse ist leider schon alles voll.
Alexander Müller:	Ihr Kollege gab mir am Telefon einen Tisch auf der Terrasse.
Kellnerin:	Sie können gerne warten. . . .
Alexander Müller:	Ich möchte nicht warten. Ihr Kollege versprach mir einen Tisch auf der Terrasse für 19 Uhr.
Kellnerin:	Im Moment geht das leider nicht . . .
Alexander Müller:	Kann ich bitte mit dem Oberkellner sprechen. Ich möchte mich beschweren.
Alexandra Müller:	Herr Müller, lassen Sie uns doch hier essen.
Alexander Müller:	Also gut.
Kellnerin:	Ich bringe Ihnen sofort die Speisekarte.

Alexander and Alexandra take a seat and wait. Twenty minutes later they still don't have the menu.

Alexander Müller:	Wo bleibt denn unsere Kellnerin?
Alexandra Müller:	Da kommt ein anderer Kellner. Entschuldigung, unsere Kellnerin sollte uns eine Speisekarte bringen. Wir warten schon seit zwanzig Minuten.

Kellner:	**Das wundert mich nicht. Der Teil des Restaurants ist heute geschlossen.**
Alexander Müller:	**Wie bitte?**
Alexandra Müller:	**Können wir bitte einen anderen Tisch haben?**
Kellner:	**Haben Sie einen Tisch reserviert?**
Alexander Müller:	**Ja, auf 19 Uhr.**
Kellner:	**Tja, es ist schon fast 19 Uhr 30. Wir halten Reservierungen nur für fünfzehn Minuten bereit. Tut mir leid.**
Alexander Müller:	**Das ist ja unglaublich. Heute geht aber auch alles schief . . .**

ACTIVITY 6: **HOW'S THAT AGAIN?**

1. *Auf welche Uhrzeit hat Herr Müller einen Tisch reserviert?*
2. *Wo soll der Tisch sein?*
3. *Warum kann er nicht auf der Terrasse sitzen?*
4. *Warum möchte er mit dem Oberkellner sprechen?*
5. *Warum kommt die Kellnerin nicht mit der Speisekarte?*
6. *Wie lange hält das Restaurant die Reservierung?*

WORD ON THE STREET

In German, things don't go wrong, they go crooked. *Heute geht aber auch alles schief!* Or you could also say: *Heute klappt aber auch gar nichts!* (Today absolutely nothing works!)

WORKSHOP 2

WORDS TO LIVE BY

DEALING WITH PROBLEMS AND VOICING COMPLAINTS

What are some of the things that could go wrong at a hotel or in a restaurant? To express your complaints to the *Empfangschef* you'll find the following expression very useful:

Ich möchte mich beschweren.	I want to complain.

Here are some ways to politely deal with those responsible for the problem. Once you have the *Empfangschefs* undivided attention, you might want to be more specific and use:

. . . *funktioniert* (sg.)/*funktionieren* (pl.) nicht.	. . . doesn't/don't work. (Lit. . . . doesn't/don't function.)

and

Ich brauche . . . auf meinem Zimmer.   I need . . . in my room.

Take a look at the examples:

Ich brauche ein Kissen/eine Decke/   I need a pillow/a blanket/soap/shampoo in my room.
Seife/Shampoo auf meinem Zimmer.

Die Heizung/der Airconditioner/das   The heater/air conditioner/telephone/TV doesn't work.
Telefon/der Fernseher funktioniert
nicht.

In a restaurant you might encounter these problems.

Wir warten schon seit einer halben   We've been waiting for our drinks for half an hour.
Stunde auf die Getränke.

Das Essen ist kalt.   Our food is cold.

Der Teller/die Tasse/das Glas/die   The plate/cup/glas/fork/knife/spoon is dirty.
Gabel/das Messer/der Löffel ist
schmutzig.

Entschuldigung, wir haben kein   Excuse me, we don't have any silverware.
Besteck.

Das habe ich nicht bestellt.   I didn't order that.

WORD ON THE STREET

Here are ways to deal with those responsible for your problems in a little less polite way.

Also, so geht's nicht.   You can't do that.
Das ist Ihr Fehler/Problem.   This was your mistake/problem.

And these phrases you ONLY want to use as a last resort.

Das lasse ich mir nicht gefallen.   I won't be treated like that.
Was glauben Sie eigentlich?   How dare you!

Did You Know?

Germans can be rather confrontational when dealing with problems. Don't be taken aback if you end up in the middle of an argument when voicing a complaint with service personnel. Even though *Der Kunde ist König* (The customer is king) even in Germany, his subjects may not be afraid to argue, and you may end up having to ask for the supervisor: *Kann ich mit Ihrem Vorgesetzten sprechen?* (Can I speak to your supervisor?)

Eigentlich could roughly be translated with "actually" or "anyway." It is frequently used if you wish to soften a contradiction or a complaint. For example: *Eigentlich stimmt das doch gar nicht* (That's actually not quite true).

TAKE IT FOR A SPIN

What would you say?

1. Imagine you are at a restaurant, and you are missing silverware.
2. Imagine you are at a restaurant, and the waiter brings you the wrong food.
3. Imagine the waiter shows attitude, and you want to complain.
4. Imagine the waiter simply shrugs off your complaint.
5. Imagine the waiter keeps brushing you off, and you want to complain to his supervisor.

THE NITTY GRITTY

THE SIMPLE PAST OF MODAL VERBS

All modal verbs you've learned so far, *wollen* (to want to), *sollen* (to be supposed to), *müssen* (to have to), *dürfen* (to be allowed to) and *können* (to be able to) form the simple past by adding *-te* plus a personal ending. See the forms of *wollen*.

THE PAST TENSE OF MODAL VERBS—*WOLLEN* (TO WANT TO)			
SINGULAR		**PLURAL**	
ich wollte	I wanted to	*wir wollten*	we wanted to
du wolltest	you wanted to	*ihr wolltet*	you wanted to
Sie wollten	you wanted to (formal)	*Sie wollten*	you wanted to (formal)
er/sie/es wollte	he/she/it wanted to	*sie wollten*	they wanted to

Please note that *dürfen, können,* and *müssen* drop the *Umlaut* in the past tense forms. As in the present tense, the modal verb takes the position of the verb. The main verb is in the infinitive and goes to the end of the sentence.

Ich wollte eigentlich einen Tisch auf der Gartenterrasse haben.	I actually wanted to have a table on the garden terrace.
Unsere Kellnerin sollte uns eine Speisekarte bringen.	Our waitress was supposed to bring us a menu.
Ich musste mich einfach beschweren.	I simply had to complain.

TAKE IT FOR A SPIN

Rewrite the sentences in the simple past.

1. *Ich muss das Restaurant anrufen.*
2. *Ich soll einen Tisch auf 20 Uhr reservieren.*
3. *Meine Freundin will einen Tisch im Garten haben.*
4. *Leider kann ich keinen Tisch im Garten reservieren.*
5. *Der Garten soll geschlossen sein.*
6. *Meine Freundin wil in ein anderes Restaurant gehen.*

WHAT'S DONE IS DONE: THE SIMPLE PAST OF STRONG VERBS

We said earlier that those German verbs that change their stem vowel in the simple past are called "strong verbs." For example, the past tense form of *kommen* (to come) changes its stem vowel from "o" to "a" as in *er kam* (he came). That change in the stem signifies that the verb is in the past tense. Once you know the past tense stem, you add the personal endings (the same endings you'd use in the present tense). Take a look at the strong verb *geben*, for example:

Infinitive: *geben* (to give)
Stem vowel change: *g<u>a</u>b* (gave)
Ending: *du gab<u>st</u>* (you gave)

Now let's look at the different forms of the verb *nehmen* in the simple past.

THE SIMPLE PAST TENSE OF STRONG VERBS—*NEHMEN* (TO TAKE)

SINGULAR		PLURAL	
ich nahm	I took	*wir nahmen*	we took
du nahmst	you took	*ihr nahmt*	you took
Sie nahmen	you took (formal)	*Sie nahmen*	you took (formal)
er/sie/es nahm	he/she/it took	*sie nahmen*	they took

Please note that the *ich*-form and *er*-form do not take an ending.
As in the present tense, separable verbs such as *ankommen* (to arrive) separate in the simple past.

Wir kamen spät im Hotel an.   We arrived late at the hotel.

The past tense forms of strong verbs are unpredictable and must be memorized. Here is a select list of strong verbs and their past tense forms. Some of them show similar changes in English as well, e.g., *to drive → drove, to give → gave, to fly → flew.*

SELECTED STRONG VERBS			
fahren	to drive	*fuhr*	drove
geben	to give	*gab*	gave
fliegen	to fly	*flog*	flew
nehmen	to take	*nahm*	took
kommen	to come	*kam*	came
sehen	to see	*sah*	saw
gehen	to go	*ging*	went
trinken	to drink	*trank*	drank
essen	to eat	*aß*	ate
sprechen	to speak	*sprach*	spoke
scheinen	to shine, to seem	*schien*	shone, seemed
rufen	to call	*rief*	called

LET'S TAKE IT FOR A SPIN

Once upon a time . . . Please complete the story by inserting the right verb in the simple past tense.

Es (to be) _____ *einmal ein Restaurant. Das Restaurant* (to have) _____ *ein schöne Gartenterrasse. Die Gäste* (to want) _____ *auf der Terrasse sitzen. Ein Gast* (to call) _____ *an und* (to reserve) _____ *einen Tisch für 20 Uhr. Er* (to want) _____ *mit seiner Frau und seiner Tochter in dem Restaurant* (to eat) _____. *Um 20 Uhr* (to arrive) _____ *sie im Restaurant an. Der Kellner* (to give) _____ *Ihnen einen Tisch auf der Terrasse. Sie* (to order) _____ *das Essen. Das Essen* (to come) _____ *lange nicht. Der Gast* (to complain) _____ *sich. Endlich* (to be able to) _____ *sie* (to eat) _____. *Nach dem Essen* (to eat) _____ *sie Nachtisch. Dann* (to go) _____ *sie satt nach Hause.*

CRIB NOTES

Receptionist:	Can I be of assistance?
Alexander Müller:	Good day. I have reservations for Müller.
Receptionist:	Müller. Ah, yes, here it is. A double room with a bath for three nights. From August 16 through August 19.
Alexander Müller:	I actually wanted to stay until the twenty-first.
Receptionist:	That's no problem. Your room is on the fourth floor. Here is your key. The elevator is here to your left. Your spouse is waiting for you in . . .
Alexander Müller:	Excuse me, who?
Receptionist:	Your wife. She is already in your room
Alexander Müller:	I am not married.
Receptionist:	Well, whether the lady is your wife or not is really none of my business . . . Ah, there is your . . . ah . . . the lady.

At that very moment a female customer approaches the counter.

Alexandra Müller:	Can I . . .
Alexander Müller:	I don't know this woman.
Alexandra Müller:	Don't interrupt me, sir!
Alexander Müller:	I'm sorry. I can't stay in the same room with her. Give me . . .
Alexandra Müller:	Excuse me? How dare you . . .
Alexander Müller:	Please don't interrupt me! Give me another room, please!
Receptionist:	We are all booked.
Alexander Müller:	Excuse me?
Receptionist:	We assumed . . . I mean you have the same last name and you are from the same town . . . it seemed logical . . . You don't belong together?
Alexander and Alexandra Müller:	No.

Alexander Müller:	Good evening, I have reservations in the name of Müller.
Waitress:	Yes, of course, Herr Müller. A table for two. Please follow me.

The waitress leads them to a table in a separate room inside the restaurant.

Alexander Müller:	I actually wanted to have a table on the terrace.
Waitress:	Unfortunately, the terrace is full at the moment.
Alexander Müller:	On the phone, your colleague gave me a table on the terrace.
Waitress:	You're welcome to wait. . . .
Alexander Müller:	I don't want to wait. Your colleague promised a table on the terrace at 7 PM.
Waitress:	At the moment that is not possible . . .
Alexander Müller:	Can I speak to the head waiter? I want to complain.
Alexandra Müller:	Herr Müller, let's eat here.
Alexander Müller:	OK.

Waitress:	I'll bring the menu immediately.

Alexander and Alexandra take a seat and wait. Twenty minutes later they still don't have the menu.

Alexander Müller:	Where is our waitress?
Alexandra Müller:	There is another waiter. Excuse me, our waitress was supposed to bring us a menu. We've been waiting for twenty minutes.
Waiter:	I'm not surprised. This part of the restaurant is closed today.
Alexander Müller:	I beg your pardon?
Alexandra Müller:	Could we please have another table?
Waiter:	Do you have reservations?
Alexander Müller:	Yes, for 7PM.
Waiter:	Well, it is almost 7:30PM. We hold reservations only for fifteen minutes. I'm sorry.
Alexander Müller:	This is unbelievable. Today everything is going wrong . . .

ACTIVITY 1

1. b   2. b   3. a
4. a   5. b

ACTIVITY 2

1. *Er hat ein Zimmer auf den Namen Müller bestellt.*
2. *Ja, Alexandra Müller hat ein Zimmer auf den Namen Müller bestellt.*
3. *Er will eigentlich bis zum einundzwanzigsten in Hannover bleiben.*
4. *Nein, das ist kein Problem.*
5. *Seine Gemahlin soll bereits angekommen sein.*
6. *Er kennt sie nicht.*
7. *Das Hotel ist ausgebucht*
8. *Der Empfangschef nahm an, Herr und Frau Müller sind verheiratet/gehören zusammen.*

ACTIVITY 3

Empfangschef:	Kann ich Ihnen behilflich sein?
Guest:	Ich habe ein Zimmer auf den Namen Schneider bestellt/reserviert.
Empfangschef:	Eine Reservierung für Schneider. Einen Augenblick, bitte. Ach ja, da haben wir's ja schon. Ein Doppelzimmer für drei Nächte.
Guest:	Eigentlich wollte ich vier Nächte bleiben.
Empfangschef:	Vier Nächte sind kein Problem.
Guest:	Ich möchte ein Zimmer mit Blick auf das Schloss.
Empfangschef:	Leider haben wir kein Zimmer mit Blick auf das Schloss mehr frei. Darf es auch Blick auf den Garten sein?
Guest:	Haben Sie noch ein Zimmer mit Blick auf den Garten und Bad frei?
Empfangschef:	Selbstverständlich. Ein Zimmer mit Blick auf den Garten und Badezimmer.
Guest:	Haben Sie Zimmerservice?
Empfangschef:	Ja, natürlich haben wir Zimmerservice. Das Restaurant ist bis 23 Uhr geöffnet.

ACTIVITY 4

1. a. *Ich wohne auf der zwölften Etage.*
   b. *Mein Bruder wohnt auf der achten Etage.*
2. a. *Frau Schneider hat am 3. August Geburtstag.*
   b. *Herrn Schneiders Sohn hat am 25. Mai Geburtstag.*
3. a. *Sie fährt am 17. August nach Hamburg.*
   b. *Sie fährt am 21. August nach München.*

ACTIVITY 5

1.	Gast:	Haben Sie ein Einzelzimmer?
	Empfangschef:	Ja, wir haben ein Einzelzimmer.
	Gast:	Wie komme ich auf mein Zimmer?
	Empfangschef:	Nehmen Sie den Aufzug in den dritten Stock.
	Gast:	Wo kann ich jetzt noch etwas essen?
	Empfangschef:	Rufen Sie den Zimmerservice an.
2.	Tochter:	Soll ich mit Horst ins Theater oder mit Peter ins Kino gehen?
	Mutter:	Geh mit Peter ins Kino.
	Tochter:	Wie kann ich es Horst sagen?
	Mutter:	Ruf ihn doch an.
3.	Familie:	Was machen wir am Wochenende?
	Vater:	Lasst uns doch ins Museum gehen./Gehen wir doch ins Museum.
	Famlie:	Fahren wir mit dem Bus oder mit dem Auto?
	Vater:	Fahren wir doch mit dem Auto./Nehmen wir doch das Auto./Lasst uns doch mit dem Auto fahren./Lasst uns doch das Auto nehmen.

ACTIVITY 6

1. *Er hat einen Tisch auf 19 Uhr reserviert.*
2. *Der Tisch soll auf der Gartenterrasse sein.*
3. *Auf der Terrasse ist alles voll.*
4. *Er will sich beschweren.*
5. *Dieser Teil des Restaurants ist geschlossen.*
6. *Nur für 15 Minuten.*

ACTIVITY 7

1. *Wir haben kein Besteck.*
2. *Das habe ich nicht bestellt.*
3. *Ich möchte mich beschweren.*
4. *Das lasse ich mir nicht gefallen.*
5. *Ich möchte mit Ihrem Vorgesetzten sprechen.*

ACTIVITY 8

1. *Ich musste das Restaurant anrufen.*
2. *Ich sollte einen Tisch auf 20 Uhr reservieren.*
3. *Meine Freundin wollte einen Tisch im Garten haben.*
4. *Leider konnte ich keinen Tisch im Garten reservieren.*
5. *Der Garten sollte geschlossen sein.*
6. *Meine Freundin wollte in ein anderes Restaurant gehen.*

ACTIVITY 9

Es war einmal ein Restaurant. Das Restaurant hatte eine schöne Gartenterrasse. Die Gäste wollten auf der Terrasse sitzen. Ein Gast rief an und reservierte einen Tisch für 20 Uhr. Er wollte mit seiner Frau und seiner Tochter in dem Restaurant essen. Um 20 Uhr kamen sie im Restaurant an. Der Kellner gab ihnen einen Tisch auf der Terrasse. Sie bestellten das Essen. Das Essen kam lange nicht. Der Gast beschwerte sich. Endlich konnten sie essen. Nach dem Essen aßen sie Nachtisch. Dann gingen sie satt nach Hause.

A GOOD STUMBLER FALLETH NOT

Ein guter Stolperer fällt nicht

Ever since I've experienced one of the worst *Zahnweh* (toothache) of my life while on a weekend trip in Vienna, I make sure that I know exactly what to do and where to go in a *Notfall* (emergency), no matter where I am. An *Arzt* (male doctor) or an *Ärztin* (female doctor) is the person to call if you have a medical problem that can be taken care of during office hours. If you have a dental problem consult a *Zahnarzt* (male dentist) or a *Zahnärztin* (female dentist). And in case of a medical emergency, go to the *Notaufnahme* (emergency admission) at a *Krankenhaus* (hospital), where a *Krankenschwester* (nurse) or a *Krankenpfleger* (male nurse) will take care of you immediately, before an *Arzt* has time to tend to your injuries. If all you need are non-prescription drugs, go to the *Apotheke* (pharmacy).

Heads Up!

Beware of those false cognates! A *Drogerie* is a drugstore in German, but you won't be able to buy medication there, not even non-prescription drugs such as headache pills. But you will find make-up, soap, shampoo and toothpaste along with other items for your bathroom, and you may even find batteries and film for your camera.

ACTIVITY 1:	LET'S WARM UP

Matchmaker time! Let's see if you can match the German and the English.

1.	*die Wunde*	a.	tooth
2.	*der Arm*	b.	fever
3.	*der Zahn*	c.	arm
4.	*das Fieber*	d.	wound
5.	*die Hand*	e.	shoulder
6.	*die Schulter*	f.	hand

HEAR . . . SAY 1

Frau Graupert is traveling alone with her seven-year-old son, Jan (pronounced as [yahn]), visiting a friend in Vienna, Austria. On a beautiful sunny day they decide to visit the Prater. At the playground there, her son falls from the *Kletterturm* (climbing tower) and hurts himself. They go to the *Notaufnahme* (emergency room) immediately.

Arzt:	**Guten Tag, Frau Graupert. Guten Tag, Jan.** (greets him with a handshake) **Ich bin Dr. Schlosser. Was ist denn passiert, mein Junge?**
Jan:	**Ich bin vom Kletterturm gefallen. Im Prater. Was machen Sie denn da?**
Arzt:	**Ich wasche mir nur die Hände. Und dabei hast du dich verletzt?**
Jan:	**Ja, ich habe mir die Stirn verletzt. Warum waschen Sie sich die Hände?**
Arzt:	(laughs) **Ich muss saubere Hände haben. Ich will schließlich keine Bakterien in deine Wunde tragen. Darf ich mir deine Stirn einmal anschauen?**
Jan:	**Aua!**
Arzt:	**Tut das weh?**
Jan:	**Ja, ein bisschen.**
Arzt:	**Tut mir leid.** (to Frau Graupert) **Das ist nur eine kleine Platzwunde. Das ist bald wieder gut.**
Simone Graupert:	**Muss das genäht werden?**
Arzt:	**Nein, nein. Wir waschen die Wunde nur schnell aus.**
Jan:	**Waschen? Ich habe mich heute morgen schon gewaschen!**
Arzt:	(laughs) **Keine Sorge, mein Junge. Die Krankenschwester macht einen Verband an deine Stirn. Dann musst du dich eine ganze Weile nicht waschen. Zumindest nicht an der Stirn.**
Jan:	**Und kämmen muss ich mich auch nicht, oder?**
Simone Graupert:	(laughs) **Nein, mein Schatz. Ausnahmsweise nicht.**

ACTIVITY 2: HOW'S THAT AGAIN?

Some of the following sentences are incorrect. Can you find them and fix them? (Hint: Only two sentences are correct.)

1. *Jan ist aus dem Auto gefallen.*
2. *Jan hat eine Platzwunde an der Stirn.*
3. *Dr. Schlosser wäscht sich die Füße.*
4. *Die Wunde muss genäht werden.*

5. *Der Arzt macht einen Verband an die Stirn.*
6. *Jan muss sich nicht kämmen.*

Did You Know?

The Vienna Prater is much more than just another amusement park. It's a Viennese institution, in existence since 1766, like the *Kaffeehaus* (coffee house) or the *Heuriger* (*neuer Wein* [wine from the current year]). One of Prater's landmarks is the *Riesenrad* (giant ferris wheel), which was first opened in 1897, and which to this day proudly towers over the booths. The Prater offers a ghost train, go-carts and grotto railways, a merry-go-round, and throwing and shooting galleries. It has something to offer for the entire family: children enjoy the fairytale train, the extra-long slides, and the hall of mirrors. Adults may go for the *Planetarium* (planetarium) or the Prater museum. Most of the attractions are open from the beginning of March through October. The *Riesenrad* is open from February through November, with a special one-night opening on New Year's Eve.

WORKSHOP 1

WORDS TO LIVE BY

BREAK A LEG! BODY PARTS

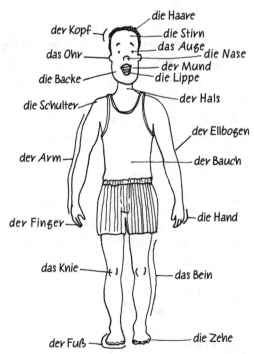

WORD ON THE STREET

Body parts feature prominently in a few fun colloquial expressions. *Den Kopf waschen* (to wash somebody's head) translates best as "to set somebody straight." *Mir stehen die Haare zu Berge* (My hair is standing up straight) means "I am shocked." *Eine Hand wäscht die andere* (One hand washes the other) refers less to cleanliness than it does to doing each other favors. And *Er lebt auf großem Fuß* (He lives on a big foot) describes someone who lives beyond his means.

ACTIVITY 3: TAKE IT FOR A SPIN

Please answer the following questions.

1. *Womit spricht der Mensch?*
2. *Was hat fünf Finger?*
3. *Wovon hat der Mensch zwei?*
4. *Was tut weh nach zu viel Schokolade?*
5. *Womit sieht der Mensch?*

OUCH! EXPRESSING PAIN

Even though pain itself is universal, the way we express it in language is not. German speakers say *aua!* (pronounced as OW-wah) rather than "ouch" when something hurts. Here are a few other helpful expressions.

Das tut (mir) weh.	That hurts.
Mein Bein tut (mir) weh.	My leg hurts (me).
der Schmerz	pain
Ich habe Schmerzen.	I am in pain.

And this is how you specify what hurts.

Ich habe Kopfweh.	I have a headache.
Er hat starke Kopfschmerzen.	He has a bad headache. (Lit. He has a strong headache.)
Meine Frau hat Bauchschmerzen.	My wife has a stomach ache.
Mein Sohn hat Halsweh.	My son has a sore throat.
Haben Sie Fieber?	Do you have a fever?
Haben Sie hohes Fieber?	Do you have a high fever?
Mir ist schwindlig.	I am/feel dizzy.
Mir ist schlecht.	I am sick (to my stomach).

THE FINE PRINT

Note that the expression *weh tun* (to hurt) is quite similar to *leid tun* (to be sorry). For example, *Es tut ihr weh* (It hurts her [Lit. It does her pain]) uses the same construction as *Es tut ihr leid* (She is sorry [Lit. It does her sorry]). Another expression in this group is *gut tun* (to be good for), as in *Es tut dir gut* (It is good for you [Lit. It does you good].) The basic meaning of *tun* is 'to do.'

Did You Know?

Fever, just like any temperature, is measured in centigrade in Germany, Austria and Switzerland. 36.8 to 37 degrees centigrade are considered *Normaltemperatur* (normal body temperature). 37 to 37.8 degrees centigrade are considered *erhöhte Temperatur* (elevated temperature). Anything above 37.8 degrees centigrade is considered a *Fieber* (fever). Make sure you consult a doctor if your temperature climbs above 40 degrees centigrade. That would be considered a *hohes Fieber* (high fever).

ACTIVITY 4: **TAKE IT FOR A SPIN**

Participate in this conversation by answering the doctor's questions in German. Use the hints in parentheses.

Arzt:	*Was ist passiert?*
Patient:	_____ (I fell from the bicycle.)
Arzt:	*Haben Sie sich verletzt?*
Patient:	_____ (My arm hurts.)
Arzt:	*Darf ich mir das einmal anschauen?*
Patient:	_____ (Ouch!)
Arzt:	*Das tut mir leid.*
Patient:	_____ (I'm dizzy.)

THE NITTY GRITTY

LOOKING AT MYSELF IN THE MIRROR: REFLEXIVE VERBS

Verbs such as "to wash oneself" in English are called reflexive verbs. They always come with a pronoun, such as "myself," "yourself," "himself," etc., which refers back to the subject of the sentence, indicating that subject and object of the sentence are identical.

When Jan, the little boy from our dialogue, says *Ich habe mich gewaschen* (I have washed myself), he is using a reflexive verb, *sich waschen* (to wash oneself).

Other examples of reflexive verbs from the lesson are:

sich verletzen	to hurt oneself
Hast du dich verletzt?	Did you hurt yourself?
sich erkälten	to catch a cold
Hatschi! Ich habe mich erkältet.	Hatschi! I caught a cold.

Other common ones are:

sich kämmen	to comb one's hair
Ich kämme mich.	I'm combing my hair.
sich beeilen	to hurry
Beeil dich bitte.	Hurry up!
sich kümmern um	to take care of
Ich kümmere mich um die Kinder.	I take care of the kids.
sich ärgern	to be annoyed
Ich ärgere mich.	I am annoyed.
sich setzen	to sit down
Setzen Sie sich doch, bitte!	Please take a seat.

English reflexive pronouns add the suffix "-self" or "-selves" to the personal pronoun. In German the reflexive pronouns are identical to the personal pronouns, except in the *er/sie/es* and *sie/Sie* forms.

THE REFLEXIVE PRONOUNS		
	PERSONAL PRONOUN	**REFLEXIVE PRONOUN**
SINGULAR	*ich*	*mich*
	du	*dich*
	Sie (formal)	*sich*
	er/sie/es	*sich*
PLURAL	*wir*	*uns*
	Ihr	*euch*
	Sie	*sich*
	sie	*sich*

THE FINE PRINT

Note that the reflexive pronoun for the formal *Sie* is NOT capitalized. For example:

    Beeilen Sie sich, bitte!   (Please, hurry up!)

Reflexive verbs are very common in German, and many verbs that are reflexive in German are NOT in English. For example:

    Ich habe mich erkältet.   I caught a cold.

One reason for the frequent use of reflexive verbs in German may be the fact that German prefers to show possession with a reflexive pronoun rather than with the possessive adjective. This is particularly true with parts of the body. The English "I am washing <u>my</u> hands" becomes the German *Ich wasche <u>mir</u> die Hände* (Lit. I am washing myself the hands.)

So, when a reflexive verb (*waschen* in the sentence above) has a direct object (*die Hände* in the sentence above) other than the reflexive pronoun, the reflexive pronoun must take the dative case (*mir* in the sentence above). Here's another example:

Ich muss mir auch die Haare kämmen.   I have to comb my hair, too. (Lit. I have to comb myself the hair, too.)

TAKE IT FOR A SPIN

Please rewrite the sentences using the cues in parentheses.

1. *Ich kämme mich. (du)*
2. *Der Arzt wäscht sich. (die Hände)*
3. *Jan hat sich verletzt. (die Stirn)*
4. *Frau Graupert sieht sich an. (die Wunde)*
5. *Frau Graupert kümmert sich um Jan. (Wir)*
6. *Wir beeilen uns. (ihr)*
7. *Ich wasche mich. (die Haare)*

Did You Know?

The Prater provided the breathtaking scenery for the showdown between Joseph Cotton and Orson Welles in the 1949 movie "The Third Man" based on Graham Greene's novel. The other non-human protagonist of this movie was a musical instrument, the zither, which provided a haunting backdrop to the drama unfolding in Carol Reed's thriller depicting crumbling Vienna in the aftermath of World War II. And the Austrian Hollywood connection goes much farther still. Everyone knows that Arnold Schwarzenegger is originally from Austria, but the Austrian roots of actors, directors and producers, such as Fritz Lang, Peter Lorre, Otto Preminger, Billy Wilder, Fred Zinneman and Fred Astaire, from the golden times of Hollywood, as well as more recently, Senta Berger and Klaus-Maria Brandauer, are much less well-known.

Let's get back to Frau Graupert and her son Jan. Remember that Jan had to be *behandelt* (treated) because of a *Platzwunde?*

After the visit in the *Notaufnahme*, Simone Graupert and her son Jan want to get back to their hotel to relax. But it seems that they cannot find their car.

Simone Graupert:	Wo steht unser Auto nur? Ich dachte, wir haben hier geparkt. Oh je, ich glaube, unser Wagen wurde gestohlen.
Jan:	Und was machen wir jetzt?
Simone Graupert:	Wir rufen die Polizei.
Jan:	(excited) Au ja!

A few minutes later the police arrive at the scene.

Polizist:	Ihr Auto wurde gestohlen?
Simone Graupert:	Ja, ich habe hier geparkt, und jetzt ist es weg.
Polizist:	Können Sie das Auto beschreiben?
Simone Graupert:	Ja, es ist ein Opel. Oder ein Ford. Viertürig. Und er ist grün. Oder braun. (to her son) Jan, ist unser Wagen grün oder braun?
Jan:	Braun, Mama. Wußtest du das nicht? Und er hat nur zwei Türen.
Simone Graupert:	Ich dachte er ist grün. . . . na ja . . . es ist ein Mietwagen.
Polizist:	Ich verstehe. Was führte Sie denn ins Krankenhaus?
Simone Graupert:	Mein Sohn. . . . Ich brachte ihn in die Notaufnahme. Er wurde wegen einer Platzwunde behandelt. Jan, bleib bitte hier.
Polizist:	Da waren Sie doch sicher recht aufgeregt?
Simone Graupert:	Ja, natürlich. Jan, wo bist du denn?
Jan:	Hier bin ich, Mama. Ich habe unseren Wagen gefunden. Er wird gerade abgeschleppt . . .
Polizist:	In der Aufregung haben Sie wohl falsch geparkt . . .

WORD ON THE STREET

Note the German expression *falsch parken,* "to park wrongfully" rather than "to park illegally." Similar expressions are: *falsch abbiegen* (to make a wrong turn) and *falsch schreiben* (to misspell).

HOW'S THAT AGAIN?

True or false? Take your pick.

	TRUE	FALSE
1. *Simone Graupert hat einen Mietwagen.*	_____	_____
2. *Simone Graupert hat den Mietwagen falsch geparkt.*	_____	_____
3. *Simone Graupert war aufgeregt.*	_____	_____
4. *Simone Graupert kann sich nicht an die Farbe des Wagens erinnern.*	_____	_____
5. *Jan kann sich auch nicht an die Farbe des Mietwagens erinnern.*	_____	_____
6. *Der Wagen wurde gestohlen.*	_____	_____
7. *Der Polizist hat den Wagen gefunden.*	_____	_____
8. *Der Wagen wird abgeschleppt.*	_____	_____

WORKSHOP 2

WORDS TO LIVE BY

HELP! DEALING WITH EMERGENCIES

In case of an emergency the most important word might be the simplest:

| *Hilfe!* | Help! |

In case of fire:

| *Es brennt!* | Fire! (Lit. It is burning.) |

In case somebody is trying to steal your handbag:

| *Haltet den Dieb!* | Stop the thief. |

In case you need assistance:

Helfen Sie mir bitte.	Please help me.
Rufen Sie die Polizei.	Call the police.
Rufen Sie einen Krankenwagen.	Call an ambulance.
Rufen Sie die Feuerwehr.	Call the fire department.

Did You Know?

In an emergency, dial 112 from any telephone within continental Europe. You will immediately be connected to the nearest dispatch station, which will send the appropriate help out to you. ONLY call this number in case of an emergency that needs immediate attention. The call is free. Do NOT call 112 if you have reason to believe your car was towed or your luggage was stolen. In these cases, contact the local police station.

WICHTIGE TELEFONNUMMERN			
NOTRUF (emergency numbers)	**DEUTSCHLAND**	**ÖSTERREICH**	**SCHWEIZ**
EURONOTRUF (European emergency number)	112	112	112
POLIZEI (police)	110	133	117
FEUERWEHR (fire department)	112	122	118
KRANKENWAGEN (ambulance)	118	144	144
HILFREICHE NUMMERN (helpful numbers)	**DEUTSCHLAND**	**ÖSTERREICH**	**SCHWEIZ**
ADAC (AAA)	0180 22 22 22 2		
KINDERNOTRUF (children's emergency number, i.e., emergency number for abused children)		02622 66 66 1	
FRAUENNOTRUF (women's emergency number, i.e., emergency number for battered women)			01 71 71 9

If you'd like to look up your high school sweetheart who moved to Germany, Austria or Switzerland, but you don't have his/her number, you need to consult a local phone book or find the local number for the *Auskunft* (Directory assistance [Lit. Information]). And if your watch is still on American time, check the local listings for the *Zeitansage* (time announcement).

| ACTIVITY 7: | **TAKE IT FOR A SPIN** |

Which number would you dial in the following situations?

1. You are in Graz, Austria, and somebody yells: *Es brennt!*
2. You want to dial the equivalent of 911 in Bern, Switzerland.
3. Your new rental car just broke down in Frankfurt, Germany.
4. You just watched a jewel thief run off with millions of euros worth of jewelry in Stuttgart, Germany.
5. You'd like to look up your high school sweetheart who moved to Vienna, Austria, but you don't have his/her number.
6. While sightseeing at the Prater, somebody standing in line next to you is having a heart attack.
7. You look at your watch and realize it is still on American time. *Wie spät ist es?* you wonder.

THE NITTY GRITTY

IT'S BEEN DONE: THE PASSIVE VOICE

All German sentences you have heard or read so far were in the active voice. This only means that the subject of the sentence is understood as an agent, i.e., it does what the verb expresses.

Der Arzt behandelte Jan.   The doctor treated Jan.

In contrast to this, in the passive voice, the subject is not an agent; instead it is the person or object acted upon. It is passive. Accordingly, the verb comes in the special form, called the passive voice.

Jan wurde behandelt.   Jan was treated.

The German passive is formed with the verb *werden* (to become) and the past participle of the main verb. First, here are the present tense forms of *werden*.

THE VERB *WERDEN* (TO BECOME) IN THE PRESENT TENSE

SINGULAR	PLURAL
ich werde	wir werden
du wirst	ihr werdet
Sie werden (formal)	Sie werden (formal)
er/sie/es wird	sie werden

The passive voice can be formed in all tenses. The verb *werden* changes to express different tenses, while the past participle remains the same.

- Present Tense Passive

Jan wird behandelt.	Jan is being treated.
Das Auto wird gestohlen.	The car is being stolen.
Das Auto wird abgeschleppt.	The car is being towed.

- Past Tense Passive

Jan wurde behandelt.	Jan was treated.
Das Auto wurde gestohlen.	The car was stolen.
Das Auto wurde abgeschleppt.	The car was towed.

- Present Perfect Passive

Jan ist behandelt <u>worden</u>.	Jan has been treated.
Das Auto ist gestohlen worden.	The car has been stolen.
Das Auto ist abgeschleppt worden.	The car has been towed.

Note that in the present perfect the form *worden*, the past participle of *werden*, is at the very end of the sentence, whereas the past participle of the main verb precedes it.

In the passive voice, the performer of the action (the agent) may or may not be mentioned:

Jan wird behandelt.	Jan is being treated. (no agent)
Jan wird vom Arzt behandelt.	Jan is being treated by the doctor. (agent = *der Arzt*)

The passive voice is often used with modal verbs. In that case, the modal verb forms the tense and takes the position of the conjugated verb, and the past participle of the main verb plus *werden* in the infinitive form stand at the very end of the sentence.

Muss das genäht werden?	Does this have to be stitched?
Kann das Auto hier geparkt werden?	Can the car be parked here?

TAKE IT FOR A SPIN

Please rewrite the story in the passive voice. Make sure you match the tense of the active and the passive sentence.

Frau Graupert hat Jan ins Krankenhaus gebracht. Der Arzt behandelte die Platzwunde. Die Kranken-schwester machte einen Verband. Frau Graupert findet das Auto nicht. Sie ruft die Polizei. Die Polizei sucht das Auto. Jan findet das Auto. Der Abschleppwagen schleppt das Auto ab.

THE SIMPLE PAST OF MIXED VERBS

There is a small group of irregular verbs we discussed earlier, which form the simple past by adding the same past tense endings as weak verbs (the past tense marker -*t*- plus the personal endings), but like strong verbs, also undergo a stem-vowel change. Due to this mixture of past tense formation, these verbs are called "mixed verbs."

Here are a few examples:

Wusstest du das nicht?	Didn't you know that?
Ich dachte es ist grün.	I thought it is green.
Ich brachte meinen Sohn ins Krankenhaus.	I brought my son to the hospital.

Here's a list of such irregular verbs:

bringen → brachte	to bring, to take
kennen → kannte	to know, to be acquainted with
nennen → nannte	to name
rennen → rannte	to run
senden → sandte	to send
verbringen → verbrachte	to spend (time)
wissen → wusste	to know

TAKE IT FOR A SPIN

Please put the story in the simple past tense.

Mein Sohn hat sich im Prater verletzt. Ich bin schnell zu ihm gerannt. Dann habe ich ihn ins Kranken-haus gebracht. Ich kenne den Arzt dort. Wir haben zwei Stunden in der Notaufnahme verbracht. Es ist nur eine Platzwunde. Der Arzt nennt das Glück.

STRUT YOUR STUFF

TAKE IT FOR A SPIN

Are you ready for a review of what you've learned so far in the last five lessons? I bet you'll be impressed with yourself. Please complete the following newspaper article retelling a story of a "stolen" car. Use the cues in parentheses.

Eine _____ (young) Frau _____ (called) gestern Abend um _____ (7:30PM) bei der Polizei an. _____ (Her) Auto _____ (was stolen). Die Polizei _____ (wanted) _____ (her name) und _____ (her address) wissen. Aber sie _____ (wanted) ihren Namen nicht nennen. Sie _____ (named) die Addresse _____ (of the Parkhaus, use the genitive). Die Polizei _____ (drove) _____ (to the) Parkhaus. Aber die junge Frau _____ (was) nicht da. Die Polizei _____ (drove) _____ (to the) Polizeistation zurück. Ein Brief _____ (waited) dort auf _____ (them). In _____ (the) Brief hieß es: _____ (Thank you) für den Computer. Ich _____ ihn _____ (stole, use present perfect). Ich habe _____ (no) Geld. Die Polizisten _____ (were annoyed).

CRIB NOTES

HEAR . . . SAY 1

Doctor:	Good day, Frau Graupert. Hello, Jan. I am Dr. Schlosser. What happened, my dear boy?
Jan:	I fell from the climber. At the Prater. What are you doing?
Doctor:	I am just washing my hands. And that's how you hurt yourself?
Jan:	Yes, I hurt myself on the forehead. Why are you washing your hands?
Doctor:	I have to have clean hands. I don't want to get bacteria into your wound. May I take a look at your forehead?
Jan:	Ouch!
Doctor:	Does that hurt?
Jan:	Yes, a little.
Doctor:	I am sorry. It is only a small laceration. It'll be fine soon.
Simone Graupert:	Does it have to be stitched?
Doctor:	No, no. We'll just clean the wound.
Jan:	Wash? I washed myself this morning!
Doctor:	Don't worry, my boy. The nurse will put a bandage on your forehead. Then you won't have to wash for quite a while. At least not your forehead.
Jan:	And I don't have to brush my hair either, right?
Simone Graupert:	No, sweetie. As an exception, you don't have to.

HEAR . . . SAY 2

Simone Graupert:	Where is our car? I thought we parked right here. Oh dear, I think our car was stolen.
Jan:	And what do we do now?
Simone Graupert:	We call the police.
Jan:	Oh, yeah!
A few minutes later the police arrives at the scene.	
Policeman:	Your car was stolen?
Simone Grauert:	Yes, I parked here, and now it is gone.
Policeman:	Can you describe the car?
Simone Graupert:	Yes, it is an Opel. Or a Ford. With four doors. And it is green. Or brown. Jan, is our car green or brown?
Jan:	Brown, Mama. Didn't you know that? And it only has two doors.
Simone Graupert:	I thought it was green . . . oh well . . . it is a rental car.
Policeman:	I see. What brought you to the hospital?
Simone Graupert:	My son. . . . I took him to the

		Simone Graupert:	Yes, of course. Jan, where are you?
	emergency room. He was treated for a laceration. Jan, please stay here.	Jan:	I'm here, Mama. I found our car. It is being towed . . .
Policeman:	I'm sure you were somewhat worried.	Policeman:	In your worry you must have parked illegally . . .

ANSWER KEY

ACTIVITY 1
1. d   2. c   3. a
4. b   5. f   6. e

ACTIVITY 2
1. False. *Jan ist vom Kletterturm gefallen.*
2. True. *Jan hat eine Platzwunde an der Stirn.*
3. False. *Dr. Schlosser wäscht sich die Hände.*
4. False. *Die Wunde muss nicht genäht werden.*
5. False. *Die Krankenschwester macht einen Verband an die Stirn.*
6. True. *Jan muss sich nicht kämmen.*

ACTIVITY 3
1. *Der Mensch spricht mit dem Mund.*
2. *Die Hand hat fünf Finger.*
3. *Der Mensch hat zwei Augen, zwei Arme, zwei Hände, zwei Beine und zwei Füße.*
4. *Der Bauch tut weh.*
5. *Der Mensch sieht mit den Augen.*

ACTIVITY 4
Arzt:	Was ist passiert?
Patient:	Ich bin vom Fahrrad gefallen.
Arzt:	Haben Sie sich verletzt?
Patient:	Mein Arm tut (mir) weh.
Arzt:	Darf ich mir das einmal anschauen?
Patient:	Aua!
Arzt:	Das tut mir leid.
Patient:	Mir ist schwindlig.

ACTIVITY 5
1. *Du kämmst dich.*
2. *Der Arzt wäscht sich die Hände.*
3. *Jan hat sich die Stirn verletzt.*
4. *Frau Graupert sieht sich die Wunde an.*
5. *Wir kümmern uns um Jan.*
6. *Ihr beeilt euch.*
7. *Ich wasche mir die Haare.*

ACTIVITY 6
1. True.
2. True.
3. True.
4. True.
5. False.
6. False.
7. False.
8. True.

ACTIVITY 7
1. *Ich rufe die Feuerwehr an unter der Nummer 122.*
2. *Ich rufe den Euronotruf an unter der Nummer 112.*
3. *Ich rufe den ADAC an unter der Nummer 01802222222.*
4. *Ich rufe die Polizei an unter der Nummer 110.*
5. *Ich rufe die Auskunft an.*
6. *Ich rufe den Krankenwagen unter der Nummer 144*
7. *Ich rufe die Zeitansage an*

ACTIVITY 8
Jan ist (von Frau Graupert) ins Krankenhaus gebracht worden. Die Platzwunde wurde (vom Arzt) behandelt. Der Verband wurde (von der Krankenschwester) gemacht. Das Auto wird nicht (von Frau Graupert) gefunden. Die Polizei wird (von ihr) gerufen. Das Auto wird (von der Polizei) gesucht. Das Auto wird (von Jan) gefunden. Das Auto wird (vom Abschleppwagen) abgeschleppt.

ACTIVITY 9
Mein Sohn verletzte sich im Prater. Ich rannte schnell zu ihm. Dann brachte ich ihn ins Krankenhaus. Ich kannte den Arzt dort. Wir verbrachten zwei Stunden in der Notaufnahme. Es war nur eine Platzwunde. Der Arzt nannte das Glück.

ACTIVITY 10
Eine junge Frau rief gestern abend um 18 Uhr 30 bei der Polizei an. Ihr Auto wurde gestohlen. Die Polizei wollte ihren Namen und ihre Adresse wissen. Aber sie wollte ihren Namen nicht nennen. Sie nannte die Adresse des Parkhauses. Die Polizei fuhr zum Parkhaus. Aber die junge Frau war nicht da. Die Polizei fuhr zur Polizeistation zurück. Ein Brief wartete dort auf sie. In dem Brief hieß es: Vielen Dank für den Computer. Ich habe ihn gestohlen. Ich habe kein Geld. Die Polizisten ärgerten sich.

11

HOME, SWEET HOME

Trautes Heim, Glück allein
(Lit. Sweet home, happiness abounds)

Kaufen (to buy) or *mieten* (to rent)? That is the question. Well, for many of us, with no cash to put down, not a very difficult one, after all. *Ein Haus* (a house) or *eine Wohnung* (an apartment) or maybe *eine Eigentumswohnung* (condo) after all? And how many *Zimmer* (rooms) should it have? Do you need a *Garten* (garden), or a *Terrasse* (a terrace) or a *Balkon* (balcony)? Do you want to live in the *Innenstadt* (downtown) or in a *Wohnviertel* (residential area) *außerhalb der Stadt* (on the outskirts of town)? Those and many other questions will keep you awake at night if you are looking for a place to live. This lesson will take one worry off your chest. If you are in a German speaking country, you'll at least know how to express your wishes in German.

ACTIVITY 1: LET'S WARM UP

Please answer the questions.

1. The *Wohnzimmer* is the room in the house where you . . .
   a. . . . sleep.
   b. . . . eat your breakfast.
   c. . . . cook.
   d. . . . watch TV or read a book.
2. You sleep in the . . .
   a. . . . *Küche.*
   b. . . . *Badezimmer.*
   c. . . . *Schlafzimmer.*
   d. . . . *Wohnzimmer.*
3. The *Makler* is the person who . . .
   a. . . . sells the house.
   b. . . . buys the house.
   c. . . . shows you many houses.
   d. . . . lends you the money to buy the house.
4. Your computer will most likely go into the . . .
   a. . . . *Arbeitszimmer.*
   b. . . . *Kinderzimmer.*
   c. . . . *Esszimmer.*
   d. . . . *Küche.*
5. The *Küche* is where you . . .
   a. . . . have your afternoon naps.
   b. . . . cook.
   c. . . . work.
   d. . . . work out.

Karin and Georg Seitzer are a young married couple looking to buy their first home. Karin is very interested in buying a house their *Makler* (real estate agent) showed her a few days earlier. Now she is coming back to convince her reluctant husband, who feels that this house may be a bit over their *Budget* (budget).

Makler:	Dieses Haus hier hat eine hervorragende Lage. Die Hölderlinstraße ist eine Sackgasse in einem ruhigen Wohnviertel.
Georg:	Teuer ist es auch, das Wohnviertel.
Karin:	(ignoring him) Das Einkaufszentrum ist zu Fuß erreichbar. Und um die Ecke wird eine neue Grundschule gebaut. Genau rechtzeitig.
Georg:	Was meinst du denn damit?
Makler:	Die Diele ist sehr geräumig. Bitte, kommen Sie doch weiter ins Wohnzimmer. Hier haben Sie einen schönen Blick in den Garten.
Georg:	Das Wohnzimmer ist ja so groß wie unsere ganze Wohnung. Kein Wunder, dass das Haus so teuer ist . . .
Makler:	Und hier ist das Esszimmer.
Karin:	Wir werden bestimmt meistens in der Küche essen. Die ist heller als das Esszimmer. Und das machen wir zu deinem Arbeitszimmer, Georg.
Georg:	Gute Idee, aber wir können uns das Haus nicht leisten.
Karin:	(still ignoring him) Die drei Schlafzimmer und das Badezimmer sind im ersten Stock.
Makler:	Die Treppen sind hier.
Karin:	Das Zimmer hier wird das Schlafzimmer. Es ist grösser als die anderen. Und das hier wird ein Kinderzimmer. Es ist hell und freundlich. Und das kleinere Zimmer daneben wird auch ein . . .
Georg:	(interrupts her) Karin, wir haben doch gar keine Kinder.
Karin:	Noch nicht. Aber bald . . . Ich bin schwanger, Georg.
Georg:	Was? . . . Wie? . . . Aber . . .
Karin:	Mit Zwillingen.
Georg:	Zwillinge! . . . Ich . . . Aber . . . Karin, das ist ja . . . Wir nehmen das Haus.
Karin:	Aber es ist doch so teuer . . .
Georg:	Wir werden uns das schon irgendwie leisten können. Hier werden unsere Kinder zur Welt kommen.
Makler:	Gratuliere!

All of the sentences below are not quite true. Can you fix them?

1. *Das Haus liegt in einer lauten Straße.*
2. *Georg und Karin finden das Haus zu teuer.*
3. *Das Haus hat vier Schlafzimmer, ein Wohnzimmer, ein Esszimmer, zwei Badezimmer und eine Küche.*
4. *Das Haus hat keinen Garten.*
5. *Georg und Karin wollen keine Kinder.*
6. *Georg und Karin kaufen die Wohnung.*

Did You Know?

Germans treasure their history, which is probably not surprising since there is quite a lot of it. Some of it is rather dark, such as Germany's more recent history—the death and destruction created by the two world wars and the division into East and West Germany, in the aftermath of the Second World War, that lasted for over 40 years. The coalescence of the German nation as we know it today was a process that took hundreds of years and drew together myriads of tribes. Some of these tribal differences are still reflected in the customs observed and dialects spoken in the different states. These differences between the individual German states of the Federal Republic and their relative cultural and linguistic similarities to their neighboring nations bear witness to the fact that the borders of Germany, just like those of any other European country, have been artificially defined and redefined throughout history. For example, the dialect spoken in Bavaria is much closer to the version of German spoken in Austria than to the version of German spoken in Saxony. And some of the Swabian culinary specialties are similar to those of Switzerland and France, whereas Eastern German cuisine resembles the cuisine of Poland more than the cuisine of another German state.

WORKSHOP 1

WORDS TO LIVE BY

These words will come in handy when you are looking for a place to live.

AROUND THE HOUSE			
die Wohnung	apartment	das Haus	house
das Zimmer	room	die Vierzimmerwohnung	3-bedroom apartment
das Wohnzimmer	living room	das Esszimmer	dining room
das Arbeitszimmer	office	das Schlafzimmer	bedroom
das Kinderzimmer	children's room	das Gästezimmer	guest room
das Badezimmer	bathroom	die Toilette	bathroom (toilet)
der Keller	basement	der Dachboden	attic
der Balkon	balcony	die Terrasse	terrace

If you rent a *Wohnung* or a *Haus*, you have to put down a *Kaution* (deposit) and pay *Miete* (rent). If you buy an *Eigentumswohnung* (condo) or a *Haus*, you have to put down an *Anzahlung* (down payment) and pay the *Hypothek* (mortgage). In case the place you wanted to rent is already *vermietet* (rented, gone), or the house you wanted to buy is already *verkauft* (sold), you'll have to start all over and scout out what's available in the *Samstagsausgabe* (Saturday edition) of the *Zeitung* (newspaper).

LET'S PUT IT IN WRITING

In Germany, Austria and Switzerland it is the *Samstagsausgabe* of most daily newspapers, rather than the *Sonntagsausgabe* like in the United States, that runs classified ads. Here's an example.

> **4-Zi-Whg. zu vermieten.** 110 m2. Gr. Balkon, hell, ruhige Lage, Stadtnähe. 1200 Euro kalt. Kaution: 2 Monatsmieten.   **Tel. 089/564433221.**

WORD ON THE STREET

Classified ads use lots of abbreviations in Germany as in the United States. I'm sure you've figured these out already, but just in case, here are those that appear in the ad above: *Zi.* is short for *Zimmer; Whg.* is short for *Wohnung; gr.* is short for *groß; Tel.* is short for *Telefon*. *1200 Euro kalt* or *Kaltmiete* means that the rent does not include utilities such as electricity or heat. *1200 Euro warm* or *Warmmiete* means that the utilities are included in the rent.

Imagine you are the *Vermieter* (landlord) running the classified ad above, and a prospective *Mieter* (tenant) is calling with a few questions. Please answer truthfully using the ad above as a blueprint.

Mieter:	*Ist die Wohnung schon vermietet?*
Vermieter:	_____
Mieter:	*Wie groß ist die Wohnung?*
Vermieter:	_____
Mieter:	*Bekommt die Wohnung viel Sonne?*
Vermieter:	_____
Mieter:	*Ist es laut in der Straße?*
Vermieter:	_____
Mieter:	*Ist es weit in die Stadt?*
Vermieter:	_____
Mieter:	*Wie hoch ist die Miete?*
Vermieter:	_____

Did You Know?

When talking about the size of an apartment in Germany, Austria and Switzerland, people count the bedrooms plus a living room. So *eine Vierzimmerwohnung* (a four-room apartment) is an apartment with three bedrooms and a living room. Most apartments and single-family homes have but one full *Badezimmer* (bathroom), and sometimes an extra *Toilette* (toilet, half-bathroom).

THE NITTY GRITTY

I'LL GET TO THAT: **THE FUTURE TENSE**

As you remember, you can talk about events in the immediate future using the present tense.

Wir nehmen das Haus.   We're taking the house.

German, like English, also has a special tense reserved for speaking about things to come: the future tense. The future tense is formed with the present tense of the verb *werden* (to become) and the infinitive of the main verb. The verb *werden* is conjugated, i.e., changes depending on the personal pronoun used, while the infinitive of the main verb moves to the end of the sentence.

> **Wir werden in der Küche essen.** We will eat in the kitchen.
> **Hier werden unsere Kinder zur Welt kommen.** Our children will be born here.

If *sein* or *werden* are the main verbs, their infinitive is optional. In other words . . .

> **Das Zimmer hier wird das Schlafzimmer.** This room here will be the bedroom.

. . . is as good as:

> **Das Zimmer hier wird das Schlafzimmer werden.** This room here will be the bedroom.

Another example from the dialogue is:

> **Ich werde bald Mutter (werden).** I will soon become a mother.

If a sentence that refers to the future uses a modal verb, both the modal verb (*können* in the sentence below) and the main verb (*leisten* in the sentence below) will be found at the end of the sentences in the infinitive form. The infinitive of the modal verb follows the infinitive of the main verb.

> **Wir werden uns das schon irgendwie leisten können.** We will be able to afford this somehow.

Heads Up!

Be careful not to confuse the passive and the future just because both use the verb *werden* as a helping verb. The passive uses the conjugated form of *werden* and the past participle of the main verb: *Um die Ecke wird eine neue Grundschule gebaut* (Around the corner a new elementary school is being built). The future, on the other hand, uses the conjugated form of the verb *werden* followed by the infinitive of the main verb: *Die Grundschule wird nächstes Jahr schon fertig sein* (The elementary school will be ready next year).

ACTIVITY 4: **TAKE IT FOR A SPIN**

Tell us about Georg's and Karin's future. Rewrite the following sentences using the future tense.

Georg und Karin haben zwei Kinder. Ihre Kinder heißen Sebastian und Gabriel. Georg und Karin kaufen ein Haus am Stadtrand. Das Haus hat fünf Zimmer. Gabriel und Sebastian haben ein eigenes Zimmer. Die Familie isst in der Küche. Das Esszimmer ist Georgs Arbeitszimmer. Karin hat kein Arbeitszimmer. Sie muss sich um die Kinder kümmern.

Heads Up!

Make sure you don't confuse German *bekommen* (to get, to have) with the English "to become." These two words are "false friends," i.e., words that have the same root but different meanings. In German, *werden* is used to mean "to become." For example: *Ich werde Mutter* (I'll become a mother) but *Ich bekomme ein Kind* (I'll have a child).

BIGGER IS BETTER: THE COMPARATIVE OF ADJECTIVES

There are three degrees of comparison—positive, comparative, and superlative. Take the example of *groß* (big):

> *groß* (big) *größer* (bigger) *am größten* (the biggest)

We will talk about the positive and the comparative in German in this lesson. The superlative will have to wait until the next one.

In the positive form an adverb or adjective simply describes a noun or a verb.

> *Das Zimmer ist groß.*   The room is big.

The construction *so . . . wie* compares similar persons and things and is equivalent to he English "as . . . as."

> *Das Wohnzimmer ist so groß wie unsere*   The living room is as big as our entire apartment.
> *ganze Wohnung.*

The comparative compares persons and things that are not alike.

> *Die Küche ist heller als das Esszimmer.*   The kitchen is lighter than the dining room.

The comparative of an adjective or adverb is formed by adding *-er* to the positive. Many one-syllable adjectives and adverbs with stem-vowels *a, o, u* add an Umlaut in the comparative.

POSITIVE	COMPARATIVE
hell (light)	*heller*
laut (loud)	*lauter*
ruhig (calm, quiet)	*ruhiger*
klein (small)	*kleiner*
teuer (expensive)	*teurer*
billig (cheap)	*billiger*
groß (big)	*größer*
stark (strong)	*stärker*
warm (warm)	*wärmer*
kalt (cold)	*kälter*
jung (young)	*jünger*
alt (old)	*älter*
lang (long)	*länger*
kurz (short)	*kürzer*

Das Zimmer ist grösser als die anderen.	This room is bigger than the others.
Das Wohnzimmer ist freundlicher als das Schlafzimmer.	The living room is friendlier than the bedroom.
Die Hölderlinstraße ist ruhiger als die Mozartstraße.	The Hölderlinstraße is calmer than the Mozartstraße.

And of course, if a comparative adjective precedes the noun, its ending changes depending on gender, number and case of the noun.

Wir können uns die teureren Häuser nicht leisten.	We can't afford the more expensive houses.
Lass uns doch das billigere Haus kaufen.	Let's buy the cheaper house.

Here are a few important irregular comparative forms:

gut	*besser*
viel	*mehr*
gern	*lieber*
hoch	*höher*

Das kleine Haus gefällt mir besser.	I like the small house more (Lit. better).

ACTIVITY 5: LET'S TAKE IT FOR A SPIN

Take a good look at the floor plan of Georg's and Karin's apartment. It clearly is not big enough for the two of them AND their twins, is it? Please label the rooms with their appropriate names, and then answer the questions below.

1. *Wie viele Zimmer hat die Wohnung?*
2. *Ist das Wohnzimmer grösser als das Schlafzimmer?*
3. *Welches Zimmer ist kleiner, das Esszimmer oder das Schlafzimmer?*
4. *Ist die Küche so groß wie das Esszimmer oder so groß wie das Bad?*

If you need to use the bathroom in Germany, Austria or Switzerland, ask for the *Toilette* (pronounced as [toh-eeh-LEH-teh]) or the *WC* (pronounced like the alphabet letters, veh-tseh). *Wo ist die Toilette? Wo ist die Damentoilette/Herrentoilette? Wo sind die Toiletten? Wo ist das WC?* Don't ask for the *Badezimmer* (bathroom) in German or people might think you wish to take a shower.

ACTIVITY 6:   LET'S WARM UP

Let's take another look at the floor plan above. Can you find the following *Möbelstücke* (furniture items)? Try to match the item with its proper name from the list below.

das Bett (you sleep in it), *die Badewanne* (you take a bath in it), *der Tisch* (you sit at it), *der Stuhl* (you sit on it), *die Couch/das Sofa* (you nap on it), *der Fernseher* (you watch it), *die Tür* (you walk through it), *das Fenster* (you see through it).

   And now let's get back to Georg and Karin.

HEAR . . . SAY 2

It is about six months later. Karin and Georg have just signed the papers to buy the house. They are walking through their empty house to see what needs fixing, painting, or renovating. Georg is very happy, Karin is very pregnant.

Georg:	**Dieser Altbau ist schön, aber wir werden viel renovieren müssen. Diese Wand hier bei der Haustür, zum Beispiel, muss neu verputzt werden.**
Karin:	**Ja, und wir müssen die Maler rufen. Ich will jedes Zimmer neu streichen. Ich habe an weiß für das Wohnzimmer und grün für dein Arbeitszimmer gedacht. Das passt gut zu deinem braunen Schreibtisch.**
Georg:	**Grün? Mir gefällt gelb aber besser.**
Karin:	(ignores him) **Und was hältst du von rot für die Küche? Das passt gut zu unseren bunten Kochtöpfen.**
Georg:	**Also gut.**
Karin:	**Unser Schlafzimmer will ich gelb streichen. Das passt gut zu unserem braunen Kleiderschrank und unserem grünen Bett.**

Georg:	(joking) **Und das Kinderzimmer hier streichen wir rosa, und das hier hell-blau. Das passt gut zu den Kindern.**
Karin:	(yells out) **Georg!**
Georg:	**Das war doch nur ein Scherz, Karin. O je. Die Wasserleitungen im Bad sind verstopft.**
Karin:	(yells even louder) **Ach herrje!**
Georg:	**So schlimm ist es nun auch wieder nicht. Ein Klempner kann das sicher reparieren.**
Karin:	**Ich bekomme ein Kind, Georg.**
Georg:	**Ja, ich weiß. Zwei sogar.**
Karin:	**Du verstehst mich ganz falsch. Wenn wir uns nicht beeilen, kommen deine Kinder direkt hier auf dem Teppichboden zur Welt.**
Georg:	**Schreck lass nach . . . Soll ich den Bodenleger rufen?**
Karin:	**Georg!**
Georg:	**Nur ein Scherz, mein Schatz. Wir fahren natürlich sofort ins Krankenhaus.**

He sweeps her up, kisses her and carries her to the car.

ACTIVITY 7: **HOW'S THAT AGAIN?**

	TRUE	FALSE
1. *Der Altbau ist schön, und er muss nicht renoviert werden.*	_____	_____
2. *Die Maler werden jedes Zimmer neu streichen.*	_____	_____
3. *Ein Klempner kann die Wasserleitungen im Bad reparieren.*	_____	_____
4. *Karin ist nicht mehr schwanger. Sie hat ihre Zwillinge schon bekommen.*	_____	_____
5. *Georg fährt Karin sofort ins Krankenhaus.*	_____	_____

Did You Know?

In Germany the term *Altbau* (old building) refers to buildings from the time prior to World War II. It is not necessarily a disadvantage to live in an *Altbau,* because such a building may have more character and charm than a *Neubau* (new building). The term *Altbau* may refer to buildings built as long ago as the 19th century, which have often been very nicely restored and renovated, with heavy subsidy from the city and state, in an effort to preserve the architectural beauty of older towns and cities.

HOME, SWEET HOME: FURNISHINGS

A *Wohnung* or *Haus* is not complete without its furniture. Here are the absolute necessities:

der Tisch	table
der Stuhl	chair
der Sessel	armchair
die Couch/das Sofa	couch
das Bett	bed
der Schrank	closet, cabinet
der Kleiderschrank	wardrobe
der Küchenschrank	kitchen cupboard
die Kommode	dresser
der Teppich	rug, carpet
der Teppichboden	wall-to-wall carpeting
der Holzfußboden	wooden floor

LOOKING THROUGH ROSE COLORED GLASSES: COLORS

A splash of color helps the looks of any *Wohnung* or *Haus*. Most German names for the colors are very similar to their English counterparts.

rot	red
blau	blue
grün	green
gelb	yellow
braun	brown
grau	grey
weiß	white
schwarz	black
rosa	pink
bunt	colorful

Colors are adjectives. Now, you already know the drill with the adjectives in German: If an adjective precedes the noun, its ending matches the gender, number and case of the noun it describes. If it follows it, it has no ending.

Ich habe an grün für dein Arbeitszimmer gedacht.	I was thinking of green for your office.

Das passt gut zu deinem braunen Schreibtisch.	That goes well with your brown desk.
Und was hältst du von rot für die Küche?	And what do you think about red for the kitchen?
Das passt gut zu unseren bunten Kochtöpfen.	That goes well with our colorful pots and pans.
Unser Schlafzimmer will ich gelb streichen.	I want to paint our bedroom yellow.
Das passt gut zu unserem braunen Kleiderschrank und unserem grünen Bett.	That goes well with our brown wardrobe and our green bed.

TAKE IT FOR A SPIN

Let's mix and match some colors. Do you remember Karin's ideas for interior decoration? Go through the dialogue again to check her sense of color.

1.	*das Wohnzimmer*	*a.*	*gelb*
2.	*das Schlafzimmer*	*b.*	*rot*
3.	*ein Kinderzimmer*	*c.*	*grün*
4.	*das andere Kinderzimmer*	*d.*	*rosa*
5.	*das Arbeitszimmer*	*e.*	*hellblau*
6.	*das Bett*	*f.*	*braun*
7.	*der Kleiderschrank*	*g.*	*weiß*
8.	*der Schreibtisch*	*h.*	*bunt*
9.	*die Kochtöpfe*		
10.	*die Küche*		

TAKE IT UP A NOTCH

And what colors do you have at home? Describe your own house by filling in the right color adjective.

1. *Mein Wohnzimmer ist _____ .*
2. *Das passt gut zu meinem _____ Sofa.*
3. *Und mein _____ Sofa passt gut zu meinem _____ Teppichboden.*
4. *Mein Schlafzimmer ist _____ .*
5. *Das passt gut zu meinem _____ Bett.*
6. *Mein Badezimmer ist _____ .*
7. *Das passt gut zu meinen _____ Augen.*

WORD ON THE STREET

Words for colors feature in many colloquial expressions. *Rot werden* (to turn red) means that you are blushing; but *rot sehen* (to see red) means that you are rather angry; *schwarz sehen* (to see black), on the other hand, reveals you as a pessimist; if you are *grün vor Neid* it means that you are green with envy; *gelb vor Eifersucht* says that you are yellow with jealousy; if you are *blau* (blue) you had too much to drink; *blau machen* (to make blue), though, means that you just didn't feel like showing up for work or school and played hooky.

TALK ABOUT YOUR FIXER UPPER: WHO FIXES WHAT?

Everybody knows how important it is to have a good relationship with the *Handwerker* (craftsman; handyman) whom you'll need to fix the endless problems in your *Haus.* The *Klempner* (plumber) fixes anything that has to do with plumbing. The *Fliesenleger* (tiler) or *Bodenleger* (floor layer) takes care of your floors no matter whether you'd like wood, a carpet or tiles. The *Elektriker* (electrician) will connect your wires. The *Dachdecker* (roofer) will fix your roof tiles. The *Maurer* (bricklayer) is in charge of your inner and outer walls together with the *Maler* (painter) who will paint them. The *Schreiner* (carpenter) will make your furniture. And if you'd like to find many different professions under one roof, go to a *Raumausstatter* or *Innenarchitekt* (interior decorator). But if your TV is broken, call the *Kundendienst* (service department) of the company that made it, or the *Kundendienst* of the store that sold it to you. Nobody else will touch it.

ACTIVITY 10:   TAKE IT FOR A SPIN

Who do you call when . . .

1.   . . . you need a new *Tisch* and matching *Stühle.*
2.   . . . yesterday's hail has completely ruined your roof.
3.   . . . your two-year-old mistook your living room wall for scrap paper.
4.   . . . one year later that three-year-old has spilled so much cranberry juice on the carpet you'd never know it wasn't always red.
5.   . . . you are so tired and worn-out from running after your child that you need a break. And yes, the German word is exactly the same as the English word.

Did You Know?

Learning a trade and becoming a *Handwerker* (craftsman) takes several years of schooling and just as many in an apprenticeship. You go from a *Lehrling* (apprentice) to *Meister* (master), a title that comes with a lot of pride. Only a *Meister* is licensed to open up shop in his or her profession. You would be ill-advised to hire somebody without this title to do repairs around your house.

THE NITTY GRITTY

THAT ONE OVER THERE: DEMONSTRATIVE ADJECTIVES AND DEMONSTRATIVE PRONOUNS

Demonstrative adjectives are words that point to a person or an object, like "this" and "that" in English. Demonstrative adjectives in German are *dieser* (m. sg.), *diese* (f. sg.), *dieses* (n. sg.) and it is used to mean both "this" and "that." They are often called *der*—words, as they take the same endings as the definite article *der* when showing gender, number and case of the noun they refer to.

Dieser Altbau ist schön.	This old building is beautiful.
Diese Wand hier bei der Haustür muss neu verputzt werden.	This wall over here by the door has to be re-plastered.
Dieses Haus hier hat eine hervorragende Lage.	This house here is in an excellent location.

Demonstrative pronouns in German have the same form as the definite articles, yet they stand alone. They are equivalent to English "this one" or "that one."

Das Kinderzimmer hier streichen wir rosa, und das hier hellblau.	We'll paint this children's room pink, and this one light blue.
Wir werden meistens in der Küche essen. Die ist heller als das Esszimmer.	We will eat in the kitchen most of the time. It (Lit. This one) is lighter than the dining room.

Words that behave in a similar fashion are the indefinite adjectives: *jede, -r, -s* (every, each); *manche, -r, -s* (some, several, many a); and *solche, -r, -s* (such, such a).

Ich will jedes Zimmer neu streichen.	I want to repaint every room.
Solche Häuser gibt es nicht jeden Tag.	Such houses are not available every day.

The question adjective *welche, -r, -s* (which) also takes the adjective endings.

Für welches Haus interessieren Sie sich denn?	Which house are you interested in?
Für das in der Hölderlinstraße.	For the one in the Hölderlinstraße.

Please complete this advertisement by a *Maklerbüro* (realtor's office) with the correct demonstrative adjective or pronoun.

Unser Maklerbüro bietet zehn neue Eigentumswohnungen in _____ (this) Altbau an. _____ (this) Altbau ist renoviert, und _____ (each) Wohnung hat ein neues Bad. _____ (some) der Wohnungen haben sogar eine neue Küche. Die Wohnungen im ersten Stock haben 90m², und _____ (the one) im Erdgeschoss 100 m². Rufen Sie uns baldmöglichst an. _____ (such) Wohnungen finden Sie nicht so schnell wieder.

CRIB NOTES

HEAR . . . SAY I

Agent:	This house here is in an excellent location. The Hölderlinstraße is a cul-de-sac in a quiet neighborhood.
Georg:	It is expensive, too, this neighborhood.
Karin:	The shopping center can be reached on foot. And they are building a new elementary school just around the corner. Just in time.
Georg:	What do you mean by that?
Agent:	The hall is very roomy. Please, step into the living room. You'll have a great view into the garden.
Georg:	The living room is as big as our entire apartment. No wonder the house is so expensive.
Agent:	And here is the dining room.
Karin:	We will probably eat in the kitchen most of the time. It is lighter than the dining room. And this one we'll just turn into your office, Georg.

Georg:	Good idea, but we can't afford this house.
Karin:	The three bedrooms and the bathroom are on the second floor.
Agent:	Here are the stairs.
Karin:	This room here will be our bedroom. It is bigger than the others. And this one will be the nursery/children's room. It is bright and friendly. And the smaller room right next to it will also be a . . .
Georg:	Karin, we don't have any children.
Karin:	Not yet. But soon . . . I am pregnant, Georg.
Georg:	What? . . . Why? . . . But . . .
Karin:	With twins.
Georg:	Twins! . . . I . . . But . . . Karin, this is . . . We'll take the house.
Karin:	But it is so expensive . . .
Georg:	We'll be able to afford it somehow. This is where our children will be born.
Agent:	Congratulations!

Georg:	This old building is beautiful, but we will have to do a lot of renovation. This wall here, next to the front door, for example, has to be replastered.
Karin:	Yes, and we'll have to call the painters. I want to paint every room in the house. I was thinking of white for the living room, and green for your office. That goes well with your brown desk.
Georg:	Green? I like yellow better.
Karin:	And what do you think of red for the kitchen? That goes well with our colorful pots and pans.
Georg:	OK.
Karin:	I want to paint our bedroom yellow. That goes well with our brown wardrobe and our green bed.
Georg:	And this nursery, we'll paint pink,

	and this one light blue. That goes well with our children.
Karin:	Georg!
Georg:	It was just a joke, Karin. Oh, dear. The pipes in the bathroom are clogged.
Karin:	Oh, dear!
Georg:	It's not that bad. The plumber will surely be able to fix it.
Karin:	I am having a baby, Georg.
Georg:	Yes, I know. Two even.
Karin:	You misunderstand me completely. If we don't hurry, your children will be born right here on the carpet.
Georg:	Heavens . . . Should I call the floor layer?
Karin:	Georg!
Georg:	Just a joke, my darling. We'll go to the hospital immediately.

ANSWER KEY

ACTIVITY 1
1. d   2. c   3. c
4. a   5. b

ACTIVITY 2
1. *Das Haus liegt in einer ruhigen Straße.*
2. *Georg findet das Haus zu teuer.*
3. *Das Haus hat drei Schlafzimmer, ein Wohnzimmer, ein Esszimmer, ein Badezimmer und eine Küche.*
4. *Das Haus hat einen Garten.*
5. *Georg und Karin wollen Kinder.*
6. *Georg und Karin kaufen das Haus.*

ACTIVITY 3
Mieter:	*Ist die Wohnung schon vermietet?*
Vermieter:	*Nein, die Wohnung ist noch nicht vermietet./Die Wohnung ist noch frei.*
Mieter:	*Wie groß ist die Wohnung?*
Vermieter:	*Die Wohnung hat 110 m²./Die Wohnung hat vier Zimmer.*
Mieter:	*Bekommt die Wohnung viel Sonne?*
Vermieter:	*Ja, die Wohnung ist hell.*
Mieter:	*Ist es laut in der Straße?*
Vermieter:	*Nein. Die Wohnung liegt in ruhiger Lage.*
Mieter:	*Ist es weit in die Stadt?*
Vermieter:	*Nein, die Wohnung liegt in Stadtnähe.*
Mieter:	*Wie hoch ist die Miete?*
Vermieter:	*Die Miete ist 1200 Euro.*

ACTIVITY 4
Georg und Karin werden zwei Kinder haben. Ihre Kinder werden Sebastian und Gabriel heißen. Georg und Karin werden ein Haus am Stadtrand kaufen. Das Haus wird fünf Zimmer haben. Gabriel und Sebastian werden ein eigenes Zimmer haben. Die Familie wird in der Küche essen. Das Esszimmer wird Georgs Arbeitszimmer (sein/werden). Karin wird kein Arbeitszimmer haben. Sie wird sich um die Kinder kümmern müssen.

ACTIVITY 5

das Schlafzimmer   das Wohnzimmer

das Badezimmer   die Küche   das Esszimmer

1. *Die Wohnung hat drei Zimmer./Es ist eine Dreizimmerwohnung.*
2. *Ja, das Wohnzimmer ist größer als das Schlafzimmer.*
3. *Das Schlafzimmer ist kleiner (als das Esszimmer).*
4. *Die Küche ist so groß wie das Bad.*

ACTIVITY 6

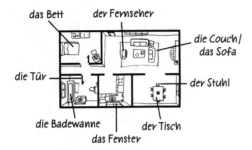

das Bett   der Fernseher

die Couch/ das Sofa

die Tür

der Stuhl

die Badewanne

der Tisch

das Fenster

ACTIVITY 7

1. False.
2. True.
3. True.
4. False.
5. True.

ACTIVITY 8

1. g
2. a
3. d
4. e
5. c
6. c
7. f
8. f
9. h
10. b

ACTIVITY 9

1. *Mein Wohnzimmer ist* (adjective without ending).
2. *Das passt gut zu meinem* (adjective with *-en* ending) *Sofa.*

3. *Und mein* (adjective with *-es* ending) *Sofa passt gut zu meinem* (adjective with *-en* ending) *Teppichboden.*
4. *Mein Schlafzimmer ist* (adjective without ending).
5. *Das passt gut zu meinem* (adjective with *-en* ending) *Bett.*
6. *Mein Badezimmer ist* (adjective without ending).
7. *Das passt gut zu meinen* (adjective with *-en* ending) *Augen.*

ACTIVITY 10

1. A *Schreiner.*
2. A *Dachdecker.*
3. A *Maler.*
4. A *Bodenleger.*
5. A *Babysitter.*

ACTIVITY 11

Unser Maklerbüro bietet zehn neue Eigentumswohnungen in diesem Altbau an. Dieser Altbau ist renoviert, und jede Wohnung hat ein neues Bad. Manche der Wohnungen haben sogar eine neue Küche. Die Wohnungen im ersten Stock haben 90m², und die im Erdgeschoss 100 m². Rufen Sie uns baldmöglichst an. Solche Wohnungen finden Sie nicht so schnell wieder.

THE EARLY BIRD CATCHES THE WORM

Morgenstund hat Gold im Mund
(Lit. Morning hours have gold in their mouth)

COMING UP . . .

- *Dressed to the nines:* Clothing items

- Some insults and comebacks

- *How to make things sound small and sweet:* Diminutives

- *The best of the best:* The superlative

- *The man who:* Relative clauses

- *Nothing and everything:* Indefinite pronouns

When in the morning the *Wecker* (alarm clock) rings, *aufstehen* (getting up), *Zähne putzen* (brushing teeth) and *sich anziehen* (getting dressed) is often the *schwierigste* (most difficult) task of the day. Who hasn't mismatched *Kleider* (clothes) once in a while, wearing a *Bluse* (blouse) that doesn't go with the *Rock* (skirt), or two different *Socken* (socks)? Who hasn't put on a great *Hemd* (shirt) or terrific *Hosen* (pants) at home only to notice in the office that they had a *Fleck* (stain)? And personally I have often found myself wearing a *Pullover* (sweater) on a day too hot to wear anything but a *T-shirt* (T-shirt).

ACTIVITY 1: **LET'S WARM UP**

Here's what my day looks like in the mornings. These sentences are about as jumbled as my mind is at that time of the day. Please put them in their correct order.

> *Dann ziehe ich mich an.*
> *Ich stehe auf.*
> *Und dann gehe ich ins Büro.*
> *Dann frühstücke ich.*
> *Der Wecker klingelt um sechs Uhr morgens.*
> *Ich putze mir die Zähne.*
> *Heute ziehe ich meinen roten Pullover und meine schwarzen Hosen an.*

HEAR . . . SAY 1

It is time to get ready for school. Dieter and his fourteen-year-old son are alone while the woman of the house is visiting her parents. Here's what happens.

Dieter:	Jens, aufstehen. Es ist schon halb acht.
Jens:	Ja, gleich. Mama lässt mich länger schlafen.
Dieter:	(a few minutes later) Jens, Zähne putzen.
Jens:	Ja doch.
Dieter:	Komm, wir machen ein Wettrennen. Sieger ist der, der sich am schnellsten die Zähne putzen kann.
Jens:	Das ist die albernste Idee, die ich je gehört habe. Mama macht so etwas nie.
Dieter:	Du willst nur nicht verlieren.

Jens:	Also gut.

The race is on.

Jens:	Ich habe gewonnen.
Dieter:	Gratuliere! Und jetzt zieh dich bitte an. Es ist kalt draußen. Du brauchst warme Kleider.
Jens:	Das ist die wärmste Hose, die ich habe, Papa.
Dieter:	Ja, gut.
Jens:	Wo ist denn mein Pullover?
Dieter:	Welcher denn?
Jens:	Na der, den ich gestern anhatte.
Dieter:	Der ist in der Wäsche.
Jens:	In der Wäsche? Aber da war doch nur der kleinste Ketchupfleck darauf.
Dieter:	Der Pullover muss gewaschen werden, Jens.
Jens:	Aber der passt am besten zu meiner Hose. Mama wäscht so etwas von Hand.
Dieter:	Ich weiß, ich weiß, Mama ist die Beste. Du hast doch bestimmt auch noch andere Kleider, die zu der Hose passen.
Jens:	Das ist aber mein schönster Pullover.
Dieter:	Und dein schmutzigster. Zieh dir bitte etwas anderes an.
Jens:	Egal was?
Dieter:	(not quite sure how to answer) Na ja, die Kleider, die du anziehst, müssen warm genug sein.
Jens:	Kein Problem.

Five minutes later, Jens comes back, fully dressed.

Dieter:	Das sieht doch prima aus . . . Moment mal. Das Hemd, das du anhast, gehört doch mir!

ACTIVITY 2:   **HOW'S THAT AGAIN?**

Here is a list of words and phrases to do with morning routines. Listen to the dialogue again and circle the ones you hear. Only three of them are not used. Beware: The words and phrases are listed in their basic forms below, whereas the dialogue may use the nouns in a different number or case and the verbs in a different tense.

kalt, die Kleider, warm, anziehen, der Rock, schnell, der Pullover, das Hemd, der Schuh, schmutzig, schön, aufstehen, klein, Zähne putzen, die Hose, die Uhr

Did You Know?

The German world of fashion is so much more than the traditional *Tracht* (costume) of *Lederhosen* and *Dirndl*. Jill Sander redefined the classic chic with well cut suits and costumes. Karl Lagerfeld is Germany's most famous success story. Before accepting his current post with Chanel, he worked for famous designer houses such as Chloe, Krizia and Fendi, while in the process of making his own name a trademark. Wolfgang Joop's success is based mainly on his perfumes. And models Claudia Schiffer, Nadja Auermann and Heidi Klum are well-known all over the world.

THE FINE PRINT

Welcher? (which one?) asks for a specific item or person among a finite number of items. The response always requires a detailed description distinguishing the particular item from those in the larger group.

—*Welcher Pullover?* Which sweater?
—*Der blaue.* The blue one.

WORKSHOP 1

WORDS TO LIVE BY

DRESSED TO THE NINES: **CLOTHING ITEMS**

Kleider machen Leute (clothes make the man) says a German proverb. So let's get dressed up.

das Hemd	shirt
die Bluse	blouse
der Pullover	sweater
die Hose	pants
die Jeans	jeans
der Rock	skirt
das Kleid	dress
der Anzug	suit
die Jacke	jacket
der Mantel	coat
die Schuhe	shoes
die Socken	socks

And of course there are a few accessories.

die Kravatte	tie
der Gürtel	belt
der Hut	hat
die Handschuhe	gloves

der Schal	scarf
der Schirm	umbrella
die Uhr	watch
die Kette	necklace
der Ring	ring

And if you feel that your wardrobe needs an update, a few phrases will come in handy as you're shopping.

Kann ich das anprobieren?	May I try this on?
Ich suche . . .	I'm looking for . . .
Ich schaue mich nur um.	I'm just browsing.

And in case you have already made up your mind.

| Wie viel kostet das? | How much is it? |
| Ich nehme es. | I'll take it. |

TAKE IT FOR A SPIN

Label all the items of clothing in the *Schaufenster* (window).

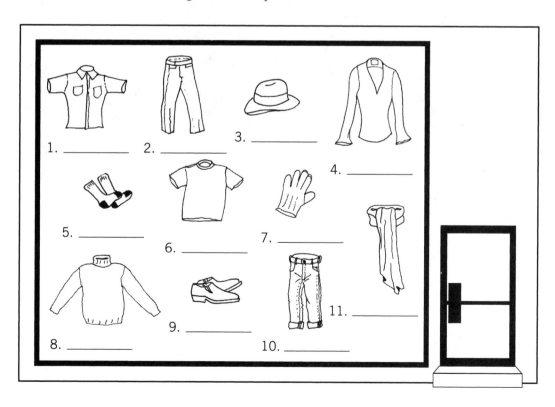

1. _____
2. _____
3. _____
4. _____
5. _____
6. _____
7. _____
8. _____
9. _____
10. _____
11. _____

Did You Know?

European clothing sizes are rather different from those in the US. The following charts will help you figure out your *Größe* (size).

WOMEN'S CLOTHING SIZES (*Frauengrößen*)

COATS, DRESSES, SKIRTS, SLACKS (*Mäntel, Kleider, Röcke, Hosen*)

U.S.	4	6	8	10	12	14	16
GERMANY	36	38	40	42	44	46	48

BLOUSES, SWEATERS (*Blusen, Pullover*)

U.S.	32/6	34/8	36/10	38/12	40/14	42/16
GERMANY	38/2	40/3	42/4	44/5	46/6	48/7

SHOES (*Schuhe*)

U.S.	4-4½	5-5½	6-6½	7-7½	8-8½	9-9½	10	11
GERMANY	35	36	37	38	39	40	41	42

MEN'S CLOTHING SIZES (*Männergrößen*)

SUITES, COATS (*Anzüge, Mäntel*)

U.S.	34	36	38	40	42	44	46	48
GERMANY	44	46	48	50	52	54	56	58

SLACKS (*Hosen*)

U.S.	30	31	32	33	34	35	36	37	38	39
GERMANY	38	39-40	41	42	43	44-45	46	47	48-49	50

SHIRTS (*Hemden*)

U.S.	14	14½	15	15½	16	16½	17	17½	18
GERMANY	36	37	38	39	40	41	42	43	44

SWEATERS (*Pullover*)

U.S.	XS/36	S/38	M/40	L/42	XL/44
GERMANY	42/2	44/3	46-48/4	50/5	52-54/6

SHOES (*Schuhe*)

U.S.	7	7½	8	8½	9	9½	10	10½	11	11½
GERMANY	39	40	41	42	43	43	44	44	45	46

WORD ON THE STREET

There are a few fun colloquial expressions using the words for clothing items.

Das ist doch Jacke wie Hose.	That doesn't matter. (Lit. The jacket is like the pants.)
Hut ab!	Hats off!
Das ging aber in die Hose.	That was a total flop. (Lit. That went in the pants.)
Das Hemd ist mir näher als der Rock.	Charity begins at home. (Lit. The shirt is closer to me than the skirt.)
Wo drückt der Schuh?	What's the trouble? What's bothering you? (Lit. Where does the shoe hurt?)
Umgekehrt wird ein Schuh daraus.	The exact opposite is true. (Lit. the other way round makes it a shoe.)
jemandem etwas in die Schuhe schieben	to blame somebody for something (Lit. to push something into somebody's shoes)

THE NITTY GRITTY

THE BEST OF THE BEST: THE SUPERLATIVE

A superlative adjective describes a person, thing or action that cannot be surpassed.

Das ist die albernste Idee.   That's the silliest idea.

The superlative adjective is formed by adding -*st*- plus the ending for gender, number and case of the noun it describes.

albern (silly) → *albernst* + *-er, -e, -es*
schnell (fast) → *schnellst* + *-er, -e, -es*

The one-syllable adjectives that add an Umlaut in the comparative do so as well in the superlative.

warm (warm) → *wärmst* + *-er, -e, -es*

Das ist die wärmste Hose.   Those are the warmest pants.

If the positive of the adjective ends in -*d*, -*t*, -*s*, -*ß*, or -*z*, the vowel -*e*- is usually added to the stem to facilitate pronunciation.

alt (old) → *ältest-*
nass (wet) → *nässest-*

Note that the adjective *groß* is an exception to this rule.

groß (big) → *größt-*

The adjectives with irregular comparatives have irregular superlatives as well.

gut (good)	*best-er, -e, -es*
viel (much)	*meist-er, -e, -es*
gern (like)	*liebst-er, -e, -es*
hoch (high)	*höchst-er, -e, -es*

Ich weiß, ich weiß, Mama ist die Beste.	I know, I know, Mama is the best.

As with the comparative, if the superlative form of the adjective precedes the noun, it has to agree with it, and the appropriate endings reflecting gender, number and case have to be added.

Das ist aber mein schönster Pullover.	That is my most beautiful sweater.
Das war nur der kleinste Ketchupfleck.	That was only the smallest ketchup stain.

The superlative of adverbs is formed by adding the suffix *-en* to the superlative and adding the preposition *am* before the word.

Wer kann am schnellsten Zähne putzen?	Who can brush teeth the quickest?
Der Pullover passt am besten zu meiner Hose.	This sweater goes best with my pants.

WORD ON THE STREET

Ketchup is one of the many words adopted from English. You can either spell it just like you do in English or use a Germanized spelling: *Kätschapp*. There are numerous other words taken from English: *T-shirt, Jeans, Ticket, Show, Computer* are but a few. Most of them retain their English spelling and even pronunciation.

ACTIVITY 4: TAKE IT FOR A SPIN

Please complete the sentences using the comparative and/or the superlative as appropriate. Use the adjective or adverb in parentheses.

1. *Mein roter Pullover gefällt mir gut. Mein blauer gefällt mir _____, und mein schwarzer gefällt mir _____.* (good)
2. *Es ist sehr kalt draußen. Zieh dir die _____ Kleider an, die du hast.* (warm)
3. *Warum hast du meine Hose gewaschen? Das war doch nur der _____ Fleck.* (small)
4. *Mein Vater ist einfach Klasse. Er ist _____.* (good)

5. *Mein Vater hat die* _____ *Hemden.* (beautiful and expensive)
6. *Sieger ist der, der sich* _____ *anziehen kann.* (fast)

Let's take a close look at the following sentence:

The man who is standing in the corner is calling his wife.

The pronoun "who" is used to join the noun (the man) with the phrase that describes it (who is standing in the corner). "Who" is a relative pronoun. The phrase introduced by such a relative pronoun is called a relative clause and it gives additional information about a noun. Here is a German example from the dialogue.

Das ist die wärmste Hose, die ich habe. Those are the warmest pants (that) I have.

In German, the relative pronoun always has to be stated. In English it can be left out as in the following example.

Das Hemd, <u>das</u> du anhast, gehört doch mir. The shirt (which) you are wearing is mine.

In German, the relative pronoun agrees in gender and number with the noun it refers to. Note also that the verb stands in the last position in a relative clause.

Der Mantel, der (m. sg.) **warm genug ist, hängt im Schrank.** The coat which is warm enough is in the closet.

Die Kleider, die (f. pl.) **warm genug sind, hängen im Schrank.** The clothes which are warm enough are in the closet.

A relative clause can refer to the subject or to the object of a sentence. The relative pronoun has to change accordingly. Let's compare the following two sentences.

Der Mann, der in der Ecke steht, ruft dich. The man who is standing in the corner is calling you.

Der Mann, den du rufst, steht in der Ecke. The man whom you are calling is standing in the corner.

Just like the English relative pronoun changes from "who" to "whom" in the second sentence to signify the change from subject to object, the German relative pronoun changes from *der* to *den*.

Let's look at another example:

Der Pullover, den du anhast, gehört mir. The sweater (which) you are wearing is mine.

In the relative clause, the subject is *du*, and *der Pullover*, represented by the relative pronoun *den*, is the direct object: *Du hast den Pullover an* (You wear the sweater) → *Der Pullower, den du anhast . . .* (The sweater that you wear . . .). Hence the relative pronoun needs to be in the masculine singular accusative form: *den*.

Der Mantel, den ich gesucht habe, hing im Kleiderschrank. The coat (which) I was looking for was in the closet.

A relative clause can begin with a preposition followed by a relative pronoun. The case of the relative pronoun is then determined by this preposition.

Das ist die Hose, in der ich am besten aussehe. These are the pants in which I look the best.

LET'S PUT IT IN WRITING

Karstadt
bietet die beste Kollektion an,
die es diesen Sommer gibt.

Sie finden in unseren Kaufhäusern Kleider,
die kein anderes Kaufhaus verkaufen wird.
Hosen, Röcke, Hemden und T-shirts,
die billig sind und trotzdem besser aussehen
als die in anderen Kaufhäusern.
Wir bieten Schuhe an,
die Ihnen gut passen werden.

KOMMEN SIE BALD VORBEI. UNSERE KLEIDER,
DIE NICHT SCHÖNER SEIN KÖNNEN, WARTEN AUF SIE.

ACTIVITY 5: TAKE IT FOR A SPIN

Please take a look at the advertisement above and circle the relative pronouns. And while you're at it, why don't you underline all the comparatives and dot all the superlatives you can find?

TAKE IT UP A NOTCH

Please connect the sentences using relative pronouns.

1. *Ich habe ein Hemd an. Das Hemd ist grün.*
2. *Der Pullover passt zu dieser Hose. Der Pullover ist schmutzig.*
3. *Meine Tochter steht spät auf. Sie kann sich schnell anziehen.*
4. *Ich kann in diesen Schuhen nicht laufen. Sie sind zu klein.*

And now, let's see how Jens is doing.

HEAR . . . SAY 2

Jens finally made it to school—a few minutes late. The geography lesson has already started. His teacher is not thrilled.

Jens:	**Tut mir leid. Ich habe verschlafen.** He takes a seat next to his friend Peter.
Frau Baun:	**Das ist schon das dritte Mal diese Woche. Kann denn bei dir zu Hause niemand einen Wecker stellen?**
Peter:	(whispering) **Hallo, du alte Schlafmütze.**
Jens:	**Doch schon, aber . . .** (whispering to Peter) **Sei doch still!**
Frau Baun:	**Ich muss irgendwann mit deiner Mutter sprechen.**
Jens:	**Meine Mutter ist gerade nicht zu Hause. Mein Vater und ich sind diese Woche alleine.**
Frau Baun:	**Na, das erklärt ja alles.** (smiles) **Morgen kommst du bitte pünktlich.**

Later, during break, Jens is chatting with his friend.

Peter:	**Das ist der langweiligste Kurs, den ich je gemacht habe. Geographie interessiert doch niemanden.**
Jens:	**Willst du etwa nicht wissen, ob Europa oben oder unten ist auf der Welt?**
Peter:	**Aber du Dummerchen, die Erde ist doch rund.**
Jens:	**Und das ist etwas, was man im Unterricht lernt. Geographie interessiert viele.**
Peter:	**Ach du liebes bisschen. Sei doch nicht so neunmalklug.**
Jens:	**Warum nicht? Irgendjemand muss ja der Schlauberger sein.**

True or false with a twist: In only one of the following groups of sentences everything is true. Which group is it?

1. *Jens hat das dritte Mal diese Woche verschlafen. Seine Mutter ist nicht zu Hause. Sein Vater kann den Wecker nicht stellen.*

2. *Jens ist zu spät in die Schule gekommen. Er findet Geographie langweilig. In Geographie hat er gelernt, dass die Erde rund ist.*

3. *Jens hat verschlafen. Morgen soll er pünktlich kommen. Die Lehrerin will mit seiner Mutter sprechen.*

4. *Jens hat verschlafen. Peter nennt ihn "Schlafmütze." Die Lehrerin nennt ihn "Dummerchen" Jens mag das nicht.*

Did You Know?

Education in Germany, Austria and Switzerland is free. In other words, people can go from *Kindergarten* (kindergarten) to the *Universität* (university) without ever paying any tuition. A typical school career leads from *die Grundschule* (elementary school, 1st through 4th grade) to either *die Hauptschule* (junior high school, 5th through 9th grade) or *die Realschule* (middle school, 5th through 10th grade) or the *Gymnasium* (highschool, 5th trough 13th grade). Students graduating from the *Hauptschule* usually go on to *die Berufsschule* (vocational school) learning a trade, those graduating from the *Realschule* often choose administrative careers, and only those graduating with the *Abitur* from the *Gymnasium* can go on to the *Universität*. This three-fold school-system has been criticized for locking children into a certain career based on their academic performance at too early an age—in grade school. Therefore a few *Gesamtschulen* (inclusive schools) have been introduced, which keep all students together until the 10th grade.

WORD ON THE STREET

Kindergarten is one of the words English has adopted from German. Some others are *Gesundheit*, *Zeitgeist*, *Weltanschauung*, *Sauerkraut* and *Autobahn*.

WORKSHOP 2

WORDS TO LIVE BY

INSULTS AND COMEBACKS

Beleidigungen (insults)—every language has them. Some are just teasing, some are a little hurtful, and some cannot be used in public. I want to make sure that you do not make enemies by accidentally using offensive words.

First, there is the word *Beleidigung* itself.

Das ist eine Beleidigung für den Geschmack.	That's an insult to taste.
Das ist eine Beleidigung für die Augen.	That's an eyesore.
Sie spielt die beleidigte Leberwurst.	She is in a huff. (Lit. She plays the insulted liverwurst.)

And then there are a few animals, or rather their supposed negative behavior, used in insults.

Du Esel!	You donkey! (implying stubbornness and lack of sophistication)
Du dumme Kuh/Gans/Pute!	You stupid cow/goose/turkey! (used for women, implying silliness beyond reason)

If you wish to question somebody's state of mind:

Du hast wohl nicht alle Tassen im Schrank!	You must be out of your mind! (Lit. You don't have all your cups in your cupboard.)
Du bist ja verrückt!	You are crazy.
Du spinnst ja wohl!	You are nuts! (Lit. You are spinning!)

And then there are a few words that state the intended criticism rather plainly.

Was für eine Schlafmütze!	What a sleepyhead! (implying that somebody sleeps a lot)
	What a dozy devil! (implying that somebody may be unnaturally slow)
So ein Schlauberger!	Such a smart aleck!
Trottel!	Dope!

And while we're at it: Tapping your index finger on your forehead towards another driver may get you a citation. This gesture basically means "You are crazy!" and is considered one of the worst insults possible.

ACTIVITY 8: **TAKE IT FOR A SPIN**

The behavior police is watching out for . . . Which insult would you use when?

1. *Das ist eine Beleidigung für die Augen.*
   a. Your little sister has once again broken one of your favorite CDs.

2. *Du spinnst ja wohl!*
   b. That's how your mother gently calls you when you're still in bed after she told you to get up a million times.

3. *Du Schlafmütze!*
   c. You see somebody walking by wearing a pink striped shirt with red checkered pants and mint green shoes.

4. *Du dumme Kuh!*

    d. A girlfriend of yours suggests you ask the most beautiful girl in your class out, even though you know she'd never give you the time of day.

HOW TO MAKE THINGS SOUND SWEET AND SMALL: DIMINUTIVES

The diminutive of nouns, the form that conveys that what you are talking about is small, is formed by adding *-chen* or *-lein* to the basic word.

das Hemd (shirt)	*das Hemdchen*	*das Hemdlein*

All nouns ending on *-chen* or *-lein* are neuter, even if they are masculine or feminine in their basic form.

der Rock (skirt)	*das Röckchen*	*das Röcklein*
die Jacke (jacket)	*das Jäckchen*	*das Jäcklein*

Please note that the stem-vowels *a, o, u* can become *Umlaute* in the diminutive. Not only does the diminutive express things small, it also makes them sweet. In fact, many endearing terms end on *-chen* or *-lein*.

Schatz (darling)	*Schätzchen*
Hans	*Hänslein*
Kuss (kiss)	*Küsschen*

Anything, even insults, can be made to sound cute by adding *-chen* or *-lein*.

Du Dummerchen.	You silly (little) thing.

But *der Ton macht die Musik* (it's the tune that makes the music). If somebody calls you *Freundchen* (little friend) in a threatening tone, it is a warning that they are rather angry or disgruntled with you. Tactical retreat is advised.

Warte nur, mein Freundchen, *dir zeig ich's gleich!*	Wait, my (little) friend. I'll show you!

WORD ON THE STREET

In the south of Germany and Austria, people usually add *-le* instead of *-chen* or *-lein*. *Dummerchen* (silly little thing) becomes *Dummerle*, *Küsschen* (kisses) becomes *Küssle*, *Häuschen* (little house) becomes *Häusle*.

TAKE IT FOR A SPIN

Here is a list of some of the most famous fairytales by the *Gebrüder* Grimm. Can you pick out the ones using diminutives?

Dornröschen (Sleeping Beauty)
Die Bremer Stadtmusikanten (The Bremen Town Musicians)
Der gestiefelte Kater (Puss in Boots)
Schneewittchen und die sieben Zwerge (Snow White and the Seven Dwarfs)
Der Froschkönig (The Frog King)
Der Wolf und die sieben Geislein (The Wolf and the Seven Little Goats)
Aschenputtel (Cinderella)
Rotkäppchen (Little Red Riding Hood)
Das tapfere Schneiderlein (The Brave Little Tailor)

THE NITTY GRITTY

NOTHING AND EVERYTHING: INDEFINITE PRONOUNS

JEMAND AND *NIEMAND*

Jemand (someone, anyone) and *niemand* (no one, not anyone) belong to a group of indefinite pronouns, which refer to objects or people that are not specifically defined.

Kann denn bei dir zu Hause niemand einen Wecker stellen?	Can nobody at your house set an alarm clock?
Geographie interessiert doch niemanden.	Geography is not interesting to anybody.
Jemand muss es ja sein.	Somebody has to.

They are used only in the singular, but watch the case endings. Luckily, at least in the dative and accusative, these endings can be omitted.

INDEFINITE PRONOUNS *JEMAND* (SOMEONE, ANYONE) AND *NIEMAND* (NO ONE)		
NOM.	*jemand*	*niemand*
ACC.	*jemand(en)*	*niemand(en)*
DAT.	*jemand(em)*	*niemand(em)*
GEN.*	*jemandes*	*niemandes*

Ist da draußen jemand?	Is somebody outside?
Nein, ich habe niemand(en) gehört.	No, I didn't hear anyone.

*In everyday speech, these forms are often replaced by *von jemanden* and *von niemandem.*

While in negative statements in English it is possible to use either "anyone" together with "not" or "nobody" without "not," only one option exists in German. In a negative sentence, you have to use *niemand* to form the negation.

OTHER INDEFINITE WORDS

German uses a variety of indefinite words such as *viele* (many), *alles* (everything), *alle* (all), *man* (one), *irgendwer* (anyone, someone), *irgendwo* (anywhere, somewhere), *irgendwann* (anytime, some time), *etwas* (something), and *nichts* (nothing).

Ich muss irgendwann mit deiner Mutter sprechen. I have to speak to your mother some time.

Just like *jemand* and *niemand*, these indefinite pronouns take case endings.

	OTHER INDEFINITE WORDS				
NOM.	irgendwer	man	viele	alle	etwas
ACC.	irgendwen	einen	viele	alle	etwas
DAT.	irgendwem	einem	vielen	allen	etwas
GEN.*	—	—	vieler	aller	etwas

Na, das erklärt ja alles. Well, that explains (it) all.
Geographie interessiert viele. Geography is interesting to many.
Das ist etwas, was man im Unterricht lernt. That is somethig one learns in class.

THE FINE PRINT

Note that *irgendwer*, *alles*, *man*, *etwas* and *nichts* are always singular, whereas *viele* and *alle* are always plural.

Man muss morgens den Wecker stellen. One has to set the alarm for the morning.
Alle müssen morgens den Wecker stellen. All have to set the alarm in the mornings.

ACTIVITY 10: **TAKE IT FOR A SPIN**

Who has done it? Please use the appropriate indefinite words.

Ich habe heute verschlafen. _____ (nobody) *hat den Wecker gestellt.* _____ (some time) *muss ich den Weckdienst anrufen.* _____ (All) *waren vor mir in der Schule. Auch* _____ (many), *die mit dem Bus in die Schule fahren müssen. Meine Lehrerin will* _____ (some time) _____ (somewhere) *mit meinem Vater sprechen. Sie sagt, es muss* _____ (something) *getan werden. Ich muss* _____ (somehow) *pünktlich werden.*

* The genitive forms *irgendwes* and *eines* exist, but are very rarely used.

CRIB NOTES

Dieter:	Jens, get up. It is already 7:30.
Jens:	Yes, right away. Mama lets me sleep longer.
Dieter:	Jens, brush your teeth.
Jens:	OK, OK.
Dieter:	Come on, we'll have a race. The winner is the one who brushes his teeth the fastest.
Jens:	That's the silliest idea I've ever heard. Mama never does things like that.
Dieter:	You are just afraid to loose.
Jens:	You're on.
Jens:	I won.
Dieter:	Congratulations! And now get dressed, please. It is cold outside. You need warm clothes.
Jens:	Those are the warmest pants I have, Dad.
Dieter:	OK.
Jens:	Where is my sweater?
Dieter:	Which one?

Jens:	Well, the one I wore yesterday.
Dieter:	It's in the wash.
Jens:	In the wash? But there was just the littlest ketchup stain on it!
Dieter:	The sweater needs to be washed, Jens.
Jens:	But it goes best with my pants. Mama washes that by hand.
Dieter:	I know, I know. Mama is the best. You must have other clothes that go with these pants.
Jens:	But that is my most beautiful sweater.
Dieter:	And your dirtiest. Put on something else, please.
Jens:	No matter what?
Dieter:	Well, the clothes you wear must be warm enough.
Jens:	No problem.
Dieter:	That looks great . . . Wait a minute. The shirt you are wearing belongs to me!

Jens:	I'm sorry. I overslept.
Mrs. Baun:	This is the third time this week. Can nobody at your house set an alarm clock?
Peter:	Hello, sleepyhead.
Jens:	Yes, of course, but . . . Be quiet!
Mrs. Baun:	I need to speak with your mother some time.
Jens:	My mother is not at home at the moment. My father and I are by ourselves this week.
Mrs. Baun:	Oh, well that explains everything. Please be on time tomorrow.

Peter:	That is the most boring class I ever took. Geography doesn't interest anyone.
Jens:	Don't you want to know whether Europe is up or down in the world?
Peter:	Dopey, the earth is round.
Jens:	And that is something one learns in class. Geography interests many.
Peter:	Oh, dear. Don't be such a smart aleck.
Jens:	Why not? Somebody has to.

ANSWER KEY

ACTIVITY 1
Der Wecker klingelt um sechs Uhr morgens. Ich stehe auf. Ich putze mir die Zähne. Dann ziehe ich mich an. Heute ziehe ich meinen roten Pullover und meine schwarzen Hosen an. Dann frühstücke ich. Und dann gehe ich ins Büro.

ACTIVITY 2
kalt, die Kleider, warm, anziehen, schnell, der Pullover, das Hemd, schmutzig, schön, aufstehen, klein, Zähne putzen, die Hose.

ACTIVITY 3

1. *das Hemd;*
2. *die Hose;*
3. *der Hut;*
4. *die Bluse;*
5. *die Socken;*
6. *das T-Shirt;*
7. *die Handschuhe;*
8. *der Pullover;*
9. *die Schuhe;*
10. *die Jeans;*
11. *der Schal*

ACTIVITY 4

1. *Mein roter Pullover gefällt mir gut. Mein blauer gefällt mir besser, und mein schwarzer gefällt mir am besten.*
2. *Es ist sehr kalt draußen. Zieh dir die wärmsten Kleider an, die du hast.*
3. *Warum hast du meine Hose gewaschen? Das war doch nur der kleinste Fleck.*
4. *Mein Vater ist einfach klasse. Er ist der Beste.*
5. *Mein Vater hat die schönsten und teuersten Hemden.*
6. *Sieger ist der, der sich am schnellsten anziehen kann.*

ACTIVITY 5

*Karstadt bietet die <u>beste</u> Kollektion an, **die** es diesen Sommer gibt. Sie finden in unseren Kaufhäusern Kleider, **die** kein anderes Kaufhaus verkaufen wird. Hosen, Röcke, Hemden und T-shirts, **die** billig sind und trotzdem <u>besser</u> aussehen als **die** in anderen Kaufhäusern. Wir bieten Schuhe an, **die** Ihnen gut passen werden. Kommen Sie bald vorbei. Unsere Kleider, **die** nicht <u>schöner</u> sein können, warten auf Sie.*

ACTIVITY 6

1. *Das Hemd, das ich anhabe, ist grün.*
2. *Der Pullover, der zu dieser Hose passt, ist schmutzig.*
3. *Meine Tochter, die spät aufsteht, kann sich schnell anziehen.*
4. *Die Schuhe, in denen ich nicht laufen kann, sind zu klein.*

ACTIVITY 7

1. *Jens hat das dritte Mal diese Woche verschlafen. Seine Mutter ist nicht zu Hause. <u>Sein Vater kann den Wecker nicht stellen.</u>* (wrong)
2. *Jens ist zu spät in die Schule gekommen. <u>Er findet Geographie langweilig.</u> In Geographie hat er gelernt, dass die Erde rund ist.* (wrong)
3. *Jens hat verschlafen. Morgen soll er pünktlich kommen. Die Lehrerin will mit seiner Mutter sprechen.* (right)
4. *Jens hat verschlafen. Peter nennt ihn "Schlafmütze." <u>Die Lehrerin nennt ihn "Dummerchen."</u> Jens mag das nicht.* (wrong)

ACTIVITY 8

1. c
2. d
3. b
4. a

ACTIVITY 9

Dornrös<u>chen</u>
Schneewitt<u>chen</u> und die sieben Zwerge
Der Wolf und die sieben Geis<u>lein</u>
Rotkäpp<u>chen</u>
Das tapfere Schneider<u>lein</u>

ACTIVITY 10

Ich habe heute verschlafen. Niemand hat den Wecker gestellt. Irgendwann muss ich den Weckdienst anrufen. Alle waren vor mir in der Schule. Auch viele, die mit dem Bus in die Schule fahren müssen. Meine Lehrerin will irgendwann irgendwo mit meinem Vater sprechen. Sie sagt, es muss etwas getan werden. Ich muss irgendwie pünktlich werden.

13

HONEST WORK NEVER HURT

Arbeit macht das Leben süß
(Lit. Work makes life sweet)

LOOKING AHEAD . . .

Arbeit (work) is an essential part of our life. So is *Vergnügen* (entertainment, relaxation, fun), of course. The right balance is what will keep us *gesund* (healthy) and *glücklich* (happy). A day at the *Büro* (office) is filled with endless *Besprechungen* (meetings), *Terminen* (due dates), discussions about the *Budget* (budget) curbing the *Preis* (price) and the *Kosten* (cost) of any project. Makes you think about your next *Urlaub* (vacation), doesn't it?

ACTIVITY 1: LET'S WARM UP

Which words do you prefer, those that relate to *Arbeit* (work), or those that relate to *Urlaub* (vacation)? Check them off in the right column.

	ARBEIT	URLAUB
der Kunde	_____	_____
der Schreibtisch	_____	_____
die Sonne	_____	_____
das Problem	_____	_____
der Termin	_____	_____
das romantische Abendessen	_____	_____
der Schlaf	_____	_____
die Sekretärin	_____	_____
die Besprechung	_____	_____
das Vergnügen	_____	_____
das Telefon	_____	_____

HEAR . . . SAY 1

Alfred Hamm owns a small company that produces buttons for the designer industry. One *Kunde* (client) has requested a large *Lieferung* (shipment) in much less time than usual. Alfred Hamm and Agnes Kammer, the manager of the *Versand* (shipping department) are trying to solve the problem in a hurry.

Sekretärin:	Herr Hamm, Sie haben noch eine Besprechung mit der Dame vom Versand.
Alfred Hamm:	Würden Sie ihr sagen, dass ich gleich komme?

A few minutes later.

Alfred Hamm:	Guten Abend, Frau Kammer. Wie schön, dass wir uns zu so später Stunde noch treffen konnten. Könnten wir gleich zur Sache kommen? Meine Frau erwartet mich in einer Stunde zum Abendessen. Wenn ich zu spät komme, gibt's Ärger.

Everyone laughs politely.

Agnes Kammer:	Natürlich. Wir haben Terminprobleme. Die Lieferfirma, mit der wir normalerweise zusammenarbeiten, kann unsere Bedingungen nicht erfüllen.
Alfred Hamm:	Wie wär's mit einer anderen Lieferfirma?
Agnes Kammer:	Daran habe ich auch schon gedacht. Ich habe Kostenvoranschläge von verschiedenen Firmen eingeholt. Leider gehen alle im Preis weit über unser Budget hinaus.
Alfred Hamm:	Haben Sie Lösungsvorschläge?
Agnes Kammer:	Wäre es Ihnen recht, wenn wir den Liefertermin nach hinten verschieben? Dann könnten wir mit der üblichen Lieferfirma zusammen arbeiten.
Alfred Hamm:	Das kommt leider nicht in Frage. Unser Kunde wäre niemals damit einverstanden.
Agnes Kanner:	Dann schlage ich vor, dass wir das Budget etwas flexibler gestalten.
Alfred Hamm:	Das geht leider auch nicht. Könnten Sie noch einen anderen Vorschlag machen?
Agnes Kammer:	Wenn weder der Termin noch das Budget flexibel sind, sehe ich nur noch eine Möglichkeit: eine teilweise Lieferung mit unserer üblichen Lieferfirma zum gewünschten Termin.
Alfred Hamm:	Das ist eine hervorragende Idee. Ich wusste doch, dass Sie die Lage retten können. Frau Kammer, würden Sie das bitte sofort veranlassen.
Agnes Kammer:	Heute Abend noch?
Alfred Hamm:	Ja, natürlich. Eine weitere Verzögerung könnte uns den Kunden kosten.
Agnes Kammer:	Ich würde lieber morgen weiter arbeiten. Mein Mann erwartet mich zum Abendessen. Wenn ich zu spät komme . . .
Alfred Hamm	. . . gibt's Ärger. Ich weiß. Hätten Sie etwas dagegen, wenn ich Ihnen helfe?
Agnes Kammer:	Nein, das würde mich freuen.

Did You Know?

The nine-to-five workday in a 40-hour workweek is a thing of the past in Germany. Companies are trying to accommodate the changing needs of their employees by offering *Gleitzeit* (flexible working hours [Lit. gliding hours]). Employees may arrive for work as early as 6AM and as late as 9AM, and leave as early as 2PM on any given day, as long as the office is covered during the *Kernarbeitszeit* (main working hours [Lit. kernel working hours]) between 9AM and 3PM, and as long as any individual employee works the required 35-hour workweek. This is meant to help working mothers and fathers and is supposed to ease a crowded employment market. The regular business hours for public administrative offices are from 8AM to 4PM. Often, public administration offices close for lunch sometime between 12 noon and 2PM for an hour. On Fridays many offices close earlier, any time between 1PM and 4PM. One day a week, at least, they will stay open until 6PM to accommodate the needs of the working population.

ACTIVITY 2: HOW'S THAT AGAIN?

Draw two columns on a piece of paper. In the first, copy down all the phrases from the dialogue that offer suggestions. In the second, copy down all the phrases which comment on these suggestions.

WORD ON THE STREET

The expression *die Lage retten* (Lit. to save the situation) is equivalent to the English "saving the day," and so is *die Eisen aus dem Feuer holen* (Lit. to take the irons out of the fire).

WORKSHOP 1

WORDS TO LIVE BY

HERE'S A SUGGESTION: MAKING SUGGESTIONS AND OFFERS

Life is full of compromises . . . and negotiations. It is a good idea to know how to negotiate well—in any language. Here are a few expressions you will find useful when making suggestions and negotiating in German:

Ich schlage vor, dass . . .	I suggest that . . .
Das beste wäre, wenn . . .	The best would be if . . .
Was halten Sie von . . . ?	What do you think of . . . ?
Wäre es Ihnen recht, wenn . . . ?	Would you agree if . . . ?
Wie wär's mit . . . ?	What about . . . ?
Hätten Sie etwas dagegen, wenn . . . ?	Would you mind if . . . ?
Was würden Sie sagen, wenn, . . . ?	What would you say if . . . ?

THE FINE PRINT

Hätte, wäre, and *würde* are the subjunctive II forms of *haben, sein,* and *werden* respectively. The subjunctive, the verbal form expressing hypothetical conditions, is not very common in everyday speech, except in polite requests and in negotiations. We'll encounter these forms throughout the lesson.

Here's a set of possible responses:

If you like the suggestion, you could say . . .

Guter Vorschlag.	Good suggestion.
Das ist eine hervorragende Idee.	That's an excellent idea.
Das klingt interessant/gut.	That sounds interesting/good.
Einverstanden.	Agreed.

If you don't like the suggestion you could respond with . . .

Das geht leider nicht.	That won't work, unfortunately.
Damit bin ich nicht einverstanden.	I don't agree with that.
Das kommt nicht in Frage.	That is out of the question.

And if you're not quite sure . . .

Ich muss darüber nachdenken.	I have to think about that.
Kann ich mir das noch überlegen?	Can I think about that?
Ich weiß nicht so recht.	I'm not quite sure.

ACTIVITY 3: **TAKE IT FOR A SPIN.**

Participate in the following conversation.

Assistant: *Ich schlage vor, wir erhöhen das Budget.*

Manager: _____. (That is out of the question.)

Assistant: *Wie wär's dann, wenn wir den Termin verschieben?*

Manager: _____. (That won't work.)

Assistant: *Was halten Sie davon, wenn wir eine andere Lieferfirma nehmen?*

Manager: _____. (Good suggestion.)

Assistant: *Das beste wäre, wenn wir uns Kostenvoranschläge einholten.*

Manager: _____. (Agreed.)

Did You Know?

Negotiations and decision-making can take a very long time in Germany. The typical structure of authority in a German company is vertical. Decisions are made by a few people at the top, which, before a decision is finalized, may consult with their department heads to reach a consensus. Thus it is not surprising that decisions are rarely made on the spot. While major decisions are made at the top, German employees have empowerment for making decisions within the domain of their jobs. It is important that you locate and deal with the person who is specifically responsible for the issue you need addressed, as "going above one's head" would surely sour a business relation from the start.*

THE NITTY GRITTY

LET'S BE POLITE: THE SUBJUNCTIVE

WÜRDE PLUS INFINITIVE

Apart from *bitte* and *danke*, German polite requests contain a specific verb form called the subjunctive II. For most verbs this means using the subjunctive of the verb *werden* and the infinitive of the main verb. This construction is similar to the English construction involving "would."

Würden Sie ihr sagen, dass ich gleich komme?	Would you please tell her that I'll be there shortly?
Würden Sie das bitte sofort veranlassen.	Would you please set that in motion immediately?
Würdest du mir bitte helfen?	Would you help me, please?

Here are the subjunctive forms of *werden*.

WERDEN IN THE SUBJUNCTIVE	
SINGULAR	PLURAL
ich würde	*wir würden*
du würdest	*ihr würdet*
Sie würden	*Sie würden*
er/sie/es würde	*sie würden*

THE SUBJUNCTIVE OF MODAL VERBS

The modal verbs, used frequently in polite speech, have their own subjunctive forms, used to make the request even more polite. Compare the two following sentences.

Können wir gleich zur Sache kommen?	Can we get to the point right away?

vs.

Könnten wir gleich zur Sache kommen?	Could we get to the point right away?

---

* From: Phillips, Jennifer. In the Know in Germany. Living Language, New York, 2001.

and

    Können Sie das heute noch veranlassen?   Can you set that in motion today?

vs.

    Könnten Sie das heute noch veranlassen?   Could you set that in motion today?

and

    Darf ich Sie etwas fragen.   Can I ask you something?

vs.

    Dürfte ich Sie etwas fragen?   May I ask you something?

THE SUBJUNCTIVE OF MODALS

ICH	könnte	müsste	dürfte	wollte	möchte	sollte
DU	könntest	müsstest	dürftest	wolltest	möchtest	solltest
SIE (FORMAL)	könnten	müssten	dürften	wollten	möchten	sollten
ER/SIE/ES	könnte	müsste	dürfte	wollte	möchte	sollte
WIR	könnten	müssten	dürften	wollten	möchten	sollten
IHR	könntet	müsstet	dürftet	wolltet	möchtet	solltet
SIE	könnten	müssten	dürften	wollten	möchten	Sollten

THE SUBJUNCTIVE II OF *HABEN* AND *SEIN*

Haben and *sein* also have a subjunctive II form of their own and do not need to use *werden* as do main verbs.

    Hätten Sie etwas dagegen, wenn ich Ihnen helfe?   Would you mind if I helped you?

    Wäre es Ihnen recht, wenn wir den Liefertermin nach hinten verschieben?   Would it be OK with you if we moved back the delivery date?

THE SUBJUNCTIVE II OF *HABEN* AND *SEIN*

ICH	hätte	wäre	WIR	hätten	wären
DU	hättest	wärst	IHR	hättet	wärt
SIE (FORMAL)	hätten	wären	SIE (FORMAL)	hätten	wären
ER/SIE/ES	hätte	wäre	SIE	hätten	wären

USES OF THE SUBJUNCTIVE II

The most common use of the German subjunctive is to express polite requests. In addition, the subjunctive II is also used to express hypothetical situations, a constant during negotiations. Just look at the following dialogue portion. English uses "would" in these circumstances.

Agnes Kammer:	*Wäre es Ihnen recht, wenn wir den Liefertermin nach hinten ver-schieben? Dann könnten wir mit der üblichen Lieferfirma zusammen arbeiten.*
	Would it be OK with you if we moved back the delivery date? We could work with our usual shipping company.
Herr Hamm:	*Das kommt leider nicht in Frage. Unser Kunde wäre niemals damit einverstanden.*
	Unfortunately that is out of the question. Our client would never accept that.

ACTIVITY 4: TAKE IT FOR A SPIN

Please make these requests even more formal and polite.

1. *Können Sie mir helfen?*
2. *Machen Sie bitte einen anderen Vorschlag.*
3. *Darf ich Sie etwas fragen?*
4. *Haben Sie etwas dagegen, wenn wir anfangen?*
5. *Seien Sie bitte so freundlich!*
6. *Beeilen Sie sich bitte!*
7. *Hilf mir bitte!*

SUBORDINATE CLAUSES: DASS-SENTENCES

Dass introduces a subordinate clause (a clause that is dependent on another, main clause and cannot stand alone) and is equivalent to the English "that."

Wie schön, dass wir uns zu so später Stunde noch treffen konnten.	How nice that we could meet at such a late hour.

Unlike in English it is NOT possible to drop *dass* in German.

Würden Sie ihr sagen, dass ich gleich komme?	Would you please tell her (that) I'll be there right away?

Please note that the verb in the *dass*-clause always takes the last position.

Dann schlage ich vor, dass wir das Budget etwas flexibler gestalten.	Then I suggest (that) we be more flexible with the budget.

Heads Up!

Make sure not to mix up *dass* and *das*. Even though they are pronounced the same, they are spelled differently and have very different meanings. *Das* is the definite article used with singular neuter nouns, and also a relative pronoun in the nominative and accusative.

Das Budget, das wir diskutieren, ist nicht flexibel.	The budget (which) we're discussing is not flexible.

Dass, on the other hand, does not refer to a noun but to the information of an entire sentence.

Ich glaube nicht, dass das Budget flexibel ist.	I don't think (that) the budget is flexible.

ACTIVITY 5: TAKE IT FOR A SPIN

Please put the two sentences together with *dass*.

1. *Wir können uns treffen.*
   Ich hoffe, _____.
2. *Das Budget ist nicht flexibel.*
   Ich glaube nicht, _____.
3. *Ich komme gleich.*
   Sagen Sie ihm bitte, _____.
4. *Bitte helfen Sie mir.*
   Ich möchte, _____.
5. *Machen Sie einen Vorschlag.*
   Ich erwarte, _____.

SUBORDINATE CLAUSES: WENN-SENTENCES

In German, *wenn*-sentences can introduce a condition upon which the main clause depends. In English, these sentences can be expressed with either *if*- or *when*-clauses.

Wenn ich zu spät komme, gibt's Ärger.	When/if I'm late, there's trouble.

If the *wenn*-sentence is mentioned first, subject and verb change places in the main clause. Compare the following two sentences.

Ich <u>sehe</u> nur noch eine Möglichkeit, wenn weder der Termin noch das Budget flexibel sind.	There is only one possibility if/when neither the due date nor the budget is flexible.

vs.

Wenn weder der Termin noch das Budget flexibel sind, <u>sehe</u> ich nur noch eine Möglichkeit.	If/when neither the due date nor the budget is flexible, there is only one possibility.

TAKE IT FOR A SPIN

Go back to the Hear . . . Say 1 dialogue and underline all *wenn*-sentences.

TAKE IT UP A NOTCH

Please connect the following sentences with *wenn*.

1. *Es gibt ein Problem. Der Termin ist nicht flexibel.*
2. *Wir verlieren den Kunden. Die Lieferung dauert länger.*
3. *Sie brauchen meine Hilfe. Ich möchte helfen.*

And now, let's go back to our office scene. I am curious whether Frau Kammer and Herr Hamm made it home in time to avoid marital problems.

HEAR . . . SAY 2

Herr Hamm gets home about one hour late. On his way home he stopped at a convenience store of a gas station to pick up some flowers. His daughter greets him at the door.

Sabine:	**Hallo Papa! Mama ist ganz schön sauer auf dich.** (pointing to the flowers in his hands) **Willst du sie mit den Blumen etwa besänftigen?**
Alfred Hamm:	**Meinst du, dass ich damit Erfolg habe?**
Sabine:	**Wo denkst du hin, Papa. Heute doch nicht.**
Alfred Hamm:	(mumbling to himself) **Warum ausgerechnet heute nicht? . . . Hallo mein Schatz. Tut mir leid, dass es etwas später als geplant geworden ist.**
Astrid Hamm:	(she does not look up, visibly annoyed) **ETWAS später?**
Alfred Hamm:	**Entschuldige.**
Astrid Hamm:	**Eine Entschuldigung genügt nicht. Heute jedenfalls nicht. Du arbeitest zu viel und hast zu wenig Zeit für uns.**
Alfred Hamm:	**Ich weiß. Glaub mir, das ist nicht meine Absicht.**
Astrid Hamm:	**Schon gut.** (finally looking up) **Blumen. . . . wenn du etwa glaubst, dass damit alles wieder gut ist, hast du dich getäuscht.** (She takes the envelope hidden in the flowers) **Was ist das denn?**
Alfred Hamm:	**Mach einfach auf.**

Astrid Hamm	(reading) **Kreuzfahrt . . . tropische Inseln . . . 3 Wochen . . . Fred, du hast also doch an unseren Hochzeitstag gedacht . . .**
Alfred Hamm:	(obviously surprised) **Oh, aber natürlich!**

Meanwhile, across town:

Robert Kammer:	**Na endlich. Ich habe die Koffer schon gepackt.**
Agnes Kammer:	**Fährst du etwa in den Urlaub? Oder willst du mich verlassen?**
Robert Kammer:	**Gedacht habe ich schon daran. . . .**
Agnes Kammer:	**Woran? An den Urlaub, hoffe ich . . .**
Robert Kammer:	**Du hättest ja gar keine Zeit für einen Urlaub.**
Agnes Kammer:	**Sei bitte nicht böse. Ich wollte wirklich nicht, dass es so spät wird, aber mein Chef. . . .**
Robert Kammer:	**Agnes, wir wollten heute Abend zusammen essen gehen. Und jetzt ist es dazu viel zu spät.**
Agnes Kammer:	**Ich weiß, und es tut mir wirklich leid.**
Robert Kammer:	**Macht ja nichts. Und wenn du mit einem Kuss um Verzeihung bittest . . .**

WORD ON THE STREET

Sauer is not only the "sour" taste of milk gone sour—*Die Milch wird sauer*—but also an expression of somebody's mood as in *Ich bin sauer* (I am annoyed). The expression *jemandem das Leben sauer machen* translates as "to make somebody's life miserable," whereas *sauer verdientes Geld* is "hard-earned money."

Did You Know?

Time is money. Everybody knows that Germans are among the most time-conscious people in the world. But this does not only mean that you'll encounter rather inflexible shopping hours, rigid train and bus schedules, and the understanding that everybody should be on time for appointments. This also means that Germans are rather serious about their free time. While an American might stay in the office late or postpone a vacation to finish a project, a German might guard his *Feierabend* (end of the work day) rather jealously and is likely to leave the office on time or take a day off even when the deadline has not been met. This does not mean that Germans are less serious about their work. It simply means that for Germans there is a time for everything— a time to work and a time to play.

ACTIVITY 8: **HOW'S THAT AGAIN?**

Draw two large columns on a piece of paper. In the first column, copy down all the phrases from the dialogue in Hear . . . Say 2 that offer apologies. In the second column, copy down all the phrases which either accept or decline the apology.

Wo denkst du hin? What an idea! (Lit. Which direction are you thinking?) This phrase implies that the idea is absolutely outrageous. It is quite strong so be sure you only use the phrase with friends and acquaintances. Your boss might not appreciate it, even though he or she might take the liberty to use it if you make an outlandish suggestion.

WORKSHOP 2

WORDS TO LIVE BY

APOLOGIES

You are bound to find yourself in a situation where an apology will save the day. Here are the essentials of apologizing.

(Es) tut mir leid.	I'm sorry.
Entschuldigung.	Sorry./Forgive me.
Verzeihung.	Forgive me.
Das wollte ich nicht.	I didn't mean that (to happen).
Das war nicht meine Absicht.	This was not my intention.
Seien Sie mir bitte nicht böse./Sei mir bitte nicht böse.	Don't be angry.
Das ist mir aber peinlich.	That is embarrassing.

THE FINE PRINT

Sei mir bitte nicht böse/Seien Sie mir bitte nicht böse use the Subjunctive I form of *sein*. Just learn the whole expression as is, because, except in these apologetic expressions and in the following polite requests, this form is rarely used: *Seien Sie/Sei bitte so freundlich?* (Would you be so kind?).

Reacting graciously if somebody else apologizes will help you make friends.

Das macht nichts.	It doesn't matter.
Kein Problem.	No problem.
Schon gut.	It's OK.
Nichts passiert.	No harm done.
Ich nehme die Entschuldigung gerne an.	I'll gladly accept the apology.

WORD ON THE STREET

The adjective *ausgerechnet* (Lit. calculated) is used idiomatically with many different nouns: *ausgerechnet heute* (today of all days), *ausgerechnet er* (he of all people), *ausgerechnet Bananen* (bananas of all things). A common phrase is: *Ausgerechnet mir muss das passieren?* (Why did it have to happen to me of all people?).

LET'S PUT IT IN WRITING

Take a look at Alfred's note to Regina.

Liebe Regine,

Es tut mir sehr leid, dass ich gestern so spät nach Hause gekommen bin. Leider wurde ich im Büro aufgehalten. Ich wollte dich anrufen, aber leider war die Batterie in meinem Handy leer. Sei mir bitte nicht böse. Ich hoffe, dass du diese Blumen als Entschuldigung annehmen wirst.

Dein Alfred

ACTIVITY 9: TAKE IT FOR A SPIN

Now answer the following questions.

1. *Wie oft bittet Alfred um Verzeihung?*
2. *Warum kam er nicht?*
3. *Warum hatte er nicht angerufen?*
4. *Warum schickt er die Blumen?*

IN AND AROUND THE OFFICE AND HOW TO GET AWAY FROM IT

The *Alltagsstress* (daily grind) is enough to make everybody *urlaubsreif* (in need of a vacation) and dream of a *Reise* (trip) in *ferne Länder* (faraway countries). *Im Sommer* you plan your *Badeurlaub* (beach vacation) *am Strand* (at the beach), and *im Winter* it is the *Skiurlaub* (skiing vacation) *in den Bergen* (in the mountains). You can *in den Urlaub fahren* (to go on vacation by car) or *fliegen* (fly). When you *in die Ferien gehen* (go on holidays), you must *packen* (pack) your *Koffer* (suitcase) before you go. Once you are at your *Urlaubsort* (vacation place), you will get *Erholung* (relaxation, rest), and upon your return to the *Büro* (office) you will feel *erholt* (rested) and you will once again, *gründliche Arbeit leisten* (do a good job).

ACTIVITY 10: **TAKE IT FOR A SPIN**

What's true?

1. *Der Alltagsstress ist der Stress . . .*
    a. *. . . im Urlaub.*
    b. *. . . in den Ferien.*
    c. *. . . im Büro.*
    d. *. . . beim Zahnarzt.*
2. *Im Sommer gehen viele Leute . . .*
    a. *. . . in den Badeurlaub.*
    b. *. . . zum Zahnarzt.*
    c. *. . . an den Strand.*
    d. All of the above.
3. *Im Winterurlaub kann man . . .*
    a. *. . . sich gut erholen.*
    b. *. . . in die Berge fahren.*
    c. *. . . Ski fahren.*
    d. All of the above.
4. *Vor jedem Urlaub muss man . . .*
    a. *. . . sich erholen.*
    b. *. . . die Koffer packen.*
    c. *. . . in die Berge fahren.*
    d. *. . . sich entschuldigen.*
5. *Gründliche Arbeit ist . . .*
    a. *. . . gute Arbeit.*
    b. *. . . keine Arbeit.*
    c. *. . . Urlaub.*
    d. *. . . Büroarbeit.*

THE NITTY GRITTY

DA-COMPOUNDS AND *WO*-COMPOUNDS

In English, any noun that follows a preposition can be replaced with a pronoun, no matter whether the noun refers to a person, a thing, or an idea.

I'll talk to the shipping manager. → I'll talk to <u>him</u>.
Something is wrong with the shipment. → Something is wrong with <u>it</u>.
He should think about a new proposition. → He should think about <u>it</u>.

In German, a pronoun can only be used if the noun refers to a person. Look at the German version of the English sentences above. If the noun refers to a thing or an idea, a *da*-compound is used.

Ich spreche mit dem Manager im Versand. → *Ich spreche <u>mit ihm</u>.*

But:

Etwas ist mit der Lieferung nicht in Ordnung. → *Etwas ist <u>damit</u> nicht in Ordnung.*
Er sollte an einen neuen Vorschlag denken. → *Er sollte <u>daran</u> denken.*

Da-compounds are formed by joining *da*- with a preposition. Frequently used *da*-compounds are:

- *damit*

  Meinst du, dass ich mit den Blumen Erfolg habe? — Do you think I'll be successful with the flowers?

  Meinst du, dass ich damit Erfolg habe? — Do you think I'll be successful with them?

- *daran*

  Du hast also doch an unseren Hochzeitstag gedacht. — You remembered our wedding anniversary after all.

  Du hast also doch daran gedacht. — You remembered it after all.

- *dazu*

  Und jetzt ist es viel zu spät zum Abendessen. — And now it is too late for dinner.

  Und jetzt ist es dazu viel zu spät. — And now it is too late for it.

Other *da*-compounds are: *dafür* (for it), *dagegen* (against it), *darin* (in it), *darauf* (on it), *darunter* (under it).

Ich interessiere mich für Sport. — I'm interested in sports.
Ich interessiere mich dafür. — I'm interested in it.

A similar type of compound is used in questions. The questions word *was* (what) refers to things and ideas. If the noun it questions is preceded by a preposition (*an Scheidung* in the example below), it is generally replaced by a *wo*-compound.

Ich denke an Scheidung.	I'm thinking about a divorce.
Woran (or an was) denkst du?	What are you thinking about?
Sie sprechen von den Lieferproblemen.	They are speaking about the shipping problems.
Wovon sprechen sie?	What are they talking about?

Other common *wo*-compounds are: *womit* (with what), *wofür* (for what), *worauf* (on what), *wogegen* (against what), *wozu* (what for). For example:

Wofür interessieren Sie sich?	What are you interested in?

Heads Up!

Please note that the *da-* and *wo*-compounds with prepositions starting on a vowel add an *-r-* after *da* and *wo,* as in *darauf* (on that) and *worauf* (on what).

ACTIVITY 11:   **TAKE IT FOR A SPIN**

Complete the following story using *da-* or *wo*-compounds. The following verbs and their prepositions will be used: *warten auf, einverstanden sein mit, diskutieren über, denken an, helfen bei, sprechen über, dankbar sein für.*

Wir haben Probleme mit dem Versand. Ich habe mit meinem Chef gestern _____ gesprochen. _____ haben wir diskutiert? Ich will das Budget erhöhen. Mein Chef hat auch schon _____ gedacht. Aber der Kunde wird nicht _____ einverstanden sein. In ein paar Wochen kann unsere Lieferfirma wieder mehr arbeiten. Aber _____ können wir nicht warten. Wir müssen also eine neue Lieferfirma finden. Mein Chef hat mir _____ geholfen. _____ bin ich ihm sehr dankbar.

CRIB NOTES

Secretary:	Mr. Hamm, you have a meeting with the lady from shipping.
Alfred Hamm:	Would you please tell her that I'll be right there?
Alfred Hamm:	Good evening, Frau Kammer. How nice that we could meet at such a late hour. Could we get to the point right away? My wife is expecting me for dinner in an hour. If I am late, there will be trouble.
Agnes Kammer:	Of course. We are experiencing shipping problems. The shipping company we usually work with cannot meet our conditions.
Alfred Hamm:	How about another shipping company?
Agnes Kammer:	I've thought about that, too. I requested estimates from several companies. Unfortunately all of them far exceed our budget in price.
Alfred Hamm:	Do you have any suggestions?
Agnes Kammer:	Would it be OK with you to postpone the shipping date? Then we could work with our usual company.
Alfred Hamm:	That is out of the question. Our client would never agree to that.
Agnes Kanner:	Then I suggest that we are more flexible with our budget.
Alfred Hamm:	Unfortunately, that's not possible either. Could you make another suggestion?
Agnes Kammer:	If neither the shipping date nor the budget are flexible, I see only one other possibility: a partial shipment with our usual shipping company at the desired shipping date.
Alfred Hamm:	That is an excellent idea. I knew that you'd save the day. Ms. Kammer, would you set that in motion immediately?
Agnes Kammer:	Tonight?
Alfred Hamm:	Yes, of course. Another delay could cost us the client.
Agnes Kammer:	I would rather continue working on this tomorrow. My husband is expecting me for dinner. If I am late . . .
Alfred Hamm	. . . there will be trouble. I know. Would you mind if I help you?
Agnes Kammer:	No, I'd be delighted.

Sabine:	Hello, Daddy! Mom is pretty upset with you. Are you trying to appease her with these flowers?
Alfred Hamm:	Do you think I'll be successful with that?
Sabine:	Not a chance, daddy! Not today!
Alfred Hamm:	Why not today of all days? . . . Hello, my darling. I'm sorry that it is a little later than planned.
Astrid Hamm:	A little later?
Alfred Hamm:	I'm sorry.
Astrid Hamm:	An apology is not enough. Not today. You work too much and have too little time for us.
Alfred Hamm:	I know. Believe me, that is not my intention.
Astrid Hamm:	OK. Flowers . . . if you believe that this will make up for everything you are mistaken. What is that?
Alfred Hamm:	Why don't you open it?
Astrid Hamm	Cruise . . . tropical islands . . . three weeks . . . Fred, you thought about our wedding anniversary after all . . .
Alfred Hamm:	Why, of course!

Meanwhile, across town:

Robert Kammer:	Finally. I packed all the suitcases already.
Agnes Kammer:	Are you going on vacation? Or are you leaving me?
Robert Kammer:	I have thought about it. . . .
Agnes Kammer:	About what? About our vacation, I hope . . .
Robert Kammer:	You wouldn't have any time for a vacation.
Agnes Kammer:	Please don't be angry. I really didn't want it to be so late, but my boss . . .
Robert Kammer:	Agnes, we wanted to go out to dinner together tonight. And now it is much too late for that.
Agnes Kammer:	I know, and I'm really sorry.
Robert Kammer:	No harm done. And if you beg my forgiveness with a kiss . . .

ACTIVITY 1

der Kunde—Arbeit
der Schreibtisch—Arbeit
die Sonne—Urlaub
das Problem—Arbeit
der Termin—Arbeit
das romantische Abendessen—Urlaub
der Schlaf—Urlaub
die Sekretärin—Arbeit
die Besprechung—Arbeit
das Vergnügen—Urlaub
das Telefon—Arbeit

ACTIVITY 2

Suggestion:
- *Könnten wir gleich zur Sache kommen?*
- *Wie wär's mit einer anderen Lieferfirma?*
- *Wäre es Ihnen recht, wenn wir den Liefertermin nach hinten verschieben?*
- *Dann schlage ich vor, dass wir das Budget etwas flexibler gestalten.*
- *Könnten Sie noch einen anderen Vorschlag machen?*
- *Hätten Sie etwas dagegen, wenn ich Ihnen helfe?*

Reaction:
- *Natürlich.*
- *Daran habe ich auch schon gedacht.*
- *Das kommt leider nicht in Frage.*
- *Das geht leider auch nicht.*
- *Das ist eine hervorragende Idee.*
- *Nein, das würde mich freuen.*

ACTIVITY 3

Assistant:	Ich schlage vor, wir erhöhen das Budget.
Manager:	Das kommt nicht in Frage.
Assistant:	Wie wär's dann, wenn wir den Termin verschieben?
Manager:	Das geht nicht.
Assistant:	Was halten Sie davon, wenn wir eine andere Lieferfirma nehmen?
Manager:	Guter Vorschlag.
Assistant:	Das beste wäre, wenn wir uns Kostenvoranschläge einholten.
Manager:	Einverstanden.

ACTIVITY 4

1. *Könnten Sie mir helfen?*
2. *Würden Sie bitte einen anderen Vorschlag machen.*
3. *Dürfte ich Sie etwas fragen?*
4. *Hätten Sie etwas dagegen, wenn wir anfangen?*
5. *Wären Sie bitte so freundlich!*
6. *Würden Sie sich bitte beeilen!*
7. *Würdest du mir bitte helfen?*

ACTIVITY 5

1. *Ich hoffe, dass wir uns treffen können.*
2. *Ich glaube nicht, dass das Budget flexibel ist.*
3. *Sagen Sie ihm bitte, dass ich gleich komme.*
4. *Ich möchte, dass Sie mir helfen.*
5. *Ich erwarte, dass Sie einen Vorschlag machen.*

ACTIVITY 6

Wenn ich zu spät komme, gibt's Ärger.
Wäre es Ihnen recht, wenn wir den Liefertermin nach hinten verschieben würden?
Wenn weder der Termin noch das Budget flexibel sind, sehe ich nur noch eine Möglichkeit.
Hätten Sie etwas dagegen, wenn ich Ihnen helfe?

ACTIVITY 7

1. *Es gibt ein Problem, wenn der Termin nicht flexibel ist.*
2. *Wir verlieren den Kunden, wenn die Lieferung länger dauert.*
3. *Wenn Sie meine Hilfe brauchen, möchte ich helfen.*

ACTIVITY 8

Apology:
- *Tut mir leid, dass es etwas später als geplant geworden ist.*
- *Entschuldige.*
- *Glaub mir, das ist nicht meine Absicht.*
- *Sei bitte nicht böse.*
- *Ich weiß, und es tut mir wirklich leid.*

Reaction:
- *Eine Entschuldigung genügt nicht.*
- *Schon gut.*
- *Macht ja nichts.*

ACTIVITY 9

1. *Drei Mal. (Es tut mir sehr leid, dass ich gestern so spät nach Hause gekommen bin. Sei mir bitte nicht böse. Ich hoffe, dass du diese Blumen als Entschuldigung annehmen wirst.)*
2. *Er wurde im Büro aufgehalten.*
3. *Die Batterie in seinem Handy war leer.*
4. *Als Entschuldigung.*

ACTIVITY 10

1. c   2. d   3. d
4. b   5. a

ACTIVITY 11

*Wir haben Probleme mit dem Versand. Ich habe
mit meinem Chef gestern **darüber** gesprochen.
Worüber haben wir diskutiert? Ich will das Budget
erhöhen. Mein Chef hat auch schon **daran** gedacht.
Aber der Kunde wird nicht **damit** einverstanden
sein. In ein paar Wochen kann unsere Lieferfirma
wieder mehr arbeiten. Aber **darauf** können wir nicht
warten. Wir müssen also eine neue Lieferfirma
finden. Mein Chef hat mir **dabei** geholfen. **Dafür**
bin ich ihm sehr dankbar.*

THERE ARE TWO SIDES TO EVERYTHING

Jedes Ding hat seine zwei Seiten
(Lit. Every thing has its two sides)

COMING UP . . .

- *In my view:* **Expressing opinions**

- *Frankly, my dear:* **Interjections and conversation fillers**

- *Subordinate clauses:* **Conjunctions such as *weil, ob,* and question words**

- **Infinitives with *zu***

- *Schifffahrtsunternehmen:* **German compound nouns**

Good morning! Is there anything better than starting the day with a *Tasse Kaffee*, a *Brötchen* and the *Zeitung* (newspaper)? I'll have you know that more than 75% of German households have a daily newspaper delivered to their home. So it is safe to assume that most Germans are rather interested in *Politik* (politics). Indeed, Germans love discussing the *Tagesgeschehen* (daily events), which is presented *auf Seite 1* (on the front page) with family and friends, and sometimes even with strangers. But there are other *Themen* (topics) that may make you pick up a paper: you can read the *Kritik* (critique) of the latest *Theaterstück* (play) or the latest *Roman* (novel) in the *Feuilleton* (culture section), about *Fußball* (soccer) in the *Sportteil* (sports section), and about the *Börse* (stock market) in the *Wirtschaftsteil* (business section). My favorite section of the paper, however, is the *Leitartikel* (editorial). I just enjoy a good *Kommentar* (commentary).

ACTIVITY 1: LET'S WARM UP

Please match the two columns.

1. *Die Bundesligaergebnisse vom letzten Samstag findet man . . .*	a. *. . . im Leitartikel.*
2. *Eine Kritik des neuesten Romans von Günter Grass findet man . . .*	b. *. . . auf Seite 1.*
3. *Die besten Börsentips findet man . . .*	c. *. . . im Feuilleton.*
4. *Die interessantesten Artikel über Tagespolitik findet man . . .*	d. *. . . im Sportteil.*
5. *Den Kommentar findet man . . .*	e. *. . . im Wirtschaftsteil.*

HEAR . . . SAY 1

It's a typical morning at the Rotters' home. Husband and wife are enjoying a leisurely Saturday morning breakfast, relaxing with the paper and exchanging views on what they read.

Frau Rotter:	**Das darf doch wohl nicht wahr sein!**
Herr Rotter:	**Was denn?**
Frau Rotter:	**Stell dir vor, sie wollen das Wahlrecht für 16-Jährige einführen.**
Herr Rotter:	**Na und?**
Frau Rotter:	**Hältst du das etwa für eine gute Idee?**
Herr Rotter:	**Ja, warum denn nicht?**

Frau Rotter:	Ich finde, ein 16-Jähriger sollte noch nicht wählen, weil ein 16-Jähriger noch nicht genug vom Leben versteht.
Herr Rotter:	Also ich weiß ja nicht, ob Entscheidungen von älteren Leuten so viel besser sind. Das Leben ist so schnelllebig heutzutage. Ich frage mich, ob Jugendliche da nicht viel besser mithalten können.
Frau Rotter:	Das glaube ich nicht. Hast du dir schon einmal überlegt, ob Jugendliche reif genug sind für politische Entscheidungen?
Herr Rotter:	Alter allein ist doch kein gutes Argument.
Frau Rotter:	Nein, da stimme ich mit dir überein. Aber meiner Meinung nach denken Jugendliche viel zu viel an materielle Dinge. Sie interessieren sich doch noch gar nicht für Politik.
Herr Rotter:	Ich verstehe nicht, wie du so etwas sagen kannst. Dein eigener Sohn ist gerade mal fünfzehn Jahre alt, und wir diskutieren ständig mit ihm über Politik.
Frau Rotter:	Genau darum geht's mir doch. Willst du etwa, dass Werner mitentscheiden darf, wer Bundeskanzler wird?
Herr Rotter:	Hmm, wenn du die Sache so formulierst, sehe ich das Problem.

HOW'S THAT AGAIN?

Create complete sentences by matching the beginning of a sentence in the left column with its end in the right column. Make sure that the sentences correspond to the opinions expressed in the dialogues.

1. *Frau Rotter will nicht, . . .*

2. *Herr Rotter weiß nicht, . . .*

3. *Das Leben ändert sich so schnell, . . .*

4. *Frau Rotter findet, . . .*

5. *Der Sohn, Werner Rotter, zeigt großes Interesse an Politik, . . .*

6. *Herr Rotter will nicht, . . .*

a. *. . . wenn er mit seinen Eltern diskutiert.*

b. *. . . dass 16-Jährige nicht reif genug sind für politische Entscheidungen.*

c. *. . . ob Alter allein ein gutes Argument ist.*

d. *. . . dass sein Sohn Werner entscheidet, wer Bundeskanzler wird.*

e. *. . . dass Jugendliche besser mithalten können.*

f. *. . . dass das Wahlrecht für 16-Jährige eingeführt wird.*

WORKSHOP 1

WORDS TO LIVE BY

IN MY VIEW: EXPRESSING OPINIONS

Everybody has got an opinion, right? And since Germans enjoy a good political discussion, I believe you'll have ample opportunity to express yours. Here's how you introduce your opinion.

Ich finde/glaube, dass . . .	I think that . . .
Meiner Meinung/Ansicht nach . . .	In my opinion . . .

Here's how you can express disagreement.

Ich finde/glaube nicht, dass . . .	I don't think that . . .
Da bin ich anderer Meinung/Ansicht.	I have a different opinion. (Lit. I am of a different opinion.)
Ich sehe das anders.	I see that differently.

If you have trouble accepting something you've heard or read, you can say . . .

Das darf doch wohl nicht wahr sein.	This can't be true!
Das gibt's doch nicht!	This can't be!

A sharp difference of opinion could be expressed as follows:

Ich verstehe nicht, wie du so etwas sagen kannst.	I don't understand how you can say something like that.
Das kann doch nicht dein Ernst sein.	You can't be serious.

If, on the other hand, you agree, say . . .

Da stimme ich mit dir/Ihnen überein.	I agree with you on that.
Ich gebe dir/Ihnen recht.	I agree with you. (Lit. I give you right.)

If you don't quite agree, but want to make sure that the argument does not get too heated, use the following.

Schon, aber . . .	Of course, but . . .
Vielleicht, aber . . .	Maybe, but . . .
Ich weiß ja nicht, ob . . .	I don't know whether . . .

And if you are interested in other people's opinions and would like to start a discussion, ask . . .

Was halten Sie denn von . . . ?	What do you think of . . .
Wie finden Sie . . . ?	What do you think of . . .
Was sagen/meinen Sie dazu?	What do you say to that?

TAKE IT FOR A SPIN

What would you say? Choose one of the expressions introduced in the previous *Words to Live By* section to react to the situations below.

1. Your wife/husband has just told you that she/he has received yet another ticket for speeding. You can't believe it!

   _____

2. Your obvious annoyance with your wife/husband upon the ticket prompts her/him to say that you care more about the money the ticket costs than her/him. You don't understand how she/he can say that.

   _____

3. You calmly tell her/him that you see things differently.

   _____

4. You simply feel that it is dangerous to speed within city limits, and that she/he shouldn't do this any more. What, you wonder, does she/he say to that?

   _____

5. Your wife/husband, diplomat that she/he is, seems to agree with you at first, but then, of course she/he comes up with an outrageous excuse.
   _____, _____ *ich war so in Eile, weil ich dir dein Auto zurückbringen wollte. Eigentlich ist das alles deine Schuld.*

6. Your fault? You tell her that she can't be serious!

   _____

Did You Know?

There are numerous daily newspapers and magazines in Germany, Austria and Switzerland. In Germany there is the *Frankfurter Allgemeine Zeitung* (www.faz.de), the *Süddeutsche Zeitung* (www.sueddeutsche.de), *Die Zeit* (www.zeit.de). And then there is, of course, the tabloid *Bild* (www.bild.de). *Der Spiegel* (www.spiegel.de) focuses on political, social and economic news, and *Der Stern* (www.stern.de) is a color magazine focusing on culture and entertainment as well as politics. Other popular magazines include *FOCUS* (www.focus.de), *Brigitte* (www.brigitte.de), *Die BUNTE* (www.bunte.de), and *Freundin* (www.freundin.de). The best-known Swiss papers are the *Weltwoche* (www.weltwoche.ch) and the *Tages-Anzeiger* (www.tages-anzeiger.ch); many Austrians read *Die Kronenzeitung* (www.krone.at), *Der Standard* (www.standard.at) and *Der Wiener Kurier* (www.kurier.at).

SUBORDINATE CLAUSES: CONJUNCTIONS SUCH AS *OB, WEIL,* AND QUESTION WORDS

In lesson 13, we discussed subordinate clauses using *dass* (that) and *wenn* (if).

Willst du etwa, dass Werner mitentscheiden darf?	Do you really want Werner to be part of the decision process? (Lit. Do you really want that your son can decide this as well?)
Wenn du die Sache so formulierst, sehe ich das Problem.	If you phrase it like that I see the problem.

In addition to *wenn* (if, when) and *dass* (that), two other subordinating conjunctions are *weil* (because) and *ob* (whether).

Weil-sentences introduce the reason for a particular action described in the main clause. In other words, *weil* (because) answers the question *warum?* (why?).

Warum sollten 16-Jährige nicht wählen?	Why should sixteen-year-olds not vote?
Ein 16-Jähriger sollte noch nicht wählen, weil ein 16-Jähriger noch nicht genug vom Leben versteht.	A sixteen-year-old shouldn't vote because a sixteen-year-old doesn't understand enough about life yet.
Ein 16-Jähriger sollte noch nicht wählen, weil ein 16-Jähriger sich nicht für Politik interessiert.	A sixteen-year-old shouldn't vote because a sixteen-year-old isn't interested in politics.

Weil (because) can be replaced by *da* (because, as).

Jugendlich können vielleicht besser mithalten, da sich das Leben schnell ändert.	Teenagers may be better equipped to keep up, because life changes so quickly.

Ob-sentences are equivalent to the English *if-* or *whether*-sentences.

Ich weiß nicht, ob Entscheidungen von älteren Leuten so viel besser sind.	I don't know whether decisions of old people are that much better.
Ich frage mich, ob Jugendliche da nicht viel besser mithalten können.	I wonder if teenagers can't keep up better.
Hast du dir überlegt, ob Jugendliche reif sind für politische Entscheidungen?	Have you thought about whether teenagers are ready for political decisions?

It is also possible to form subordinate clauses with question words such as *warum* (why), *wer* (who), *wann* (when), *wie* (how), *wo* (where).

Ich verstehe nicht, wie du so etwas sagen kannst.	I don't understand how you can say something like that.
Soll dein Sohn mitentscheiden, wer Bundeskanzler wird?	Should your son decide who becomes chancellor?
Ich weiß nicht, wann die Wahlen stattfinden.	I don't know when the elections will take place.

As in *wenn*- and *dass*-sentences, the verb in all other subordinate clauses moves to the final position.

Jugendliche können besser mithalten. Teenagers can keep up better.

Ich weiß nicht, ob Jugendliche besser I don't know whether teenagers can keep up better.
mithalten können.

TAKE IT FOR A SPIN

Please connect the sentences using any of the following subordinate conjunctions: *dass*, *wenn*, *weil*, *ob*, or question words.

1. *Ich weiß es nicht. Jugendliche sind reif für politische Entscheidungen.*
2. *Verstehst du das? Wie kann er so etwas glauben?*
3. *Wer soll entscheiden? Wer wird Bundeskanzler?*
4. *Ältere Menschen können besser Entscheidungen treffen. Sie haben genug gelernt.*
5. *Ich bin der Meinung. Jugendliche sollen nicht wählen.*
6. *Jugendliche interessieren sich nicht für Politik. Sie denken an materielle Dinge.*

HEAR . . . SAY 2

Jedes Ding hat seine zwei Seiten. I'd be curious to hear what the Rotters' son, Werner, thinks about the *Wahlrecht* (right to vote) for sixteen-year-olds. Wouldn't you? It just so happens that Werner is taking part in a *Meinungsumfrage* (opinion poll) among teenagers about this very subject.

Fragesteller:	**Hast du Lust, an einer Umfrage teilzunehmen?**
Werner:	**Kommt darauf an, worum es geht.**
Fragesteller:	**Es geht um das Wahlrecht für 16-Jährige. Die Frage ist, was du davon hältst.**
Werner:	**Ich halte das für eine gute Idee.**
Fragesteller:	**Interessant. Und warum das?**
Werner:	**Na, was die Politiker entscheiden, betrifft uns ja auch. Also sollten wir auch die Politiker wählen dürfen. Oder etwa nicht?**
Fragesteller:	**Glaubst du denn, genug Erfahrung zu haben, um solche Entscheidungen treffen zu können?**

Werner:	Also ehrlich, nur weil jemand Erfahrung hat, heißt das doch nicht, dass er gute Entscheidungen trifft. Mein Vater, zum Beispiel, hat trotz seines Alters schon manchen Bock geschossen.
Fragesteller:	Ich verstehe. Eine gute Entscheidung ist also keine Altersfrage. Wovon hängt eine gute Entscheidung dann ab?
Werner:	Das ist doch ganz klar Ansichtssache.
Fragesteller:	Wie meinst du das?
Werner:	Ob etwas eine gute Entscheidung ist oder nicht kommt doch darauf an, wie man das sieht. Ich meine, es kommt auf deine Meinung an, ob etwas gut oder schlecht ist. Meinungssache eben. Und deshalb sollte man in einer Wahl auch ganz viele Meinungen hören. Auch die von ganz jungen Leuten.
Fragesteller:	Ich muss zugeben, das ist ein gutes Argument. Und du glaubst für diese Verantwortung reif zu sein?
Werner:	Noch nicht, aber ich plane, mit der Verantwortung zu wachsen.

ACTIVITY 5: HOW'S THAT AGAIN?

Do you think Werner would agree or disagree? Answer based on what he said in the dialogue above.

	WERNER AGREES	WERNER DISAGREES
1. *Jugendliche heutzutage interessieren sich nicht für Politik.*	_____	_____
2. *Politiker treffen Entscheidungen, die für Jugendliche wichtig sind.*	_____	_____
3. *Gute Entscheidungen kommen mit dem Alter.*	_____	_____
4. *Ob Jugendliche wählen sollen, ist Meinungssache.*	_____	_____
5. *Jugendliche sollten nicht wählen dürfen, weil sie noch nicht reif genug sind für die Verantwortung.*	_____	_____
6. *Es ist wichtig, dass Politiker viele Meinungen hören.*	_____	_____
7. *Mit Verantwortung wächst man.*	_____	_____

When Werner claims that his father *hat schon manchen Bock geschossen,* he does not mean that his father has literally, "shot many a deer buck," but rather that his father "has dropped many a clanger." The *Bock* (deer buck) is part of several other German phrases that are used rather frequently. If you have *null Bock* (Lit. zero deer buck), then you absolutely don't feel like doing anything. If you make *den Bock zum Gärtner* (Lit. making the deer buck the gardener), you are asking for trouble. And *ein sturer Bock* is "a stubborn old devil."

Did You Know?

The most important political parties in Germany are the *SPD* (*Sozialdemokratische Partei Deutschlands* [Social Democratic Party of Germany]), the *Grüne/Bündnis 90* (the Green Party/Coalition 90), *CDU* (*Christlich-Demokratische Union* [Christian Democratic Union]), *CSU* (*Christlisch-Soziale Union* [Christian Social Union]), *FDP* (*Freie Demokratische Partei* [Free Democratic Party]), and the *PDS* (*Partei des Demokratischen Sozialismus* [Party of Democratic Socialism]). The *SPD* is the party traditionally catering to the left wing, carrying a platform favoring the working class. The party's agenda was pushed to the center when throughout the 1980s the *Grünen* became more and more popular among liberals with their environmental platform. The final push towards the center took place when the *Bündnis 90* and the *PDS,* two former socialist East German parties received a huge number of votes in the Eastern states during the first elections of a reunited Germany in 1990/91. The *CDU* and the *FDP* have traditionally represented the interests of business. Due to the fact that any party who receives at least 5% of the vote is represented in the parliament, many elections in Germany have resulted in a *Koalitionsregierung* (coalition government) of at least two parties to enjoy a majority in the parliament.

WORKSHOP 2

WORDS TO LIVE BY

FRANKLY, MY DEAR: INTERJECTIONS AND CONVERSATION FILLERS

Even the most serious political discussion can be lightened up with a few interjections and conversation fillers. Some of them simply refer back to what the person has said before. They show you are listening and are willing to accept what has been said.

Interessant.	Interesting.
Ich verstehe.	I understand.
Zugegeben.	Admittedly.
Sicherlich/ohne Frage.	Without a doubt.

Others are meant to elicit a comment by your opponent.

Oder etwa nicht?	Or do you disagree?
Wie meinst du das?	What do you mean? (Lit. How do you mean?)

Yet others comment on what you are about to say.

Na, . . .	Well,
Also ehrlich, . . .	Frankly/Honestly . . .
Also bitte, . . .	Please . . .
Um ehrlich zu sein, . . .	To be honest . . .
Wenn ich ehrlich bin, . . .	If I am honest . . .

And then there are the ones, which simply liven up the conversation.

zum Beispiel	for example
übrigens	by the way

ACTIVITY 6: **TAKE IT FOR A SPIN**

Fill in the blanks using the choices provided: *zum Beispiel, zugegeben, Na, Ich verstehe, Um ehrlich zu sein, Entschuldigung, eigentlich*

1. _____, hättest du Lust, an der Umfrage teilzunehmen. Die Frage ist, ob Jugendliche wählen sollen.
2. *Nein,* _____ *möchte ich an der Umfrage nicht teilnehmen.*
3. _____. *Warum denn nicht?*
4. _____, *interessiert mich die Frage nicht.*
5. _____, *die Frage klingt langweilig, aber die Ergebnisse werden uns viel über Jugendliche sagen.*
6. *Was denn,* _____?
7. _____, *zum Beispiel werden wir lernen ob sich Jugendliche überhaupt für Politik interessieren.*

Did You Know?

Das Wahlrecht (right to vote) is one of the rights protected by the *Grundgesetz der Bundesrepublik Deutschland* (German Constitution [Lit. Basic Law of the Federal Republic of Germany]) which came into force in 1949, originally as a temporary measure in West Germany only. When in 1990 Germany was reunited, the *Grundgesetz* was retained since people's trust in it had become so great. The first sentence of the *Grundgesetz* reads: *Die Würde des Menschen ist unantastbar.* (The dignity of every individual is sacred). Some other *Grundrechte* (basic rights) are: *Presse- und Meinungsfreiheit* (freedom of opinion and press), *Versammlungsfreiheit* (right to assembly [Lit. freedom of assembly]), *Religionsfreiheit* (freedom of religion), *Gleichheit aller vor* dem Gesetz (equality before the law), *Eigentumsrecht* (right to possession). **For changes to be made to the** *Grundgesetz,* **a two-third majority of the members of the** *Bundesrat* **(Congress) and** *Bundestag* **(Senate) is needed. If citizens consider any of their rights as laid down in the** *Grundgesetz* **violated, they can ask for independent arbitration by the** *Bundesverfassungsgericht* **(Federal Constitutional Court).**

THE NITTY GRITTY

INFINITIVES WITH *ZU*

While *dass*-sentences require a subject, infinitive constructions with *zu* never have a subject, but relate to the subject and action of the introductory main clause.

Hast du Lust, an einer Umfrage teilzunehmen?	Do you feel like taking part in an opinion poll?
Glaubst du denn, genug Erfahrung zu haben?	Do you believe to have enough experience?
Und du glaubst für diese Verantwortung reif zu sein?	And you believe to be ready for such a reponsibility?
Ich plane, mit der Verantwortung zu wachsen.	I plan to grow with the responsibility.

Constructions with *um* followed by *zu* and the infinitive are comparable to the English "in order to."

Und du glaubst, genug Erfahrung zu haben, um solche Entscheidungen treffen zu können?	And you believe to have enough experience in order to make such decisions?

Just like any infinitive with *zu, um . . . zu* demands that main and subordinate clauses share the same subject.

Um gute Entscheidungen zu treffen, muss ich nicht alt sein.	In order to make good decision, you don't have to be old.

Ohne . . . zu and *anstatt . . . zu* are two other infinitive constructions.

Er wählt, ohne sich für Politik zu interessieren.	He votes without being interested in politics.
Jugendliche interessieren sich für materielle Dinge, anstatt sich für Politik zu interessieren.	Teenagers are interested in material things instead of being interested in politics.

THE FINE PRINT

I'm sure you've noticed already that all subordinate clauses are separated from their main clauses by a comma in German. Unlike in English, this is true even for *dass*-sentences and infinitive constructions with *zu*.

TAKE IT FOR A SPIN

Answer the questions with an infinitive construction.

1. *Wozu glaubt Frau Rotter sind 16-Jährige zu jung?*
2. *Wozu glaubt der Fragesteller braucht man Erfahrung?*
3. *Werner glaubt wozu reif zu sein?*

TAKE IT UP A NOTCH

Go to the website of any of the newspapers mentioned above and find at least five sentences with an infinitive construction with *zu*, and write them down. Then consult the *Crib Notes* for further discussion.

COMPOUND NOUNS

Having looked at the newspaper article you have probably noticed that the German language likes putting long nouns together to make an even longer one. A new noun, made by combing two or more nouns, is called a compound noun. For example:

die Wahl + **das Recht** = **das Wahlrecht** (right to vote, from "election + right")

Please note that the second noun dictates the gender of the compound noun.

die Presse + **die Freiheit** = **die Pressefreiheit** (freedom of the press)
die Wirtschaft + **der Teil** = **der Wirtschaftsteil** (business section)

Many of the compound nouns have a possessive connection, which could be expressed by using the genitive case: *das Geschehen des Tages* (the events of the day). The possessive connection is often still noticeable in a compound noun by the possessive *-s-* that attaches to the first word in the compound:

der Tag + **das Geschehen** = **das Tagesgeschehen** (current events [Lit. events of the day])
die Zeitung + **der Artikel** = **der Zeitungsartikel** (newspaper article)

TAKE IT FOR A SPIN

Create the compound.

1. *die Meinung + die Umfrage =*
2. *die Religion + die Freiheit =*
3. *der Fußball + der Fan =*

Find the individual parts of these compounds.

4. *die Ansichtssache =*
5. *die Altersfrage =*
6. *das Theaterstück =*

TAKE IT FOR A SPIN

Go back to the same website you visited when doing *Activity 8*. Find at least five compound nouns and write them down. Then consult the *Crib Notes* for further discussion.

THE FINE PRINT

One of the most curious German spelling rules requires that a compound word retains all individual letters, even when they are identical, in order to keep the words making the compound noun intact. Here's what happens:

das Schiff + die Fahrt = die Schifffahrt (cruise)

No, this is NOT a mistake. German is probably the only language that allows three identical consonants to meet. Here are a few other examples:

schnell + lebig = schnelllebig (fast-paced)
der Schluss + der Satz = der Schlusssatz (final sentence)

If this rule seems too, well, curious, you can also use a hyphen: *der Schluss-Satz*. If the compound consists of two nouns joined by a hyphen, capitalize both.

CRIB NOTES

Mrs. Rotter:	This can't be true!
Mr. Rotter:	What?
Mrs. Rotter:	Imagine, they want to implement the right to vote for sixteen-year-olds.
Mr. Rotter:	So what?
Mrs. Rotter:	Don't tell me you think this is a good idea?
Mr. Rotter:	Well, why not?
Mrs. Rotter:	I think a sixteen-year-old shouldn't vote, because a sixteen-year-old doesn't know enough about life.
Mr. Rotter:	Well, I don't know whether decisions by older people are that much better. Life is so fast-paced these days. I wonder whether teenagers can't keep up much better.
Mrs. Rotter:	I don't think so. Have you ever wondered whether teenagers are mature enough for political decisions?
Mr. Rotter:	Age alone is not a good argument.
Mrs. Rotter:	No, I agree with you there. But in my opinion, teenagers think about material things way too much. They are not interested in politics.
Mr. Rotter:	I don't understand how you can say such a thing. Your own son is barely 15 years old, and we constantly are discussing politics with him.
Mrs. Rotter:	My point exactly. Do you really want Werner to be allowed to help decide who becomes the new chancellor?
Mr. Rotter:	Hmm, if you phrase it that way I can see the problem.

Interviewer:	Do you feel like taking part in an opinion poll?
Werner:	That depends on what it is about.
Interviewer:	It is about the right to vote for sixteen-year-olds. The question is, what you think about it.
Werner:	I think that's a good idea.
Interviewer:	Interesting. And why is that?
Werner:	Well, politicians decide matters that concern us as well. So we should be allowed to vote for them. Don't you think?
Interviewer:	Do you believe to have enough experience in order to make such decisions?
Werner:	Honestly, just because you have experience doesn't mean that you make good decisions. My father, for example, has made many a mistake despite his age.
Interviewer:	I understand. A good decision is not a question of age. What does a good decision depend on?
Werner:	That is clearly a matter of point of view.
Interviewer:	What do you mean?
Werner:	Whether a decision is good or not depends on how you see it. I mean, it depends on your opinion whether something is good or bad. A matter of opinion, simply put. And that's why during an election many opinions should be heard. Even those of relatively young people.
Interviewer:	I have to admit that this is a good argument. And you believe to be ready for this responsibility?
Werner:	Not yet. But I am planning to grow with the responsibility.

ACTIVITY 1

1. d 2. c 3. e
4. b 5. a

ACTIVITY 2

1. f 2. c 3. e
4. b 5. a 6. d

ACTIVITY 3

1. *Das gibt's doch nicht!*
2. *Ich verstehe nicht, wie du so etwas sagen kannst.*
3. *Ich sehe das anders.*
4. *Was sagst du dazu?*
5. *Schon, aber ich war so in Eile, weil ich dir dein Auto zurückbringen wollte. Eigentlich ist das alles deine Schuld.*
6. *Das kann doch nicht dein Ernst sein!*

ACTIVITY 4

1. *Ich weiß nicht, ob Jugendliche reif für politische Entscheidungen sind.*
2. *Verstehst du, wie er so etwas glauben kann?*
3. *Wer soll entscheiden, wer Bundeskanzler wird?*
4. *Ältere Menschen können besser Entscheidungen treffen, weil sie genug gelernt haben.*
5. *Ich bin der Meinung, dass Jugendliche nicht wählen sollen.*
6. *Jugendliche interessieren sich nicht für Politik, weil sie an materielle Dinge denken.*

ACTIVITY 5

1. Werner disagrees.
2. Werner agrees.
3. Werner disagrees.
4. Werner agrees.
5. Werner disagrees.
6. Werner agrees.
7. Werner agrees.

ACTIVITY 6

1. *Entschuldigung, hättest du Lust, an der Umfrage teilzunehmn. Die Frage ist, ob Jugendliche wählen sollen.*
2. *Nein, eigentlich möchte ich an der Umfrage nicht teilnehmen.*
3. *Ich verstehe. Warum denn nicht?*
4. *Um ehrlich zu sein, interessiert mich die Frage nicht.*
5. *Zugegeben, die Frage klingt langweilig, aber die Ergebnisse werden uns viel über Jugendliche sagen.*
6. *Was denn, zum Beispiel*
7. *Na, zum Beispiel werden wir lernen ob sich Jugendliche überhaupt für Politik interessieren.*

ACTIVITY 7

1. *Frau Rotter glaubt, 16-Jährige sind zu jung, um zu wählen.*
2. *Der Fragesteller glaubt, man braucht Erfahrung, um gute Entscheidungen zu treffen.*
3. *Werner glaubt, für die Verantwortung reif zu sein.*

ACTIVITY 8

Have you found five sentences using an infinitive construction with *zu?* Have you written them down? Do they simply use *zu,* or are they constructions with *um . . . zu* or *ohne . . . zu* or *anstatt . . . zu?* How would you translate these sentences? Can you use an infinitive in English as well, or is it better to use the *-ing* form?

ACTIVITY 9

1. *die Meinung + die Umfrage = die Meinungsumfrage*
2. *die Religion + die Freiheit = die Religionsfreiheit*
3. *der Fußball + der Fan = der Fußballfan*
4. *die Ansichtssache = die Ansicht + die Sache*
5. *die Altersfrage = das Alter + die Frage*
6. *das Theaterstück = das Theater + das Stück*

ACTIVITY 10

Have you found 5 compound nouns? Have you written them down? What are their individual parts? Look up the meaning of their individual parts in the dictionary, and then see if you can find the meaning of the compound noun in there as well.

TO EACH HIS OWN

Jedem Tierchen sein Pläsierchen
(Lit. To every little animal its little pleasure)

- *I won't take no for an answer:* How to convince and (not) be convinced

- *You are so beautiful!* Paying compliments and accepting them gracefully

- *Coordinating conjunctions: aber, und,* and *oder*

- *When you're ill, you've got an illness:* Word formation

- Alternatives to the passive voice

LOOKING AHEAD . . .

Tastes are different. What's your favorite *Freizeitbeschäftigung* (pastime)? Are you the type that enjoys listening to *Musik* (music), and if so, do you prefer *Jazz* (jazz) or *klassische Musik* (classical music), or do you go for a good *Oper* (opera)? If the latter, do you prefer Wagner (Germany) or Mozart (Austria)? Or maybe you'd rather spend an afternoon at a *Kunstmuseum* (art museum) to check out a *Bild* (painting) by Klimt (Austria) or Dürer (Germany) or Klee (Switzerland)? And if you are a *Leseratte* (bookworm [Lit. reading rat]), would you rather spend time with Goethe or Günther Grass? Yes, Germany, Austria and Switzerland have plenty of *hohe Kunst* (high art) to offer. But believe it or not, not all of us are all that serious. We have as much taste for *Massenkultur* (mass culture) as do the Americans. Personally, I like going to the *Kino* (cinema). And not only to watch Wim Wenders and Fassbinder. No, I like watching *Komödien* (comedies) or *Krimis* (thrillers). And I also have a weakness for soap operas . . . The very first German *Seifenoper* (soap opera) was *Gute Zeiten–Schlechte Zeiten* (Good Times–Bad Times) and started its daily TV-broadcast in 1992. Check it out. It is *unschlagbar* (unbeatable)!

ACTIVITY 1: LET'S WARM UP

How would you categorize the following items?

	HOHE KUNST	MASSENKULTUR
1. The highly popular German *Fernsehkrimiserie DERRICK*, which dishes out easily digestible morals on the good, the bad and the rich every Friday evening.	_____	_____
2. Mozart's *Oper DIE ZAUBERFLÖTE* (The Magic Flute) and Wagner's *Oper DER FLIEGENDE HOLLÄNDER* (The Flying Dutchman)	_____	_____
3. Any old *Lied* (song) by *ERSTE ALLGEMEINE VERUNSICHERUNG*, an Austrian pop group taking a satirical look at political and social issues.	_____	_____
4. The German *Tageszeitung BILD*.	_____	_____
5. The works of the Swiss *Lyriker* (poet) C.F. Meyer.	_____	_____

Remember how Gabriele and Sebastian, our friends from Lesson 1, met? Right, they bumped into each other, Sebastian tried out a few *erfolglose* (unsuccessful) pick-up lines, and then they discovered that they have *etwas gemeinsam*. What was it again? Oh, right. They are both dentists. And remember how *unvorstellbar* (unimaginable) it seemed for you at the time to ever speak a complete German sentence? Look how far you've come! And let's see how far they've come. Sebastian is calling Gabriele to make plans for this evening.

Sebastian:	Hallo, Gabriele. Was gibt's Neues?
Gabriele:	Nicht viel.
Sebastian:	Was hast du denn heute abend vor?
Gabriele:	Eigentlich wollte ich zu Hause bleiben und ein bisschen fernsehen.
Sebastian:	Fernsehen? Aber es ist doch Freitagabend. Da geht man doch aus!
Gabriele:	Man vielleicht. Ich nicht. Beim Fernsehen kann ich mich am besten entspannen.
Sebastian:	Zur Entspannung habe ich genau das richtige. Wie wär's mit einem romantischen Abendessen in einem fabelhaften Restaurant, gefolgt von einem unvergesslichen Theaterbesuch oder einem anregenden Besuch in einem Jazzlokal?
Gabriele:	Das klingt zwar unwiderstehlich, aber ich bin einfach zu müde, um etwas zu unternehmen.
Sebastian:	Komm schon, Gabriele, sei doch kein Spielverderber.
Gabriele:	Nein, wirklich nicht, Sebastian. Ein anderes Mal vielleicht.
Sebastian:	Schade. Heißt das etwa, dass ich mein Dasein heute ganz alleine fristen muss?
Gabriele:	(laughs) Sieht so aus.
Sebastian:	Und wie wär's, wenn ich beim Italiener vorbeifahre und uns eine Pizza hole?
Gabriele:	Du lässt dich wohl nicht abwimmeln. . . .
Sebastian:	Nein . . . zur Pizza könnte ich uns auch ein Video ausleihen. Wim Wenders vielleicht . . .
Gabriele:	Alles, nur kein Wim Wenders. Aber wenn du Lust hast, mit mir fernzusehen, lasse ich mich vielleicht zu einer Pizza überreden.
Sebastian:	Was kommt denn im Fernsehen?
Gabriele:	Tatort. Mit Schimanski.

Sebastian:	Ach herrje. Du glaubst also, dass ich ruhig zuschaue, wie du einen anderen Mann anhimmelst?
Gabriele:	Genau.
Sebastian:	Mit mir kann man's ja machen. Also gut, ich bin in einer halben Stunde bei dir.
Gabriele:	Mit der Pizza, hoffentlich . . .

WORD ON THE STREET

Jemanden anhimmeln (Lit. to gaze skywards at somebody) means "to gaze at somebody adoringly" or "to swoon over somebody." *Jemanden anbeten* (Lit. to pray to somebody) can be used similarly: *Ich bete ihn an.* I absolutely adore him.

ACTIVITY 2: HOW'S THAT AGAIN?

Sounds like Sebastian has his work cut out for him with Gabriele. Or do you think she is just playing hard to get? Please answer the questions.

1. *Was will Sebastian zum Abendessen machen?*
2. *Welche Aktivitäten schlägt er nach dem Abendessen vor?*
3. *Und was will Gabriele machen?*
4. *Warum?*
5. *Was machen Sie schließlich?*
6. *Wen wird Gabriele wohl anhimmeln: Schimanski oder Sebastian?*

WORKSHOP 1

WORDS TO LIVE BY

I WON'T TAKE NO FOR AN ANSWER: HOW TO CONVINCE AND (NOT) BE CONVINCED

People will make suggestions to you all the time. The expressions you'll hear most often when they do is . . .

Wie wär's mit . . . ?	How about . . . ?

And sometimes people will try to be very convincing

Komm schon.	Come on.
Sei kein Spielverderber.	Don't be a spoilsport.
Ich habe genau das Richtige.	I have just the (right) thing.

WORD ON THE STREET

A *Spielverderber* is a "spoilsport," *Muffel* is a grouch, and a *Miesepeter* is a killjoy. All three terms are acceptable among friends and family. But it is not advisable to use them with your office colleagues.

Say no, but do it politely . . .

Das klingt zwar . . . , aber . . .	It sounds really . . . , but . . .
Nein, wirklich nicht.	No, really, I can't.

And a few handy excuses are . . .

Ich bin zu müde.	I am too tired.
Ich habe zu viel zu tun.	I have too much to do.
Es ist zu spät.	It's too late.
Eigentlich wollte ich . . .	I actually had planned to . . .

Why don't you let them off easy with a ray of hope.

Ein anderes Mal vielleicht.	Another time, perhaps.

And if they just won't leave you in peace and you agree grudgingly . . .

Du lässt dich wohl nicht abwimmeln.	You won't be turned away, will you?
Also gut.	Oh, OK.
Wenn es denn sein muss.	If I have to. (Lit. If it has to be.)
Mit mir kann man's ja machen!	The things I put up with! (Lit. You can do it with me!)

ACTIVITY 3: **TAKE IT FOR A SPIN**

How would you respond? It is time not only to practice your German language skills, but also to test your personality. First, fill in the blanks with the appropriate German phrase, and then decide which one you would most likely use in such a situation.

1. It is Friday evening after a hectic work week. You are looking forward to a quiet evening at home with your favorite TV show. Your best friend calls, asking you to go dancing with her. Do you . . .
   a. . . . tell her that you have too much to do?

   _____

   b. . . . tell her the truth and tell her that you actually wanted to stay at home and watch TV?

   _____

   c. . . . tell her that you'd be willing to go some other time?

   _____

2. It is Sunday morning and you are still in bed. Your mother calls, asking you to come with her to visit your Aunt Klara. Do you . . .
   a. . . . act as if you can't hear her, claiming that your phone is broken?

   _____

   b. . . . grudgingly agree and tell your mother how much you put up with?

   _____

   c. . . . try to get out of it by claiming that it sounds irresistible, but that you'd rather go some other time?

   _____

3. The man/woman of your dreams calls to ask you to go out on a date, but you have a very bad hair day. Do you . . .
   a. . . . tell him/her that you are too tired and only go out on Saturdays?

   _____

   b. . . . admit your problem and tell him/her that you absolutely can't go out that day?

   _____

   c. . . . thank him/her for his call, and ask him/her if you can call him/her back the next day?

   _____

Did You Know?

Even though some (uninformed) people might argue that a German comedy is a contradiction in terms, some of the most successful German movies ever made were comedies: Doris Dörrie's *Männer* (Men) in 1985, Katja von Garnier's *Abgeschminkt* (No Make-up) in 1993, Sönke Wortmann's *Der bewegte Mann* (Maybe . . . Maybe Not) in 1994, and Tom Tykwer's *Lola rennt* (Run, Lola, Run) in 1999. And then, of course, there's the old master of comedy, Billy Wilder (1906–2002), who emigrated from his native Austria in 1933 to become famous in the United States with movies such as 1959's *Some Like It Hot,* which is *Manche mögen's heiß* in German. So, take a trip to the video store and have a laugh—in German!

THE NITTY GRITTY

COORDINATING CONJUNCTIONS: *ABER, UND,* AND *ODER*

In the last two lessons you learned the subordinating conjunctions such as *dass, ob, weil,* and *wenn,* which link a main clause with a subordinate clause. Coordinating conjunctions are, on the other hand, used to connect two main, or independent, clauses. The coordinating conjunctions include *aber* (but, however), *und* (and), *oder* (or), *sondern* (but, on the contrary), and *denn* (because). They do not affect word order, and are generally separated by a comma.

Das klingt zwar unwiderstehlich, aber ich bin einfach zu müde, um etwas zu unternehmen.	That sounds irresistible, but I am too tired to do anything tonight.

No comma is used before *und* and *oder* if the subject is the same in both clauses and is not mentioned a second time.

Ich bleibe zu Hause und sehe fern.	I'll stay home and watch TV.
Wie wär's mit einem romantischen Abendessen oder mit einem unvergesslichen Theaterbesuch?	How about a romantic dinner or an unforgettable visit to the theater?

Sondern is used after a negative sentence only, to mean "but," "rather," or "on the contrary."

Ich will nicht fernsehen, sondern ins Kino gehen.	I don't want to watch TV, rather (I want) to go to the movies.

When *denn* replaces *weil* to connect two main clauses, the word order remains the same.

Ich will nicht essen gehen, denn ich bin zu müde.	I don't want to go out for dinner because I am too tired.

If you use *weil*, the verb moves to the final position as it does in subordinate clauses.

Ich will nicht essen gehen, weil ich zu müde bin.

ACTIVITY 4: **TAKE IT FOR A SPIN**

Please connect the sentences using the coordinating conjunctions in parentheses.

1. *Ich will zu Hause bleiben. Ich will fernsehen.* (and)
2. *Willst du ins Kino gehen? Willst du ein Video ausleihen?* (or)
3. *Das klingt prima. Ich bin zu müde.* (but)
4. *Ich möchte nicht essen gehen. Ich möchte eine Pizza holen.* (but)
5. *Sebastian will nicht fernsehen. Sebastian will Schimanski nicht anhimmeln.* (because)

WHEN YOU'RE ILL, YOU'VE GOT AN ILLNESS: **WORD FORMATION**

Often words from different word groups, an adjective and a noun, for example, may share the same root and therefore be related in meaning. Look at the English "ill" and "illness," for example. The same relationships between words can happen in German: *krank* (ill) and *die Krankheit* (illness). Let's look at some of the rules that help order the chaos of word formation.

FROM VERB TO NOUN

You can create a noun from a verb by adding the suffix *-ung* to the stem. All nouns ending in *-ung* are feminine and form their plural with *-en*.

> *wohnen* (to live, to reside) → *die Wohnung* (apartment)
> *wandern* (to hike) → *die Wanderung* (hike)

Verbs ending in *-ieren* usually form nouns with *-ion* suffixes.

> *informieren* (to inform) → *die Information* (information)
> *diskutieren* (to discuss) → *die Diskussion* (discussion)

Exceptions are:

> *reservieren* (to reserve) → *die Reservierung* (reservations)
> *respektieren* (to respect) → *der Respekt* (respect)

FROM ADJECTIVE TO NOUN

Many adjectives can be used as nouns in German if an article is used before them. The noun ending, which is that of the corresponding adjective, denotes the case, number, and gender, just like an adjective would. If the nouns are general and descriptive, they are usually neuter.

> *Zur Entspannung habe ich genau das Richtige.* — I know just the thing to relax you. (Lit. I have just the right thing for relaxation.)
> *Was gibt's Neues?* — What's new?

You can also create a noun from an adjective by adding the suffix *-heit* or *-keit*. Such nouns are usually feminine.

> *krank* (ill) → *die Krankheit* (illness)
> *schön* (beautiful) → *die Schönheit* (beauty)
> *sauber* (clean) → *die Sauberkeit* (cleanliness)
> *sicher* (safe, secure) → *die Sicherheit* (safety, security)
> *müde* (tired) → *die Müdigkeit* (tiredness)

FROM NOUN TO ADJECTIVE

You can create an adjective from a noun by adding the suffixes *-los* or *-haft*. *-los* usually means "without (a given property)," while *-haft* means "with (a given property)."

die Fabel (fable) → *fabelhaft* (fabulous)
das Kind (child) → *kindhaft* (childish)
das Ende (end) → *endlos* (endless)
der Kopf (head) → *kopflos* (headless)

FROM VERB TO ADJECTIVE

You can create an adjective from a verb by adding the suffix *-bar* or *-haft* to the verb stem. *-bar* is similar in meaning to the English "-able."

machen (to make, to do) → *machbar* (doable)
tragen (to carry) → *tragbar* (carryable)
glauben (to believe) → *glaubhaft* (believable)

FROM POSITIVE TO NEGATIVE

As in English, the prefix *un-* gives a word a negative or opposite meaning.

widerstehlich (resistable) → *unwiderstehlich* (irresistable)
interessant (interesting) → *uninteressant* (uninteresting)
ruhig (calm) → *unruhig* (restless)
sicher (safe, secure) → *unsicher* (unsafe, insecure)

Heads Up!

The difference a single letter makes: Don't mix up *wieder* (again) and *wider* (against, contrary to). *Wiederholen* means "to repeat," *widersprechen*, on the other hand, means "to contradict" and *widerrufen* "to deny, to cancel."

ACTIVITY 5: TAKE IT FOR A SPIN

Create all the words you can from the ones listed below.

1. *interessant*
2. *krank*
3. *glauben*
4. *widerstehlich*
5. *schön*
6. *müde*
7. *das Ende*

8. *vergessen*
9. *romantisch*
10. *essen*
11. *sicher*

Did You Know?

Everyone knows about Johann Wolfgang von Goethe and Richard Wagner, but there's a lighter side even to German literature and music. Look up Friedrich Dürrenmatt (born in Bern in 1921), a Swiss writer mostly known for satirical plays commenting on the ills of modern-day society, who wrote a great crime story called *Der Richter und sein Henker* (The Judge and His Henchman). And the Austrian pop group *Erste Allgemeine Verunsicherung* (First General Insecurity) has become famous all over the German-speaking world with comical and sometimes non-sensical songs about love, money, politics, society, and just about everything that is relevant in modern-day society. Check them out. They are great!

Now, let's see how Sebastian's and Gabriele's evening progresses.

HEAR . . . SAY 2

Sebastian has just arrived at Gabriele's doorstep with the pizza. Gabriele opens the door.

Sebastian:	Hallo, meine Liebe. Hier bin ich.
Gabriele:	Hallo. Komm doch bitte herein.
Sebastian:	Hier ist die Pizza.
Gabriele:	Mmmm. Die sieht aber gut aus.
Sebastian:	Mmmm. Du auch. (In response to her questioning look) Ich meine, du siehst sehr hübsch aus. Wie immer.
Gabriele:	Vielen Dank.
Sebastian:	Das blaue T-Shirt unterstreicht die Farbe deiner Augen.
Gabriele:	Danke. Wie lieb von dir, das zu sagen.
Sebastian:	Bitte, gern geschehen. Und die Jeans bringen deine Figur gut zur Geltung.
Gabriele:	(in a mock frown) Jetzt trägst du aber ein bisschen dick auf, findest du nicht?
Sebastian:	Ganz und gar nicht. Und außerdem weiß ich, dass du meine Komplimente gerne hörst.
Gabriele:	(laughs) Das ist natürlich schwer zu leugnen. Kann ich dir etwas zu trinken anbieten?

Sebastian:	Und eine hervorragende Gastgeberin bist du auch. Was will man mehr?
Gabriele:	Etwas zu trinken, vielleicht?
Sebastian:	Ach ja, richtig. Ein Glas Rotwein, bitte.
Gabriele:	Hier.
Sebastian:	Diese Gläser sind sehr elegant. Sie zeugen von gutem Geschmack.
Gabriele:	Sebastian, willst du mich auf den Arm nehmen? So viele Komplimente sind nicht ernst zu nehmen.
Sebastian:	(smiling) Vielleicht nicht, aber sonst kann ich doch mit Schimanski gar nicht mithalten.
Gabriele:	Was? Ach herrje. Jetzt ist die Pizza auch noch kalt geworden. Du bringst mich ganz durcheinander.
Sebastian:	Das freut mich zu hören. Und die Pizza kann man doch sicher aufwärmen.
Gabriele:	Ja, natürlich, das läßt sich machen.
Sebastian:	Übrigens, das Kompliment mit der hervorragenden Gastgeberin läßt sich nicht mehr aufrecht erhalten . . .

WORD ON THE STREET

The phrase *dick auftragen* is used just like its English equivalent "to lay it on thick." It is used among family and friends. Among people you are not on familiar terms with, you might simply use the verb *übertreiben* (to exaggerate): *Jetzt übertreiben Sie aber!* (Now you are exaggerating!)

ACTIVITY 6: HOW'S THAT AGAIN?

Let's go on a search and rescue operation. Take a piece of paper and draw two columns on it. Then listen to the dialogue, paying particular attention to the compliments Sebastian makes. Write them down in one column. In the other column, write down the phrases Gabriele uses to react. Then listen to the dialogue again, checking whether you caught them all. Finally, try to think on your own of two more compliments, and add them to your list.

WORDS TO LIVE BY

YOU ARE SO BEAUTIFUL! **PAYING COMPLIMENTS AND ACCEPTING THEM GRACEFULLY**

Compliments are certainly a good way to somebody's heart in a romantic relationship. But don't think that you can't use compliments in other situations as well. Everybody enjoys an appreciative comment on just about anything. *Aber nicht übertreiben!* (But don't exaggerate!)

Here are a few good phrases to comment on somebody's looks:

- *aussehen* (to look)
Du siehst aber gut aus./Sie sehen aber gut aus.   You look good.

- *sein* (to be)
Wie nett du bist! Wie nett Sie sind!   How nice you are!

- *etwas unterstreichen* (to underline, to emphasize)
Das T-shirt unterstreicht die Farbe deiner Augen.   The T-shirt emphasizes the color of your eyes.

- *etwas gut zur Geltung bringen* (to show something off)
Die Jeans bringen deine Figur gut zur Geltung.   The jeans show off your figure.

- *schmeicheln* (to flatter)
Das Kleid schmeichelt deiner Figur.   The dress flatters your figure.

And if you'd like to comment on somebody's behavior:
Du bist eine hervorragende Gastgeberin.   You are an excellent host.

And of course, you can always comment on somebody's taste:
Das zeugt von gutem Geschmack.   This proves good taste.
Sie haben aber einen exquisiten Geschmack.   You have exquisite taste.

And finally, a nice comment on people's cooking goes a long way.
Das schmeckt aber gut.   This tastes so good.
Was für ein guter Koch Sie sind!   What a good cook you are!

A simple reaction is often the best:

Vielen Dank.   Thank you very much.

But if you'd like to say a bit more:

Das ist aber nett von dir/Ihnen.   That is nice of you!
Wie aufmerksam!   How attentive!
Jetzt übertreiben Sie aber.   But you are exaggerating.

You can never use too many adjectives when paying a compliment.

hübsch	pretty
schön	beautiful
elegant	elegant
gut	good
hervorragend	excellent
geschmackvoll	tasteful
exquisit	exquisite
prima	great
aufmerksam	attentive
nett	nice
lieb	sweet

WORD ON THE STREET

A common expression used in reaction to a compliment among friends is *Vielen Dank für die Blumen*. (Thanks for the compliment. [Lit. Thanks for the flowers.])

Did You Know?

Germans are a bit more reserved than Americans when it comes to paying compliments. It is not that Germans aren't appreciative of beauty, a job well done or a gentle gesture; rather, Germans are simply less verbal about it. Often a smile or an encouraging nod with the head is meant to say it all. Subtleties are the order of the day in Germany, Austria, and Switzerland, and people paying too many compliments might be met with distrust. By the same token, don't think it rude if Germans respond to a compliment with a form of denial, saying something like *Aber nicht doch!* (Not at all!) or *Meinen Sie das wirklich?* (Do you really mean that?) or *Aber das war doch ganz billig* (But it was so cheap). These responses are a form of modesty appropriate in a society which doesn't carry its emotions on its sleeves.

Use the cues below to pay another compliment following the model provided.

1. *Die Farbe deines T-Shirts unterstreicht die Farbe deiner Augen.* (blouse, color of your hair)
2. *Du bist eine hervorragende Gastgeberin.* (good, dancer)
3. *Diese Weingläser sind sehr elegant.* (plates, tasteful)
4. *Dieses Kleid schmeichelt Ihrer Figur.* (pants, waist)
5. *Wie hübsch Sie sind!* (beautiful, you [informal])
6. *Wie lieb von dir!* (attentive, you [formal])

Did You Know?

Here are a few do's and don'ts you should know about in case you get invited for dinner: It is customary to bring a bottle of wine for the host and flowers for the hostess. Flowers are always given in uneven numbers and are usually presented to the hostess unwrapped. Don't bring red roses unless your dinner has romantic overtones. It is unusual to bring dessert, as the host or hostess will have planned the entire meal including hors d'oeuvres and dessert. Don't expect that your host will serve the wine you brought for dinner, as even the choice of wine is part of the cook's dinner plan. Your wine may be served before dinner, of course.

In less formal situations, it is perfectly acceptable to ask whether you should bring anything to complete the meal, be that drinks, hors d'oeuvres or desserts. Potlucks are rather unusual, though. The main course is usually the host's responsibility—and honor.

THE NITTY GRITTY

ALTERNATIVES TO THE PASSIVE VOICE

In lesson 10, we learned how to make passive sentences, such as "That can be done." While in the active voice the subject of the sentence is understood as an agent or a doer, in the passive voice the subject is not an agent but the person or object acted upon. It is passive. The passive voice, which is rather common in the German language, can be replaced by other constructions:

The construction using *man* is the most common way to express a general truth that can otherwise be expressed by the passive.

Die Pizza kann sicher aufgewärmt werden.	***Die Pizza kann man sicher aufwärmen.***
The pizza can be heated up.	One/You can heat up the pizza.
Was kann mehr gewollt werden?	***Was will man mehr?***
What more can be wished for?	What more can one/you wish for?

SEIN + *ZU* + INFINITIVE

Passive constructions with *können* and *müssen* can be replaced with *sein* + *zu* + infinitive.

Das kann schwer geleugnet werden.	***Das ist schwer zu leugnen.***
That can be denied only with difficulty.	That is hard to deny.
So viele Komplimente können nicht ernst genommen werden.	***So viele Komplimente sind nicht ernst zu nehmen.***
So many compliments cannot be taken seriously.	So many compliments are not to be taken seriously.

SICH LASSEN + INFINITIVE

This can replace *können* and a passive infinitive.

Das kann gemacht werden.	***Das läßt sich machen.***
That can be done.	That can be done. (Lit. That lets itself be done.)
Das Kompliment kann nicht mehr aufrecht erhalten werden.	***Das Kompliment läßt sich nicht mehr aufrecht erhalten.***
The compliment can no longer be maintained.	The compliment can no longer be maintained. (Lit. The compliment no longer lets itself be maintained.)

ACTIVITY 8: **TAKE IT FOR A SPIN**

Please transform the following story using the alternatives to the passive discussed above. Watch the tenses.

Gestern haben Schneiders angerufen. Ich wurde zum Abendessen eingeladen. (use *man*) *Es wurde mir gesagt, dass ich Wein mitbringen soll.* (use *man*) *Ich habe eine Flasche Weißwein mitgebracht. Der Wein musste kalt gestellt werden.* (use *sein* + *zu*) *Das Essen wurde um 20 Uhr serviert.* (use *man*) *Es schmeckte hervorragend.*

Take a look at this thank-you note.

> *Liebe Frau Schneider,*
>
> *Vielen Dank für das hervorragende Essen gestern abend. Es schmeckte ausgezeichnet. Sie sind ein hervorragender Koch. Es hat mir bei Ihnen wirklich gut gefallen. Ihre Wohnung ist sehr elegant eingerichtet. Sie zeugt von Ihrem guten Geschmack.*
>
> *Nochmals vielen Dank. Ich hoffe, ich darf Sie bald bei mir begrüßen.*
>
> *Liebe Grüße,*
> *Barbara*

ACTIVITY 9: TAKE IT UP A NOTCH

Please write a thank you note for a fun party. Use the following words and phrases: *toll, viel Spaß machen, aufmerksamer Gastgeber, interessante Gäste, guter Geschmack.*

And here comes the last activity of the course. Don't you feel good about having gotten this far with your German? Give it your best . . .

STRUT YOUR STUFF

Let's end on a good note. How about playing a game (where you'll be a certain winner)? Do you know *das Millionenspiel?* The *Without the Fuss* Edition? Well, here are ten questions I'd like you to answer.

ACTIVITY 10: TAKE IT FOR A SPIN

1. What is the capital of Germany?
    a. *Berlin*
    b. *Zürich*
    c. *Wien*
    d. *Bonn*
2. They say that *Kleider machen* . . .
    a. . . . *Menschen.*
    b. . . . *Leute.*
    c. . . . *glücklich.*
    d. . . . *schön.*
3. In German-speaking countries they _____ when they meet you.
    a. kiss
    b. shake hands
    c. hug
    d. pat you on the back
4. *Der beliebteste Sport in Deutschland ist _____.*
    a. *Handball*
    b. *Tennis*
    c. *Fußball*
    d. *Radfahren*
5. When do you say *Guten Appetit?*
    a. When talking to a stranger.
    b. When talking to people who are about to eat.
    c. When angry with somebody.
    d. When talking to a waiter.
6. You would use *du* to . . .
    a. the new boss you just met.
    b. the waiter in a first-class restaurant.
    c. your very best friend.
    d. your 60-year-old new neighbor.
7. How do you say "May I take a message?"
    a. *Kann ich mitkommen?*
    b. *Kann ich etwas ausrichten?*

    c. *Kann ich Ihnen helfen?*

    d. *Wie komme ich in die Stadt?*

8. A *Doppelzimmer* is . . .

    a. a room with a view.

    b. two rooms.

    c. a room for two people.

    d. a room rented out twice.

9. If you disagree with somebody you would say . . .

    a. *Wie schön du bist!*

    b. *Da bin ich anderer Meinung.*

    c. *Vielen Dank, und auf Wiedersehen.*

    d. *Die Rechnung, bitte!*

10. *Alle, die mit diesem Buch Deutsch gelernt haben* . . .

    a. *. . . haben einen deutschen Namen.*

    b. *. . . fahren nach Deutschland in den Urlaub.*

    c. *. . . haben ein deutsches Auto.*

    d. *. . . sprechen gut Deutsch.*

Well, this is it for your German lessons. Or is it? I hope this is just the beginning of a long and lasting reationship with the German language and German-speaking cultures. Remember that regular and abundant exposure to the language is the best way to learn it. So keep using what's around you—TV, radio, newspapers and the Internet. Travel to Germany, Austria, Switzerland if you can, make friends with your German neighbors, join chat rooms, write e-mails, go to a German restaurant . . . and don't be afraid to make mistakes. It's the effort that counts and most people will appreciate it. As for me, I hope to meet with you again.

Auf Wiedersehen! Tschüs! Ade! Servus! Und alles Gute!

CRIB NOTES

HEAR . . . SAY 1

Sebastian:	Hello, Gabriele. What's new?
Gabriele:	Not much.
Sebastian:	What are your plans for tonight?
Gabriele:	Actually I wanted to stay home and watch some TV.

Sebastian:	TV? But it is Friday evening. You go out on Fridays.
Gabriele:	You maybe. Not me. I can relax best while watching TV.
Sebastian:	I have exactly the right thing for

	relaxation. How about a romantic dinner at a fabulous restaurant, followed by an unforgettable visit to the theater or a stimulating visit at a jazz club?
Gabriele:	That sounds irresistible, but I am too tired to do anything.
Sebastian:	Come on, Gabriele, don't be a spoilsport.
Gabriele:	No, really, I can't. Maybe some other time.
Sebastian:	Too bad. Does this mean that I will have to be all by myself tonight?
Gabriele:	Looks like it.
Sebastian:	And how about if I go by the Italian restaurant and pick up a pizza for us?
Gabriele:	You won't let me get rid of you . . .

Sebastian:	Nope . . . and I could rent a video with that pizza. Maybe a Wim Wenders . . .
Gabriele:	Anything but Wim Wenders. But if you feel like watching TV with me I may be persuaded to have a pizza.
Sebastian:	What's on?
Gabriele:	Tatort. With Schimanski.
Sebastian:	Oh no. So you think I will sit by silently while you swoon over some other guy?
Gabriele:	Exactly.
Sebastian:	The things I put up with! Alright, I'll be at your place in half an hour.
Gabriele:	With the pizza, I hope . . .

HEAR . . . SAY 2

Sebastian:	Hello my dear. Here I am.
Gabriele:	Hello. Come on in.
Sebastian:	Here is the pizza.
Gabriele:	Mmmm. That looks good.
Sebastian:	Mmmm. You too. I mean, you look pretty. As usual.
Gabriele:	Thanks.
Sebastian:	The blue T-shirt emphasizes the color of your eyes.
Gabriele:	Thanks. How sweet of you to say that.
Sebastian:	You're welcome. And your jeans show off your figure.
Gabriele:	Now you're laying it on a bit thick, don't you think?
Sebastian:	Not at all. And besides, I know you like to hear my compliments.
Gabriele:	That is hard to deny. Can I offer you something to drink?
Sebastian:	And you are an excellent hostess. What more could you want?

Gabriele:	Something to drink, maybe?
Sebastian:	Oh, yes, right. A glass of red wine, please.
Gabriele:	Here.
Sebastian:	These glasses are very elegant They prove your good taste.
Gabriele:	Sebastian, are you trying to tease me? So many compliments can't be taken seriously.
Sebastian:	Maybe not. But otherwise I don't stand a chance next to Schimanski.
Gabriele:	What? Oh dear. The pizza went cold. You are getting me all flustered.
Sebastian:	I'm glad to hear that. And I'm sure you can heat up the pizza.
Gabriele:	Yes, of course. That can be done.
Sebastian:	By the way, the compliment about the excellent hostess cannot be maintained any more . . .

ANSWER KEY

ACTIVITY 1
1. *Massenkultur.*
2. *Hohe Kunst.*
3. *Massenkultur.*
4. *Massenkultur.*
5. *Hohe Kunst.*

ACTIVITY 2
1. *Er will ein romantisches Abendessen in einem fabelhaften Restaurant.*
2. *Er schlägt einen unvergesslichen Theaterbesuch oder einen anregenden Besuch in einem Jazzlokal vor.*
3. *Eigentlich wollte sie zu Hause bleiben und ein bisschen fernsehen.*

4. *Weil sie sich beim Fernsehen am besten entspannen kann.*
5. *Sie essen Pizza und sehen fern.*
6. *Wer weiß . . .*

ACTIVITY 3

1.
   a. *Ich habe zu viel zu tun.*
   b. *Eigentlich wollte ich zu Hause bleiben und ein bisschen fernsehen.*
   c. *Vielleicht ein anderes Mal.*
2.
   a. *Mama? Ich kann dich nicht hören. Mein Telefon ist kaputt.*
   b. *Also gut. Mit mir kann man's ja machen.*
   c. *Das klingt unwiderstehlich. Ein anderes Mal vielleicht?*
3.
   a. *Ich bin zu müde und gehe nur samstags aus.*
   b. *Nein, meine Haare sind unmöglich. Heute wirklich nicht.*
   c. *Danke für den Anruf. Kann ich dich morgen zurückrufen?*

And here is your personality chart:
1. If you answered "a" more than once: You seem to have a few problems with telling the truth!
2. If you answered "b" more than once: You are way too easy to convince. Get yourself some backbone!
3. If you answered "c" more than once: According to your answers you are a very polite and friendly person. No way you answered truthfully!

ACTIVITY 4

1. *Ich will zu Hause bleiben und (ich will) fernsehen.*
2. *Willst du ins Kino gehen oder (willst du) ein Video ausleihen?*
3. *Das klingt prima, aber ich bin zu müde.*
4. *Ich möchte nicht essen gehen, sondern (ich möchte) eine Pizza holen.*
5. *Sebastian will nicht fernsehen, denn er will Schimanski nicht anhimmeln./Sebastian will nicht fernsehen, weil er Schimanski nicht anhimmeln will.*

ACTIVITY 5

1. *interessant uninteressant*
2. *krank krankhaft, die Krankheit*
3. *glauben glaubhaft, unglaubhaft*
4. *widerstehlich unwiderstehlich*
5. *schön die Schönheit*
6. *müde die Müdigkeit*
7. *das Ende endlos*
8. *vergessen vergesslich, unvergesslich, die Vergesslichkeit*
9. *romantisch unromantisch*
10. *essen das Essen*
11. *sicher unsicher, die Sicherheit*

ACTIVITY 6
Compliment:
Du siehst sehr hübsch aus. Wie immer.
Das blaue T-Shirt unterstreicht die Farbe deiner Augen.
Und die Jeans bringen deine Figur gut zur Geltung.
Und eine hervorragende Gastgeberin bist du auch.
Diese Gläser sind sehr elegant. Sie zeugen von gutem Geschmack.
Your own compliment. You could comment on somebody's apartment: Das ist aber eine gemütliche Wohnung.
Or you could comment on somebody's cooking: Das Essen schmeckt sehr gut. Sie sind/Du bist eine gute Köchin/ein guter Koch.

Reaction:
Vielen Dank.
Danke. Wie lieb von dir, das zu sagen.
Jetzt trägst du aber ein bisschen dick auf.
Willst du mich auf den Arm nehmen?

ACTIVITY 7
1. *Die Farbe deiner Bluse unterstreicht die Farbe deiner Haare.*
2. *Du bist ein guter Tänzer.*
3. *Diese Teller sind sehr geschmackvoll.*
4. *Diese Hose schmeichelt Ihrer Taille.*
5. *Wie schön du bist!*
6. *Wie aufmerksam von Ihnen!*

ACTIVITY 8
Gestern haben Schneiders angerufen. Man hat mich zum Abendessen eingeladen. Man sagte mir, ich soll Wein mitbringen. Ich habe eine Flasche Weißwein mitgebracht. Der Wein war kalt zu stellen. Man servierte das Essen um 20 Uhr. Es schmeckte hervorragend.

ACTIVITY 9
Vielen Dank für die tolle Party gestern abend. Es hat viel Spaß gemacht. Sie sind ein aufmerksamer Gastgeber. Es hat mir bei Ihnen wirklich gut gefallen. Sie hatten interessante Gäste. Das zeugt von Ihrem guten Geschmack.
Nochmals vielen Dank. Ich hoffe, ich darf Sie bald bei mir begrüßen.
Liebe Grüße,

ACTIVITY 10

1.	a	2.	b	3.	b
4.	c	5.	b	6.	c
7.	b	8.	c	9.	b
10.	d				

APPENDIX A

A SHORTCUT TO GERMAN GRAMMAR

PERSONAL PRONOUNS				
	SUBJECT PRONOUNS (NOM.)	**DIRECT OBJECT PRONOUNS (ACC.)**	**INDIRECT OBJECT PRONOUNS (DAT.)**	**REFLEXIVE PRONOUNS**
SINGULAR	*ich* (I)	*mich* (me)	*mir* (to me)	*mich* (myself)
	du (you)	*dich* (you)	*dir* (to you)	*dich* (yourself)
	er (he)	*ihn* (him)	*ihm* (to him)	*sich* (himself)
	sie (she)	*sie* (her)	*ihr* (to her)	*sich* (herself)
	es (it)	*es* (it)	*ihm* (to it)	*sich* (itself)
	Sie (fml.) (you)	*Sie* (you)	*Ihnen* (to you)	*sich* (yourself)
PLURAL	*wir* (we)	*uns* (us)	*uns* (to us)	*uns* (ourselves)
	ihr (you)	*euch* (you)	*euch* (to you)	*euch* (yourselves)
	sie (they)	*sie* (them)	*ihnen* (to them)	*sich* (themselves)

DEFINITE AND INDEFINITE ARTICLES		SINGULAR			PLURAL
		M	**F**	**N**	**M/F/N**
DEFINITE	Nom.	*der*	*die*	*das*	*die*
ARTICLE	Acc.	*den*	*die*	*das*	*die*
(THE)	Dat.	*dem*	*der*	*dem*	*den*
	Gen.	*des*	*der*	*des*	*der*
INDEFINITE	Nom.	*ein*	*eine*	*ein*	-
ARTICLE	Acc.	*einen*	*eine*	*ein*	
(A/AN)	Dat.	*einem*	*einer*	*einem*	
	Gen.	*eines*	*einer*	*eines*	

DER-WORDS *DIESER, -E, ES* (THIS, THAT; THIS ONE, THAT ONE)		SINGULAR			PLURAL
		M	**F**	**N**	**M/F/N**
NOM.		*dieser*	*diese*	*dieses*	*diese*
ACC.		*diesen*	*diese*	*dieses*	*diese*
DAT.		*diesem*	*dieser*	*diesem*	*diesen*
GEN.		*dieses*	*dieser*	*diese*	*dieser*

Other words in this group are *dieser, jener, welcher, mancher,* and *solche.* The endings of the indefinites *mancher, solche* and of the demonstratives *dieser, jener, welcher,* agree with the following noun the way the definite article does. That's why they are called *der*-words.

	EIN-WORDS MEIN, -E, -ES (MY, MINE)			
	SINGULAR			**PLURAL**
	M	**F**	**N**	**M/F/N**
NOM.	*mein*	*meine*	*mein*	*meine*
ACC.	*meinen*	*meine*	*mein*	*meine*
DAT.	*meinem*	*meiner*	*meinem*	*meinen*
GEN.	*meines*	*meiner*	*meines*	*meiner*

Other words in this group are *dein, sein, ihr, unser, euer,* and the negative *kein.* The endings of the possessives *mein, dein, sein, ihr, unser, euer, ihr, ihr* as well as the negative *kein* agree with the following noun the way the indefinite article does. That's why they are called *ein*-words.

INTERROGATIVE PRONOUNS WER (WHO) AND WAS (WHAT)		
	ANIMATE	**INANIMATE**
NOM.	*wer*	*was*
ACC.	*wen*	*was*
DAT.	*wem*	*(mit/von/an) was*
GEN.	*wessen*	*wessen*

RELATIVE PRONOUNS				
	M	**F**	**N**	**P**
NOM.	*der*	*die*	*das*	*die*
ACC.	*den*	*die*	*das*	*die*
DAT.	*dem*	*der*	*dem*	*denen*
GEN.	*dessen*	*deren*	*dessen*	*deren*

QUESTION WORDS

warum	why
weshalb	why
weswegen	why
wieso	why
wann	when
wo	where
wieviel	how much
wie viele	how many
wer	who
wie	how
wozu	what for
was	what

ADJECTIVES PRECEDED BY AN ARTICLE

	M	F	N	PLURAL
NOM.	der alte Mann	die alte Stadt	das alte Haus	die alten Weine
	ein alter Mann	eine alte Stadt	ein altes Haus	alte Weine
ACC.	den alten Mann	die alte Stadt	das alte Haus	die alten Weine
	einen alten Mann	eine alte Stadt	ein altes Haus	alte Weine
DAT.	dem alten Mann	der alten Stadt	dem alten Haus	den alten Weinen
	einem alten Mann	einer alten Stadt	einem alten Haus	alten Weinen
GEN.	des alten Mannes	der alten Stadt	des alten Hauses	der alten Weine
	eines alten Mannes	einer alten Stadt	eines alten Hauses	alter Weine

ADJECTIVES NOT PRECEDED BY AN ARTICLE

	M	F	N	PLURAL
NOM.	alter Mann	alte Stadt	altes Haus	alte Weine
ACC.	alten Mann	alte Stadt	altes Haus	alte Weine
DAT	altem Mann	alter Stadt	altem Haus	alten Weinen
GEN.	alten Mannes	alter Stadt	alten Hauses	alter Weine

THE COMPARATIVE AND SUPERLATIVE OF ADJECTIVES

POSITIVE	COMPARATIVE	SUPERLATIVE
schön (beautiful)	*schöner*	*schönste, -r, -s; am schönsten*
groß (big)	*größer*	*größte, -r, -s; am größten*
klein (small)	*kleiner*	*kleinste, -r, -s; am kleinsten*

ADVERBS OF TIME

jetzt	now
heute	today
später	later
bald	soon
morgen	tomorrow
übermorgen	the day after tomorrow
früher	earlier
gestern	yesterday
vorgestern	the day before yesterday
nie(mals)	never
oft	often
manchmal	sometimes
immer	always

ADVERBS OF QUANTITY

viel	a lot
wenig	a little
nichts	nothing
mehr	more
weniger	less
zu viel	too much
zu wenig	too little
alles	everything

THE PRESENT TENSE OF ALL VERBS

FRAGEN (TO ASK)

ich frage

du fragst

Sie fragen (formal)

er/sie/es fragt

wir fragen

ihr fragt

sie fragen

THE PRESENT PERFECT TENSE

WEAK VERBS **FRAGEN (TO ASK)**	STRONG VERBS **KOMMEN (TO COME)**	MIXED VERBS **DENKEN (TO THINK)**
ich habe gefragt	ich bin gekommen	ich habe gedacht
du hast gefragt	du bist gekommen	du hast gedacht
Sie haben gefragt	Sie sind gekommen	Sie haben gedacht
er/sie/es hat gefragt	er/sie/es ist gekommen	er/sie/es hat gedacht
wir haben gefragt	wir sind gekommen	wir haben gedacht
ihr habt gefragt	ihr seid gekommen	ihr habt gedacht
sie haben gefragt	sie sind gekommen	sie haben gedacht

THE SIMPLE PAST

WEAK VERBS **FRAGEN (TO ASK)**	STRONG VERBS **KOMMEN (TO COME)**	MIXED VERBS **DENKEN (TO THINK)**
ich fragte	ich kam	ich dachte
du fragtest	du kamst	du dachtest
Sie fragten	Sie kamen	Sie dachten
er/sie/es fragte	er/sie/es kam	er/sie/es dachte
wir fragten	wir kamen	wir dachten
ihr fragtet	ihr kamt	ihr dachtet
sie fragten	sie kamen	sie dachten

THE FUTURE TENSE OF ALL VERBS

FRAGEN (TO ASK)

ich werde fragen

du wirst fragen

Sie werden fragen

er/sie/es wird fragen

wir werden fragen

ihr werdet fragen

sie werden fragen

THE SUBJUNCTIVE IN POLITE REQUESTS

HELFEN (TO HELP)

ich würde helfen

du würdest helfen

Sie würden helfen

er/sie/es würde helfen

wir würden helfen

ihr würdet helfen

sie würden helfen

Use the subjunctive to make polite requests. All verbs but modals and *haben* and *sein* use the subjunctive form of *werden* plus the infinitive of the main verb to form the subjunctive.

THE SUBJUNCTIVE OF MODAL VERBS

	KÖNNEN	*MÜSSEN*	*DÜRFEN*	*WOLLEN*	*MÖGEN*	*SOLLEN*
ICH	*könnte*	*müsste*	*dürfte*	*wollte*	*möchte*	*sollte*
DU	*könntest*	*müsstest*	*dürftest*	*wolltest*	*möchtest*	*solltest*
SIE	*könnten*	*müssten*	*dürften*	*wollten*	*möchten*	*sollten*
ER/SIE/ES	*könnte*	*müsste*	*dürfte*	*wollte*	*möchte*	*sollte*
WIR	*könnten*	*müssten*	*dürften*	*wollten*	*möchten*	*sollten*
IHR	*könntet*	*müsstet*	*dürftet*	*wolltet*	*möchtet*	*solltet*
SIE	*könnten*	*müssten*	*dürften*	*wollten*	*möchten*	*sollten*

THE SUBJUNCTIVE OF *HABEN* (TO HAVE) AND *SEIN* (TO BE)

ICH	*hätte*	*wäre*
DU	*hättest*	*wärst*
SIE	*hätten*	*wären*
ER/SIE/ES	*hätte*	*wäre*
WIR	*hätten*	*wären*
IHR	*hättet*	*wärt*
SIE	*hätten*	*wären*

THE PASSIVE VOICE *FRAGEN* (TO ASK)

PRESENT TENSE	SIMPLE PAST	PRESENT PERFECT
ich werde gefragt	*ich wurde gefragt*	*ich bin gefragt worden*
du wirst gefragt	*du wurdest gefragt*	*du bist gefragt worden*
Sie werden gefragt	*Sie wurden gefragt*	*Sie sind gefragt worden*
er/sie/es wird gefragt	*er/sie/es wurde gefragt*	*er/sie/es ist gefragt worden*
wir werden gefragt	*wir wurden gefragt*	*wir sind gefragt worden*
ihr werdet gefragt	*ihr wurdet gefragt*	*ihr seid gefragt worden*
sie werden gefragt	*sie wurden gefragt*	*sie sind gefragt worden*

The German passive is formed with the verb *werden* (to become) and the past participle of the main verb.

THE IMPERATIVE

	DU-FORM	*IHR*-FORM	*WIR*-FORM	*SIE*-FORM
GEHEN (TO GO)	*Geh doch!*	*Geht doch!*	*Gehen wir doch!*	*Gehen Sie doch!*
SEIN (TO BE)	*Sei so gut!*	*Seid so gut!*	*Seien wir so gut!*	*Seien Sie so gut!*
LASSEN (TO LET [GO])	*Lass mich!*	*Lasst mich!*	*Lasst uns!*	*Lassen Sie mich!*

WORD ORDER RULES

- Regular word order in German is subject-verb-object: *Ich liebe dich sehr.*

- In questions, the subject and verb switch places: *Liebst du mich? Wen liebst du?*

- It is possible to emphasize any part of the sentence simply by moving it to the beginning of the sentence: *Dich liebe ich sehr.* In that case, as in ALL cases when a word precedes the subject, subject and verb have to switch places.

- In subordinate clauses, the verb moves to the end of the clause: *Ich liebe dich, weil du nett bist.*

- In a sentence with both a direct and an indirect object pronoun, the direct object pronoun comes first: *Ich gebe ihn dir.*

- In a sentence with both an adverb of time and an adverb of location, the adverb of time usually comes first: *Ich fahre morgen nach Hamburg.*

COMMAS AND PERIODS AND ALL THE OTHER STUFF

THE PERIOD

The period is used at the end of any sentence that is not a question (see *Question mark*) or an exclamation (see *Exclamation mark*).

The period is also used after ordinal numbers in dates. For example: *1. Januar 2005* or *Mein 30. Geburtstag war am 21.03.98.* My 30th birthday was on March 21, 1998.

The period is used to separate the thousands. For example: *1.000 (eintausend)* or *25.320 (fünfundzwanzigtausenddreihundertzwanzig)*. A gap can be used instead of a period: 1 000 or 25 320.

THE COMMA

- The comma is always used to separate words, names or items in a list. There is no comma before the word *und* at the end of a list. For example:

Wir müssen heute Brot, Gemüse, Obst und Wurst einkaufen.	We have to buy bread, vegetables, fruit, and cold cuts today.

- The comma separates subordinate clauses. For example:

Als ich zehn Jahre alt war, kam ich ins Gymnasium.	When I was ten years old, I started high school.
Die Schule, in die ich ging, war ganz in der Nähe.	The school, which I went to, was close to my home.

So kam es auch, dass ich zu Fuß gehen musste, auch wenn es regnete.	That's how it happened that I had to walk to school, even when it was raining.

· A comma is used to separate the details of an address or a date. For example:

Seine Adresse lautet: Mommsenstrasse 85, 509337 Köln.	His address is Mommsenstrasse 85, 509337 Cologne.
Ich bin von Montag, 6. Januar, bis Mittwoch, 8. Januar, im Urlaub.	I'll be on vacation from Monday, January 6, through Wednesday, January 8.

· The comma is used to denote decimals in currency. For example:

Das kostet € 3,20.	This costs € 3.20.

THE QUESTION MARK

The question mark is used after a direct question. For example:

Wie spät ist es?	What time is it?

The question mark is NOT used in reported speech. For example:

Er fragte, wie spät es sei.	He asked, what time it was.

THE EXCLAMATION MARK

· The exclamation mark is used after sentences or words to indicate emotional intensity.

For example:

Hilfe!	Help!
Wie schön, dich zu sehen!	How nice to see you!

· The exclamation mark is also used after commands. For example:

Komm bitte sofort her!	Please come here right now!

· It can be used to address a person in letters. For example:

Sehr geehrter Herr Bauer!	Dear Mr. Bauer,

QUOTATION MARKS

· German uses double quotation marks. The opening marks are on the line and below, the closing marks are above the line.

THE HYPHEN

The German word for hyphen is *Bindestrich* (connecting line).

- It is used in compounds, if they are both nouns. For example:

  T-Shirt, Freizeit-Schuh, Jogging-Set   T-shirt, leisure time shoes, jogging set

- Noun compounds taken from the English may or may not use a hyphen. For example:

  Hand-out/Handout, Lay-out/Layout.

- It is used when compounds are repeated immediately to avoid repetition. For example:

bergauf und -ab	uphill and downhill
Ein- und Ausfuhr	import and export
Holztüren und -fenster	wooden doors and windows

- It is used in compounds with numbers or single letters. For example:

  das 4-Eck, 3/4-Takt, 4-Zylinder, D-Zug, Fußball-WM

- It can be used if three identical vowels or consonants meet in a compound. For example:

  Schiff-Fahrt, See-Elefant, Kaffee-Ernte, Schritt-Tempo

CAPITALIZATION

- All sentences begin with a capital letter.

- All nouns begin with a capital letter. For example:
  das neue Auto, die schöne Stadt, meine Mutter (the new car, the beautiful city, my mother)

- The polite pronoun *Sie* and all its forms are capitalized. All other pronouns, including the pronoun *du* and its forms are NOT capitalized, except in letters.

- Words that are usually not capitalized (e.g., adjectives) should be capitalized when used in proper names. For example: *das Bibliographische Institut, der Stille Ozean* (the Bibliographical Institute, the Red Sea)

- All titles, honorary as well as job titles or descriptive titles, are capitalized. For example: *Dr. Bauer, Karl der Große, der Heilige Vater, Ihre Königliche Hoheit, der*

Regierende Bürgermeister (Dr. Bauer, Karl the Great, the Holy Father, Your Highness, the Mayor)

- Special calendar days are capitalized. For example: *der Heilige Abend* (Christmas Eve)

- Historical events are capitalized. For example: *der Dreißigjährige Krieg, der Erste Weltkrieg, die Goldenen Zwanziger* (the Thirty-Year War, the First World War, the Golden Twenties)

- Country and city names, as well as compounds formed with country or city names. For example: *die Schweiz, Schweizer Berge* (Switzerland, Swiss mountains)

- Language names are capitalized in connection with prepositions. For example: *auf Englisch, im Deutschen* (in English, in German)

APPENDIX B

EXCEPTIONS THAT CONFIRM THE RULE

MASCULINE *N*-NOUNS		
	SINGULAR	**PLURAL**
NOM.	der Architekt	die Architekten
ACC.	den Architekten	die Architekten
DAT.	dem Architekten	den Architekten
GEN.	des Architekten	der Architekten

Other examples are: *der Mensch, der Bauer, der Jurist, der Präsident, der Diplomat, der Fotograf, der Experte, der Nachbar, der Zeuge, der Journalist.*

IRREGULAR COMPARATIVES AND SUPERLATIVES		
POSITIVE	**COMPARATIVE**	**SUPERLATIVE**
gut	*besser*	*beste, -r, -s am besten*
groß	*größer*	*größte, -r, -s am größten*
hoch	*höher*	*höchste, -r, -s am höchsten*
nahe	*näher*	*nächste, -r, -s am nächsten*
viel	*mehr*	*meiste, -r, -s am meisten*
gern	*lieber*	*liebste, -r, -s am liebsten*

INFINITIVE	PRESENT	SIMPLE PAST	PAST PARTICIPLE
anfangen (to begin)	fängt an	fing an	angefangen
backen (to bake)	bäckt	buk (backte)	gebacken
beginnen (to begin)		begann	begonnen
bekommen (to receive)		bekam	bekommen
beweisen (to prove)		bewies	bewiesen
bieten (to offer)		bot	geboten
bleiben (to remain)		blieb	ist geblieben
brechen (to break)	bricht	brach	gebrochen
bringen (to bring)		brachte	gebracht
denken (to think)		dachte	gedacht
diskutieren (to discuss)		diskutierte	diskutiert
dürfen (to be allowed to)	darf	durfte	gedurft
einladen (to invite)	lädt ein	lud ein	eingeladen
empfehlen (to recommend)	empfiehlt	empfahl	empfohlen
essen (to eat)	isst	aß	gegessen
fahren (to drive)	fährt	fuhr	ist gefahren
fallen (to fall)	fällt	fiel	ist gefallen
finden (to find)		fand	gefunden
fliegen (to fly)		flog	ist geflogen
frieren (to freeze)		fror	gefroren
geben (to give)	gibt	gab	gegeben
gefallen (to please)	gefällt	gefiel	gefallen
gehen (to go)		ging	ist gegangen
genießen (to enjoy)		genoss	genossen
gewinnen (to win)		gewann	gewonnen
greifen (to seize)		griff	gegriffen
haben (to have)	hat	hatte	gehabt
halten (to hold, to stop)	hält	hielt	gehalten
hängen (to be hanging, to hang)		hing, hängte	gehangen, gehängt
heißen (to be called)		hieß	geheißen
helfen (to help)	hilft	half	geholfen
kennen (to know)		kannte	gekannt
kommen (to come)		kam	ist gekommen
können (to be able to, can)	kann	konnte	gekonnt
lassen (to let)	lässt	ließ	gelassen
laufen (to run, to walk)	läuft	lief	ist gelaufen
leiden (to suffer)		litt	gelitten
leihen (to lend, to borrow)		lieh	geliehen
lesen (to read)	liest	las	gelesen
liegen (to lie (down))		lag	gelegen
mögen (to like)	mag	mochte	gemocht

INFINITIVE	PRESENT	SIMPLE PAST	PAST PARTICIPLE
müssen (to have to, must)	*muss*	*musste*	*gemusst*
nehmen (to take)	*nimmt*	*nahm*	*genommen*
nennen (to name, to call)		*nannte*	*genannt*
raten (to advise, to guess)	*rät*	*riet*	*geraten*
rennen (to run)		*rannte*	*ist gerannt*
reservieren (to reserve)		*reservierte*	*reserviert*
rufen (to call)		*rief*	*gerufen*
schaffen (to create)		*schuf*	*geschaffen*
schlafen (to sleep)	*schläft*	*schlief*	*geschlafen*
schließen (to close)		*schloss*	*geschlossen*
schneiden (to cut)		*schnitt*	*geschnitten*
schreiben (to write)		*schrieb*	*geschrieben*
schreien (to scream)		*schrie*	*geschrien*
schwimmen (to swim)		*schwamm*	*ist geschwommen*
sehen (to see)	*sieht*	*sah*	*gesehen*
sein (to be)	*ist*	*war*	*ist gewesen*
senden (to send)		*sandte*	*gesandt*
sitzen (to sit)		*saß*	*gesessen*
sollen (to be supposed to)	*soll*	*sollte*	*gesollt* (uncommon)
sprechen (to speak)	*spricht*	*sprach*	*gesprochen*
springen (to jump)		*sprang*	*ist gesprungen*
stehen (to stand)		*stand*	*gestanden*
steigen (to climb)		*stieg*	*ist gestiegen*
sterben (to die)	*stirbt*	*starb*	*ist gestorben*
stoßen (to push, to run into)	*stößt*	*stieß*	*hat/ist gestoßen*
streiten (to fight)		*stritt*	*gestritten*
tragen (to carry, to wear)	*trägt*	*trug*	*getragen*
treffen (to meet)	*trifft*	*traf*	*getroffen*
treten (to walk, to tread, to kick)	*tritt*	*trat*	*getreten*
trinken (to drink)		*trank*	*getrunken*
tun (to do)		*tat*	*getan*
verbieten (to forbid)		*verbot*	*verboten*
verbinden (to connect)		*verband*	*verbunden*
vergessen (to forget)	*vergisst*	*vergaß*	*vergessen*
verlieren (to lose)		*verlor*	*verloren*
verschwinde (to disappear)		*verschwand*	*ist verschwunden*
wachsen (to grow)	*wächst*	*wuchs*	*ist gewachsen*
waschen (to wash)	*wäscht*	*wusch*	*gewaschen*
werden (to become, to get)	*wird*	*wurde*	*ist geworden*
wissen (to know)	*weiß*	*wusste*	*gewusst*
wollen (to want, to wish, intend to)	*will*	*wollte*	*gewollt*
ziehen (to pull)		*zog*	*gezogen*

APPENDIX C

WHEN YOU'RE STUCK FOR WORDS

DECIDING ON A LANGUAGE

Do you speak English?	*Sprechen Sie English?*
I don't speak German.	*Ich spreche nicht Deutsch*
I don't understand.	*Ich verstehe nicht.*
Can you repeat that, please?	*Können Sie das bitte wiederholen?*
What does . . . mean in German/English?	*Was heißt. . . . auf Deutsch/Englisch?*

TRAVELLING

Here's my passport.	*Hier ist mein Reisepass.*
I'm American.	*Ich bin Amerikaner/in.*
I'm Canadian.	*Ich bin Kanadier/in.*
My name is . . .	*Ich heiße . . . /Mein Name ist . . .*
Where can I exchange dollars?	*Wo kann ich Dollar wechseln?*
What's the exchange rate?	*Wie ist der Wechselkurs?*
These are my suitcases.	*Das sind meine Koffer.*
I've lost my luggage.	*Ich habe mein Gepäck verloren.*
Where is . . .	*Wo ist . . .*
• the taxi stand?	• *der Taxistand?*
• the train station?	• *der Bahnhof?*
• the bus stop?	• *die Bushaltestelle?*
• the underground?	• *die U-Bahn?*
• the car rental?	• *die Autovermietung?*
• the phone/a public telephone?	• *das Telefon/eine Telefonzelle?*
I'd like a . . . ticket for the train to . . .	*Ich möchte eine Zugfahrkarte nach . . .*
• one-way	• *einfach*
• round-trip	• *hin und zurück*
When is the next train to . . . ?	*Wann fährt der nächste Zug nach . . . ab?*
This seat is taken.	*Dieser Platz ist besetzt.*
At what time do we arrive?	*Um wieviel Uhr kommen wir an?*
My car won't start.	*Mein Auto springt nicht an.*
I'm out of gas.	*Ich habe kein Benzin mehr.*
Fill it up.	*Volltanken, bitte.*
How do I get to . . . ?	*Wie komme ich nach . . . /zu . . .*
Is this the road to . . . ?	*Ist das die Straße nach . . .*
Do I go straight?	*Muss ich geradeaus gehen/fahren?*

Do I go to the right/left?	*Muss ich rechts/links abbiegen?*
Where can I park?	*Wo kann ich parken?*

IN A RESTAURANT

Can you recommend a good restaurant?	*Können Sie ein gutes Restaurant empfehlen?*
Is it expensive/affordable?	*Ist es teuer/erschwinglich?*
Do I need to reserve a table?	*Muss ich einen Tisch reservieren?*
I'd like to reserve . . .	*Ich möchte . . . bestellen.*
• a table for two/four.	• *einen Tisch für zwei/vier Personen.*
• for tonight.	• *einen Tisch für heute abend*
• for tomorrow.	• *einen Tisch für morgen*
• a table in the garden.	• *einen Tisch im Garten*
The menu, please.	*Die Speisekarte, bitte.*
What can I get you?	*Was darf's denn sein?*
I'm vegetarian.	*Ich bin Vegetarier.*
I'll have this. (point to item on menu)	*Ich nehme das hier.*
Where's the restroom?	*Wo sind die Toiletten?*
The check, please.	*Die Rechnung, bitte.*
Please keep the change.	*Stimmt so.*

AT THE HOTEL

Are there any free rooms?	*Haben Sie noch Zimmer frei?*
I'd like a . . .	*Ich möchte ein . . .*
• single room.	• *Einzelzimmer.*
• double room.	• *Doppelzimmer.*
• room with a shower.	• *Zimmer mit Dusche.*
I have reserved a room.	*Ich habe ein Zimmer reserviert.*
Do you have a city map?	*Haben Sie einen Stadtplan?*
Do you offer room service.	*Bieten Sie Zimmerservice an?*
Where's . . .	*Wo ist . . .*
• the museum?	• *das Museum?*
• the center?	• *das Stadtzentrum?*
• the bank?	• *die Bank?*
• the post office?	• *die Post?*
Can you go on a city tour here?	*Kann man hier eine Stadtrundfahrt machen?*

ON A SHOPPING SPREE

I'd like to see . . .	*Ich möchte gerne . . . sehen.*
Can you show me . . .	*Könnten Sie mir . . . zeigen?*

I'm looking for . . .	Ich suche . . .
• a gift.	• ein Geschenk.
• a souvenir.	• ein Souvenir.
Can I try this on?	Kann ich das anprobieren?
My (clothing/shoe) size is . . .	Ich habe Größe . . .
How much is it?	Wie teuer ist es/sind sie?
Can you gift-wrap it for me?	Könnten Sie das bitte als Geschenk verpacken?
I'm just looking.	Ich schaue mich nur um.

BETTER SAFE THAN SORRY

Help!	Hilfe!
Look out!	Vorsicht!
Fire!	Feuer!/Es brennt!
Thief!	Dieb!
Stop!	Halt!
Call . . .	Rufen Sie . . .
• an ambulance!	• einen Krankenwagen!
• the police!	• die Polizei!
• the fire department!	• die Feuerwehr!
I need . . .	Ich brauche . . .
• a doctor.	• einen Arzt.
• a dentist.	• einen Zahnarzt.
I don't feel well.	Ich fühle mich nicht wohl.
I have . . .	Ich habe . . .
• a headache.	• Kopfschmerzen.
• a stomach ache.	• Bauchschmerzen.
• a pain in my throat.	• Halsschmerzen.
• a fever.	• Fieber.
• a cold.	• eine Erkältung.
• the flu.	• die Grippe.
• a rash.	• einen Ausschlag.
My . . . hurts.	Mein . . . tut (mir) weh.
• head	• Kopf
• leg	• Knöchel
• ankle	• Bein
• arm	• Arm
• elbow	• Ellbogen
I am allergic to . . .	Ich bin allergisch gegen . . .
Is it serious?	Ist es ernst?
Is it contagious?	Ist es ansteckend?
Do I need a prescription?	Brauche ich ein Rezept?

| Can I have a bill for my insurance? | *Könnte ich bitte eine Rechnung für meine Versicherung haben?* |

SHOPPING LIKE A REAL TOURIST

I want to develop this film.	*Ich möchte diesen Film entwickeln lassen.*
I need batteries for my camera.	*Ich brauche Batterien für meine Kamera.*
At what time do you close?	*Um wieviel Uhr machen Sie zu?*
Where can I buy stamps and postcards?	*Wo kann ich Briefmarken und Postkarten kaufen?*

APPENDIX D

HOW TO SOUND LIKE A NATIVE SPEAKER

Everything OK?	*Alles klar?*
Let's go.	*Los geht's.*
OK.	*Geht in Ordnung.*
No problem.	*Kein Problem.*
Enjoy your meal!	*Guten Appetit!*
Cheers!	*Prost!*
This can't be true!	*Das darf doch wohl nicht wahr sein!*
I'm fed up!	*Mir reicht's!*
I can't believe it.	*Also so was!*
What nonsense!	*So ein Quatsch!*
Right?	*Stimmt's?*
Exactly.	*Genau.*
May I use "du"?	*Darf ich "du" sagen?*
Well, there you have it.	*Na also!*
That is out of the question.	*Das kommt gar nicht in Frage.*
Over my dead body.	*Nur über meine Leiche.*
Darn!	*Verflixt!*
Ouch!	*Aua!*
Oh my goodness!	*Ach du liebes bisschen!/Ach du dickes Ei.*
What's so urgent?	*Wo brennt's denn?*
How dare you?	*Wie kommen Sie dazu . . . ?*
Gesundheit!/Bless you!	*Gesundheit!*
Are you nuts?	*Du spinnst wohl!*
Are you kidding?	*Soll das ein Witz sein?*
Great!	*Klasse!/Toll!/Prima!*
Leave me alone!	*Lass mich in Ruhe!*
Congratulations!	*Gratuliere!*
Don't exaggerate!	*Jetzt übertreiben Sie mal nicht!*
Show me!	*Zeig mal! Gib mal her!*
Better safe than sorry!	*Vorsicht ist die Mutter der Porzellankiste!/ Vorsicht ist besser als Nachsicht!*
Who do you think you are?	*Was glauben Sie eigentlich?*
Keep talking.	*Sprechen Sie ruhig weiter.*

APPENDIX E

SURFING THE WEB IN GERMAN

The Web is a great place to learn more about the German language and the culture of the countries where German is spoken. A good place to start is about.com, which provides loads of great information on these countries, all in English. And when you're feeling a little more confident, try one of your favorite major websites with the extension *.de* for Germany, *.ch* for Switzerland, or *.at* for Austria. You'd be surprised what you'll find. Here's just a small selection:

- *www.yahoo.de/www.yahoo.ch/www.yahoo.at*
- *www.msn.de*
- *www.cnn.de*
- *www.aol.de*

And here are some other sites you can check out, depending on your mood and interests:

GERMANY IN GENERAL

www.deutschland.de is the official and independent portal for all things German. *www.schweiz.ch* gives you information on Switzerland, and *www.oesterreich.at* introduces you to Austria.

GERMAN, AUSTRIAN OR SWISS CITIES

Virtually any German, Austrian or Swiss city has a website, which can usually be accessed by www + name of the city + country code. For example: *www.esslingen.de* will get you to the official website of Esslingen, Germany, (which happens to be my home town), *www.zuerich.ch* will get you straight to Zurich, Switzerland, and *www.wien.at* will get you to Vienna, Austria.

LANGUAGE LEARNING

For language learning tips and links to very interesting websites on all things German, Austrian and Swiss go to *www.learn-german-online.net*, or go to *www.dw-world.de*. The site *www.schulweb.de* provides information on German schools.

TRAVEL

www.deutschland-tourismus.de will give you information and tips for business and pleasure travel in Germany.

www.tiscover.de is a travel network to help you with all your travel needs.

BUSINESS

If you need to do business in a German speaking country, the website of the German American Chamber of Commerce, or of the Swiss American Chamber of Commerce, or of the Austrian American Chamber of Commerce will provide valuable information.

ART

For those of you who wish to know more about German, Austrian and Swiss art and artists, go to *www.art-navigator.com/europe*.

MUSIC

The music lovers among you could check out *www.musichits.de*.

FILM

These websites will interest those among you who love to go to the movies. *www.filmgeschichte.de*, or *www.deutsches-filmmuseum.de*, and *www.film.de*.

LITERATURE

Do you like to read, and would like to check out some of those famous German writers? Go do some research here: *www.sewanee.edu/german/literatur.html*.

HISTORY

This website will allow you to browse through 2000 years of history. Pick any country, and you'll find out valuable information: *www.geschichte.2me.net*.

NEWS

www.zeitung.de provides links to virtually any German language newspaper and magazine in the world.

COOKING

Craving a Wiener Schnitzel? *www.kueche.de* tells you how to prepare it yourself.

APPENDIX F

SUBJECT *WHAT?*: WHAT THOSE GRAMMAR TERMS REALLY MEAN

ADJECTIVE	A word that describes a noun, e.g., *gut* (good), *rot* (red), *nett* (nice). Don't forget that in German, adjectives always agree with the noun in gender, number and case, e.g., *ein netter Mann* (a nice man) but *eine nette Frau* (a nice woman).
ADVERB	A word that modifies an action (a verb), a quality (an adjective) or another adverb, e.g., *schnell* (quickly), *sehr* (very), and *oft* (often). Adverbs never change for agreement.
AGREEMENT	Changing a word to match the grammatical features of another word. In German, adjectives and articles agree with the gender, number and case of the nouns they describe, e.g., *der nette Mann, die nette Frau, das nette Kind* vs. *die netten Männer/Frauen/Kinder* vs. *mit dem netten Mann, mit der netten Frau, mit dem netten Kind*.
ARTICLE	"A/an" or "the." Definite articles mean "the" and indefinite articles mean "a/an." In German, articles match the gender, number and case of the noun, e.g., *ein/der Mann* but *eine/die Frau, ein/das Kind*.
CASE	The form articles, adjectives, pronouns, and a few nouns in German take depending on their grammatical function in the sentence. German has four cases: the nominative, or subject case, the accusative, or direct object case, the dative, the indirect object case, and the genitive, the possessive object case. For example, the nominative *Das ist mein Freund* (This is my friend) becomes the accusative *Ich sehe meinen Freund* (I see my friend).
COMPARATIVE	An expression comparing two people or things or two qualities. In German, the comparative is formed by adding *-er* plus adjective agreement to the positive form of the adjective, e.g., *Helga ist netter als Karin* (Helga is nicer than Karin).
CONJUGATION	Changing a verb to show who the subject is and when the action takes place (i.e., tense—past, present, future). For example, *ich spreche,* but *du sprichst* (you speak) and *du sprachst* (you spoke).
CONJUNCTION	A word that connects other words, phrases, or sentences. The most common coordinating conjunctions are: *und* (and), *aber* (but), *oder* (or). Two subordinating conjunctions are *dass* (that) and *wenn* (when/if).

DEMONSTRATIVE	"This" and "that." In German, demonstratives match the gender, number and case of the nouns they describe or replace, e.g., *dieser Mann* but *diese Frau*.
DIRECT OBJECT	In the sentence *Ich schreibe meinem Bruder eine Karte* (I'm writing a postcard to my brother), the direct object is *eine Karte* (a postcard). Direct objects receive the action of the verb, usually without the "help" of a preposition, like *an* (to) or *für* (for). They take the accusative case.
GENITIVE OBJECT	In the sentence *Das ist die Schwester meines Vaters* (This is the sister of my father), the possessive object is *meines Vaters* (my father's). Possessive objects specify relation and possession and take the genitive case in German.
GENDER	Strictly a grammatical category. In German, nouns, adjectives, and articles have a gender: they can be masculine (*der Mann* [the man]), feminine (*die Frau* [the woman]) or neuter (*das Kind* [the child]).
INDIRECT OBJECT	In the sentence *Ich schreibe meinem Bruder eine Karte* (I'm writing a postcard to my brother), the indirect object is *meinem Bruder* (to my brother). Indirect objects receive the action of the verb, take the dative case, and often follow a preposition, like *an* (to) or *mit* (with).
INFINITIVE	The basic form of a verb (the one you'll find in a dictionary), before it's been changed (or conjugated) to show who the subject is or when the action takes place. For example: *gehen* (to go) and *haben* (to have).
INTRANSITIVE VERB	A verb that stands alone, i.e., cannot take a direct object, e.g., *kommen* (to come).
NOUN	A word that signifies a person, place, thing or idea. For example: *der Mann* (man) or *das Auto* (car).
NUMBER	There are two grammatical numbers in German denoting "one" or "more than one," also called "singular" and "plural." For example: *der Mann* (man), *die Männer* (men).
PASSIVE	A construction in which the subject and the object "switch places"; used to emphasize the object, as in "the cathedral was built in 1873." In German, the passive is formed with the verb *werden* and the past participle, for example *Hier wird Englisch gesprochen* (English is spoken here).
PAST PARTICIPLE	The form of a verb used to form the present perfect or the passive in German, e.g., *Ich habe gesprochen* (I have spoken) or *Hier wird Englisch gesprochen* (English is spoken here).

POSSESSIVE	*Mein/dein* (my/mine, your/yours), etc. A word that shows ownership. In German, possessives are adjectives and agree in gender and number with the object or person possessed, not the owner.
PREFIX	A syllable added to the beginning of a word to change its meaning, e.g., *un-* meaning "un-," which turns an adjective into its opposite. For example: *interessant* (interesting) vs. *uninteressant* (uninteresting).
PREPOSITION	Words such as "to, from, on, in," etc. A connective word that shows spatial, temporal, or other relationships between other words.
PRONOUN	"I, him, mine, this one," etc. A word that takes the place of a noun.
REFLEXIVE VERB	A verb conjugated with a reflexive pronoun: *mich* (myself), *dich* (yourself [sg. infml.]), *sich* (him/herself, itself; yourself [sg./pl. fml.]) *uns* (ourselves), *euch* (yourselves), *sich* (themselves). Sometimes, the action actually "reflects" back on the subject, as in *Ich ziehe mich an* (I'm getting dressed [i.e. dressing myself]); often, there is nothing inherently "reflexive" about the action expressed by the reflexive verb, as in *sich unterhalten* (to have a conversation), *sich erinnern* (to remember), etc.
SUFFIX	An ending that is attached to a word to change its meaning, e.g., *-chen, -lein* meaning "small," or *-heit*, which turns an adjective into a noun as in *krank* v. *Krankheit*.
SUBORDINATE CLAUSE	Also: dependent clause. A phrase or a clause which cannot stand on its own but gives additional information about an element of the main clause. For example, relative clauses or temporal *wenn*-sentences are subordinate clauses.
SUPERLATIVE	Words such as "most, least," etc. An expression indicating the highest degree, used when comparing three or more things, people or qualities, e.g., *Sie ist die schönste Frau der Welt* (She's the most beautiful woman in the world). In German, the superlative is formed by adding *-st* to the positive form of the adjective.
TENSE	The time of an action or state of being, e.g., past, present, future, etc.
VERB	A word showing an action or a state of being, e.g., *sprechen* (to speak) or *sein* (to be).

GERMAN–ENGLISH GLOSSARY

A

der Abbau *mining, dismantling*
abbauen *to mine, to dismantle*
abbiegen *to make a turn*
abbuchen *to debit the account*
die Abbuchung, –en *debit*
der Abend, –e *evening*
Abend *evening, hello (infml.)*
    guten Abend *good evening (fml.)*
    Heiligabend *Christmas Eve*
    zu Abend essen *to have supper*
    das Abendessen, – *dinner*
    zum Abendessen *for supper*
    das Abendgymnasium, –en *night school*
    der Abendkurs, –e *evening class, evening course*
abends *in the evening, evenings*
aber *but*
    Aber nicht doch! *Don't mention it.*
abfahren *to depart, to leave*
abfliegen *to depart (by airplane)*
der Abflug, ¨ –e *departure (by airplane)*
abgeben *to hand in*
abhängen von *to depend upon*
das Abitur, –e *high school examination, diploma*
    Abitur machen *to take the high school examination*
der Abiturient, –en *high school graduate*
die Ablage, –en *a shelf or board giving room for temporary storage, (office) filing*
ablegen *to take off (coat, jacket), to put down; to file*
abmelden *(computers) to sign off, to log off*
abnehmen *to lose weight; to buy*
der Abnehmer, – *buyer*
abrasieren *to shave off*
absagen *to cancel (a meeting, an appointment)*
abschicken *to send off*
abschleppen *to tow (a car)*
abschließen *to lock up, to close, (insurance, agreement) to finish up*
abschließend *in closing*

der Absender, – *return address, sender of mail*
die Absicht, –en *intention*
    Das war nicht meine Absicht. *That wasn't my intention.*
absteigen *to descend, to go down; to stay (in a hotel)*
    In welchem Hotel ist er abgestiegen? *Which hotel is he staying at?*
der Abstellraum, ¨ –e *storage space, storage room*
der Abstieg, –e *descent*
das Abteil, –e *compartment*
die Abteilung, –en *department (section of a museum, university, store)*
abtrocknen *to dry dishes*
abtrocknen (sich) *to dry (oneself)*
abwarten *to wait, to bide one's time*
abwechseln *to take turns*
abwechselnd *one then the other, taking turns*
abwimmeln (jmdn.) *to turn someone away*
acht *eight*
die Achtung *attention, respect, esteem*
    Alle Achtung! *I compliment you.*
achtzehn *eighteen*
achtzig *eighty*
die Adresse, –n *address*
Ade! *Good-bye!, Bye! (Swiss)*
der Affe, –n *ape*
die Ahnung, –en *idea, clue*
    Ich habe keine Ahnung! *I have no idea!*
die Akademie, –n *academy*
der Akt, –e *act*
die Akte, –n *file*
die Aktenablage, –n *filing shelf*
der Aktenschrank, ¨ –e *filing cabinet*
die Aktie, –n *(stock market) share*
die Aktiengesellschaft (die AG), –en *stock company*
aktuell *current, topical*
das Aktuelle *current events*
albern *silly*
das Album, –ben *album*

das alkoholfreie Getränk, –e *soft drink*
das alkoholische Getränk, –e *alcoholic beverage*
alle *all*
allein *alone*
die Allergie, –n *allergy*
allergisch *allergic*
    Sind Sie gegen irgendetwas allergisch? *Are you allergic to anything?*
alles *all*
der Alltagsstress *daily grind*
die Alm, –en *Alpine pasture*
die Alpen *the Alps*
das Alphabet *alphabet*
als *when, as, than*
also *so (conclusion)*
    Also ehrlich! *Quite frankly! Honestly*
    Na also! *See? Well then!*
alt *old*
der Altbau, –ten *old building*
das Alter, – *age*
altertümlich *ancient; antiquated*
altmodisch *old-fashioned*
die Altstadt, ¨ –e *old town, city*
Amerika *America*
der Amerikaner, – *American*
die Amerikanerin, –nen *female American*
an *at, at the side of, to, on*
die Ananas *pineapple*
anbauen *to grow, to produce; to build on*
anbieten *to offer*
anbeten (jmdn.) *to idolize, to adore*
das Andenken, – *souvenir*
andere *others*
ändern *to change, to alter*
anders *different*
andrehen *to sell something of inferior quality/value to someone*
die Anerkennung, –en *respect, recognition*
anfangen *to begin, to start*
    Fangen wir an! *Let's start!*
die Angabe, –n *statement*
das Angebot, –e *offer*
der Angeklagte, –n/–n *accused*
angenehm *pleasant*
    Angenehm! *Pleased to meet you!*

angesichts (gen.) *in view of*
angestellt sein *to be employed*
der/die Angestellte, –n/–n *clerk, employee*
angewandt *applied*
angreifen *to attack*
angrenzen *to border on*
anhaben *to have on, be dressed with*
der Anhang, ¨ –e *attachment (letter, e-mail)*
der Anhänger, – *trailer*
anhimmeln (jmdn.) *to idolize, look lovingly at someone*
ankommen *to arrive*
ankommen auf *depending on*
Es kommt auf . . . an! *It depends on . . . !*
die Ankunft, ¨ –e *arrival*
die Anlage, –n *investment*
anlassen *to start (a car)*
der Anlasser, – *starter*
anlegen *to invest money; to land (a boat)*
das Anmeldeformular, –e *registration form*
anmelden *to register, (computers) to log on*
die Anmeldung, –en *registration*
die Annahme, –n *assumption; also: receiving (goods)*
annehmen *to assume, to presume, to accept*
anonym *anonymous*
anprobieren *to try on (clothing)*
anregend *exciting, stimulating*
der Anruf, –e *telephone call*
der Anrufbeantworter, – *answering machine*
anrufen *to call, to telephone*
ansagen *to announce*
anschauen *to look at, to review*
   sich etwas anschauen *to look at something*
der Anschluss, ¨ –e *connection*
die Anschrift, –en *address*
ansehen *to look at*
ansehen (sich [dat.]) *to look at*
die Ansicht, –en *view, opinion*
die Ansichtskarte, –n *postcard*
die Ansichtssache, –n *matter of opinion*
anspringen *to start (car)*
anspruchsvoll *demanding, sophisticated*
die Anstalt, –en *institution*
(an)statt *instead of*
anstellen *to employ someone*
die Anstellung, –en *job, employment*
anstoßen *to toast (with a drink), to bump into, to run into*

anstrengend *strenuous*
die Antiquität, –en *antique object*
der Antiquitätenladen, ¨ – *antique store, also: second-hand store*
der Anwalt, ¨ –e *lawyer*
antworten *to answer*
anwenden *to use, to apply, to put into effect*
die Anzahl *number of*
die Anzahl der Einwohner *the number of inhabitants*
die Anzahlung, –en *down payment*
die Anzeige, –n *advertisement*
   eine Anzeige aufgeben *to file a classified ad*
   eine Anzeige machen *to report someone (to the police)*
anzeigen *to report; to show*
anziehen *to put on; to dress someone*
anziehen (sich) *to get dressed*
der Anzug, ¨ –e *suit*
der Apfel, ¨ – *apple*
der Apfelsaft, ¨ –e *apple juice*
die Apfelschorle, –n *apple juice with mineral water*
die Apfelsine, –n *orange*
der Apfelstrudel, – *apple strudel*
die Apotheke, –n *pharmacy*
der Apotheker, – *pharmacist (male)*
die Apothekerin, –nen *pharmacist (female)*
der Apparat, –e *telephone; machine*
   Wer ist am Apparat? *Who is on the phone?*
der Akquisiteur, –e *someone soliciting new clients (esp. advertising), canvasser*
der April *April*
die Arbeit, –en *work*
   Arbeit macht das Leben süß. *Honest work never hurts.*
arbeiten *to work*
der Arbeitgeber, – *employer*
der Arbeitseifer *love of work, love of efficiency*
die Arbeitslosigkeit *unemployment*
der Arbeitsplatz, ¨ –e *position, job*
die Arbeitsplatzbeschaffung *job creation (program)*
das Arbeitszimmer, – *home office*
das Archiv, –e *archive(s)*
der Architekt, –en/–en *architect*
die Architektur *architecture*

der Ärger, – *trouble; anger*
das Argument, –e *argument*
arm *poor*
der Arm, –e *arm*
   jemanden auf den Arm nehmen *to pull someone's leg*
der Ärmel, – *sleeve*
   etwas aus dem Ärmel schütteln *to come up with something off-handedly*
arrangieren *to arrange*
die Art, –en *type, kind*
der Artikel, – *article; object*
der Arzt, ¨ –e *physician*
   beim Arzt *at the physician's*
die Ärztin, –nen *physician*
der Aschermittwoch *Ash Wednesday*
das Aspirin, – *aspirin*
die Assistentin, –nen *(female) assistant*
die Attraktivität *attractiveness, attraction*
auch *also*
auf *on top of, onto, on*
   auf Wiederhören *good-bye (on the telephone)*
   auf Wiedersehen *good-bye*
der Aufenthalt, –e *stay*
   Ich wünsche einen angenehmen Aufenthalt. *Have a pleasant stay.*
die Aufgabe, –n *task, duty*
aufhören *to stop*
aufladen *to load*
auflegen *to hang up (the telephone)*
aufmachen *to open*
aufmerksam *attentive, observant*
die Aufmerksamkeit *attention*
   Darf ich um Ihre Aufmerksamkeit bitten? (fml.) *May I have your attention?*
die Aufnahme, –n *photo; recording*
aufnehmen *to take down, to take in*
aufpassen *to pay attention*
aufrecht erhalten *to keep up, to keep alive*
aufregen (sich) *to get excited, to be upset*
aufregend *exciting*
die Aufregung *excitement (often negative)*
der Aufschlag, ¨ –e *surcharge, also: impact (as stone on windshield)*
der Aufschnitt *cold cuts*
aufstehen *to get up*

aufsteigen to ascend, to climb
der Aufstieg, –e ascent
der Auftrag, ¨ –e order
der Auftraggeber, – person who places order, here: person authorized to sign on account
aufwachen to wake up
aufwärmen to warm up
die Aufwendung, –en cost, (raised) funds
aufziehen to parade, to march
der Aufzug, ¨ –e elevator; act (in a play)
das Auge, –n eye
der Augenblick, –e moment
    Augenblick, bitte! Just a moment, please!
augenblicklich current, currently, just now, immediately
der August August
der Auktionär, –e auctioneer
aus out, from
ausbauen to expand, to add (to a building)
die Ausbildung professional training, education
der Ausblick, –e view
ausbrechen to escape, to break out
die Ausdauer perseverance
die Ausfahrt, –en highway exit
der Ausgang, ¨ –e exit
ausgeben to spend (money)
ausgebucht booked, sold out
ausgehen to go out
ausgerechnet out of all (things)
    Ausgerechnet heute muss das passieren? Out of all days this has to happen today?
ausgezeichnet excellent
der Ausguss sink
aushalten to endure
die Aushilfearbeit temporary employment
auskennen (sich) to be well versed in, to know well
die Auskunft, ¨ –e information
ausladen to unload
das Ausland abroad, foreign territories
ausländisch foreign
die Auslandsüberweisung, –en transfer (to foreign bank)
ausleihen to lend
die Ausnahme, –n exception
ausnahmsweise as an exception
ausräumen to clear out
ausrichten (jmdm.) to notify, to give a message
ausruhen (sich) to rest, to relax
aussagen to testify

der Ausschlag rash
das Außenfach, ¨ –e outside compartment
außer (+ dat.) except for, besides
außerhalb (+ gen.) outside of
außerdem besides
ausschließlich exclusively
ausschreiben to advertise
aussehen to look like, to resemble; to appear
    Sieht so aus! Looks like it!
das Aussichtsdeck observation deck
aussteigen to get off, to deboard, to leave (also fig.)
ausstellen to exhibit
die Ausstellung, –en exhibition
das Ausstellungsstück, –e displayed item, exhibit
aussuchen to pick, to choose
der Austausch exchange
der Ausverkauf, ¨ –e sale
    im Ausverkauf sein to be on sale
ausverkauft sold out
die Auswahl selection, choice
der Ausweis, –e ID, passport
auszahlen to pay out
die Auszahlung, –en payment, debit
das Auszahlungsformular, –e withdrawal slip
ausziehen to undress, to take off
ausziehen (sich) to get undressed
der Auszubildende, –n/–n trainee, intern
das Auto(mobil), –s(e) car
die Autobahn, –en highway, freeway
der Automechaniker, – auto mechanic
die Autoreparaturwerkstatt, ¨ –en automobile repair shop
der Autor, –en author

B

der Bach, ¨ –e brook, stream
die Backe, –en cheek
backen to bake
der Backenzahn, ¨ –e molar
das Bad, ¨ –er bathroom; bath
der Bademantel, ¨ – bathrobe, beach robe
die Bademütze, –en bathing cap
baden to bathe
der Badeort, –e spa, health resort
das Badetuch, ¨ –er bath towel, beach towel
der Badeurlaub, –e vacation at seaside

die Badewanne, –n bathtub
das Badezimmer, – bathroom
die Bahn, –en railroad
die Deutsche Bundesbahn (DB) German Federal Railway
der Bahnhof, ¨ –e train station
am Bahnhof at the train station
der Bahnsteig, –e platform
die Bakterie, –n bacterium
bald soon
baldmöglichst as soon as possible
der Balkon, –e balcony, deck
der Ball, ¨ –e ball
die Banane, –n banana
das Band, ¨ –er tape, ribbon
die Bank, –en bank
    auf der Bank at the bank
der/die Bankangestellte, –n, –n bank clerk, teller
die Bankgebühr, –en charge, fee
die Bankleitzahl (BLZ), –en sorting code
die Banküberweisung, –en bank transfer
das Bargeld cash
der Bart, ¨ –e beard
die Batterie, –n battery
der Bauch, ¨ –e stomach
die Bauchschmerzen stomachache
bauen to build
das Bauhaus German design group, 1919–1933
der Bauherr, –en (architectural) client for whom something is built
der Bau, Bauten building
der Baum, ¨ –e tree
der Bauzaun, ¨ –e construction site, fence
bay(e)risch Bavarian
Bayern Bavaria
beachten to watch out for, to bear in mind
der Beamte, –n/–n official, civil servant (male)
die Beamtin, –nen official, civil servant (female)
beanspruchen to demand
beantworten to answer
die Bearbeitungsgebühr, –en administrative fee
beauftragen to order, to engage
der Becher, – cup
bedanken (sich) to thank
bedauerlich sad, regretful, regrettable
die Bedingung, –en condition (depending)
    unter der Bedingung under the condition

die Bedienung *service, operation; waiter/waitress*
die Bedienungsanleitung, –en *operational manual, owner's manual*
bedrohlich *threatening*
bedürfen *to require*
beeilen (sich) *to hurry*
beeindrucken *to impress*
beeindruckend *impressive*
beenden *to end, (computers) to shut down*
befähigen *to enable*
befördern *to promote*
befragen *to question*
der/die Befragte, –n, –n *the one questioned, participant*
begleichen *to pay (a bill)*
begrüßen *to greet*
die Begrüßung, –en *greeting*
behandeln *to treat*
behilflich sein *to help someone, to lend a hand*
bei *with; at; near; during*
beide *both*
beifügen *to attach, to add*
die Beilage, –n *insert, side dish*
das Bein, –e *leg*
das Beispiel, –e *example*
   zum Beispiel (z.B.) *for example*
der Beitrag, ¨ –e *entry, share, participant's share, contribution*
bekannt *well-known*
bekannt sein *to be known, familiar, accustomed to*
der Bekannte, –n *acquaintance*
beklagen *to lament*
beklagen (sich) *to complain*
bekommen *to get, to receive*
die Belastung, –en *pressure*
beleidigen *to insult*
die beleidigte Leberwurst spielen (coll.) *to be in a huff*
die Beleidigung, –en *insult*
beliebt *beloved, much loved, popular*
belustigen *to amuse*
bemerken *to observe, to notice*
bemerkenswert *noteworthy*
benachrichtigen *to inform*
die Benachrichtigung, –en *information, message, memorandum*
benötigen *to need, to require*
das Benzin *gas (for engines)*
beobachten *to watch*
die Beratung, –en *consultation*
die Beratungskosten *consultancy fee*
berechnen *to charge (interest or fees)*

der Bereich, –e *area, field (fig. rather than geographically), range (temperature)*
bereinigen *to clear, clean up*
der Berg, –e *hill, mountain*
die Bergbahn, –en *mountain railway*
der Beruf, –e *profession, job*
   Was sind Sie von Beruf? *What's your profession?*
beruflich *professionally*
die Berufsaussicht, –en *professional prospects*
die Berufsschule, –en *vocational school*
beruhigen *to quiet, to calm*
sich beruhigen *to calm down*
berühmt *famous*
besänftigen *to calm (someone) down*
beschädigt *damaged*
beschäftigen *to employ, to occupy time*
der Bescheid *notification*
Bescheid geben *to inform someone, to let someone know*
   Bescheid wissen *to be informed, to be familiar with*
bescheinigen *to certify, to guarantee*
die Bescheinigung, –en *certificate*
beschönigen *to make sth. better than it is, to gloss over*
beschreiben *to describe*
die Beschwerde, –n *complaint*
beschweren (sich) *to complain*
besetzt *busy, occupied*
besichtigen *to view*
die Besichtigung, –en *sightseeing; inspection*
besonders *especially*
besorgt *worried*
besprechen *to discuss*
die Besprechung, –en *meeting; review*
bestätigen *to confirm*
die Bestätigung, –en *confirmation, acknowledgment*
das Besteck, –e *silverware*
bestehen *to pass*
bestellen *to order, to reserve a table*
   Möchten Sie bestellen? *Would you like to order?*
bestimmt *certain, certainly*
der Bestimmungsort, –e *destination*
der Besuch, –e *visit, visitor*
   zu Besuch kommen *to come for a visit*
besuchen *to visit*

betäuben *to numb; to anesthetize*
die Betäubung, –en *anesthesia*
   die örtliche Betäubung *local anesthesia*
betonen *to emphasize; to add inflection*
die Betonung, –en *emphasis, inflection*
der Betrag, ¨ –e *amount*
betreffen *to concern*
das Bett, –en *bed*
bevor *before*
die Bevölkerung *population*
bewerben (sich) *to apply*
der Bewerber, – *applicant*
die Bewerbung, –en *(job) application*
bewölkt *cloudy*
bewundern *to admire*
bewusst *conscious; aware*
das Bewusstsein *consciousness; awareness*
bezahlen *to pay (for something)*
beziehen *to receive (money)*
das Bier, –e *beer*
   ein Maß (Bavaria) *large beer (1 or 2 l)*
   eine Halbe *half a large glass of beer*
der Biergarten, ¨ – *beer garden*
bieten *to offer*
die Bilanz, –en *(financ., statist.) balance*
das Bild, –er *picture, print, painting*
der Bildschirm, –e *monitor, screen*
der Bildhauer, – *sculptor*
die Bildhauerei *(the art of) sculpture*
der Bildungsweg, –e *educational track*
billig *cheap*
die Binde, –n *bandage*
   die elastische Binde *elastic bandage*
der Binnenmarkt *home market (as opposed to export market)*
die Birne, –n *pear*
bis *until*
   Bis bald. *See you soon.*
   bis Montag *until Monday; by Monday; See you Monday.*
   bis morgen *until tomorrow; by tomorrow; See you tomorrow.*
   Bis später. *See you later.*
das Bisschen *the little bite (of food)*
ein bisschen *a little bit*

ein kleines Bisschen *a little bite*
    Ach du liebes bisschen!
    Oh, no!, Oh, dear!
Bitte! *Please! You're welcome!*
Here you are!
bitten *to ask, to request*
bitter *bitter*
blamieren (sich) *to embarrass (oneself)*
blasen *to blow*
blass *pale*
das Blatt, ¨ –er *leaf, sheet*
blau *blue*
    blau sein, betrunken sein *to be drunk*
    blau machen *to play hooky*
bleiben *to stay, to remain*
    Bleiben Sie am Apparat. *Hold on. Stay on the line.*
    Wie lange bleiben Sie? *How long will you stay?*
der Blick, –e *look, view*
blond *blond*
die Blume, –n *flower*
    Vielen Dank für die Blumen. *Thanks a lot for the flowers, Thanks a lot for the compliment (fig.).*
das Blumengeschäft, –e *flower shop*
die Bluse, –n *blouse*
das Blut *blood*
    Blut ist dicker als Wasser. *Blood is thicker than water.*
der Bock, ¨ –e *deer buck*
    einen Bock schießen *to drop a clangor*
    den Bock zum Gärtner machen *to ask for trouble*
    sturer Bock *stubborn old devil*
    null Bock haben *not to feel up to doing anything*
der Boden, ¨ –n *floor, base, attic*
der Bodenleger, – *floor layer*
die Bohne, –n *bean*
bohnern *to clean; to wax*
bohren *to drill*
die Bombardierung, –en *bombardment*
das Bonbon, –s *candy*
böse *angry*
    Seien Sie mir bitte nicht böse. *(fml.) Please, don't be angry with me.*
die Börse, –n *stock market*
der Bote, –n *messenger*
die Botin, –nen *messenger*
das Boxen *boxing*
der Boxkampf, ¨ –e *boxing match*

die Bratkartoffeln (pl.) *fried potatoes*
brauchen *to need*
braun *brown*
die Bräune *suntan*
die Braut, ¨ –e *bride*
der Bräutigam, –e *groom*
die Brautjungfer, –n *bridesmaid*
das Brautpaar, –e *bridal pair*
die Bremse, –n *brake*
bremsen *to brake*
das Bremspedal, –en *brake pedal*
brennen *to burn*
    Wo brennt's denn? *What's so urgent? What's wrong?*
die Brezel, –n *pretzel*
die Brezen, – (So.. German) *pretzel (large)*
der Brief, –e *letter*
der Briefkasten, ¨ – *mailbox*
die Briefmarke, –n *stamp*
die Brille, –n *glasses*
bringen *to bring*
das Brot, –e *bread*
    das belegte Brot *open-faced sandwich*
das Brötchen, – *breakfast roll*
die Brotzeit *snack meal, dinner*
der Bruder, ¨ – *brother*
brünett *brunette*
das Buch, ¨ –er *book*
buchen *to book*
das Bücherregal, –e *bookshelf*
der Buchhalter, – *accountant*
die Buchung, –en *booking, here: transaction*
das Budget, –s *budget*
das Bügeleisen, – *iron*
bügeln *to iron*
die Bühne, –n *attic; stage*
die Bulette, –n *meatball (originally from Berlin)*
die Bundesrepublik (Deutschland) *the Federal Republic (of Germany)*
das Bundesland, ¨ –er *state*
die Bundesbahn *the Federal Railroad System*
die Bundesliga *national soccer league*
der Bundestag *House of Representatives*
die Bundestagswahl, –en *federal election*
das Bundesverfassungsgericht *Federal Constitutional Court*
bunt *colorful*
die Burg, –en *castle*
der Bürger, – *burgher, citizen*
das Büro, –s *office*
der Bus, –se *bus*

die Busfahrkarte *bus ticket*
die Buslinie, –n *bus line*
die Bushaltestelle, –n *bus stop*
die Butter *butter*
das Butterbrot, –e *a buttered sandwich*

C

das Café, –s *café, coffee shop*
im Café *in a café*
Celsius *centigrade*
der Cent, – *cent*
der Champagner, – *champagne*
die Chemie *chemistry*
der Chemiker, – *chemist*
die Christlich–Demokratische Union (CDU) *the Christian Democratic Union*
der Computer, – *computer*
die Couch, –(e)s *couch*

D

da *there*
    da oben *up there*
das Dach, ¨ –er *roof*
der Dachboden, ¨ –en *attic*
der Dachdecker, – *roofer*
die Dachterrasse, –n *roof terrace*
dagegen *against it*
    Hätten Sie etwas dagegen? *Would you be against that?*
dahinter *behind, beyond it*
damals *back then*
die Dame, –n *lady*
der Damenfriseur, –e (der Damenfrisör, –e) *women's hairdresser*
der Damenfriseursalon, –s (der Damenfrisörsalon, –s) *women's hairdresser's salon*
damit *so that*
dampfen *to steam*
der Dampfer *steamboat*
die Dampferfahrt, –en *steamboat trip*
danach *following that, afterward*
daneben *next to, besides it*
der Dank *thanks; gratitude*
    Recht herzlichen Dank! *Thank you very much.*
    Besten Dank! *Thank you kindly!*
    Vielen Dank für die Blumen! *Thanks for the compliment!*
die Dankbarkeit *gratitude*
danken *to thank*
Danke. *Thanks. Thank you.*
Dankeschön. *Thanks a lot.*

Danke gleichfalls. *Thanks, same to you.*

dann *then*

darüber *about that*

das *the (neuter)*

das Dasein *existence*

    sein Dasein allein fristen müssen *to have to manage by oneself (oftenjokingly used)*

dass *that (conj.)*

die Datei, –en *(computer) file*

die Datenverarbeitung, –en *data processing*

der Dauerauftrag, ¨ –e *automatic bank transfer (for regular monthly payments)*

dauern *to last, to take (time)*

die Dauerwelle, –n *permanent wave*

davor *before*

die Decke, –n *blanket, ceiling*

der Deckel, – *lid*

dein *your (infml. sg.)*

die Delikatesse, –n *delicatessen, gourmet food*

demnach *therefore, thus*

die Demokratie *democracy*

die Demokratisierung *change into a democracy*

denken *to think*

    denken an (acc.) *to think of*

    Wo denkst du hin? *Oh no, what are you thinking!*

denn *because, since*

das Deodorant, –s *deodorant*

der *the (m.)*

der –, die –, dasselbe *same (as in identical items)*

deren *whose, their*

deshalb *that's why*

deswegen *because of that*

deutlich *clearly visible, recognizable*

    deutlich werden *to become clear, to crystallize, to emerge*

der/die Deutsche, –n/–n *German*

Deutschland *Germany*

der Dezember *December*

das Dia, –s *color slide*

der Dialog, –e *dialogue*

der Diaprojektor, –en *slide projector*

dick *thick, thickly*

    dick auftragen (coll.) *to lay it on thick, to exaggerate*

    Ach du dickes Ei! (coll.) *Oh, no!*

die *the (f.)*

der Dieb, –e *thief (male)*

die Diebin, –nen *thief (female)*

der Diebstahl, ¨ –e *theft*

die Diele, –n *hallway*

der Dienst, –e *service*

der Dienstag *Tuesday*

    dienstags *Tuesdays*

diese –r, –s *this*

die Differenz, –en *difference*

das Ding, –e *thing*

    Gut' Ding will Weile haben. *Haste makes waste.*

direkt *direct(ly)*

der Dirigent, –en *conductor*

die Diskussion *discussion*

diskutieren *to discuss*

doch *of course; (reaffirming) yes*

der Dokumentarfilm *documentary*

der Dom, –e *cathedral*

der Donnerstag *Thursday*

doppelt *double*

das Doppelzimmer, – *double room*

das Dorf, ¨ –er *village*

dort *there*

    dort drüben *over there*

    dorthin *there (to)*

die Dose, –n *can, tin, jar, box*

der Dramatiker, – *playwright*

draußen *outside*

das Drehbuch *(movie) script*

der Drehort *(film) location, set*

    am Drehort *(film) on location*

der Dresdner Stollen *fruit cake (Christmas)*

drei *three*

dreimal *three times*

dreißig *thirty*

dreizehn *thirteen*

dringend *urgent, urgently*

der Drogenhändler, – *drug dealer*

die Drogerie, –n *drugstore*

    in der Drogerie *at the drugstore*

    der Drogeriemarkt, ¨ –e *self-service drugstore*

der Drogist, –en *chemist, druggist (male)*

die Drogistin, nen *chemist, druggist (female)*

drüben *over there, there*

der Drucker, – *printer*

du *you (infml.)*

dumm *stupid; silly*

    Wie dumm (von mir)! *How silly (of me)!*

das Dummerchen *little stupid*

dunkel *dark*

dunkelhaarig *dark-haired*

dünn *thin*

das Duplikat, –e *carbon copy, duplicate*

durch *through*

durcheinander bringen *to mix up, to confuse*

durchkommen *to get through, to make it, to survive*

durchleben *to survive, to overcome*

durchqueren *to cut through*

der Durchschlag *carbon copy, duplicate (old-fashioned)*

durchschneiden *to cut through (paper)*

der Durchschnitt *average*

durchsetzen *to push through, to enforce*

durchsichtig *transparent*

dürfen *may, to be allowed to*

    Was darf ich Ihnen bringen? *What may I bring you?*

    Darf ich um Ihre Hand bitten? (antiq.) *May I ask you to marry me?*

die Dusche, –n *shower*

duschen *to shower*

    duschen (sich) *to take a shower*

E

ebenfalls *equally, also*

echt *real, genuine*

die Ecke, –n *corner*

der Edelstahl *stainless steel*

egal (adj./adv.) *indifferent, all the same*

    Das ist mir egal. *That really doesn't matter to me.*

ehe *before*

eher *sooner*

ehemalig *former*

der Ehrengast, ¨ –e *guest of honor*

ehrlich *honest, honestly*

    Ehrlich währt am längsten. *Honesty is the best policy.*

    Um ehrlich zu sein . . . *To be honest . . .*

das Ei, –er *egg*

eigen *own*

das Eigenheim, –e *house (owned)*

eigenständig *independent, independently, under no supervision*

eigentlich *actually*

das Eigentum, ¨ –er *belongings*

das Eigentumsrecht, –e *right to ownership*

die Eigentumswohnung, –en *condominium*

die Eile *hurry*
    Ich bin in Eile. *I'm in a hurry.*
    Ich habe es eilig. *I'm in a hurry.*
einbrechen *to break in*
der Einbrecher, – *burglar*
der Einbruch, –e *break-in, burglary*
eindämmen *to halt, to block*
eindrucksvoll *striking*
einfach *simple, easy*
der Eingang, ̈ –e *entrance*
eingeben *to enter (computers)*
der/die Einheimische, –n, –n *local resident*
einige *several*
der Einkauf, ̈ –e *purchase*
Einkäufe machen *shopping*
einkaufen *to shop (mostly used for grocery shopping)*
die Einkaufsliste, –n *shopping list*
das Einkaufszentrum, –zentren *shopping center*
einladen *to load; to invite*
die Einladung, –en *invitation*
einmal *once*
    noch einmal *once more*
einmalig *unique, once*
einnehmen *to take, to swallow*
einreiben *to rub*
einreiben (sich) *to rub oneself (with lotion, sun screen)*
einreichen *to present check for payment*
eins *one*
einschalten *to switch on*
die Einschaltquote, –en *viewer rating*
das Einschreiben, – *registered letter*
einsteigen *to board, to get on*
    Alles einsteigen, bitte! *All aboard, please!*
eintragen *to register*
eintragen (sich) *to register oneself*
eintreffen *to arrive*
einverstanden *okay, agreed*
    Damit bin ich nicht einverstanden! *I don't agree with that!*
einzahlen *to pay in, to deposit*
die Einzahlung, –en *deposit, credit*
das Einzahlungsformular, –e *deposit slip*
die Einzelheit, –en *detail*
einzeln *piece by piece, singly*
das Einzelzimmer, – *single room*
einzig *sole*
einzigartig *unique*

das Eis *ice; ice cream*
das Eisen *iron (metal)*
    (für jemanden) das Eisen aus dem Feuer holen *to save somebody else's hide (lit. to take the irons out of the fire)*
eisig *icy*
elegant *elegant*
der Elektriker, – *electrician*
das Elektrogerät, –e *electrical appliance*
elf *eleven*
die Eltern *parents*
die E-Mail, –s *e-mail*
    E-Mail abfragen *to check e-mail*
    E-Mail beantworten *to answer e-mail*
    E-Mail weiterleiten *to forward e-mail*
der Empfang *reception*
empfangen *to receive, to greet*
    in Empfang nehmen *to receive (objects or delivery)*
der Empfänger, – *receiver of mail*
der Empfangschef, –s *reception clerk (male)*
die Empfangsdame, –n *reception clerk (female)*
die Empfangshalle, –en *entrance hall*
empfehlen *to recommend*
    Was empfehlen Sie? *What do you recommend?*
    der Küchenchef empfiehlt . . . *The chef recommends . . .*
empfindlich *sensitive*
das Ende *end*
endlich *finally*
endlos *endless*
eng *narrow*
England *England*
der Enkel, – *grandson*
die Enkelin, –nen *granddaughter*
enorm *vast, far-reaching*
entfernen *to remove*
entfernt *distant, far away*
die Entfernung, –en *distance*
entkommen *to get away*
entscheiden *to decide*
die Entscheidung *decision*
    eine Entscheidung treffen *to make a decision*
entschließen (sich) *to decide (to do something)*
entschuldigen *to excuse*
    entschuldigen (sich) *to apologize*

    Entschuldigen Sie. (fml.) *Excuse me.*
    Entschuldige. (infml.) *Excuse me.*
die Entschuldigung, –en *excuse*
entsprechend *equivalent*
entspannen *to relax*
die Entspannung, –en *relaxation*
entstehen *to come up, to arise*
entwenden *to steal, to remove (illegally)*
entwickeln *to develop*
der Entwurf, ̈ –e *draft, rough draft, rough drawing, design*
die Entzündung, –en *inflammation*
er *he*
der Erbe, –n *heir*
erben *to inherit*
erbrechen (sich) *to vomit*
die Erbschaft, –en *inheritance*
die Erbse, –n *pea*
das Erbstück, –e *heirloom*
die Erdbeermarmelade, –n *strawberry jam*
die Erde *earth*
das Erdgeschoss *first floor*
erfahren *to find out, to experience*
die Erfahrung, –en *experience*
der Erfolg, –e *success*
erfolgen *to occur, to result*
erfolglos *unsuccessful*
erfolgreich *successful*
erfrischend *refreshing*
erfüllen *to complete, to fulfill*
    einen Wunsch erfüllen *to fulfill a wish*
    einen Auftrag erfüllen *to complete or fill an order*
das Ergebnis, –se *result, outcome*
erhalten *to receive; to maintain*
erheben *to lift*
    das Glas erheben *to make a toast*
erholen (sich) *to relax, to recuperate*
die Erholung, –en *relaxation, rest*
erinnern (sich) *to remember*
die Erinnerung, –en *memory*
    zur Erinnerung *in memory of*
erkälten (sich) *to catch a cold*
die Erkältung, –en *cold*
erkennen *to recognize*
erklären *to explain*
erleichtern *to facilitate, to make easier*
ermüdend *tiring*

erneuern *to redefine, to renew*
die Erneuerung, –en *renovation, renewal*
der Ernst *seriousness*
Ernst nehmen *to take something seriously*
> **Das kann doch nicht Ihr Ernst sein!** *You can't be serious!*
eröffnen *to open up (an account)*
erreichen *to reach*
erreichbar *reachable*
errichten *to erect (building)*
der Ersatz *replacement, substitute*
erschöpft *exhausted*
erschrecken (sich) *to scare someone; to be frightened*
erschweren *to complicate, to make more difficult*
ersetzen *to replace*
erst *only (in reference to time), first*
erstaunlich *amazing*
erster, –e, –es *first*
die Erststimme *first vote*
erwarten *to await*
die Erwartung, –en *expectation, anticipation*
erweitern *to expand, to extend*
erwerben *to acquire*
erzählen *to tell; narrate*
erzählen von (+ dat.) *to tell about*
es *it*
der Esel, – *donkey*
das Essen *food, meal*
> das Festessen *feast (celebration meal)*
essen *to eat*
das Esszimmer, – *dining room*
die Etage, –n *floor*
etwa *about, perhaps*
> **Oder etwa nicht?** *Isn't that so? Or do you disagree?*
etwas *some, a little*
> **Sonst noch etwas?** *Anything else?*
euer *your (fam. pl.)*
der Euro, – *euro*
der Euroscheck, –s *European checks*
Europa *Europe*
europäisch *European*
Europäische Union *European Union*
die Euroscheckkarte, –n *check card*
exquisit *exquisite*

F

die Fabel, –n *fable*
fabelhaft *fabulous*
der Fabrikant, –en *manufacturer*

das Fach, ¨ –er *compartment; subject (school)*
die Fachkenntnis, –se *knowledge in a particular field*
der Faden, ¨ – *thread*
die Fahne, –n *flag*
fahren *to drive, to go, to ride*
> fahren mit (dat.) *to go by means of*
der Fahrer, – *driver*
die Fahrerin, –nen *driver*
die Fahrkarte, –n *ticket*
der Fahrplan *schedule (bus, train)*
fallen *to fall*
falsch *wrong*
falsch parken *to park wrongly, illegally*
falsch schreiben *to misspell*
die Familie, –n *family*
der Fan, –s *fan, admirer*
fangen *to catch*
fantastisch *fantastic*
die Farbe, –n *color, paint*
färben *to dye*
das Färben *coloring, dyeing*
der Fasching *carnival*
die Fassung, –en *version*
die Fastenzeit, –en *Lent*
faszinierend *fascinating*
das Faxgerät, –e *fax machine*
der Februar *February*
fehlen *to be absent, to be missing*
> **Was fehlt?** *What's missing?*
> **Was fehlt denn?** *What is wrong?*
> **Was fehlt dir?** *What's wrong with you?*
der Fehler, – *mistake*
die Feier, –n *celebration, ceremony*
feiern *to celebrate*
der Feiertag, –e *holiday, day of rest*
> der kirchliche Feiertag *Christian holiday*
fein *fine, precious*
vom Feinsten *(of) the very best*
der Felsen, – *rock*
das Fenster, – *window*
der Fensterrahmen, – *window frame*
die Ferien (pl.) *holidays (school)*
die Feriensaison *vacation season*
fern *distant, far away*
die Ferne *far distance*
die Fernbedienung, –en *remote control*
das Ferngespräch, –e *long distance call*
fernsehen *to watch TV*

das Fernsehen *TV (the media)*
der Fernseher, – *TV (the set)*
fertig (adj./adv.) *ready, finished*
fest *firm*
das Fest, –e *party, celebration, festival*
festlich *celebrational*
die Festplatte, –n *hard drive*
die Festspiele (pl.) *festival*
der Festtag, –e *holiday, festivity*
fett *fat, big*
die Feuerwehr, –en *fire department, fire truck*
das Feuilleton, –s *culture section, feature pages (newspaper)*
das Fieber, – *fever*
die Filiale, –n *branch*
der Film, –e *film, movie*
der Film-Enthusiast, –en *movie fan*
der Filmemacher, – *filmmaker*
finden *to find*
der Finger, – *finger*
die Firma, Firmen *company*
der Fisch, –e *fish*
der Fischer, – *fisherman*
der Fischmarkt, ¨ –e *fish market*
die Fläche, –n *plane, surface*
die Flasche, –n *bottle*
der Flaschner, – *(So.. German) plumber*
der Fleck, –en *mark, spot, stain*
das Fleisch *meat*
flexibel *flexible*
die Fliege, –n *fly*
fliegen *to fly*
der Fliesenleger, – *tiler*
flink *quick*
flirten *to flirt*
der Flohmarkt, ¨ –e *flea market*
floppen *to flop*
die Flucht *flight (escape)*
flüchten *to escape*
der Flug, ¨ –e *flight*
der Fluggast, ¨ –e *airplane passenger*
der Flughafen, ¨ – *airport*
> auf dem Flughafen *at the airport*
der Flugsteig, –e *gate (airport)*
das Flugzeug, –e *airplane*
der Flur, –e *hallway*
folgen *to follow*
die Förderung, –en *mining (raw material); sponsoring, subsidization (financial)*
das Förderungsprojekt, –e *subsidized project*
die Form, –en *form, shape*
das Format, –e *format*
das Formular, –e *form, document*
formulieren *to phrase, to word*

das Foto, –s *photograph*
der Fotoapparat, –e *camera*
der Fotograf, –en, –en *photographer*
die Frage, –n *question*
    Ohne Frage! *Without doubt!*
    Das kommt überhaupt nicht in Frage! *That's out of the question.*
der Fragesteller *the Interviewer (poll)*
die Frankiermaschine, –n *postage meter*
Frankreich *France*
französisch *French*
die Frau, –en *woman, wife, Ms. (used as a form of address)*
die Frauengröße, –n *women's size (clothing)*
die Freie Demokratische Partei (FDP) *the Free Democratic Party*
die Freiheit, –en *freedom*
    Meinungsfreiheit *freedom of opinion*
    Pressefreiheit *freedom of the press*
    Religionsfreiheit *freedom of religion*
    Versammlungsfreiheit *right of assembly*
der Freitag *Friday*
die Freizeit *leisure time*
die Freizeitbeschäftigung, –en *leisure-time activity; pastime*
die Fremdwährung, –en *foreign currency*
die Fremdsprache, –en *foreign language*
freuen (sich) *to be happy about something, to be joyful*
    Freut mich. *Glad to meet you.*
der Freund, –e *male friend, boyfriend*
die Freundin, –nen *female friend, girlfriend*
freundlich *friendly*
die Freundschaft, –en *friendship*
frieren *to freeze*
    Es friert. *It's freezing.*
frisch *fresh*
der Friseur, –e (der Frisör, –e) *male hairdresser*
der Friseursalon, –s (der Frisörsalon, –s) *barbershop, hairdresser's salon, beauty parlor*
    im Friseursalon *at the barbershop/hairdresser*
die Friseuse, –n (die Frisöse, –n) *female hairdresser*
frisieren *to do someone's hair*

die Frucht, "–e *fruit*
der Frühling *spring*
das Frühstück *breakfast*
    inklusive Frühstück *including breakfast*
    zum Frühstück *for breakfast*
führen *to lead, to guide*
die Führung, –en *guided tour*
das Führungsteam, –s *management team*
füllen *to fill*
die Füllung, –en *filling*
das Fundbüro, –s *lost and found*
    auf dem Fundbüro *at the lost and found*
fünf *five*
fünfzehn *fifteen*
fünfzig *fifty*
die Funktion, –en *function*
funktionieren *to function, to work*
für *for*
    Für mich bitte . . . *For me please . . . (when ordering)*
furchtbar *terrible*
fürchten *to fear*
fürchten (sich) *to be afraid*
der Fuß, "–ße *foot*
    auf großem Fuß leben *to live beyond one's means*
der Fußball, "–e *soccer*
das Fußballfeld, –er *soccer field*
die Fußballmannschaft, –en *soccer team*
das Fußballspiel, –e *soccer match*
das Fußballstadion, –stadien *soccer stadium*
der Fußboden, "– *floor*
der Fußgänger, – *pedestrian*
die Fußgängerzone, –n *pedestrian zone, mall*
der Fußnagel, "– *toenail*
die Fußpflege *pedicure*
der Fußpfleger, – *male pedicurist*
die Fußpflegerin, –nen *female pedicurist*
die Fußzeile, –n *(computers) footer*

G

die Gabel, –n *fork*
gähnen *to yawn*
die Gallerie, –n *gallery*
der Gang, "–e *aisle, hallway, corridor*
die Gans, "–e *goose*
ganz *very, whole*
    ganz im Gegenteil *quite to the contrary*
    ganz und gar *utterly, totally*

die Garage, –n *garage*
die Garantie, –n *guarantee*
gar nicht *not at all*
garantiert *warranted, guaranteed*
der Garantieschein, –e *warranty*
die Garderobe, –n *cloakroom, coatrack, wardrobe*
der Garten, "– *garden*
das Gartencafé, –s *garden café*
das Gaspedal, –e *gasoline pedal*
der Gastarbeiter, – *foreign worker*
das Gästezimmer, – *guest room*
der Gastgeber, – *host*
die Gastronomie *catering, restaurant trade*
die Gaststätte, –n *pub, local restaurant*
das Gebäck *pastry, cookies*
das Gebäude, – *building*
geben *to give*
    es gibt *there is, there are*
    Das gibt's doch nicht! *This can't be! (surprise)*
das Gebiet, –e *area*
das Gebirge, – *mountains, mountain*
    im Gebirge *in the mountains*
der Gebirgsverein, – *hiking and climbing club*
das Gebiss, –e *set of teeth*
geboren *born*
die Geborgenheit *security (comfort)*
der Gebrauch *usage*
gebrauchen *to use*
die Gebrauchsanweisung, –en *owner's manual, operational manual*
der Gebrauchtwagen, – *used car*
die Gebühr, –en *charge, fee*
gebührenfrei *free of charge, no fee payable*
der Geburtsort, –e *place of birth*
der Geburtstag, –e *birthday*
der Gedanke, –n *thought*
die Geduld *patience*
geduldig *patient*
gefallen (dat.) *to please, to like*
gefallen lassen (sich) *to put up with*
    Das lasse ich mir nicht gefallen! *I don't let someone treat me that way!*
das Gefängnis, –se *prison, jail*
gegen *against, around*
    gegen zehn Uhr, *around ten o'clock*
gegenseitig *each other, one another, reciprocal*

der Gegenstand, ¨ –e *object*
    persönliche Gegenstände *personal items*
das Gegenteil, –e *the direct opposite (to something)*
gegenüber *opposite (only with location)*
das Gehalt, ¨ –er *salary*
das Geheimnis, –se *secret*
gehen *to go, to leave*
    Wie geht es Ihnen? *How are you? (fml.)*
    Wie geht's? *How are you? (infml.)*
    Das geht leider nicht. *That won't work, unfortunately. That can't be done.*
    Mir geht's nicht so gut. *I'm not feeling so well.*
    Also so geht's nicht! *That's not acceptable!*
    Das ging aber in die Hose! *Well, that was a total flop!*
gehören *to belong*
gelb *yellow*
    gelb vor Eifersucht werden *to turn yellow with jealousy*
das Geld, –er *money*
    Geld allein macht nicht glücklich, (aber es beruhigt). *Money isn't everything (but it comforts).*
der Geldautomat, –en *automatic teller machine*
der Geldbeutel, – *purse*
die Geldbörse, –n *purse*
das Gelee, –s *jelly*
der Gemahl, –e *husband*
die Gemahlin, –nen *wife*
das Gemälde, – *painting*
gemeinsam (adj./adv.) *together*
    etwas gemeinsam haben *to have something in common*
gemischt *mixed*
das Gemüse *vegetable(s)*
gemütlich *cozy*
genau *exact, exactly*
genauso *exactly like, just as*
das Genie, –s *genius*
genießen *to enjoy*
genug *enough*
genügen (v.) *to be sufficient*
    Das genügt mir. *That's sufficient for me.*
geöffnet *open*
die Geographie *geography*
das Gepäck *luggage*
der Gepäckwagen, – *baggage cart*
gerade *straight, just*
geradeaus *straight ahead*
das Gerät, –e *device, appliance, machine*

geräumig *roomy, spacious*
die Gerechtigkeit *justice*
das Gericht *court of law; meal, dish*
der Gerichtshof *court of law*
gern *gladly, willingly*
    Gern geschehen! *My pleasure!*
die Gesamtschule, –n *inclusive school (all grades up to 10th)*
das Geschäft, –e *store; business; deal*
die Geschäftsbesprechung, –en *business discussion; meeting, conference*
der Geschäftsführer, – *business manager*
das Geschenk, –e *gift*
der Geschenkeinkauf, ¨ –e *gift purchase*
geschieden *divorced*
geschlossen *closed*
der Geschmack, ¨ –er *taste*
geschmackvoll *tasteful*
geschnitten *sliced, cut*
die Geschwindigkeits– begrenzung *speed limit*
die Geschwister *siblings*
der/die Geschworene, –n *juror*
gesellig *gregarious*
gespannt *exited, excitedly*
das Gespräch, –e *conversation, talk*
die Gesprächsrunde *panel (discussion)*
gestalten *to create, to form*
gestatten *to allow, to permit*
    Gestatten Sie? *Permit me. May I introduce myself?*
gestern *yesterday*
gesund *healthy*
die Gesundheit, –en *health*
das Getränk, –e *beverage*
das Getreide, – *grain*
das Gewerbe, – *line of business, line of manufacturing*
die Gewerbeanmeldung, –en *business registration*
die Gewerkschaft, –en *union*
gewinnen *to win*
das Gewürz, –e *spice (food)*
der Gipfel, – *summit, mountaintop*
die Girlande, –n *garland*
das Girokonto, –en *checking account*
der Glanz *shine*
glänzend *splendid*
die Glanzzeit *peak period*
das Glas, ¨ –er *glass*
der Glasbläser, – *glassblower*
glatt *smooth*

die Glatze, –n *bald head*
glauben *to believe*
glaubhaft *believable*
gleich *in a minute; equal, similar*
    Gleich und gleich gesellt sich gern. *Birds of a feather flock together.*
die Gleichheit *equality*
der Gleichstrom *direct current (DC)*
gleichzeitig *simultaneous, simultaneously*
das Gleis, –e *track (train)*
die Gleitzeit, –en *flexible working hours*
der Gletscher, – *glacier*
das Glück *luck, happiness*
glücklich *happy*
das Gold *gold*
golden *golden*
die Goldfüllung, –en *gold filling*
der Goldhenkel, – *gold handle*
die Goldkrone, –n *gold crown*
die Grafik, –en *graphic art, illustration*
der Grafiker, – *graphic designer*
das Gramm *gram*
die Grammatik *grammar*
das Gras, ¨ –er *grass*
gratulieren *to congratulate*
grau *gray*
greifen *to grasp*
die Grenze *border*
Griechenland *Greece*
die Grippe, –n *flu*
groß *big, large*
großartig *magnificent, great*
die Größe, –n *size*
die Großeltern *grandparents*
der Größenwahn *delusions of grandeur*
der Großkonzern, –e *large concern, company*
die Großmutter, ¨ – *grandmother*
die Großtante, –n *great aunt*
der Großvater, ¨ – *grandfather*
Grüezi *hello (Swiss)*
grün *green*
    grün vor Neid werden *to become green with envy*
die Grünen *the Green Party*
die Grünanlage, –n *green space/area, park, recreational facility*
die Grünfläche, –n *green space, lawn, park*
gründen *to found*
das Grundgesetz *constitution*
gründlich *thorough, thoroughly*

die Grundschule, –n *elementary school*

das Grundstück, –e *land, estate*

der Grundstückspreis, –e *cost of land*

das Grundrecht, –e *constitutional rights*

die Gruppentour, –en *group tour*

der Gruß, ̈ –ße *greeting*
    Mit freundlichen Grüßen *Sincerely*

grüßen *to greet*
    Grüß Gott! *Hello (So. German)*
    Grüß dich. (infml.) *Hello.*

gucken *to look (So. German)*
    Guck mal! *Look!*

gültig *valid*

die Gunst, ̈ – *favor*
    zu Ihren Gunsten *in your favor*

die Gurke, –n *pickle, cucumber*

der Gürtel, – *belt*

gut *good, well*
    Also gut! *All right then!*

gutaussehend *handsome, good-looking*

der Gutachter, – *evaluator*

die Gutschrift, –en *credit (form)*

das Gymnasium, Gymnasien *high school*

die Gymnastik, – *gymnastics, calisthenics*
    Gymnastik machen *to do calisthenics*

H

das Haar, –e *hair*
    jemandem stehen die Haare zu Berge *someone is quite shocked (coll.)*

die Haarfarbe, –n *hair color*

der Haarschnitt *haircut*

der Haartrockner, – *hair dryer*

das Haarwuchsmittel, – *hair growth product*

haben *to have*

der Hafen, ̈ – *harbor*

haften *to be liable*

die Haftung, –en *liability*
Haftung übernehmen *to accept liability*

der Hagel *hail*

hageln *to hail (hail falling)*

die Halbzeit, –en *halftime*

halb *half*
    ein halbes Kilo *half a Kilo (500 gram)*

die Hälfte, –n *half*

zur Hälfte *by half*

die Halle, –n *hall*

hallo *hello*

der Hals, ̈ –e *throat, neck*

die Halsschmerzen (pl.) *sore throat*

das Halsweh *sore throat*

halten *to hold, to stop*
    sich (jmd.) auf dem Laufenden halten *to keep abreast of the news, to stay (keep someone) informed*

halten von *to think of, to evaluate*

die Haltestelle, –n *stop (as in bus/tram/subway stop)*

die Hand, ̈ –e *hand*
    Eine Hand wäscht die andere. *You do me a favour, I do you a favour.*

handeln *to bargain*

handeln von *to be about, deal with (topic)*

handeln mit *to deal with (goods)*

der Händler, – *trader, shopkeeper*

die Handlung, –en *activity, story, action*

der Handschuh, –e *glove*

das Handtuch, ̈ –er *towel*

das Handwerk *handicraft, trade*

der Handwerker, – *handyman, workman, craftsman*

handwerklich *manual*

handwerkliches Geschick *manual dexterity, skilled hands*

das Handy, –s *cell phone*

hängen *to hang*

hängen bleiben *to be stuck with something, to be left with*

der Hanseat, –en *person of old lineage from a Hanseatic city*

hart *hard*

der Hass *hate, hatred*

hassen *to hate*

häßlich *ugly*

der Hauptbahnhof, ̈ –e *main, central railroad station*

der Hauptdarsteller, – *protagonist, lead/main character*

die Hauptpost *main post office*

die Hauptrolle, –n *lead, main role*

hauptsächlich *mainly, predominantly*

die Hauptschule, –n *junior high school*

die Hauptspeise, –n *main course*

das Haus, ̈ –er *house*

die Haustür, –en *front door*

heben *to lift*

heilbar *curable*

heilen *to heal*

die Heilquelle, –n *medicinal spring*

das Heim, –e *home*
    Trautes Heim, Glück allein. *Home, sweet home.*

das Heimatland *homeland*

heiß *hot (temperature only)*

heißen *to be named, to be called*

die Heizung, –en *heating*

helfen *to help*
    helfen bei (dat.) *to help with*

hell *light, pale, bright*

das Hemd, –en *shirt*
    Das Hemd ist mir näher als der Rock. *Charity begins at home.*

heraus *out(ward)*

herausbrechen *to break off*

der Herbst *autumn*

der Herd, –e *stove*

herein *In(ward)*

der Herr, –en, *gentleman, mister (usually used only in address)*

der Herrenfriseursalon, –s (der Herrenfrisörsalon, –s) *barbershop*

Herrje! *My Goodness!*

herrlich *glorious, wonderful*

herumsprechen (sich) *to be talked about, to become common knowledge*

herunter *down(ward)*

herunterladen *to download*

herüber *across, over*

hervorheben *to point out, to emphasize*

hervorragend *excellent, outstanding*

heute *today*

heutzutage *nowadays*

die Hexe, –n *witch*

hier *here*

hierzulande *in this country*

die Hilfe *help*

die Hilfeleistung, –en *aid, support*

hilfreich *helpful*

hilfsbereit *willing to help*

der Himmel, – *sky, heaven*

Himmelfahrt *Ascension Day*

hin *(to) there*
    hin und zurück *round trip*

hinaus *out(ward)*

hinten *at the back*

hinter *behind*

hintereinander *one behind the other*

der Hintergrund, ̈ –e *background, backdrop*

hinterlassen *to leave (a message), to bequeath*
hinterlegen *to leave (a note, document, etc.) for someone*
hinüber *across, over*
hinunter *down(ward)*
hinweg *over, beyond*
die Hitze *heat*
hitzefrei *school's out due to heat*
das Hobby, –s *hobby*
hoch *high (up), tall*
der Hochbetrieb *rush hour, busy season, rush*
das Hochdeutsch *High German, Standard German*
die Hochschule *university, academy*
die Hochzeit, –en *wedding*
der Hochzeitstag, –e *wedding anniversary*
der Hof, ̈ –e *court, yard, courtyard*
hoffen *to hope*
hoffentlich *hopefully*
die Hoffnung, –en *hope*
das Hoftheater *court theater*
höher *higher*
der Holländer, – *Dutchman*
der fliegende Holländer **The flying Dutchman**
der Holzfußboden, ̈ – *wooden floor*
die Homepage, –s *homepage*
hören *to hear, listen*
   Auf Wiederhören. *Goodbye. (on the telephone)*
der Hörer, – *receiver*
die Hose, –n *pants, slacks*
das Hotel, –s *hotel*
   im Hotel *in the hotel*
der Hotelpage, –n *bellhop*
hübsch *pretty*
der Hubschrauber, – *helicopter*
das Huhn, ̈ –er *hen, chicken*
das Hühnchen, – *chicken*
der Hund, –e *dog*
hundert *hundred*
   hunderteins *one hundred one*
   zweihundert *two hundred*
der Hunger *hunger*
Hunger haben *to be hungry*
hungrig *hungry*
die Hupe, –n *horn*
Hurra *hurray*
husten *to cough*
der Husten *cough*
der Hut, ̈ –e *hat*
Hut ab! *Well done!*
die Hütte, –n *shelter, hut*
die Hypothek, –en *mortgage*

I

ich *I*
die Idee, –n *idea, creative thought (not clue)*
ihr *you (infml. sg./pl.), her, their (poss.)*
Ihr *your (fml.)*
immer *always*
immerhin *still, after all, if nothing else*
die Immobilie, –n *real estate*
der Immobilienmakler, – *real estate agent*
der Immobilienmarkt, ̈ –e *real estate market*
die Impfung, –en *vaccination*
imposant *impressive*
in *in, inside, into*
indem *in such a way that; as, while*
individuell *individual*
die Industrie, –n *industry*
der Industrielle, –n *industrialist*
industriell *industrial*
das Industrieprojekt, –e *industrial project*
der Industriezweig, –e *industrial branch*
die Information, –en *information*
informieren *to inform*
   sich informieren über (+ acc.) *to inform oneself about, to stay informed*
die Infrastruktur, –en *infrastructure*
der Inhalt, –e *contents*
die Initiale, –n *initials*
innen *inside, interior*
der Innenarchitekt, –en *interior architect*
der/die Innenausstatter/in, –, –nen *interior designer*
das Innenfach, ̈ –er *inside compartment*
innerhalb (+gen.) *inside*
die Innenstadt, ̈ –e *center of town, downtown district*
die Insel, –n *island*
das Inserat, –e *the advertisement*
inserieren *to place an ad*
insgesamt *altogether, sum total*
intelligent *intelligent*
der Intendant, –en *director*
interessieren für (sich) *to be interested in*
interessant *interesting*
das Internet *Internet*
die Internetadresse, –n *Internet address, URL*

das Internet–Café, –s *Internet Café*
das Interview, –s *interview*
interviewen *to interview*
der Interviewleiter, – *interview director*
investieren *to invest*
die Investition, –en *investment*
das Investment, –s *investment*
irgendwann *sometime*
irgendwas *something*
irgendwie *somehow*
irgendwo *somewhere*
irren *to err*
   Irren ist menschlich. *To err is human.*
Italien *Italy*

J

die Jacht, –en *yacht*
die Jacke, –n *jacket*
das Jahr, –e *year*
die Jahreszeit, –n *season*
das Jahrhundert, –e *century*
die Jahrhundertwende, –n *turn of the century*
jährlich *yearly, every year*
der Januar *January*
der Jazz *jazz*
das Jazzlokal, –e *jazzclub*
die Jeans, – *(denim) jeans*
je *ever; each; respectively*
   je . . . desto *the (+adj.) the (+adj.) (as in "the bigger the better")*
   je nachdem *depends on, depending upon*
jedenfalls *anyway, in any case*
jeder, –e, –s *each, every*
   Jedem Tierchen sein Pläsierchen. *To each its own.*
jederzeit *anytime*
jener *that*
jemals *ever*
jetzt *now*
der Jog(h)urt (also: das) *yogurt*
die Jugend *youth*
jugendlich *young, adolescent*
der Jugendliche, –n *adolescent*
der Jugendstil *Art Nouveau*
der Juli *July*
jung *young*
der Junge, –n/–n *boy*
der Juni *June*
Jura *the study of law*
   Er studiert Jura. *He is studying law.*
der Jurist, –en *lawyer, attorney at law*

K

das Kabel, – cable
die Kabelfabrik, –en cable factory
das Kabelfernsehprogramm, –e cable program
der Kabelsender, – (TV) cable station
der Kaffee, –s coffee
Kaffee trinken to have coffee
das Kaffeehaus, ˝–er coffee house
der Kahn, ˝–e barge
der Kaiser, – emperor
die Kaiserzeit imperial times
das Kalbfleisch veal
kalt cold
die Kaltmiete, –en rent (without utilities)
die Kälte cold (weather)
die Kamera, –s camera
kämmen to comb
   sich (die Haare) kämmen to comb (one's hair)
kämpfen to fight
Kanada Canada
der Kanadier, – Canadian
der Kandidat, –en candidate
das Kännchen, – small pot of coffee or tea (restaurant)
die Kanne, –n pot (as in coffeepot), pitcher
die Kapelle, –n band
das Kapital capital, assets
die Kapitalangabe, –n details on assets or profit and loss (of a company)
kaputt broken; tired
   Ich bin kaputt. I'm exhausted.
die Karaffe, –n caraffe
der Karfreitag Good Friday
die Karies tooth decay, cavity, caries
der Karneval carnival (period before Lent)
die Karotte, –n carrot
das Kartentelefon, –e public telephone operated with telephone cards
die Kartoffel, –n potato
der Kartoffelbrei mashed potatoes
der Kartoffelsalat potato salad
der Karton, –s box, cardboard box, carton
der Käse cheese
die Kasse, –n cash till, cashier's desk
der Kassierer, – cashier
die Kathedrale, –n cathedral

kaufen to buy
das Kaufhaus, ˝–er department store
kaum hardly, barely
die Kaution, –en security (rent)
kein no, not any, not a
keine, keinerlei none
der Keller, – cellar, basement
der Kellner,– waiter
die Kellnerin, –nen waitress
kennen to know, to be familiar with
kennenlernen to get to know
die Kenntnis, –se knowledge
die Keramik ceramics
das Keramikstück, – ceramic piece
die Kernarbeitszeit non-flexible working time
die Kette, –n necklace, chain
der Kiez old inner city residential area
das Kilo, –s kilo
der Kilometer, – kilometer (km)
das Kind, –er child
der Kindergarten, ˝– kindergarten
das Kinderzimmer, – child's room
kindhaft childlike
der Kineast, –en film enthusiast
das Kino, –s movie theater
das Kinopublikum moviegoers, movie theater audience
der Kiosk, –s kiosk, newsstand
die Kirche, –en church
die Kirsche, –n cherry
der Kirschstrudel cherry strudel
das Kissen, – pillow
die Kiste, –n box, container, crate
der Kittel, – gown, apron
die Klage, –n complaint, (jur.) lawsuit
der Kläger, – plaintiff
klappen to work, to happen (successfully)
klar clear
   Klar! Certainly! Of course!
die Klasse, –n class; grade
   Klasse! Great! First rate!
   die erste Klasse the first grade
   erster Klasse first class
das Kleid, –er dress
die Kleider (pl.) clothing (antiq.)
Kleider machen Leute. Clothing makes the man.
der Kleiderschrank, ˝–e wardrobe
die Kleidung clothing
klein small

das Kleingeld coins, change
die Kleinstadt, ˝–e small town
klemmen to jam
der Klempner, – plumber
der Kletterturm, ˝–e climbing tower (playground)
klingen to sound
das Kloster, ˝– cloister, monastery, convent
das Knie, – knee
der Knopf, ˝–e button
knusprig crunchy, crispy
die Koalition, –en coalition
die Koalitionsregierung, –en coalition government
der Koch, ˝–e (male) cook
   Viele Köche verderben den Brei. Too many cooks spoil the broth.
die Köchin, –nen (female) cook
kochen to cook
der Kochtopf, ˝–e cooking pot
der Kode code
der Kodename codename
das Kodewort codeword
der Koffer, – suitcase
das Kofferfließband, ˝–er baggage conveyor belt
der Kollege, –n co-worker, colleague
das Kombinationsschloss, ˝–er combination lock
kommen to come
   Komm schon! Come on!
   Wie kommen Sie denn dazu? How dare you!
die Kommunalwahl, –en local election
der Kommentar, –e commentary
die Kommode, –n dresser
die Komödie, –n comedy
komplex complex
der/die Komparse, –n (film) extra
die Konditorei, –en confectionary, café with bakery and pastry shop
die Konferenz, –en conference
der Konferenzraum, ˝–e conference room
der Kongress, –e convention
der König, –e king
der Konkurrent, –en competitor
die Konkurrenz competition
konkurrenzfähig competitive
können to be able to, can (ability)
der Konsul, –n consul
das Konsulat, –e consulate
der Kontakt, –e connection, contact

das Konto, Konten account
    ein Konto auflösen to close an account
    ein Konto einrichten to open an account
    ein Konto eröffnen to open an account
der Kontoauszug, "-e bank statement
der Kontostand balance (of account)
der Kontrast, -e contrast
der Konzern, -e company, corporation
das Konzert, -e concert
der Konzertveranstalter, - concert promoter
kooperieren to cooperate
das Kopfrechnen mental arithmetic
der Kopf, "-e head
    jemandem den Kopf waschen (coll.) to set someone straight
kopflos headless
die Kopfschmerzen (pl.) headache
das Kopfweh headache
die Kopfzeile, -n (computers) header
die Koproduktion, -en co-production
der Körper, - body
die Körperpflege personal hygiene
der Körperpuder, - dusting powder
die Kosten (pl.) costs
kosten to cost
    Was kostet das? How much does it cost?
der Kostenvoranschlag, "-e cost estimate
der Krabbensalat, -e shrimp salad
kräftig strong, big
der Kragen, " - collar
krank ill
    Ich bin krank. I am ill.
das Krankenhaus, "-er hospital
der Krankenpfleger, - (male) nurse
die Krankenschwester, -n (female) nurse
der Krankenwagen, - ambulance
krankhaft pathological
die Krankheit, -en illness, disease
der Kranz, "-e circle, frame, wreath
kraus wavy, frizzy

die Krawatte, -n tie
die Kreditkarte, -n credit card
das Kreditinstitut, -e bank
der Kreis, -e circle
das Kreuz, -e cross
die Kreuzfahrt, -en cruise
die Kreuzung, -en intersection; cross breed
der Krieg, -e war, (often) World War II
der Krimi, -s crime drama (movie, novel)
der Kriminalfall, "-e criminal case
das Kriminalgericht, -e criminal court
die Krimiserie, -n suspense series (TV)
der Krimskrams knickknacks, odds and ends
die Kritik, -en criticism
der Kritiker, - critic, reviewer
die Krone, -n crown
der Kronzeuge, -n main witness
die Küche, -n kitchen
der Küchenschrank, "-e kitchen cabinet, cupboard
der Kuchen, - cake
der Kugelschreiber, - ballpoint pen
die Kuh, "-e cow
der Kühlschrank, "-e refrigerator
der Kuli, -s ballpoint pen
die Kultur, -en culture
die Kulturnotiz, -en cultural item (newspaper)
der Kunde, -n customer (male)
die Kundin, -nen customer (female)
der Kundendienst, -e customer service
die Kunst, "-e art, the arts
der Künstler, - artist
das Künstlerviertel, - artists' district, district inhabited by artists
die Kunstausstellung, -en art exhibition
die Kunstbibliothek, -en art library
das Kunstmuseum, Kunstmuseen art museum
das Kunstwerk, -e work of art
die Kur, -en cure, treatment
    eine Kur machen to take a cure
der Kurfürst, -en (prince) elector, electoral prince
der Kurgast, "-e spa visitor
das Kurkonzert, -e concert at a spa

der Kurort, -e spa, health resort
    in einem Kurort in a spa
der Kurs, -e exchange rate
    der Kurs ist niedrig/hoch. The exchange rate is low/high.
der Kurswagen, - through coach (on a train)
die Kurtaxe, -n spa surcharge
kurz short
    sich kurz fassen to keep it short (in words)
    in Kürze shortly
die Kurzfassung, -en synopsis, short version
der Kurzfilm -e short feature, short film
kurzfristig on short notice
die Kusine, -n cousin (female)
der Kuss, "-e kiss

L

labil unstable
laden to load
der Laden, " - store
der Ladenschluss (store) closing time
    vor Ladenschluss before the store closes
der Ladentisch, -e (store) counter
die Lage, -n location, position
das Lamm lamb
die Lampe, -n lamp
der Lampenschirm -e lampshade
das Land, "-er country; state
    auf dem Land in the country
landen (plane) to land
die Landtagswahl, -en state election
landesweit statewide; all across the country
lang long
lange long (adv.)
    Es dauert lange. It takes a long time.
langfristig long-term
langsam slow, slowly
längst for long, already; longest
langweilig boring
lassen to leave, to let, to have done
    Das lässt sich machen! That can be done!, That's managable!
der Lastkraftwagen, -en truck
der Lastwagen, - truck
laufen to run, to walk
    jemanden auf dem Laufenden halten to keep someone posted/informed

im Lauf(e) (gen.) in the course of
laut loud
lauten to sound
läuten to ring
leben to live
das Leben, – life
der Lebenslauf, ¨ -e résumé
die Lebensmittel (pl.) groceries
der Lebensretter, – life-saver
lecker delicious
  Die Kuchen sind lecker. The cakes are delicious.
das Leder leather
  aus Leder made from leather
ledig single (not married)
leer empty
legen to put down, to lay down
legen (sich) to lie down
die Legende, –n legend
der Lehm mud
die Lehmpackung, –en mud pack
lehren to teach
die Lehre, –n apprenticeship; lesson
der Lehrer, – (male) teacher
die Lehrerin, –nen (female) teacher
der Lehrling, –e apprentice
leicht light, easy
die Leichtathletik track and field
leiden to suffer
leiden an (dat.) to suffer from
leider unfortunately
leid tun to be sorry, to feel sorry for someone
der Leierkasten, ¨ – barrel organ
der Leierkastenmann, ¨ –er organ-grinder
leihen to lend
das Leinen linen
das Leinenkleid linen dress
die Leinwand, ¨ –e canvas, screen (movies)
leise soft (not loud)
leisten (sich) to afford
leiten to lead, manage
der Leitartikel, – editorial, cover story
die Leitung, –en cable, pipe; leadership, management; line
  Die Leitung ist besetzt. The line is busy.
  Die Leitung ist gestört. The line is temporarily out of order.
lernen to learn
lesen to read
die Leselampe, –en reading lamp
die Leseratte, –n bookworm

letzte, –r, –s last
leugnen to deny
  sich nicht leugnen lassen can't be denied
die Leute people
das Licht, –er light
lieb sweet, dear
Wie lieb von dir! (infml.) How sweet of you!
die Liebe, –n love
lieber preferably
das Lieblingsstück, –e favorite piece
der Lieferant, –en, –en supplier, deliverer
die Lieferfirma, –firmen supplier
die Lieferung, –en delivery, shipment
der Lieferschein, –e delivery note
der Liefertermin, –e delivery date
der Lieferwagen, – delivery van
die Liegehalle, –n solarium
liegen to lie
der Liegewagen, – couchette (on a train)
die Liga, –s league
die Limonade, –n lemonade
links to the left, on the left
die Lippe, –n lip
der Liter, – liter
das Lizenzrecht, –e licensing right
der LKW, –s truck
das Loch, ¨ –er hole
ein Loch im Zahn cavity
die Locke, –n curl
lockig curly
der Löffel, – spoon
der Logensitz, –e box seat
logisch logical
lohnen to reward
  Es lohnt sich. It's worthwhile.
das Lokal, –e pub
der Lokomotivführer, – engine driver
los loose
  Los geht's! Let's go!
  Was ist los? What's the matter?
löschen to delete, also: extinguish
lösen to solve
der Lösungsvorschlag, ¨ –e suggested solution, suggestion
losrennen to dash off
die Lösung, –en answer, solution
luftdicht airtight
luftig breezy
die Luftpost air mail
  mit Luftpost by airmail

die Lunge, –n lung
die Lust, ¨ –e pleasure, delight
Lust haben to feel like

M

machbar doable
machen to do, to make
  (Es) macht nichts. (It) doesn't matter.
  Das macht 125 Euro. That'll be 125 euros.
  Mit mir kann man's ja machen! The things I put up with!
  Was (wie viel) macht das? How much does it come to?
das Mädchen, – girl
die Magenschmerzen (pl.) stomach-ache
der Mai May
der Mais corn
  einmal once
  x-mal x times
das Mal, –e time, event
  malen to paint
der Maler, – painter
die Malerei, –en painting
der Makler, – broker, real estate agent
der Maler, – painter
die Mama, –s mom
der Manager, – manager
manche some (usually pl.)
manchmal sometimes
der Mann, ¨ –er man
die Männergröße, –n male clothing size
männlich male
die Mannschaft, –en team
der Mantel, ¨ –e coat
der Markt, ¨ –e market
die Marktanalyse, –n market analysis
die Marmelade, –n preserves, jam
das Marzipan marzipan
der März March
der Maskenball, ¨ –e costume ball
die Massage, –n massage
das Maßband, ¨ –er tape measure
die Massenkultur mass culture
die Massenmedien mass media
das Material, –ien material
materiell material
die Matinée, –s matinee
der Maurer, – brick-layer
die Maus, ¨ –e mouse
das Medikament, –e medication
das Meer, –e ocean, sea

das Mehl *flour*
mehr *more*
mehrere *several*
mehrmals *several times*
mein *my*
meinen *to mean*
    Wie meinst du das?
    (infml.) *How do you mean that?*
    Meinen Sie das wirklich?
    (fml.) *Do you really think so?*
meinetwegen *in regards to me, for my sake; OK by me.*
die Meinung, –en *opinion*
meiner Meinung nach *in my opinion*
die Meinungssache, –n *matter of opinion*
die Meinungsumfrage, –n *opinion poll*
meist *most, mostly*
meistens *most of the time*
der Meister, – *master craftsman*
die Menge *quantity, a lot; crowd*
der Mensch, –en *human being*
die Menschheit *mankind*
die Messe, –n *trade fair, exhibition*
    auf der Messe *at the trade fair*
das Messegelände, – *fairgrounds*
messen *to measure*
der Messestand, ¨ –e *booth*
das Messer, – *knife*
das Metall, –e *metal*
der Metallfaden, ¨ – *metal thread*
die Miete, –n *rent*
mieten *to rent*
    ein Segelboot mieten *to rent a sailboat*
der Mieter, – *tenant*
die Mietpreisbindung, –en *rent control*
das Mietshaus, ¨ –er *tenement building, apartment complex*
der Mietvertrag, ¨ –e *rental agreement*
der Mietwagen, – *rental car*
die Milch *milk*
das Milchprodukt, –e *dairy product*
die Million, –en *million*
der Millionär, –e *millionaire*
mindestens *at least, minimally*
das Mineralwasser, – *mineral water, soda water*
das Mineralwasserbad, ¨ –er *bath or pool filled with mineral water*
die Minute, –n *minute*
der Mist *manure, garbage*

mit *with, by means of (transportation)*
der Mitarbeiter, – *colleague, co-worker*
mitbringen *to bring (along)*
mitentscheiden *to participate in a decision*
die Mitgift *dowry*
mithalten (mit) *to keep up with*
mitmachen *to participate*
mitnehmen *to bring along, to take with*
der Mittag, –e *noon*
das Mittagessen, – *lunch (main meal)*
    zum Mittagessen *for lunch*
mittags *at noon*
die Mitte, –n *middle*
mitteilen *to inform*
die Mitteilung, –en *message, announcement*
die Mittel, – *means, medicine*
das Mittelalter *the Middle Ages, medieval times*
der Mittelgang, ¨ –e *middle aisle*
das Mittelmeer *Mediterranean Sea*
die Mittelmeerinsel, –n *Mediterranean island*
mitten: mitten auf (dat.) *in the middle of*
die Mitternacht, ¨ –e *midnight*
mitwirken *to participate, to take part in*
der/die Mitwirkende, –n *participant (theater, film), pl.: the cast*
der Mittwoch *Wednesday*
die Möbel *(pl.) furniture*
der Möbelstil, –e *furniture style*
das Möbelstück, –e *piece of furniture*
das Modell, –e *model*
mögen *to like (inclination), may (possibility)*
die Möglichkeit, –en *possibility*
die Mohrrübe, –n *carrot*
der Moment, –e *moment*
    Einen Moment bitte! *Just a moment, please!*
    im Moment *at the moment, at the present time*
der Monat, –e *month*
der Mond, –e *moon*
der Monitor, –e *computer monitor, screen*
monströs *monstrous, gigantic, ugly*
der Montag *Monday*
morgen *tomorrow*
    morgen früh *tomorrow morning*

der Morgen *morning*
    Guten Morgen. *Good morning. (fml.)*
    Morgenstund' hat Gold im Mund. *The early bird catches the worm.*
    morgens *in the morning*
Morgen *morning, hello (infml.)*
das Motorrad, ¨ –er *motorcycle*
müde *tired*
    Ich bin müde. *I am tired.*
die Müdigkeit *tiredness*
der Muffel, – *grouch*
der Müll *garbage*
das Müllfahrzeug, –e *garbage truck*
der Mund, –e *mouth*
das Mundwasser, ¨ – *mouthwash*
die Musik *music*
    klassische Musik *classical music*
das Museum, Museen *museum*
    im Museum *at the museum*
der Musiker, – *musician*
das Müsli, –s *muesli*
müssen *to have to, must (necessity)*
    Wenn es denn sein muss! *If I have to!*
die Mutter, ¨ – *mother*
die Mütze, –n *cap*

N

nach *after, to*
der Nachbar, –n *neighbor*
nachdem *after (conj.)*
nachdenken *to think about*
nachfragen *inquire*
der Nachmittag, –e *afternoon*
nachmittags *during the afternoon*
die Nachricht, –en *news item*
    eine Nachricht hinterlassen *to leave a message*
die Nachrichten *news broadcast*
nachsehen *to look up*
die Nacht, ¨ –e *night*
    Gute Nacht. *Good night.*
die Nachspeise, –n *dessert*
nächst *next to, nearest*
der/die/das Nächste *the next (one)*
der Nachtisch, –e *dessert*
nachts *at night*
der Nacken, – *neck*
nah(e) *near, close*
nähen *to sew, to stitch (a wound)*
der Nahverkehrszug, ¨ –e *short distance train*
der Name, –n *name*
die Nase, –n *nose*

nass *wet*
der Nationalfeiertag, –e
national holiday
natürlich *of course, natural*
der Nebel, – *fog*
neb(e)lig *foggy*
neben *next to*
die Nebenrolle, –n *supporting role*
die Nebenstraße, –n *side street*
der Neffe, –n, *nephew*
nehmen *to take*
    Ich nehme . . . *I'll have . . .*
nein *no*
nennen *to call, to address, to name*
der Nerv, –en *nerve*
der Nervenkitzel *thrill, suspense*
nett *nice*
das Netz, –e *net, network, system*
neu *new*
der Neubau, –ten *new building*
der Neue, –n *the new person*
das Neujahr *New Year*
neulich *recently*
neun *nine*
der Neunmalklug, –en *know-it-all*
neunzehn *nineteen*
neunzig *ninety*
nicht *not*
    gar nicht *not at all*
die Nichte, –n *niece*
das Nichtraucherabteil, –e *non-smoking compartment*
nichts *nothing*
nie *never*
die Niederlage, –n *defeat*
niemals *never*
niemand *no one, nobody*
nirgendwo *nowhere*
noch *still, yet*
    noch nicht *not yet*
nochmal *once again, one more time*
nördlich *northerly*
die Nordsee *North Sea*
normal *standard, normal*
normalerweise *normally, generally*
die Notaufnahme, –n *(hospital) emergency (admission), emergency room*
der Notausgang, ¨ –e *emergency exit*
die Note, –n *grade, also: note (music)*
der Notfall, ¨ –e *emergency*
die Notiz, –en *note*
das Notizbuch, ¨ –er *notebook*
Notizen machen *to take (a few) notes*

der Notruf, –e *emergency call*
der November *November*
die Nudel, –n *pasta*
Nudelspeisen *pasta dishes*
null *zero*
    null Bock haben (coll.) *not to feel up to doing anything*
    Numerus Clausus *"closed numbers" system limiting university admissions*
die Nummer, –n *number*
das Nummernkonto, –konten *secret bank account*
nur *only*
nützlich *useful*
nutzlos *useless*
der Nutznießer, – *beneficiary*
    einen Nutznießer einsetzen *to name a beneficiary*

O

ob *if, whether*
der Obdachlose, –n *homeless person*
das Obdachlosenheim, –e *homeless shelter*
obgleich *although*
das Obst *(sing.) fruit*
obwohl *although, even though*
der Ochse, –n *ox*
oder *or*
offenbar *obvious(ly)*
offensichtlich *obvious, obviously*
öffentlich *public, open*
oft *often*
ohne *without*
das Ohr, –en *ear*
    viel um die Ohren haben *to be very occupied, to be very busy*
das Öl, –e *oil, ointment*
der Oktober *October*
die Oma, –s *grandmother*
der Omnibus, –se *bus*
der Onkel, – *uncle*
online *online*
der Opa, –s *grandfather*
die Oper, –n *opera, opera house*
der Orangensaft, ¨ –e *orange juice*
die Ordnung, –en *order*
    Alles ist in Ordnung. *Everything is all right.*
    Etwas ist nicht in Ordnung. *Something is wrong.*
orientieren *to inform, to instruct*
die Originalverpackung, –en *factory box/wrapping*
der Ort *place, location, town*

Ostern *Easter*
Österreich *Austria*
östlich *easterly*
die Ostsee *Baltic sea*
der Overheadprojektor, –en *overhead projector*

P

das Paar, –e *pair*
ein paar *a few*
das Päckchen, – *package*
packen *to pack*
die Packung, –en *packet, wrapping*
    Es steht auf der Packung. *It's written on the box.*
das Paket, –e *parcel, package*
das Panorama *panorama*
der Papa, –s *dad*
der Paprika, – *bell pepper, paprika (spice)*
die Parade, –en *parade*
der Park, –s *park (recreational area)*
das Parkett, –s *parquet, orchestra*
parken *to park*
parkieren (Swiss) *to park*
die Parknähe *adjacent to a park*
das Parkhaus, ¨ –er *parking garage*
der Parkplatz, ¨ –e *parking lot, parking space*
die Partei, –en *political party*
das Parterre *first floor*
der Pass, ¨ –e *passport*
die Passkontrolle, –n *passport control*
passen *to fit, to suit*
    der Mantel passt mir. *The coat fits me.*
passend *fitting, suitable*
passieren *to happen*
der Patient, –en *patient (male)*
die Patientin, –nen *patient (female)*
die Pause, –n *intermission*
peinlich *embarrassing*
perfekt *perfect*
das Perlmutt *mother of pearl*
die Person, –en *person*
das Personal *personnel*
der Personenzug, ¨ –e *passenger train*
persönlich *personal, personally*
der Pfad, –e *path, trail*
der Pfadfinder, – *boy scout*
der Pfandbrief, –e *(finance) bond*
der Pfeffer *pepper (spice)*
die Pfeife, –n *pipe*

Pfingsten *Pentecost, Whitsuntide*
die Pflaume, –n *plum, prune*
das Pfund, –e *pound, half a kilo*
der Pilot, –en *pilot*
die Pizza, –s *pizza*
die Pizzeria, Pizzerien *pizza shop*
das Photo, –s *photo*
der Photoapparat, –e *camera*
der Photograph *photographer*
der Plan, ¨–e *plan*
planen *to plan*
das Planetarium, –arien *planetarium*
die Plastik, –en *sculpture*
der Platz, ¨–e *seat, square, place*
die Platzwunde, –n *laceration (wound)*
der Platzanweiser, – *usher*
plaudern *to chat*
plötzlich *suddenly*
die Politik *politics*
politisch *political*
der Polizist, –en *policeman*
die Polsterung *upholstery*
portugiesisch *Portuguese*
die Position, –en *position*
die Post *post office, mail*
das Postamt, ¨ –er *post office*
die Postkarte, –n *postcard*
die Postleitzahl, –en *ZIP code*
das Postscheckkonto *postal checking account*
das Postsparkonto *postal savings account*
das Porzellan *china, porcelain*
die Pracht, – *splendor, pomp*
prachtvoll *splendid*
praktisch *practical, convenient*
das Präparat, –e *medical or chemical preparation, medication*
der Präsident, –en *president*
der Prater *Vienna amusement park*
der Preis, –e *price; prize*
der Preisträger, – *prize recipient (male)*
die Preisträgerin, –nen *prize recipient (female)*
preisgünstig *reasonable*
die Preisverleihung, –en *award ceremony*
die Presse, –n *press*
pressieren *to be urgent*
prima *excellent, great*
der Privatgegenstand, ¨ –e *personal belongings*
das Problem, –e *problem*
die Produktion, –en *production*
der Produzent, –en *producer (male)*

die Produzentin, –en *producer (female)*
der Professor, –en/–en *(male) professor*
die Professorin, –nen *(female) professor*
das Programm, –e *program*
　　das zweite Programm *Channel Two*
promenieren *to stroll about, to promenade*
das Projekt, –e *project*
Prost! *Cheers!*
prüfen *to assess, to test, to check, to examine*
die Prüfung, –en *test, examination*
das Publikum *audience*
der Pullover, – *sweater*
pünktlich *on time, punctual*
die Pute, –n *turkey (female)*
putzen *to clean, to shine (shoes)*
　　sich die Zähne putzen *to brush one's teeth*
der Putzdienst, –e *(hotel) cleaning service*

Q

das Quadrat, –e *square*
quadratisch *square*
der Quadratmeter, – *square meter*
die Qualität *quality*
qualitativ *qualitywise*
die Quantität *size, quantity*
quantitativ *sizewise, in quantity*
der Quark *(fresh curd) cottage cheese*
das Quartier *quarter, accommodations*
die Quelle, –n *spring, well*
quer *across, diagonal, sideways*
der Querulant, –en *grumbler, querulous person*
quietschen *to screech, to squeak*
quittieren *to give a receipt for; sign*
die Quittung, –en *receipt*

R

das Rad, ¨ –er *wheel, bicycle*
　　das Fahrrad *bicycle*
Rad fahren *to bicycle, to cycle*
das Radio, –s *radio*
　　im Radio *on the radio*
der Radsport *cycling*
der Rahmen, – *frame*
　　im Rahmen *as part of . . . , within the framework*
der Rand, ¨ –er *edge, border*

der Rang, ¨ –e *dress circle, also: rank*
rar *rare*
die Rarität, –en *rarity*
rasen *to speed*
der Rasierapparat, –e *electric razor*
die Rasiercreme, –s *shaving cream*
rasieren *to shave*
　　sich rasieren *to shave oneself*
die Raststätte, –n *rest area, service station (along Autobahn)*
der Rat *advice; senate, committee*
raten *to guess, to give advice*
das Rathaus, ¨ –er *town hall*
der Raucher, – *smoker*
der Raum, ¨ –e *room*
der Raumausstatter, – *interior decorator*
die Realität, –en *reality*
die Realschule, –n *middle school (up to 10th grade)*
rechnen *to count, to calculate*
die Rechnung, –en *check, invoice*
　　Die Rechnung bitte! *The check please!*
der Rechnungseingang, ¨ –e *receipt of invoice*
das Recht, –e *right, law*
Recht haben *to be right*
　　jemandem recht geben *to agree with*
　　Wäre es Ihnen recht, wenn . . . ? *Would it be alright with you, if . . . ?*
rechts *to the right, on the right*
der Rechtsanwalt, ¨ –e *lawyer*
die Rechtsanwältin, –nen *lawyer*
rechtzeitig *in time*
die Redaktion, –en *editorial department*
der Redaktionsschluss *time to go to press*
der Redakteur, –e *editor*
die Rede, –n *speech*
　　große Reden schwingen (coll.) *to brag, to exaggerate*
reden *to speak, to talk*
der Redner, – *speaker*
reell *real*
das Regal, –e *shelf*
regelmäßig *regular, regularly*
der Regen *rain*
der Regenmantel, ¨ – *raincoat*
die Regie *(film) direction*
Regie führen *to direct*
der Regisseur, –e *film director*

regnen *to rain*
    Es regnet. *It's raining*
reich *rich, richly*
reichen *to be sufficient*
    Es reicht. *It's enough.*
reif *ripe, mature*
der Reifen, – *tire*
reinigen *to clean*
    chemisch reinigen *to dry clean*
die Reinigung, –en *cleaning; cleaners*
    die chemische Reinigung *dry cleaning; dry cleaners*
der Reis *rice*
die Reise, –n *journey, trip*
    Gute Reise. *Have a nice trip.*
das Reisebüro, –s *travel agency*
der Reiseführer, – *travel guide (book)*
die Reisegruppe, –n *travel group*
reisen *to travel*
der/die Reisende, –n, –n *traveler*
der Reisepass, ¨ –e *passport*
der Reisescheck, –s *traveler's check*
die Reisetasche, –n *traveling bag*
das Reiseziel, –e *destination*
der Reißverschluss, ¨ –e *zipper*
die Religion, –en *religion*
rennen *to run*
renommiert *renowned*
renovieren *to renovate*
reparieren *to repair*
die Reportage, –n *(TV/film) report*
reservieren *to reserve*
reserviert *reserved*
die Reservierung, –en *reservation*
der Respekt *respect*
respektieren *to respect*
das Restaurant, –s *restaurant*
    im Restaurant *in a restaurant*
retten *to rescue*
das Rezept, –e *prescription, recipe*
die Rezeption, –en *reception*
die Rheintour *Rhine tour*
richtig *correct, correctly; accurate, accurately*
das Richtige *the right thing*
    Ich habe genau das Richtige! *I have exactly the (right) thing.*
die Richtung, –en *direction*
das Riesenrad, ¨ –er *ferris wheel*
das Rindfleisch *beef*

der Ring, –e *ring*
das Ritual, –e *ritual*
der Rock, ¨ –e *skirt*
die Rolle, –n *role*
der Rollstuhl, ¨ –e *wheelchair*
der Roman, –e *novel*
romantisch *romantic*
die Röntgenaufnahme, –n *X ray*
das Röntgenbild, –er *X-ray*
rosa *pink*
der Rosenmontag *Rose Monday (Monday before Lent)*
der Rostbraten, – *roast*
rot *red*
    rot sehen *to see red, to be in rage*
    rot werden *blushing, to be embarrassed*
die Rotation, –en *rotation*
das Rotationsverfahren, – *taking turns, in rotation*
rötlich *reddish*
der Rotwein, –e *red wine*
die Routine, –n *routine*
der Rückflug, ¨ –e *return flight*
der Rucksack, ¨ –e *backpack*
der Rücksitz, –e *backseat*
der Ruf *reputation*
die Rufnummer, –n *phone number*
rufen *to call*
die Ruhe *silence*
    Ich bitte um Ruhe! *Silence, please!*
ruhig *calm*
die Ruine, –n *ruin(s)*

S

satt *full (not hungry)*
die S-Bahn, –en *urban railway, city train*
die Sache, –n *thing, item, stuff*
    die Sachen *things, belongings*
    zur Sache kommen *to get to the point*
die Sachertorte, –n *Sacher torte*
der Sachschaden, ¨ – *damage to property*
sagen *to say*
    Was würden Sie sagen, wenn . . . ? *What would you say, if . . . ?*
die Sahne *cream*
die Salami, –s *salami*
der Salat, –e *lettuce, salad*
die Salbe, –n *salve*
das Salz *salt*
der Samstag *Saturday*

die Samstagsausgabe, –n *Saturday edition (newspaper)*
der Sammler, – *collector*
die Sammlung, –en *collection*
das Sammlungsstück, –e *collection piece*
der Sand *sand*
sandig *sandy*
der Sänger, – *singer*
sanktionieren *to sanction, to stipulate*
der Satz, ¨ –e *sentence*
sauber *clean*
die Sauberkeit *cleanliness*
sauer *sour*
    sauer sein *to be annoyed*
das Sauerkraut *sauerkraut*
die Säule, –n *column; pillar*
Schade! *Too bad!*
der Schaden, ¨ – *damage*
    Personenschaden *personal injury*
    Sachschaden *material damage*
der Schadstoff, –e *harmful substance, hazardous waste*
schaffen *to accomplish, to create; to work*
der Schal, –s *scarf*
der Schalter, – *desk, customer service desk, teller*
der Schalterbeamte, –n *postal or bank clerk at the window*
die Schalterstunden, – *opening hours*
der Schauspieler, – *actor*
der Schatz, ¨ –e *treasure, darling*
der Scheck, –s *check*
    einen Scheck einlösen *to cash a check*
die Scheckkarte, –n *check/debit card*
das Scheckkonto, –konten *checking account*
der Schein, –e *(money) bill*
scheinen *to shine, to seem*
schenken *to give*
die Schere, –n *pair of scissors*
der Scherz, –e *joke*
schicken *to send, to ship*
schief *crooked, crookedly, not even*
    etwas geht schief *something goes wrong*
das Schiff, –e *ship, boat*
die Schifffahrt, –n *shipping (marine)*
schießen *to shoot*
das Schild, –er *sign*
schimpfen mit *to scold*
der Schinken, – *(smoked) ham, prosciutto*

der Schirm, – umbrella
schlafen to sleep
  Schlafmütze! Sleepyhead!
der Schlafsack, ¨ –e sleeping bag
der Schlafwagen, – sleeping car
das Schlafzimmer, – bedroom
schlagen to beat
die Schlagfertigkeit, –en wit, ready wit
die Schlagsahne whipped cream
die Schlagzeile, –n (newspaper) headline
die Schlange, –n waiting line, snake
schlank slender
schlau smart, sly
  Schlauberger! Smart Alek!
schlecht bad, badly
  Es geht mir schlecht. I'm not feeling well.
  Mir ist schlecht. I'm feeling sick.
  Nicht schlecht! Not bad!
schleppen to haul
schleudern to skid, to spin; to fling
schließen to close
schließlich finally, eventually
schlimm terrible
der Schluss, ¨ –e end, conclusion
der Schlusssatz, ¨ –e final sentence
der Schlüssel, – key
schmecken to taste
schmeicheln to flatter
die Schmerzen pain, hurt
schmerzen to hurt
der Schmuck jewelry
das Schmuckstück, –e piece of jewelry, treasure
der Schmuggel smuggling
schmunzeln to smile (to oneself)
schmutzig dirty
der Schnee snow
der Schneefall, ¨ –e snowfall
schneiden to cut
schneien to snow
  Es schneit. It's snowing.
schnell quick, fast
schnelllebig fast-paced
der Schnellimbiss, –e snack bar
die Schnellreinigung, –en express dry cleaning
das Schnitzel, – cutlet
der Schnupftabak snuff
die Schnupftabakdose, –n snuffbox
der Schnurrbart, ¨ –e moustache
der Schöffe, –n juror (male)
die Schöffin, –en juror (female)
die Schokolade chocolate
schon already

schön beautiful
  Na schön! Okay, then! All right, then!
die Schönheit, –en beauty
der Schrank, ¨ –e wardrobe, cupboard, armoire, closet
der Schreck, –en shock, fright
schrecklich horrible
schreiben to write
  schreiben an (acc.) to write to
  schreiben über (acc.) to write about
die Schreibmaschine, –n typewriter
der Schreibtisch, –e desk
schreien to scream, to yell
der Schreiner, – carpenter
der Schriftverkehr correspondence
das Schritttempo walking speed
schüchtern shy
die Schublade, –n drawer
der Schuh, –e shoe
  jmdm. etwas in die Schuhe schieben putting the blame on someone innocent
  Umgekehrt wird ein Schuh daraus. The exact opposite is true.
  Wo drückt der Schuh? What's the trouble?
die Schule, –n school
der Schulabgänger, – graduate
der Schüler, – (school) student
die Schulter, –n shoulder
der Schwabe, –n Swabian
schwäbisch Swabian
schwach weak
der Schwager, ¨ – brother-in-law
die Schwägerin, –nen sister-in-law
schwanger pregnant
die Schwangerschaft, –en pregnancy
schwarz black
schwarz sehen to expect the worst
die Schwarzwälder Kirschtorte, –n Black Forest cake
das Schwein, –e pig, pork
Schwein haben to be lucky (undeservedly)
das Schweinefleisch pork
die Schweiz Switzerland
der Schweizer, – Swiss (person)
schweizerisch Swiss
  Schwyzerdütsch Swiss German
  Schweizer Franken Swiss Franc
die Schwellung, –en swelling

schwer heavy, difficult
die Schwester, –n sister
der Schwiegersohn, ¨ –e son-in-law
die Schwiegertochter ¨ – daughter-in-law
schwierig difficult
schwimmen to swim
das Schwimmen swimming
schwindlig dizzy
schwül muggy
sechs six
sechzehn sixteen
sechzig sixty
der See, –n lake
die See ocean
das Seerecht maritime rights
der Seetang seaweed
das Segel, – sail
der Segelanzug sailing suit
das Segelboot, –e sailboat
segeln to sail
das Segelschiff, –e sailing ship
sehen to see
  auf Wiedersehen good-bye (fml.)
die Sehenswürdigkeit, –en sight, point of interest
die Sehne, –n tendon
die Seide, –n silk
die Seife, –n soap
die Seifenoper, –n soap opera
sein his, its
sein to be
  frei sein to be available
  fertig sein to be ready
seit since, for (expressions of time)
die Seite, –n page; side
  Jedes Ding hat zwei Seiten. There are two sides to everything.
der Sekt sparkling wine
der Sekretär, –e male secretary
selber (coll.) self
selbst self
selbstverständlich naturally, of course
die Sellerie celery (also: der Sellerie)
seltsam strange, odd
das Seminar, –e seminar, seminary
die Semmel, –n bread roll
die Sendeanstalt, –en (radio, TV) station, network
senden to send
der Sender, – (radio, TV) station
der Senf mustard
der September September
servieren to serve
Servus good-bye (Austrian)
der Sessel, – armchair

die Sesselbahn, –en *chair lift*
setzen *to set, to place, to put*
setzen (sich) *to sit down*
sexy *sexy, attractive*
das Shampoo, –s *shampoo*
sicher *sure, safe, secure; certain, certainly*
der Sicherheitsgurt, –e *safety belt*
sicherlich *certainly*
die Sicht *view*
die Sicherheit, –en *security, safety*
    mit Sicherheit *absolutely, definitely*
sicherlich *certainly*
sie *she, they*
Sie *(formal) you*
sieben *seven*
siebzehn *seventeen*
siebzig *seventy*
der Sieg, –e *victory*
der Sieger, – *winner*
siegen *to win*
das Silber *silver*
sitzen *to sit*
der Sitzplan, ̈–e *seating plan*
die Sitzung, –en *meeting*
der Ski, –er *ski(s)*
Ski laufen, Ski fahren *to ski*
der Skiurlaub, –e *skiing vacation*
die Skulptur, –en *sculpture*
der Slogan, –s *slogan*
so *so*
so dass *so that*
die Socke, –n (der Socken, –) *sock*
    ein Paar Socken *a pair of socks*
das Sofa, –s *sofa, couch*
sofort *right away*
sogar *even*
der Sohn, ̈–e *son*
solch, –e, –r, –s *such*
solange *as long as; while*
sollen *to be supposed to (do something)*
somit *thus, therefore*
der Sommer *summer*
das Sonderangebot, –e *special offer*
die Sonderausstellung, –en *special exhibition*
sondern *but, on the contrary, rather*
    nicht nur . . . sondern auch *not only . . . but also*
die Sonderschule, –n *special needs school*
der Sonnabend *Saturday*
die Sonne, –n *sun*
der Sonnenbrand, ̈–e *sunburn*

der Sonnenschein *sunshine*
die Sonnenschutzcreme, –s *sunscreen lotion*
das Sonnenschutzöl, –e *sun protection oil*
sonnig *sunny*
der Sonntag *Sunday*
sonst *otherwise*
    Sonst noch etwas? *Anything else?*
die Sorge, –n *worry*
sorgen (sich) *to worry about*
sorgen für *to care for, to look after, to see to something*
Sorgen haben *to be worried, to worry*
sowieso *in any case, anyhow*
sozial *social, societal*
die Sozialdemokratische Partei Deutschland (SPD) *the Social Democratic Party of Germany*
die Sozialwissenschaften *social sciences*
die Spalte, –n *(newsprint) column*
Spanien *Spain*
spannend *thrilling*
das Sparbuch, ̈–er *passbook, savings*
die Sparkasse, –n *savings and loan*
sparen *to save*
der Spargel, – *asparagus*
das Sparkonto, –konten *savings account*
der Spaß, ̈–e *fun*
Spaß machen *to be fun, to be enjoyable; to kid, to make a joke*
spät *late*
    Wie spät ist es? *What time is it?*
später *later*
der Spaziergang, ̈–e *walk*
spazieren gehen *to go for a walk*
der Spediteur, –e *moving, shipping agent*
die Spedition, –en *carrier, shipping company*
speichern *(computers) to save*
die Speise, –n *dish, food*
die Speisekarte, –n *menu*
der Speisewagen, – *dining car*
der Spekulant, –en *(stock market) speculator*
spekulieren *to speculate*
die Spezialität, –en *specialty*
das Spiel, –e *game*
der Spieler, – *male player*
der Spielfilm, –e *feature film*
das Spielkasino, –s *gambling casino*
der Spielverderber, – *spoilsport*

die Spielzeit, –en *season*
der Spinat *spinach*
der Spion, –e *spy*
die Spionage, – *espionage*
spionieren *to spy*
die Spirituosen (pl.) *hard liquor*
die Spitze, –n *top*
die Splitterpartei, –en *splinter party*
der Sponsor, –en *sponsor*
der Sport, – *sports*
der Sportteil, –e *(newspaper) sports section*
der Sportverein, –e *sports club*
sprechen *to talk, to speak*
sprechen über (acc.) *to talk about*
das Sprechzimmer, – *consulting room*
das Sprichwort, ̈–e *proverb*
sprichwörtlich *proverbial*
die Spritze, –n *shot*
    eine Spritze geben *to give a shot, to inject*
der Spruch, ̈–e *saying, proverb*
große Sprüche klopfen (coll.) *to brag*
die Spur, –en *trace*
spüren *to feel, to sense*
der Staat, –en *state (as in country)*
staatlich *state-, the State's . . .*
das Staatstheater, – *state theater*
stabil *stable*
das Stadion, –dien *stadium (sport)*
die Stadt, ̈–e *city*
das Städtchen, – *small town*
die Stadtgrenze, –n *city limits*
die Stadtmauer, –n *city fortification*
die Stadtmitte, –n *city center*
der Stadtplan, ̈–e *city map*
die Stadtplanung, –en *city planning*
das Stadttheater, – *municipal theater*
das Stadtzentrum, –zentren *city center*
der Stahl *steel*
die Stahlindustrie *steel industry*
der Stamm, ̈–e *stem, also: tribe, tree trunk*
der Stammkunde, –n *regular customer*
der Stammtisch, –e *regular customer's table at bar/restaurant*
ständig *constantly*
der Ständer, – *stand*
das Standesamt, ̈–er *registrar's office*
der Stapel, – *stack*

stark *strong*
starten *to start, to take off (plane)*
stattfinden *to occur, to take place*
die Statue, –n *statue*
der Stau, –s *traffic jam*
der Staub *dust*
das Staubkorn, ̈ –er *speck of dust*
die Steckdose, –n *wall socket, outlet*
stecken *to stick, to put*
der Stecker, – *plug*
stehen *to stand*
    Schlange stehen *to stand in line*
stehenbleiben *to stop, to stall*
stehend *standing; stagnant (water)*
die Stehlampe, –n *torch lamp, floor lamp*
stehlen *to steal*
steigen *to climb*
steil *steep*
der Stein, –e *stone, rock*
die Stelle, –n *spot, place*
stellen *to place, to put*
die Stellenanzeige, –n *employment ad*
die Stellung, –en *position*
die Steuer, –n *tax*
der Steuerberater, – *C.P.A.*
die Steuererhöhung, –en *tax increase*
die Steuersenkung, –en *tax cut*
stiften *to donate*
still *quiet*
    Sei doch still! *Be quiet!*
die Stimme, –n *voice, vote*
stimmen *to vote*
    seine Stimme abgeben *to cast one's vote*
stimmen *to be correct, to be true*
    Das stimmt. *That's right.*
    Stimmt so! *Keep the change!*
die Stirn, –en *forehead*
der Stock, ̈ –e *floor*
der erste Stock *the second floor*
der Stoff, –e *material*
stolpern *to stumble*
    Ein guter Stolperer fällt nicht. *A good stumbler falleth not.*
die Strafe, –n *penalty, punishment*
der Strand, ̈ –e *beach*
    am Strand *on the beach*
der Strandkorb, ̈ –e *large wicker beach chair*
die Straße, –n *street*
die Straßenbahn, –en *streetcar, trolley*

das Straßencafé, –s *street café*
die Straßenwachthilfe, –n *highway assistance service*
streng *strict*
streichen *to paint*
streuen *to sprinkle*
der Strom *electricity; (wide) river*
stromlinienförmig *streamlined*
der Strudel, – *strudel*
das Stück, –e *piece*
    im/am Stück *not sliced*
der Student, –en *student*
studieren *to go to college*
das Studium, Studien *study course*
der Stuhl, ̈ –e *chair*
die Stunde, –n *hour*
zu später Stunde *late at night*
stundenlang *for hours*
der Sturm, ̈ –e *storm*
stürmen *to storm*
    Es stürmt. *It's stormy.*
stürmisch *rough, stormy*
die Sturmwarnung, –en *storm warning*
stutzen *to trim*
suchen *to search for, to look for*
Südamerika *South America*
südlich *southerly*
das Substantiv, –e *noun*
süddeutsch *Southern German*
sündigen *to sin*
super *great, super*
der Supermarkt, ̈ –e *supermarket*
die Suppe, –n *soup*
süß *sweet*
die Süßwaren *sweets*
sympathisch *likable*
    Er ist mir sympathisch. *I like him.*
    sympatisch sein *to be likable*
das Symptom, –e *symptom*
die Szene, –n *scene*

T

die Tabaksdose, –n *tobacco box, snuffbox*
die Tablette, –n *pill*
der Tacho, –s *speedometer*
der Tachometer, – *speedometer*
die Tafel, –n *announcement board, blackboard*
die Tafel Schokolade *bar of chocolate*
der Tag, –e *day*
    Guten Tag. *Hello. (fml.)*
    Tag. *Hello. (infml.)*
    Tagein, tagaus *day in, day out*

das Tagesgeschehen, – *daily events*
die Tagesroutine *daily routine*
die Tagesschau *daily news program*
täglich *daily*
    dreimal täglich *three times a day*
die Tagung, –en *conference, convention*
das Tal, ̈ –er *valley*
tanken *to get gas*
die Tankstelle, –n *gas station*
die Tante, –n *aunt*
tanzen *to dance*
die Tapete, –n *wallpaper*
tapezieren *to hang wallpaper*
die Tasche, –n *bag, purse*
der Taschenrechner, – *pocket calculator*
die Taschenuhr, –en *pocket watch*
die Tasse, –n *cup*
    eine Tasse Kaffee *a cup of coffee*
die Tastatur, –en *(computer, typewriter) keyboard*
die Taste, –n *button, key*
der Täter, – *culprit, wrongdoer*
tatsächlich *actually, in fact, indeed*
täuschen *to deceive*
tausend *thousand*
Tausend Dank! *Thanks a million!*
das Taxi, –s *taxi*
der Taxistand, ̈ –e *taxi stand*
das Team, –s *team*
der Tee, –s *tea*
die Teekanne, –n *teapot*
das Teil, –e *piece, component*
der Teil, –e *part*
teilen *to divide, to share*
teilnehmen *to participate*
der Teilnehmer, – *participant*
die Teilnahme *participation*
teilweise *partly, partially*
das Telefon, –e *telephone*
der Telefonanschluss, ̈ –e *telephone connection*
das Telefonbuch, ̈ –er *phone book*
die Telefongesellschaft, –en *telephone company*
das Telefongespräch, –e *telephone conversation*
telefonieren *to call, to telephone*
telefonisch *by telephone, over the phone*
telefonisch erreichen *to reach by telephone*
die Telefonkarte, –n *telephone card*

die Telefonnummer, –n
telephone number
die Telefonrechnung, –en
telephone bill
die Telefonzelle, –n phone booth
der Teller, – (dinner) plate
die Temperatur, –en
temperature
    Höchsttemperatur highest
    temperature
    Tiefsttemperatur/
    Niedriegsttemperatur lowest
temperature
    durchschnittliche
    Temperatur, –en average
    temperature
der Teppich, –e carpet, rug
der Teppichboden, ¨ – wall to
wall carpeting
der Termin, –e date, meeting,
appointment, deadline
einen Termin haben to have an
appointment
die Terrasse, –n terrace, patio
teuer expensive
das Theater, – theater
der Theaterbesucher, –
theatergoer
die Theaterkasse, –n theater box
office
    an der Theaterkasse at the
    theater box office
das Theaterstück, –e play
das Thema, Themen subject,
topic
tief deep
die Tiefgarage, –n underground
parking
das Tier, –e animal
    Jedem Tierchen sein
    Pläsierchen. To each its own.
der Tisch, –e table
der Tisch ist gedeckt! The table
is set.
der Titel, – title
die Tochter, ¨ –er daughter
der Tod, –e death
    Bis (dass) der Tod uns
    scheidet. Till death do us
    part.
die Toilette, –n toilet, rest room
die Tomate, –n tomato
der Ton, ¨ –e tone, tune
    einen (solchen) Ton
    anschlagen to speak in such
    a tone
    große Töne spucken to
    brag (coll.)
    Ich verbiete mir diesen
    Ton. I won't accept this kind
    of tone.
toll (coll.) great

der Töpfer, – potter
die Töpferei pottery
das Tor, –e gate, goal
die Torte, –n cake, (fruit) tart
der Torwart, –e goalie
der Tourist, –en tourist
der Tourismus tourism
die Tournee, –n tour
die Tracht, –en regional dress,
costume
die Tradition, –en tradition
traditionsreich traditional,
steeped in tradition
tragen to wear
tragbar wearable, portable;
tolerable
der Transformator, –en
transformer
der Transport, –e transport
die Transportmöglichkeit, –en
means of transport
die Trauung, –en wedding
ceremony
    die kirchliche Trauung
    church wedding
    die standesamtliche
    Trauung civil wedding
treffen to meet
das Treffen, – meeting
der Treffpunkt, –e meeting place
treiben to do (an activity)
    Sport treiben to engage in
    sports
trennen to separate
    sich trennen to part
die Treppe, –n stairs
    Nehmen Sie die Treppe!
    Take the stairs!
das Treppenhaus, ¨ –er (public)
staircase
treten to step
trinken to drink
das Trinkgeld, –er tip
trocknen to dry
    sich die Haare trocken to
    dry one's hair
der Tropfen, – drop
tropisch tropical
der Trottel, – idiot, dope,
trotz despite, in spite of
trotzdem although; nevertheless
das T–Shirt, –s t-shirt
Tschau. (infml.) Bye. (-Ciao)
tschechisch Czech
Tschüs. (infml.) Bye.
tun to do, to make
    gut tun to do good
    Schwimmen tut ihr gut.
    Swimming is good for her.
    weh tun to hurt
    Es tut weh. It hurts.
die Tür, –en door

der Turm, ¨ –e tower
turnen gymnastics
das Turnen gymnastics
die Tüte, –n bag

U

die U–Bahn, –en subway
über over, above, across
überall all over, everywhere
das Überangebot surplus glut
der Überblick, –e overview
übereinstimmen to agree
    nicht übereinstimmen to
    disagree
überflüssig superfluous,
redundant
überhaupt actually, anyway
    überhaupt nicht not at all
überholen to overtake (another
vehicle)
überlegen to contemplate
    Kann ich mir das noch
    überlegen? Can I think about
    that?
übernehmen to take over, to
accept
überqueren to cross over
überprüfen to check, to double-
check
überraschen to surprise
die Überraschung, –en
surprise
überreden lassen to be talked
into
übertragen to broadcast
die Überschwemmung, –en
flood, flooding
übersehen to estimate, to
evaluate
übersetzen to translate
übertreiben to exaggerate
überwechseln to change, to
transfer
überweisen to transfer
die Überweisung, –en (bank)
transfer
der Überweisungsauftrag, ¨ –e
(bank) transfer form, remittance
order
überwiegend most, mostly, for
the most part
überziehen to overdraw; to pull
over, to put on
üblich usual, normal
übrigens by the way
die Uhr, –en clock, watch
    Wieviel Uhr ist es? What
    time is it?
der Uhrmacher, – watchmaker,
watch/clock repair shop
um (zu) in order to

um *around*
  Um wie viel Uhr? *At what time?*
der Umbau, –ten *redesign, renovation*
umbauen *to rebuild, to remodel*
die Umfrage, –n *survey, poll*
umgehen *to handle, to deal with; to avoid*
die Umgehungsstraße, –n *city highway diverting traffic from the center*
die Umhängetasche, –n *shoulder bag*
die Umkleidekabine, –n *fitting room*
umschalten *to switch, to convert*
umschauen (sich) *to browse (in a store) to look around*
  Ich schaue mich nur um. *I'm just browsing.*
umsetzen *convert*
  in die Realität umsetzen *to implement, to carry out (an idea)*
umsonst *without charge, free*
umsteigen *to change trains*
der Umtausch, ¨–e *exchange*
umtauschen *to exchange*
die Umwelt *environment*
die Umweltforschung *ecological research*
der Umweltschutz *environmental protection*
umziehen *to move*
umziehen (sich) *to change one's clothes*
der Umzug, ¨–e *move*
unangenehm *unpleasant*
die Unannehmlichkeit, –en *inconvenience, trouble*
unbedingt *absolutely, without fail*
unbekannt *unknown*
und *and*
  Na und? *So what?*
der Unfall, ¨–e *accident*
ungeduldig *impatient*
unglaublich *unbelievable*
uninteressant *uninteresting*
die Universität, –en *university*
unklar *unclear*
unmodern *old-fashioned*
unordentlich *untidy, unorganized*
der Unrat *waste, garbage*
unreif *immature, not ripe*
unruhig *restless*
unsachgemäß *inappropriate, improper*
unschlagbar *invincible*
unser *our*
unsicher *unsure, insecure*

unsichtbar *invisible*
unter *under, beneath, underneath*
unter anderem *among other things*
unterbrechen *to interrupt*
untereinander *among (themselves)*
unterhalten (sich) *to talk, to chat; to enjoy oneself*
unternehmen *to go and do something, to venture out*
das Unternehmen, – *company; venture, plan*
der Unternehmer, – *entrepreneur*
die Unternehmensberatung, –en *management consultancy*
die Unterlagen *documents, papers, records, files*
der Unterricht (no pl.) *(school) classes; instruction*
unterschreiben *to sign*
die Unterschrift, –en *signature*
unterstellen *to assume, to imply (with bad intent); to seek shelter; to place under/beneath*
unterstreichen *to underline, to emphasize*
unterstützen *to support*
die Unterstützung *support*
untersuchen *to examine closely, to investigate*
unvergesslich *unforgettable*
unvorstellbar *unimaginable, incredible*
das Unwetter, – *violent storm*
unwiderstehlich *irresistible*
unzählig *numerous, innumerable*
die Urgroßmutter, ¨ – *greatgrandmother*
der Urgroßvater, ¨ – *greatgrandfather*
der Urlaub *vacation*
  in Urlaub fahren *to go on vacation*
der Urlaubsort, –e *vacation place*
urlaubsreif *in need of a vacation*
das Urlaubsziel, –e *vacation destination*
die Urne, –n *ballot box*
  zur Urne gehen *to cast one's vote*
die Ursache, –n *cause*
  Keine Ursache. *Don't mention it. That's alright.*
die USA *the U.S.A.*

V

der Vater, ¨ – *father*
der Vatikan *Vatican*

der Vegetarier, – *vegetarian*
die Verabredung *appointment, date*
verabschieden (sich) *to say good-bye*
  Ich verabschiede mich. *I'm saying good-bye.*
die Verabschiedung, –en *dismissal; passing (of a bill)*
veranlassen *to initiate, to take care of, arrange*
veranstalten *to host, to organize*
die Veranstaltung, –en *event*
verantworten *to be responsible for*
verantwortlich *responsible*
die Verantwortung, –en *responsibility*
der Verband, ¨–e *bandage*
der Verbandkasten, ¨ – *first-aid kit*
der Verbandstoff *bandage*
verbessern *to improve*
verbieten *to forbid*
verbinden *to connect*
  falsch verbunden *wrong number*
die Verbindung, –en *connection*
das Verbrechen, – *crime*
verbringen *to spend (time)*
verdienen *to earn*
verdoppeln *to double*
verehren *to adore*
der Verein, –e *club, organization*
die Vereinbarung, –en *agreement*
vereint *united*
verfallen *to expire, to become void*
die Verfassung *constitution*
das Verfassungsgericht *constitutional court*
die Verfügung, –en *decree, order, instruction*
zur Verfügung stellen *to provide, to supply*
zur Verfügung stehen *to be available, to be at someone's disposal*
vergangen *passed, past (time), last (time)*
vergeben *to give away; to forgive*
vergessen *to forget*
vergesslich *forgetful*
der Vergleich, –e *comparison*
  einen Vergleich ziehen *to draw a comparison*
  im Vergleich zu *compared with/to, in comparison with*
vergleichen *to compare*

das Vergnügen, - *pleasure*
   Viel Vergnügen! *Enjoy yourself!*
   Mit Vergnügen! *With pleasure!*
vergrößern *to enlarge, to increase*
verhandeln *to negotiate*
verheiratet *married*
verkaufen *to sell*
der Verkäufer, - *salesman*
die Verkäuferin, -nen *(female) salesperson*
die Verkaufszahlen (pl.) *sales figures*
der Verkehr *traffic*
verkehrsfreie Zone *traffic free zone*
das Verkehrsmittel *means of transportation*
   öffentliche Verkehrsmittel *public transportation*
die Verkehrsregel, -n *traffic rule*
das Verkehrsschild, -er *traffic sign*
der Verkehrsstau, -s *traffic congestion*
der Verkehrsunfall, ¨-e *traffic accident*
verkehrswidrig *in violation of traffic regulations*
verkleinern *to reduce, to decrease, to make smaller*
verkorkst (coll.) *ruined, spoiled*
verlassen *to leave*
verleihen *to award*
die Verleihung, -en *award ceremony*
verletzen (sich) *to hurt*
verletzt *injured*
verlieren *to lose*
verlobt *engaged*
vermerken *to note (only in writing)*
vermieten *to rent out*
der Vermieter, - *landlord*
das Vermögen, - *fortune (money)*
veröffentlichen *to publish*
die Veröffentlichung, -en *publication*
verordnen *to rule, to order*
die Verordnung, -en *rule, regulation*
verpacken *to pack*
verpackt *packed*
die Verpackung, -en *packaging, packing material*
verpassen *to miss (train, appointment)*
verputzen *to plaster*
verringern *to decrease, to reduce*

verrückt *crazy*
   Du bist ja verrückt! (coll.) *You are crazy.*
   Du hast wohl nicht alle Tassen im Schrank! (coll.) *You must be out of your mind!*
   Du spinnst ja wohl! (coll.) *You're nuts.*
versagen *to fail*
der Versammlungsraum, ¨-e *meeting room, conference room, hall*
der Versand *shipping department*
versäumen *to miss, to omit, to fail to do something*
verschieben *to postpone*
verschlafen *to oversleep*
verschreiben *to prescribe*
versichert *insured*
die Versicherung, -en *insurance*
versiert *fluent, familiar with, experienced*
versprechen *to promise*
   das Blaue vom Himmel versprechen *to promise the moon*
die Versorgung, -en *supply, provision, care*
das Versorgungsnetz, -e *supply system, network*
die Verstärkung, -en *intensification, support, backup*
verstehen *to understand*
versteigern *to auction (off)*
die Versteigerung, -en *auction*
verstopft *clogged, closed up by traffic*
verstoßen (gegen) *to break a law, rule*
versuchen *to try*
der Vertrag, ¨-e *contract*
vertragen *to tolerate*
vertreten *to represent*
die Verwaltung *administration*
die Verwaltungshilfe *administrative aid*
der/die Verwandte, -n *relative*
verwenden *to use*
die Verwendung, -en *use*
   für etwas Verwendung haben *to have use for something*
der Verzehr *(food) consumption*
verzeihen *to forgive*
   Verzeihung! *Forgive me!*
   um Verzeihung bitten *to ask for forgiveness*
die Verzögerung, -en *delay*
der Vetter, -n *cousin*
das Video, -s *video tape*
die Videokassette, -n *video tape*
das Videogerät, -e *VCR*

der Videorekorder - *VCR*
viel *much*
viele *many*
vielleicht *perhaps, maybe*
vielseitig *versatile, multifaceted*
die Vielseitigkeit *versatility, various aspects*
vier *four*
das Viertel, - *quarter, fourth of*
viertürig *four-door*
vierzehn *fourteen*
vierzig *forty*
die Vierzimmerwohnung, -en *3-bedroom apartment*
die Visitenkarte, -n *business card*
die Vokabel, -n *vocabulary word*
das Volk, ¨-er *people, nation*
die Völkerverständigung *understanding between nations*
das Volkslied, -er *folk song*
voll *full*
die Vollbeschäftigung *full employment*
völlig *totally, completely*
die Vollreinigung, -en *dry cleaning*
vollständig *complete*
das Volt, - *volt*
von *from, by (the agent of the action)*
   von morgens bis abends *from morning to evening*
vor *in front of, before*
vor allem *above all, predominantly, primarily*
voraus *ahead*
voraussichtlich *probably*
vorbeifahren *to drive by*
vorbeikommen *to drop by*
der Vordersitz, -e *front seat*
der Vorderzahn, ¨-e *front tooth*
die Vorfahrt *right of way*
der Vorfall, ¨-e *occurrence*
die Vorführung, -en *show, showcase, presentation*
der Vorgesetzte, -n/-n *supervisor, superior*
vorhaben *to intend, to plan*
vorhanden *present, available*
vorlegen *to present, to submit*
vorletzter, -e, -es *the one before last*
die Vorliebe, -n *preference*
vorne *in the front*
der Vorort, -e *suburb*
vorrätig *available*
   vorrätig sein *to be in stock*
   Die Ware ist nicht vorrätig. *The merchandise isn't in stock.*
der Vorsatz, ¨-e *intention, intent*
der Vorschlag, ¨-e *suggestion*

vorschlagen *to suggest*
vorschreiben *to prescribe*
die Vorschrift, –en *rule, law, regulation*
die Vorsicht *caution*
die Vorspeise, –n *appetizer*
der Vorstand, ¨-e *board of directors*
das Vorstandsmitglied, –er *board member*
vorstellen *to introduce*
vorstellen (sich) *to imagine, to conjure; to introduce oneself*
die Vorstellung, –en *introduction, performance*
das Vorstellungsgespräch, –e *(job) interview*
der Vortrag, ¨-e *speech, lecture*
vorteilhaft *advantageous, flattering*
die Vorwahl(nummer) *(phone) area code*
vorzeigen *to show, to present*

W

die Waage, –n *scale*
wachhalten *to keep awake*
wachsen *to grow*
der Wagen, –e *car*
die Wahl, –en *choice, election*
die Wahlbeteiligung *voter turnout*
wählen *to choose, to vote*
der Wähler, – *male voter*
das Wahlergebnis, –se *election result*
die Wählerin, –nen *female voter*
der Wahlkampf, ¨-e *political campaign*
das Wahlrecht *right to vote*
wahr *true, genuine*
    Das ist wahr. *That's true.*
    Das darf doch wohl nicht wahr sein! *That can't be true! That can't be happening!*
während (gen.) *while, during, in the course of*
währenddessen *meanwhile*
wahrscheinlich *probably*
der Wald, ¨-er *forest, woods*
die Wand, ¨-e *wall (in a house or room)*
wandern *to wander, to walk, to hike*
die Wanderung, –en *hike*
die Wandmalerei, –en *mural*
das Wandregal, –e *wall (shelf) unit*
wann *when*
die Ware, –n *goods, product*

das Warenmuster, – *sample (of product, merchandise)*
warm *warm*
die Wärme *warmth*
die Warmmiete, –n *rent including heating costs*
die Warnung, –en *warning*
warten *to wait*
    warten auf (acc.) *to wait for*
warum *why*
was *what*
waschen *to wash*
    mit der Hand waschen *to wash by hand*
    sich waschen *to wash oneself*
die Wäsche *laundry*
die Waschküche, –n *laundry room*
das Wasser *water*
Wasser brauchen *to need water*
die Wasserleitung, –en *water pipe*
das WC *toilet, rest room*
weben *to weave*
der Weber, – *weaver*
die Weberei *weaving*
die Web–Seite, –n *web page*
der Wechselkurs *exchange rate*
wechseln *to change, to exchange*
der Wechselstrom *alternating current (AC)*
die Wechselstube, – *money changing establishment*
wecken *to wake*
    Wecken Sie mich um . . . *Wake me up at . . .*
der Wecker, – *alarm clock*
weg *away, gone*
der Weg, –e *way*
wegdenken *to unthink, to imagine it weren't there*
weglaufen *to run away*
wegen (gen.) *because of*
weh tun *to hurt*
    Tut das weh? *Does it hurt?*
weich *soft*
Weihnachten *Christmas*
weil *because*
die Weile *while, short time*
    Gut' Ding will Weile haben. *Haste makes waste.*
der Wein, –e *wine*
der Weinberg, –e *vineyard*
die Weinlese *grape harvest*
die Weinprobe, –n *wine tasting*
die Weinschorle, –n *wine cooler, spritzer*
der Weisheitszahn, ¨-e *wisdom tooth*
weiß *white*
der Weißwein, –e *white wine*

weit *far*
    Wie weit ist es? *How far is it?*
weitere *further, additional*
weitergeben *to hand on, to pass on*
weiterhelfen *to help along*
welche *which*
die Welle, –n *wave*
der Weltkrieg, –e *world war*
wem (dat.) *whom*
wen (acc.) *whom*
wenig *little*
weniger werden *to become less, to decrease*
wenigstens *at least*
wenn *when, as soon as, if, whenever*
wer (nom.) *who*
die Werbeeinnahmen *income from commercials or advertising*
der Werbeslogan, –s *advertising slogan*
die Werbung *advertising, commercials, advertisement*
werden *to become*
das Werk *plant, factory, the works, oeuvre*
der Werkzeugkasten, ¨- *toolbox*
der Wert, –e *value*
wert sein *to be worth*
das Wertpapier, –e *bond, security*
westlich *westerly*
    weiter westlich *farther west*
der Wettbewerb, –e *competition, contest*
wettbewerbsfähig *competitive*
das Wetter *weather*
der Wetterbericht, –e *weather report*
das Wettrennen, – *race (running)*
wichtig *important*
wider *in contrast to, against*
der Widerstand, ¨-e *resistance*
widerrufen *to deny, to cancel*
widersprechen *to contradict*
widerstehen *to resist*
widerstehlich *resistable*
wie *how*
wie viel(e) *how much/many*
Wie wär's (mit) . . . ? *How about . . . ?*
wieder *again*
der Wiederaufbau *restoration*
wiederkommen *to return, to come back*
wiederholen *to repeat*
die Wiederholung, –en *repetition*
die Wiederholungsaufgabe, –n *review exercise*

wiedersehen *to meet again*
wiederum *then again*
wieso *why*
die Wiedervereinigung *reunification*
wiegen *to weigh*
die Wiese, –n *meadow*
der Wille *will*
    Wo ein Wille ist, ist auch ein Weg. *Where there's a will, there's a way.*
Willkommen! *Welcome*
Willkommen heißen *to welcome somebody*
der Wind *wind*
der Winkel, – *corner; angle*
der Winter *winter*
der Wintermorgen *winter morning*
der Winzer, – *wine grower, vineyard owner*
wir *we*
wirklich *real(ly)*
    Nein wirklich nicht! *No, really not!*
die Wirtschaft *economy*
    wirtschaftlich *economic, economically*
der Wirtschaftsteil, –e *(newspaper) business section*
das Wirtschaftswachstum *economic growth*
wissen *to know (a fact)*
    Das sollten Sie wissen. *You should know this.*
der Wissenschaftler, – *scientist*
die Witwe, –n *(female) widow*
der Witwer, – *(male) widow*
der Witz, –e *joke*
    Du machst wohl Witze. *You must be joking.*
witzig *witty, funny*
wo *where*
die Woche, –n *week*
das Wochenende, –n *weekend*
die Wochenschau, –en *(TV) weekly news program*
der Wochentag, –e *day of the week*
woher *from where*
wohin *to where*
das Wohl *well-being; welfare*
    Zum Wohl! *To your health!, Cheers!*
wohl *probably*
wohnen *to reside, to live*
die Wohnung, –en *apartment*
    sozialer Wohnungsbau *subsidized apartments*
das Wohnviertel, – *residential area, residential quarter(s)*
das Wohnzimmer, – *living room*

die Wolke, –n *cloud*
wollen *to want (intention)*
    Wie Sie wollen. *As you wish.*
    Was will man mehr? *What more can one want (hope for)?*
wozu *what for*
wunderschön *beautiful, wonderful*
die Wunde, –n *wound*
das Wunder, – *miracle*
wundern (sich) *to be surprised*
der Wunsch, ̈–e *wish*
    auf Wunsch *if so desired, upon request*
wünschen *to wish*
    Sie wünschen? *What would you like?*
die Würde, –n *dignity*
    Die Würde des Menschen ist unantastbar. *The dignity of every individual is sacred.*
die Wurst, ̈–e *sausage*
    der Wurstaufschnitt *(no pl.) cold cuts*
die Wurzel, –n *root*
die Wurzelbehandlung, –en *root treatment*
wütend *furious*
wütend sein *to be furious*

X

x-mal *umpteen times*

Y

Ypsilon *the letter Y*

Z

die Zahl, –en *number*
zahlen *to pay*
    Zahlen bitte! *Check, please!*
zahllos *countless, innumerable*
die Zahlung, –en *payment*
der Zahn, ̈–e *tooth*
zahnlos *toothless*
die Zähne putzen *brushing teeth*
der Zahnarzt, ̈–e *male dentist*
    beim Zahnarzt *at the dentist's*
die Zahnärztin, –nen *female dentist*
der Zahnbelag *plaque*
die Zahnbürste, –n *toothbrush*
das Zahnfleisch *gum*
die Zahnmedizin *dentistry*
die Zahnpasta *tooth paste*
die Zahnschmerzen *toothache*
das Zahnweh *toothache*
die Zauberflöte, –n *magic flute*

der Zeh, –en *toe*
zehn *ten*
das Zeichen *sign, reference, signal*
zeichnen *to draw*
die Zeichnung, –en *drawing*
zeigen *to show*
die Zeit, –en *time*
    Zeit ist Geld. *Time is money.*
die Zeitschrift, –en *magazine*
die Zeitung, –en *newspaper*
der Zeitungsverlag, –e *newspaper publisher*
der Zement *cement*
das Zementwerk, –e *cement factory*
zentral *central*
das Zentrum, Zentren *center*
das Stadtzentrum *city center*
zerbrechen *to break*
zerfallen *to decay, to rot, to fall apart*
zerreißen *to tear apart*
zerren *to sprain, to tear, to pull*
die Zerrung, –en *sprain, strain*
zersetzen *to decompose*
    sich zersetzen *to disintegrate*
zerstören *to destroy*
die Zerstörung, –en *destruction*
der Zettel, – *(scrap) piece of paper*
der Zeuge, –n *witness*
zeugen *to give evidence*
das Zimmer, – *room*
das Zimmermädchen, –n *maid*
die Zimmernummer, –n *room number*
der Zimmerservice *room service*
die Zinsen (pl.) *interest*
der Zinssatz, ̈–e *interest rate*
die Zivilisation, –en *civilization*
der Zoll *customs*
die Zollerklärung, –en *customs declaration*
die Zone, –n *zone, area*
zu *at, to; too*
der Zucker *sugar*
zuerst *at first*
der Zufall, ̈–e *coincidence*
der Zug, ̈–e *train*
der Zugang, ̈–e *access*
zugeben *to admit*
Zugegeben! *Admittedly!*
zugreifen *to take the opportunity, to take advantage*
das Zuhause, – *home*
    zu Hause sein *to be at home*
zuhören *to listen*
zulassen *to permit*
    Das kann ich nicht zulassen! *I can't let you do that!*

die Zündkerze, –n *spark plug*
der Zündschlüssel, – *ignition key*
die Zündung, –en *ignition*
die Zukunft *future*
zukünftig *in the future*
der Zukunftsplan, ¨-e *future plan*
zuletzt *last of all*
zuliebe *in love of, for . . . sake*
zumindest *at least*
zunächst *first, first of all*
zurück *back*
zurückgehen lassen *to return food at a restaurant*
zurückgeben *to give back*
zurücklassen *to leave behind*
zurückrufen *to call back (phone)*
zurückzahlen *to reimburse*
zusammen *together*
    Zusammen oder getrennt?
    One check or separate?

die Zusammenarbeit *cooperation, collaboration*
zusammenbrechen *to break down, to collapse*
zusammenfassen *to sum up*
die Zusammenfassung, –en *synopsis, summary*
die Zusammenkunft, ¨-e *meeting*
zusammenlegen *to put together, to combine, to fold up*
zusammen liegen *to lie together*
zusätzlich *additional*
zuschauen *to watch*
der Zuschauer *viewer*
die Zuschauer *audience, viewers*
der Zuschauersport *spectator sport*
der Zuschlag, ¨-e *surcharge*
der Zuschuss, ¨-e *subsidy*

der Zustand, ¨-e *state (of being)*
zustoßen (jemandem etwas–) *happen to someone*
zuviel *too much*
zuvor *previously*
zwanzig *twenty*
    einundzwanzig *twenty-one*
zwei *two*
die Zweigstelle, –n *branch office*
zweiter, –e, –es *second*
die Zweitstimme, –n *second vote*
die Zwiebel, –n *onion*
der Zwilling, –e *twin*
zwingen *to force*
zwischen *between, among*
die Zwischenzeit *meantime*
    in der Zwischenzeit *in the meantime*
zwölf *twelve*

ENGLISH–GERMAN GLOSSARY

A

about *über (to talk)*
above *über*
academy *die Hochschule*
to accept *akzeptieren, annehmen*
to access *Zugang haben zu*
access *der Zugang*
account *das Konto, die Konten*
    anonymous bank account
    das Nummernkonto
    checking account *das*
    Scheckkonto, das Girokonto
    savings account *das*
    Sparkonto
to acquire *erwerben*
across *über*
act (in a play) *der Akt, -e*
actor *der Schauspieler*
actually *tatsächlich, wirklich*
to adapt *adaptieren, sich*
anpassen
address *die Adresse, -n*
    return address *der*
    Absender, -
to address (person, audience)
ansprechen, (letter) beschriften
adjacent *nahegelegen, nebenan,*
in der Nähe liegend
to admire *bewundern*
to admit *zugeben*
    Admittedly! *Zugegeben!*
adolescent *der/die Jugendlichle,*
-n/-n
to adore *anbeten, verehren*
advantageous *vorteilhaft*
advertising *die Werbung, -en*
    advertising slogan *der*
    Werbespruch, ¨-e
to afford *sich leisten*
after *nach, nachdem*
afternoon *der Nachmittag, -e*
afterward(s) *danach, nachher*
again *wieder*
against *gegen, wider, entgegen*
    to be against *dagegen sein*
age *das Alter*
ago *vor*
to agree *übereinstimmen,*
einverstanden sein, zustimmen,
jmdm. Recht geben
    Agreed! *Einverstanden!*
to agree with *jemandem Recht*
geben

to disagree with *nicht damit*
einverstanden sein
agreement *der Vertrag, ¨-e*
ahead *voraus*
airplane *das Flugzeug, -e*
    airplane passenger *der*
    Fluggast, ¨-e
airport *der Flughafen, ¨-*
airtight *luftdicht*
aisle *der Gang, ¨-e*
    middle aisle
    der Mittelgang, ¨-e
alarm clock *der Wecker, -*
album *das Album, Alben*
alcoholic beverage *das*
alkoholische Getränk
alive *lebendig*
all *alle, alles*
allergy *die Allergie, -n*
to allow *gestatten, erlauben*
alone *allein*
alphabet *das Alphabet*
Alps (the) *die Alpen*
already *schon, bereits*
also *auch*
to alter *ändern, abändern*
always *immer*
amazing *erstaunlich*
ambulance *der Krankenwagen, -*
America *Amerika*
American *der Amerikaner, -*
(male), die Amerikanerin, -nen
(female)
among *unter*
and *und*
anesthesia *die Betäubung, -en*
    local anesthesia *die örtliche*
    Betäubung
anger *der Ärger, -*
angry *böse, ärgerlich*
    to be angry *böse sein*
animal *das Tier, -e*
answer *die Antwort, -en, die*
Lösung, -en
to answer *antworten*
    answering machine *der*
    Anrufbeantworter, -
antique *die Antiquität, -en*
anyhow *sowieso, überhaupt*
anyone *jemand, irgendwer,*
irgendjemand
    Anything else? *Sonst noch*
    etwas?
apartment *die Wohnung, -en*

3-bedroom apartment
dieVierzimmerwohnung, -en
subsidized apartments
sozialer Wohnungsbau
to apologize *sich entschuldigen*
apparently *anscheinend*
appetite *der Appetit*
appetizer *die Vorspeise, -n*
apple *der Apfel, ¨-*
    apple juice *der Apfelsaft, ¨-e*
    apple juice with mineral
    water *die Apfelschorle, -n*
    apple strudel *der*
    Apfelstrudel, -
appliance (electrical) *das*
Elektrogerät, -e
application *die Bewerbung, -en,*
der Antrag, ¨-e
to apply *sich bewerben;*
anwenden
appointment (professional) *der*
Termin, -e, (with friends) die
Verabredung, -en
apprentice *der Auszubildende,*
-n, der Lehrling, -e
apprenticeship *die Lehre,*
-n; (fig.) die Lehrjahre (pl.)
April *der April*
apron *der Kittel (So. German),*
die Schürze
area *die Gegend, -en, die*
Umgebung, -en, der Bereich, -e
area code *die Vorwahl, die*
Vorwahlnummer, -n
argument *das Argument, -e*
arm *der Arm, -e*
arm chair *der Sessel, -*
to arrange *arrangieren*
to arrive *ankommen, eintreffen*
arrival *die Ankunft, ¨-e*
art *die Kunst, ¨-e*
    work of art *Kunstwerk, -e*
art museum *das Kunstmuseum,*
Kunstmuseen
artist *der Künstler, -*
article *der Artikel, -*
Ascension Day *Himmelfahrt*
ascent *der Aufstieg, -e*
to ascent *aufsteigen*
Ash Wednesday *der*
Aschermittwoch
ask *fragen*
asparagus *der Spargel*
aspirin *das Aspirin, -*

at *bei*
at the side of *an der Seite von*
to attach *beifügen*
attachment (letter, e-mail) *der Anhang, ̈-e*
to attack *angreifen*
to attend *besuchen, teilnehmen an*
attention *die Aufmerksamkeit, -en*
>**May I have your attention?** *Darf ich um Ihre Aufmerksamkeit bitten? (fml.)*
>**Attention!** *Achtung!*

attentive *aufmerksam*
attic *der Dachboden, ̈-*
attire *die Bekleidung, -en*
auction *die Auktion, -en*
auctioneer *der Auktionär, -e*
audience *die Zuschauer, das Publikum*
August *der August*
aunt *die Tante, -n*
great aunt *die Großtante, -n*
Austria *Österreich*
author *der Autor, -en*
automatic *automatisch*
automobile *das Auto, -s*
automobile mechanic *der Automechaniker, -*
automobile repair shop *die Autoreparaturwerkstatt, ̈-en*
autumn *der Herbst*
available *verfügbar, vorrätig*
average *der Durchschnitt*
awake *wach*
>**to keep awake** *wach halten*

to await *erwarten*
aware *bewusst*

B

bacteria *die Bakterie -Bakterien (pl.)*
back *zurück*
background *der Hintergrund, ̈-e*
backpack *der Rucksack, ̈-e*
bad *schlecht, böse*
>**Not bad!** *Nicht schlecht!*

bag *die Tasche, -n, die Tüte, -n*
>**shoulder bag** *die Umhängetasche*
>**sleeping bag** *der Schlafsack, ̈-e*

to bake *backen*
balcony *der Balkon, -e*
bald *Kahl*
bald head *die Glatze, -n*
ball *der Ball, ̈-e*
>**costume ball** *der Maskenball, ̈-e*

Baltic Sea *die Ostsee*
to ban *verbieten*
banana *die Banane, -n*
band *die Kapelle, -n*

bandage *die Binde, -n, der Verband*
>**elastic bandage** *die elastische Binde*

bank *die Bank, -en, das Kreditinstitut, -e*
>**savings and loan bank** *die Sparkasse, -n*
>**bank transfer** *die Banküberweisung, -en*
>**bank account** *das Bankkonto, -en*

bar *die Tafel (Schokolade), -n*
>**snack bar** *der Schnellimbiss, -e*

barbershop *der Friseursalon, -s, der Frisörsalon, -s, der Herrenfriseursalon, -s, der Herrenfrisörsalon, -s*
barber *der Friseur, -e, der Frisör, -e*
to bargain *handeln*
basic(ally) *grundsätzlich, grundlegend*
basis *die Basis, die Grundlage, -n*
bath *das Bad, ̈-er*
>**mineral bath** *das Mineralwasserbad, ̈-er*

to bathe *baden*
bathrobe *der Bademantel, ̈-*
bathroom *das Badezimmer, -, die Toilette, -n, die WC, -s*
bathtub *die Badewanne, -n*
battery *die Batterie, -n*
to be *sein*
to be available *frei sein*
to be in stock *vorrätig sein*
to be ready *fertig sein*
beach *der Strand, ̈-e*
bean *die Bohne, -n*
beard *der Bart, ̈-e*
to beat *schlagen*
beautiful *schön*
to beautify *verschönern*
beauty *die Schönheit*
because *weil, denn*
because of *wegen*
to become *werden*
bed *das Bett, -en*
bedroom *das Schlafzimmer, -*
beef *das Rindfleisch*
beer *das Bier, -e*
>**large Bavarian glass of beer** *die Maß (1–21)*

before *bevor, davor, vor*
behind *dahinter, hinter*
>**one behind the other** *hintereinander*

believable *glaubhaft*
to believe *glauben*
bell *die Glocke, -n*
bellhop *der Hotelpage, -n*
to belong *gehören*

belonging (personal) *der Privatgegenstand, ̈-e*
belt *der Gürtel, -*
>**baggage conveyor belt** *das Gepäckband, ̈-er*

beneath *under*
beside *neben*
besides *abgesehen davon, dass . . . , außer, außerdem, daneben*
best *am besten, der/die/das Beste, beste*
better *besser*
between *zwischen*
beverage *das Getränk, -e*
beyond *dahinter*
bicycle *das Fahrrad, ̈-er*
to bicycle *Rad fahren*
big *groß*
bill (money) *der Schein, -e*
bird *der Vogel*
>**Birds of a feather flock together.** *Gleich und gleich gesellt sich gern.*

birthday *der Geburtstag, -e*
birth place *der Geburtsort*
bit (a little) *das/ein Bisschen*
bitter *bitter*
black *schwarz*
blond *blond*
blood *das Blut*
>**Blood is thicker than water.** *Blut ist dicker als Wasser.*

blouse *die Bluse, -n*
to blow *blasen*
blue *blau*
board *die Tafel, -n*
to board *einsteigen*
boat *das Boot, -e, das Schiff, -e*
body *der Körper, -*
book *das Buch, ̈-er*
to book *buchen*
booked out *ausgebucht*
bookshelf *das Bücherregal, -e*
bookworm *die Leseratte, -n*
booth *die Kabine, -n, der Messestand, ̈-e*
border *die Grenze, -n, der Rand, ̈-er*
boring *langweilig*
born *geboren*
to borrow *leihen, borgen*
both *beide*
to bother *stören*
bottle *die Flasche, -n*
box *die Kiste, -n, der Karton, -s, die Packung, -en*
>**ballot box** *die Wahlurne, -n*
>**box seat** *der Logensitz, -e*
>**factory packing** *die Originalverpackung, -en*

boxing *das Boxen*
    boxing match *der Boxkampf, ¨-e*
boyfriend *der Freund, -e*
to brag *angeben, große Sprüche klopfen (coll.), große Töne spucken (coll.)*
brake *die Bremse, -n*
    brake pedal *das Bremspedal, -e*
to brake *bremsen*
bread *das Brot, -e*
to break *zerbrechen*
breakfast *das Frühstück, -e*
    including breakfast *inklusive Frühstück*
to breakfast *frühstücken*
breezy *luftig*
brick–layer *der Maurer, -*
bridal pair *das Brautpaar, -e*
bride *die Braut, ¨-e*
bridesmaid *die Brautjungfer, -n*
bright *hell*
to brighten *erhellen*
to bring *bringen*
    to bring along *mitbringen*
    What may I bring you? *Was darf ich Ihnen bringen?(waiter)*
to broadcast *übertragen, senden*
broken *kaputt*
broker *der Makler, -*
brook *der Bach, ¨-e*
brother *der Bruder, ¨-*
brother–in–law *der Schwager, ¨-*
brown *braun*
to browse *sich umsehen*
    I just want to browse. *Ich möchte mich nur umsehen. (store)*
brunette *brünett*
budget *das Budget, -s*
building *das Gebäude, -*
    old building *der Altbau, -ten*
    new building *der Neubau, -ten*
to burden *belasten*
to burn *brennen*
bus *der Bus, -se, der Omnibus, -se*
bus line *die Buslinie, -n*
bus stop *die Bushaltestelle, -n*
bus ticket *die Busfahrkarte*
business *das Geschäft, -e, die Firma, Firmen*
business card *die Visitenkarte, -n*
business discussion *die Geschäftsbesprechung, -en*
business section *der Wirtschaftsteil, -e (newspaper)*
busy *beschäftigt, besetzt (telephone)*
but *aber, sondern*

butter *die Butter*
button *der Knopf, ¨-e*
to buy *kaufen*
buyer *der Käufer, -, der Abnehmer, -*
by *bei, von, bis*
by the way *übrigens*

C

cab *die Taxe, -n; das Taxi, -s*
café *das Café, -s*
    coffee house *das Kaffeehaus, ¨-er*
    garden café *das Gartencafé, -s*
    sidewalk café *das Straßencafé, -s*
cake *der Kuchen, -*
    Dresden fruit cake *der Dresdner Stollen (Christmas)*
calculator (pocket) *der Taschenrechner, -*
to calculate *berechnen, kalkulieren*
call *der Anruf, -e*
    long–distance call *das Ferngespräch, -e*
to call *anrufen, rufen*
    to be called *heißen*
    to call back *zurückrufen (phone)*
calm *ruhig*
to calm *beruhigen, (jmdn.) besänftigen*
    to calm down *sich beruhigen*
camera *der Fotoapparat, -e*
campaign (political) *der Wahlkampf, ¨-e*
can *die Büchse, -n*
can (to be able to) *können*
Canada *Kanada*
Canadian *der Kanadier, -, die Kanadierin, -nen (female)*
candidate *der Kandidat, -en*
candy *das Bonbon, -s*
cap *die Mütze, -n, Kappe, -n*
    bathing cap *die Bademütze, -n*
car *das Auto, -s, der Wagen, -*
    dining car *der Speisewagen, -*
    sleeping car *der Schlafwagen, -*
    used car *der Gebrauchtwagen, -*
card (credit) *die Kreditkarte, -n*
card (post) *die Postkarte, -n*
care *die Sorge, -n*
to care *sich sorgen, sich interessieren*
carnival *der Karneval, Fasching*
carpenter *der Schreiner, -*

carpet *der Teppich*
    wall to wall carpet *der Teppichboden ¨-*
carrot *die Karotte, -n, Mohrrübe, -n*
case *der Fall, ¨-e*
    in any case *sowieso*
cash *das Bargeld*
cashier *der Kassierer, -*
casino *das Spielkasino, -s*
castle *die Burg, -en, das Schloss, ¨-er*
cat *die Katze, -n*
to catch *fangen*
cathedral *der Dom, -e, die Kathedrale, -n*
cause *der Grund, ¨-e*
cavity *die Karies*
ceiling *die Decke, -n*
to celebrate *feiern*
celebration *die Feier, -n*
celebrational *festlich, feierlich*
celery *die Sellerie*
cell phone *das Handy, -s*
cellar *der Keller, -*
cent *der Cent, -*
center *das Zentrum, Zentren, der Mittelpunkt, -e*
centigrade *Celsius*
ceramics *die Keramik*
ceremony *die Zeremonie, -n, die Feier, -n*
chain *die Kette, -n*
chair *der Stuhl, ¨-e*
champagne *der Champagner, -*
change *die Veränderung, -en, die Änderung, -en, der Wechsel, -, das Wechselgeld, -er*
to change *überwechseln, umsteigen, wechseln*
    to change one's clothes *sich umziehen*
    to change reservations *umbuchen*
    Keep the change! *Stimmt so!*
Channel Two *das Zweite Programm, ZDF*
chapel *die Kirche, -n, die Kapelle, -n*
charge *die Gebühr, -en*
    to charge extra *einen Aufschlag berechnen*
    to charge *berechnen*
cheap *billig*
cheaper *billiger*
check *der Scheck, -s, die Rechnung, -en*
    to cash a check *einen Scheck einlösen*
    Check, please! *Die Rechnung bitte! Zahlen bitte!*
    One check or separate? *Zusammen oder getrennt?*

to check *prüfen, überprüfen,
checken*
>> **to check the air** *die Luft
prüfen*
cheek *die Backe, -en*
Cheers! *Prost! Zum Wohl!*
cheese *der Käse*
cherry *die Kirsche, -n*
chicken *das Huhn, ¨-er*
child *das Kind, -er*
childlike *kindhaft*
chocolate *die Schokolade*
>> **bar of chocolate** *die Tafel
Schokolade*
choice *die Wahl*
to choose *wählen, auswählen*
Christmas *Weihnachten*
>> **Christmas Eve** *der
Heiligabend*
city *die Stadt, ¨-e*
>> **city center** *die Stadtmitte, -n,
das Stadtzentrum, Stadtzentren*
>> **city map** *der Stadtplan, ¨-e*
>> **city wall** *die Stadtmauer, -n*
>> **small town** *das Städtchen*
civilization *die Zivilisation, -en*
class *die Klasse, -n*
>> **first class** *erster Klasse, die
erste Klasse*
>> **First rate!** *Klasse!*
classes *der Unterricht*
to clean *putzen, reinigen*
>> **to clean/brush one's teeth**
sich die Zähne putzen
>> **to dry clean** *chemisch
reinigen*
>> **cleaning service** *der
Putzdienst, -e (hotel)*
cleaning *die Reinigung, -en*
>> **dry cleaning** *die chemische
Reinigung, -en*
>> **express dry cleaning** *die
Schnellreinigung, -en*
clear *klar*
clerk *der/die Angestellte, -n, -n*
>> **bank clerk** *der
Bankangestellte, -n, -n*
>> **postal clerk** *der
Postangestellte, -n, -n*
>> **reception clerk** *der
Empfangschef, -s*
to climb *aufsteigen, steigen*
clock *die Uhr, -en*
>> **alarm clock** *der Wecker, -*
clogged *verstopft*
cloister *das Kloster, ¨-*
close *nahe, eng verbunden*
to close *schließen*
closed *geschlossen*
closet *der Schrank, ¨-e*
closing *(sentence)
der Schlusssatz, ¨-e*

clothing *die Kleidung, die Kleider*
>> **men's clothing size** *die
Männergröße, -n*
>> **women's clothing size** *die
Frauengröße, -n*
cloud *die Wolke, -n*
cloudy *bewölkt*
coach (through) *der
Kurswagen, -*
coalition *die Koalition, -en*
>> **coalition government** *die
Koalitionsregierung, -en*
coast *die Küste, -n*
coat *der Mantel, ¨-*
coatrack *die Garderobe, -n*
code *der Kodename, -n, das
Kodewort, ¨-er, die Kodierung, -en*
coffee *der Kaffee*
>> **coffee house** *das
Kaffeehaus, ¨-er*
>> **coffee pot** *das Kännchen, -
(small)*
coin *die Münze, -n*
coincidence *der Zufall, ¨-e*
coins *das Kleingeld*
cold *die Erkältung, -en, die Kälte,
kalt*
>> **cold cuts** *der Aufschnitt*
collar *der Kragen, -*
college *die Universität, -en*
>> **to go to college** *studieren*
color *die Farbe, -n*
colorful *bunt*
coloring *das Färben*
to comb *kämmen*
>> **to comb one's hair** *sich die
Haare kämmen*
to come *kommen*
>> **to come by** *vorbeikommen*
>> **to come for a visit** *zu
Besuch kommen*
>> **to come from** *kommen aus
(+ dat.) (with locations)*
>> **Come in!** *Herein!*
>> **Come on!** *Komm schon!*
>> **How much does it come
to?** *Was/wie viel macht das?*
comedy *die Komödie, -n*
commentary *der Kommentar, -e*
common *gemein*
>> **to have something in
common** *etwas gemeinsam
haben*
company *der Konzern, -e, die
Firma, Firmen*
>> **large company** *der
Großkonzern, -e*
comparable *vergleichbar*
to compare *vergleichen*
comparison *der Vergleich, -e*
compartment *das Abteil, -e, das
Fach, ¨-er*

>> **inside compartment** *das
Innenfach, ¨-er*
>> **non-smoking
compartment** *das
Nichtraucherabteil, -e*
>> **outside compartment** *das
Außenfach, ¨-er*
compatible *kompatibel,
vereinbar*
to compete *wetteifern*
competition *der Wettbewerb, -e,
die Konkurrenz*
to complain *sich beklagen, sich
beschweren*
to complete *erfüllen, beenden*
complex *komplex*
computer *der Computer, -*
to concern *betreffen*
concern *der Konzern, -e*
>> **large concern** *der
Großkonzern, -e*
concert *das Konzert, -e*
>> **concert at a spa** *das
Kurkonzert, -e*
condition *die Bedingung, -en*
>> **under the condition** *unter
der Bedingung*
condominium *die
Eigentumswohnung, -en*
conductor *der Dirigent, -en*
confectionary
die Konditorei, -en
conference
*die Konferenz, -en, die Tagung, -en,
die Besprechung, -en*
to congratulate *gratulieren*
to connect *verbinden, Kontakt
aufnehmen*
connection *der Anschluss, ¨-e*
constantly *ständig*
constitution *die Verfassung, das
Grundgesetz*
consul *der Konsul*
consulate *das Konsulat, -e*
contents *der Inhalt, -e*
to contradict *widersprechen*
contrary (on the) *sondern, im
Gegenteil*
contrast *der Kontrast, -e*
convenience *die Annehmlichkeit,
-en, die Bequemlichkeit, -en*
convenient *angenehm, bequem,
passend*
convention *die Konferenz, -en,
die Tagung, -en*
conversation *die Unterhaltung,
-en, das Gespräch, -e*
to converse *sich unterhalten*
converter *der Umschalter, -, der
Transformator, -en*
cook *der Koch, ¨-e (male), die
Köchin, -nen (female)*

Too many cooks spoil the broth. *Zu viele Köche verderben den Brei.*
to cook *kochen*
to cooperate *kooperieren, zusammenarbeiten*
corn *der Mais, -*
corner *die Ecke, -n, der Winkel, -*
correct *richtig, korrekt*
    to be correct *stimmen, Recht haben*
cost *die Kosten*
    cost estimate *der Kostenvoranschlag, ¨-e*
to cost *kosten*
costume *die Tracht, -en*
couch *die Couch, -(e)s*
couchette *der Liegewagen, -*
cough *der Husten*
to cough *husten*
to count *rechnen*
country *das Land, ¨-er*
cousin *die Kusine, -n*
cousin *der Vetter, -n*
cow *die Kuh, ¨-e*
cozy *gemütlich*
craft *das Handwerk, -e*
craftsman *der Handwerker, -*
cream (whipped) *die Schlagsahne*
to create *gestalten, (er)schaffen*
credit *der Kredit, -e, die Einzahlung, -en (deposit)*
credit card *die Kreditkarte, -n*
crime drama/novel *der Krimi, -s*
Christmas *Weihnachten*
crisp *knusprig*
crooked(ly) *schief*
cross *das Kreuz, -e*
crown *die Krone, -n*
    gold crown *die Goldkrone, -n*
cruise *Die Kreuzfahrt, -en*
crunchy *knusprig, knirschend*
cucumber *die (Salat)Gurke, -n*
culture *Kultur, -en*
    mass culture *die Massenkultur*
culture section *das Feuilleton, -s (newspaper)*
cup *der Becher, -, die Tasse, -n*
    a cup of coffee *eine Tasse Kaffee*
curable *heilbar*
cure *die Heilung, -en*
curl *die Locke, -n*
curly *lockig*
currency *die Währung, -en*
current *laufend, aktuell ¨-e*
current (electrical) *der Strom,*
    alternating current (AC) *der Wechselstrom*

direct current (DC) *der Gleichstrom*
currently *augenblicklich, jetzt, zurzest*
custom *die Sitte, -n, die Tradition, -en, der Brauch, ¨-e, die Gewohnheit, -en*
customer *der Kunde, -n*
customer service *der Kundendienst, -e*
customs *der Zoll*
customs declaration *die Zollerklärung, -en*
customary *gewöhnlich*
to cut *schneiden*
cutlet *das Schnitzel, -*

D

dad *der Papa, -s*
daily *täglich*
    daily events *das Tagesgeschehen*
    daily grind *der Alltagsstress*
    daily news broadcast *die Tageschau*
    daily routine *die Tagesroutine, -n*
dairy product *das Milchprodukt, -e*
damage *der Schaden, -¨*
to damage *schaden, beschädigen*
    to be damaged *beschädigt sein*
to dance *tanzen*
dark *dunkel*
dark-haired *dunkelhaarig*
to darken *verdunkeln*
darling *der Schatz, ¨-e*
to dash off *losrennen*
daughter *die Tochter, ¨-*
    daughter-in-law *die Schwiegertochter, ¨-*
day *der Tag, -e*
    Good day. *Guten Tag*
deadline *der Termin, -e*
death *der Tod, -e*
debit *die Abhebung, -en, die Auszahlung, -en*
debt *die Schulden (pl.)*
to decide *entscheiden*
decision *die Entscheidung, -en*
    to make a decision *eine Entscheidung treffen*
    to participate in the decision *mitentscheiden*
to deceive *täuschen*
December *der Dezember*
deck (observation) *das Aussichtsdeck, -s*
to decompose *(sich) zersetzen*

defeat *die Niederlage, -en*
to define *definieren*
definitely *sicher, bestimmt*
to delete *löschen*
delay *die Verzögerung, -en*
delicate *empfindlich*
delicious *lecker*
delight *die Lust, ¨-e, die Freude, -n*
delivery *die Lieferung, -en*
    delivery van *der Lieferwagen, -*
    delivery service *die Zustellfirma, -firmen*
    delivery note *der Lieferschein, -e*
    delivery date *der Liefertermin, -e*
democracy *die Demokratie*
dentist *die Zahnärztin, -nen*
dentist *der Zahnarzt, ¨-e*
dentistry *die Zahnmedizin*
to deny *leugnen, ableugnen*
    That can't be denied. *Das lässt sich nicht leugnen.*
deodorant *das Deodorant, -s*
to depart *abfahren*
    to depart by airplane *abfliegen*
department *die Abteilung, -en*
departure *der Abflug, ¨-e*
to depend on *ankommen auf, sich verlassen auf*
to deposit *einzahlen*
to descend *absteigen*
descent *der Abstieg*
to describe *beschreiben*
desk *der Schreibtisch, -e*
dessert *der Nachtisch, -e, die Nachspeise, -n*
destination *das Reiseziel, -e*
detail *die Einzelheit, -en*
devil *der Teufel, -*
dialogue *der Dialog, -e*
difference *die Differenz, -en, der Unterschied, -e*
difficult *schwierig, schwer*
dignity *die Würde, -n*
dining room *das Esszimmer, -, das Speisezimmer, -*
diploma *das Abitur, das Diplom*
to direct *Regie führen (film)*
direction *die Richtung, -en*
directions *die Gebrauchsanweisung, -en*
direct(ly) *direkt*
director *der Regisseur, -e (film); der Direktor, -en*
dirty *schmutzig*
to disagree *nicht übereinstimmen, anderer Meinung sein*

Do you disagree? *Oder etwa nicht?*
to discuss *diskutieren, besprechen*
discussion *die Diskussion, -en*
disease *die Krankheit, -en*
dish *die Speise, -n (food)*
to disintegrate *sich zersetzen*
to dissolve *sich zersetzen, (sich) auflösen*
district *das Viertel, -*
to divide *teilen*
divorced *geschieden*
dizzy *schwindlig*
to do *machen, tun*
    to do calisthenics *Gymnastik machen*
    to do good *gut tun*
    to do someone's hair *frisieren*
doable *machbar*
dog *der Hund, -e*
donkey *der Esel, -*
door *die Tür, -en*
    front door *die Haustür, -en*
doorbell *die Türklingel, -n*
dope *der Tölpel, -*
double *doppel*
    double room *das Doppelzimmer, -*
down *herunter*
download *herunterladen*
dowry *die Mitgift*
draft *der Entwurf, ¨-e*
to draw *zeichnen*
drawing *die Zeichnung, -en*
dress *das Kleid, -er*
to dress *(jemanden) anziehen*
    local dress (costume) *die Tracht, -en*
    to get dressed *sich anziehen*
    to be dressed with *anhaben*
dresser *die Kommode, -n*
to drill *bohren*
to drink *trinken*
to drive *fahren, treiben*
driver *der Fahrer, -, die Fahrerin, -nen*
drop *der Tropfen, -*
drug dealer *der Drogenhändler, -*
druggist *der Drogist, -en (male), die Drogistin -en (female)*
drugstore *die Drogerie, -n*
    self–service drugstore *der Drogeriemarkt, ¨-e*
dry *trocken*
to dry *abtrocknen*
    to dry oneself *sich abtrocken*
due *fällig*
due to *wegen, auf grund von*
during *während*
dumpling *der Knödel, -*

dye *die Farbe, -n*
to dye *färben*
dyeing *das Färben*

E

each *jede, -r, -s*
    To each its own. *Jedem Tierchen sein Pläsierchen.*
early *früh*
to earn *verdienen*
earth *die Erde*
Easter *Ostern*
easterly, eastern *östlich*
to eat *essen*
economy *die Wirtschaft, -en*
edge *der Rand, ¨-er*
editor *der Redakteur, -e, der Lektor, -en*
editorial *die Redaktion, -en; der Leitartikel, - (part of newspaper)*
effect *der Effekt, -e*
egg *das Ei, -er*
either *entweder*
to elect *wählen*
election *die Wahl, -en*
    election result *das Wahlergebnis, -se*
    federal election *die Bundestagswahl, -en*
    local election *die Kommunalwahl, -en*
    state election *die Landtagswahl, -en*
electrician *der Elektriker, -*
elegant *elegant*
elevator *der Fahrstuhl, ¨-e*
else *noch*
e–mail *die E-Mail, -s, die Mail, -s (coll.)*
    to check e–mail *E-Mail abfragen*
    to answer e–mail *E-Mail beantworten*
    to forward e–mail *E-Mail weiterleiten*
to embarrass *(sich) blamieren*
embarrassing *peinlich*
embassy *die Botschaft, -en*
to emerge *aufkommen, sich ergeben*
emergency *der Notfall, ¨-e*
    emergency admission *die Notaufnahme, -n*
    emergency call *der Notruf, -e*
    emergency exit *der Notausgang, ¨-e*
emphasis *die Betonung, -en, die Hervorhebung, -en*
to emphasize *betonen, hervorheben, unterstreichen*

employer *der Arbeitgeber,-*
employment *die Beschäftigung, -en, die Stellung, -en*
    full–time employment *die Vollbeschäftigung, -en, die Ganztagsbeschäftigung, -en*
    part–time employment *die Teilzeitbeschäftigung, -en, die Halbtagsbeschäftigung, -en*
    temporary employment *die Aushilfsarbeit, -en*
empty *leer*
encyclopedia *das Lexikon, Lexika, die Enzyklopädie, -n*
to end *enden, beenden*
end *das Ende, der Schluss*
endless *endlos*
to endure *aushalten*
to enforce *durchsetzen*
engaged *verlobt*
engine *Motor, -en*
England *England*
to enjoy *genießen*
    enjoy yourself *viel Vergnügen*
enough *genug*
to enter *eintreten, hineinkommen, eingeben (computers)*
entrance *der Eingang, ¨-e*
entrance hall *die Empfangshalle, -n*
environment *die Umwelt*
equal *gleich*
equality *die Gleichheit*
to err *irren*
    To err is human. *Irren ist menschlich.*
escalator *die Rolltreppe, -n*
to escape *entkommen, fliehen*
especially *besonders*
esteem *die Achtung*
euro *der Euro, -*
even *sogar; gerade*
evening *der Abend, -e*
    Good evening. *Guten Abend.*
    in the evening *am Abend*
event *das Geschehen, der Vorfall, ¨-e*
eventually *endlich, schließlich*
ever *jemals, immer*
every *jede, -r, -s*
everybody *jeder*
everything *alles*
everywhere *überall*
exact(ly) *genau (adj./adv.)*
to exaggerate *übertreiben, dick auftragen (coll.)*
    over–exaggerate *große Reden schwingen (coll.)*
examination (pre–college) *das Abitur*

example das Beispiel, -e
> **for example** zum Beispiel

to examine prüfen
excellent ausgezeichnet
except for außer
exception die Ausnahme, -n
> **as an exception** ausnahmsweise

exciting (stimulating) anregend
exchange der Umtausch, ¨-e
to exchange umtauschen, eintauschen
> **exchange rate** der Wechselkurs, -e

excitement die Spannung, die Aufregung
exciting spannend
to excuse entschuldigen
> **Excuse me!** Entschuldigung!, Entschuldigen Sie! (fml.), Entschuldige! (infml.)

excuse die Entschuldigung, -en
exhausted erschöpft
> **to be exhausted** erschöpft sein

exhibition die Ausstellung, -en
> **special exhibition** die Sonderausstellung, -en

existence das Dasein
exit der Ausgang, ¨-e
to expect erwarten
expensive teuer
experience die Erfahrung, -en
to explain erklären
exquisite exquisit
eye das Auge, -n
eyeglasses die Brille, -n

F

fable die Fabel, -n
fabulous fantastisch, großartig
fair (trade) die Messe, -n
> **fairgrounds** das Messegelände

to fall fallen
false falsch
family die Familie, -n
famous berühmt
fan der Fan, -s
fantastic fantastisch
far weit, fern
> **How far is it?** Wie weit ist es?

far away weit weg, weit entfernt
fast schnell
fast-paced schnelllebig
fat fett
father der Vater, ¨-er
favorite liebste, -r, -s
February der Februar
Federal Constitutional Court
das Bundesverfassungsgericht

fee die Gebühr, -en, die Bankgebühr, -en (bank)
to feel like Lust haben
ferris wheel das Riesenrad, ¨-er
festival das Fest, -e
fever das Fieber,-
few (a) ein paar
to fight kämpfen
file die Datei, -en
to fill füllen
filling die Füllung, -en
> **gold filling** die Goldfüllung, -en

film der Film, -e
finally endlich
to find finden
fine fein, gut
finger der Finger, -
to finish abschließen, beenden
finished fertig
fire department die Feuerwehr, -en
first zuerst, als Erstes, Erste, -r, -e (pl.)
fish der Fisch, -e
fish market der Fischmarkt, ¨-e
to fit passen, anprobieren
flag die Fahne, -n
to flatter schmeicheln
flattering vorteilhaft
flea market der Flohmarkt, ¨-e
flexible flexibel
flight der Flug, ¨-e; die Flucht
> **return flight** der Rückflug, ¨-e

to flirt flirten
flood die Überschwemmung, -en
floor der Boden, ¨-, der Fußboden, ¨-, der Stock
> **first floor** das Erdgeschoss, das Parterre
> **second floor** der erste Stock
> **floor layer** der Bodenleger, -
> **wooden floor** der Holzfußboden, ¨-, das Parkett

flour das Mehl
flower die Blume, -n
to fly fliegen
fly die Fliege, -n
fog der Nebel, -
foggy neblig
to follow folgen
> **as follows** wie folgt

foot der Fuß, ¨-e
footer die Fußzeile, -n
for für
> **For me please ... ** Für mich bitte . . . (when ordering)

forehead die Stirn, -en
fork die Gabel, -n
to forbid verbieten
force der Zwang, ¨-e

to force zwingen
foreign ausländisch
forest der Wald, ¨-er
forever für immer, ewig
to forget vergessen
forgetful vergesslich
forgettable nicht wert, sich daran zu erinnern
form das Formular, -e
> **deposit slip** das Einzahlungsformular, -e
> **registration form** das Anmeldeformular, -e
> **withdrawal slip** das Auszahlungsformular, -e

formal förmlich
former ehemalig
fortune das Vermögen, -
four vier
four-door viertürig
France Frankreich
freedom Freiheit, -en
> **freedom of opinion** Meinungsfreiheit
> **freedom of the press** Pressefreiheit
> **freedom of religion** Religionsfreiheit

to freeze frieren
fresh frisch
Friday der Freitag
> **Good Friday** Karfreitag

friend die Freundin, -nen
friend der Freund, -e
friendly freundlich
friendship die Freundschaft, -en
frizzy kraus
from von, aus
> **from morning to evening** von morgens bis abends

front of (in) vor
fruit das Obst, die Frucht, ¨-e
to fulfill erfüllen
> **to fulfill a wish** einen Wunsch erfüllen
> **to fulfill an order** einen Auftrag erfüllen

full voll, satt (not hungry anymore)
fun der Spaß, ¨-e, das Vergnügen, -
function die Funktion, -en
to function funktionieren
funny witzig, lustig
furious wütend
> **to be furious** wütend sein

furniture die Möbel (pl.)
furniture style der Möbelstil, -e

G

gallery die Gallerie, -n
game das Spiel, -e

garage *die Garage, -n*
garden *der Garten, ¨-*
gate *der Flugsteig, -e (airport),
das Tor (garden)*
to get gas *tanken*
gasoline *das Benzin*
    gas pedal *das Gaspedal, -e*
    gasoline pump *die
Tanksäule, -n*
    gas station *die Tankstelle, -n*
geography *die Geographie*
genius *das Genie, -s*
gentleman *der Herr, -en, -en*
genuine *wahr, echt*
geranium *die Geranie, -n*
German *Deutsch, deutsch*
    High German *Hochdeutsch*
    Standard German
Hochdeutsch
Germany *Deutschland*
to get *bekommen*
    to get up *aufstehen*
    to get to know *kennen- lernen*
giant *der Gigant, -en, (adj./adv.)
gigantisch*
gift *das Geschenk, -e*
    gift purchase *der
Geschenkeinkauf, ¨-e*
girl *das Mädchen, -*
girlfriend *die Freundin, -nen*
to give *geben*
    to give a shot *eine Spritze
geben*
glacier *der Gletscher, -*
glad *froh*
gladly *gern*
glass *das Glas, ¨-er*
    glassblower *der Glasbläser*
glasses (eye) *die Brille, -n*
glorious *herrlich*
glove *der Handschuh, -e*
to go *gehen*
    to go by (means of) *fahren
mit*
    to go on vacation *in Urlaub
fahren*
    to go out *ausgehen*
goal *das Tor, -e (soccer);
das Ziel, -e*
goalie *der Torwart, -e*
gold *das Gold*
golden *golden*
good *gut*
    My Goodness! *Herrje!*
good–bye *Ade, auf Wiederhören,
auf Wiedersehen, Servus, Tschau,
Tschüs*
goose *die Gans, ¨-e*
gown *der Kittel, -, das Kleid, -er*
grade *die Note, -n*
graduate (pre–college) *der
Abiturient, -en*

to grant *bewilligen, gewähren*
grant *die Förderung, -en, das
Stipendium, Stipendien*
gram *das Gramm, -*
grammar *die Grammatik*
granddaughter *die Enkeltochter,
¨-, die Enkelin, -nen*
grandfather *der Großvater, ¨-
der Opa, -s*
grandmother *die Großmutter, ¨-
die Oma, -s*
grandparents *die Großeltern*
grandson *der Enkelsohn, ¨-e, der
Enkel, -*
grass *das Gras, ¨-er*
gratitude *die Dankbarkeit*
to grasp *begreifen*
gravel *der Kies*
gray *grau*
great *groß, großartig, prima!,
schön, fantastisch, toll (coll.)*
greatgrandmother *die
Urgroßmutter, ¨-*
greatgrandfather *der
Urgroßvater, ¨-*
Greece *Griechenland*
green *grün*
to greet *grüßen, begrüßen*
greeting *die Begrüßung, -en, der
Gruß, ¨-e*
gregarious *gesellig*
groceries *die Lebensmittel*
groom *der Bräutigam, -e*
grouch *der Muffel, -*
ground *der Boden, ¨-en, die Erde*
to grow *wachsen, anbauen*
guest *der Gast, ¨-e*
    guest of honor *der
Ehrengast, ¨-e*
    guest room *das
Gästezimmer, -*
gums *das Zahnfleisch*
gymnastics *die Gymnastik, das
Turnen*
    to do gymnastics *turnen*

H

hail *der Hagel*
to hail *hageln (weather)*
hair *das Haar, -e*
    hair color *die Haarfarbe, -n*
    hair dryer *der Haartrockner, -*
haircut *der Haarschnitt, -e*
hairdresser (female) *die
Friseuse, -n, die Frisöse, -n*
hairdresser (male) *der Friseur,
-e, der Frisör, -e*
hairdresser's (shop) *der
Friseursalon, -s, der Frisörsalon, -s*
hall *die Halle, -n*
    city hall *das Rathaus, ¨-er*

hallway *die Diele, -n, der Flur, -e,
der Gang, ¨-e*
half *halb*
    half a Kilo (500 gram) *ein
halbes Kilo*
ham *der (gekochte) Schinken*
    smoked ham (prosciutto)
der Räucherschinken
hand *die Hand, ¨-e*
to hand in *abgeben*
handicraft *das Handwerk, -e*
to hang up *auflegen, aufhängen*
to hang wallpaper *tapezieren*
handshake *der Handschlag*
    shake hands *die Haud geben*
handsome *gutaussehend*
to happen *passieren*
happy *glücklich*
happiness *das Glück*
harbor *der Hafen, ¨-*
hard *hart, schwer*
hard drive *die Festplatte, -n*
hardly *kaum*
hat *der Hut, ¨-e*
to haul *schleppen*
to have *haben*
    I'll have … *Ich
nehme . . . (when ordering)*
    to have a right *ein Recht
haben*
    to have an appointment
einen Termin haben
    to have supper *zu Abend
essen*
    to have use for something
für etwas Verwendung haben
head *der Kopf, ¨-e*
headache *die Kopfschmerzen,
das Kopfweh*
header *die Kopfzeile, -n*
headless *kopflos*
to heal *heilen*
health *die Gesundheit (no pl.)*
healthy *gesund*
to hear *hören*
heat *die Hitze*
heating *die Heizung, -en*
heaven *der Himmel, -*
heavy *schwer*
helicopter *der Hubschrauber, -*
hello *Grüezi, Grüß Gott, Hallo*
to help *helfen*
    to help with *helfen bei (+ dat.)*
    to help along *weiterhelfen*
help *die Hilfe*
Help (me)! *Hilfe!, Hilf mir!*
here *da, hier*
high *hoch, stark*
higher *höher*
highway *die Autobahn, -en*
    highway assistance *die
Straßenwacht*

hike *die Wanderung, -en*
    hike and climbing club *der Gebirgsverein, -e*
hill *der Hügel, -, der Berg, -e*
historic *geschichtlich*
history *die Geschichte*
hobby *das Hobby, -s*
hole *das Loch, ¨-er*
holiday *der Feiertag, -e, der Festtag, -e;*
    Christian holiday *der Kirchliche Feiertag*
    national holiday *der Nationalfeiertag*
holidays *die Ferien (school)*
home *das Heim, das Zuhause, das Haus*
home country *die Heimat*
homeland *das Heimatland*
homepage *die Homepage, -s*
homework *die Hausaufgabe, -n*
honest *ehrlich*
    to mean something honestly *etwas ehrlich meinen*
honesty *die Ehrlichkeit*
    Honesty is the best policy. *Ehrlich währt am längsten.*
to hope *hoffen*
hope *die Hoffnung, -en*
hopefully *hoffentlich*
horn *die Hupe*
horrible *schrecklich*
hospital *das Krankenhaus, ¨-er*
host *der Gastgeber, -*
hot *heiß*
hotel *das Hotel, -s*
hour *die Stunde, -n*
hours (for) *stundenlang*
house *das Haus, ¨-er*
how *wie*
however *aber*
hundred *hundert*
    one hundred *einhundert*
    two hundred *zweihundert*
hunger *der Hunger*
hurray *hurra*
hurry *die Eile*
    I'm in a hurry. *Ich bin in Eile. Ich habe es eilig.*
to hurry *sich beeilen, eilen*
to hurt *schmerzen, weh tun*
    to hurt somebody *schaden, verletzen*
    to hurt oneself *sich verletzen*
husband *der Mann, ¨-er, der Ehemann, ¨-er, der Gemahl, -e*
hygiene (personal) *die Körperpflege*

I

I *ich*
ice (cream) *das Eis*
icy *eisig*
ID *der Ausweis, -e*
idea *die Idee, -n, die Ahnung, -en (clue)*
    I have no idea! *Ich habe keine Ahnung!*
if *wenn*
ignition *die Zündung, -en*
    ignition key *der Zündschlüssel, -*
ill *krank*
illegal *illegal*
illness *die Krankheit, -en*
to imagine *sich vorstellen*
immature *unreif*
immediate(ly) *sofort*
immense *immens, groß*
impatient(ly) *ungeduldig*
to implement *in die Realität umsetzen*
impressive *imposant, eindrucks voll*
in *in*
inconvenience *die Unannehmlichkeit, -en, Lästigkeit, -en*
to increase *erweitern*
indifferent(ly) *egal*
    I'm quite indifferent about that. *Das ist mir egal.*
individual *individuell*
industrial *industriell*
industrialist *der Industrielle, -n*
industry *die Industrie, -n*
inflammation *die Entzündung, -en*
information *die Information, -en*
to inform *informieren*
    to inform oneself about *sich informieren über*
initial *die Initiale, -n*
to initiate *beginnen, veranlassen*
injured *beschädigt (thing), verletzt (person)*
to inquire *nachfragen*
inside *innen, innerhalb*
inspection *die Besichtigung, -en; die Prüfung, -en, die Kontrolle, -n*
instead (of) *(an)statt*
to instruct *orientieren, lehren*
insurance *die Versicherung, -en*
insured *versichert*
intelligent(ly) *intelligent*
intention *die Absicht, -en*
interest *das Interesse, -n*
interest *die Zinsen*
interesting *interessant*
interest rate *der Zinsatz, ¨-e*

interior *innen, das Innere*
interior design *die Innenausstattung, -en, das Interior Design, -s, die Innenarchitektur, -en*
interior designer/decorator *der Innenausstatter, -, der Innenarchitekt, -en*
intermission *die Pause, -n*
Internet *das Internet*
    Internet address *die Internetadresse, -n*
    Internet café *das Internet-Café, -s*
to interrupt *unterbrechen*
intersection *die Kreuzung, -en*
interview *das Interview, -s*
to interview *interviewen*
    interviewee *der/die Befragte, -n, -n, der Kandidat, -en, -en*
interviewer *der Interviewer, -, der Fragesteller, -, der Leiter, -es*
into *hinein, herein, in*
to introduce *vorstellen, einleiten*
introduction *die Einleitung, -en, die Vorstellung, -en*
to invest *investieren*
investment *die Investition, -en, das Investment, -s, die Anlage, -n*
iron (electrical) *das Bügeleisen, -*
iron (metal) *das Eisen, -*
to iron *bügeln*
irresistible *unwiderstehlich*
island *die Insel, -n*
to issue *ausstellen, lierausgeben*
Italy *Italien*

J

jacket *die Jacke, -n*
to jam *klemmen*
jam *die Marmelade, -n*
January *der Januar*
jazz *der Jazz*
jazz–club *der Jazzklub, -s, das Jazzlokal, -e*
jeans *die Jeans, -*
jewelry *der Schmuck (no pl.)*
job *die Arbeit, der Arbeitsplatz, ¨-e, der Job, -s, die Stellung, -en*
jobless *arbeitslos*
to join *mitmachen, Mitglied werden*
joke *der Witz, -e, der Scherz. -e*
journalism *der Journalismus*
journalist *der Journalist, -en*
journey *die Reise, -n*
judge *der Richter, -*
judgment *das Urteil, -e*
July *der Juli*
June *der Juni*
jury *die Jury, die Geschworenen, die Schöffen*

to justify *rechtfertigen*
just *einfach, gerade (time), gerecht*
just now *gerade eben*
justice *die Gerechtigkeit*
juvenile court *Jugendgericht*
juvenile *der/die Jugendliche, -n*

K

to keep *behalten, halten*
    to keep up/alive *aufrecht erhalten*
    to keep up with *mithalten mit*
key *der Schlüssel, -*
keyring *der Schlüsselbund, ¨-e*
kilo *das Kilo, -s*
    half a kilo *das Pfund, -e*
kilometer (km) *der Kilometer*
kind *die Art, -en, der Typ, -en; freundlich, nett, aufmerksam*
kindergarten *der Kindergarten, ¨-*
kindness *die Freundlichkeit, -en, die Güte*
king *der König,-e*
kiosk *der Kiosk, -e*
kiss *der Kuss, ¨-e*
kit (first-aid) *der Verbandskasten, ¨-*
kitchen *die Küche, -n*
    kitchen cabinet *der Küchenschrank, ¨-e*
knee, *das Knie, -*
knife *das Messer, -*
to knock *(an)klopfen*
to know *wissen, kennen*
    to get to know *kennenlernen*
    know-it-all *der Neunmalkluge, -n (coll.)*
knowledge *das Wissen, die Kenntnis, -se*
known *bekannt*

L

laceration *die Platzwunde, -n*
lady *die Dame, -n*
to lament *klagen*
lamb *das Lamm(fleisch)*
lamp *die Lampe, -n*
    reading lamp *die Leselampe, -n*
to land *anlegen (boat), landen (plane)*
to last *dauern*
late *spät*
later *später*
    See you later! *Bis später!*
large *groß*

laundry *die Wäsche*
law *das Recht, -e*
lawyer *der Jurist, -en, -en, der Rechtsanwalt, ¨-e*
to lay *legen*
to lead *führen*
lead *die Hauptrolle, -n*
leaf *das Blatt, ¨-er*
league *die Liga, -en*
to learn *lernen*
at least *wenigstens, zumindest*
leather *das Leder, -*
    (made) of leather *aus Leder*
to leave *weggehen, lassen, hinterlassen (Nachricht), verlassen*
    to leave behind *zurücklassen, hinterlassen*
left *links (direction)*
leg *das Bein, -e*
legend *die Legende, -n*
lemonade *die Limonade, -n*
to lend *leihen, ausleihen*
lent *die Fastenzeit*
to let *lassen*
letter *der Brief, -e*
    express letter *der Eilbrief, -e*
    registered letter *das Einschreiben, -*
level *die Ebene, -n*
library *die Bibliothek, -en*
    art library *die Kunstbibliothek, -en*
license *die Lizenz, -en*
licensing rights *die Lizenzrechte, -*
to lie *liegen*
life *das Leben*
life-saver *der Lebensretter*
lift (chair) *die Sesselbahn, -en*
light *das Licht, -er; leicht*
lightbulb *die Glühbirne, -en*
likable *sympathisch*
to like *mögen, gefallen (+ dat.), gern haben*
    What would you like? *Sie wünschen?*
    I like that. *Das gefällt mir!*
liked *beliebt*
likelihood *die Wahrscheinlichkeit, -en*
likely *wahrscheinlich, möglich*
line *die Leitung, -en; die Schlange (waiting line)*
linen *das Leinen*
    linen dress *das Leinenkleid*
lip *die Lippe, -n*
liquor *die Spirituosen (hard)*
to listen *hören*
liter *der Liter*
little *klein*
little bit (a) *ein bisschen*
    little bite *ein Bisschen*

to live *leben*
living room *das Wohnzimmer, -*
to load *aufladen, einladen, laden*
location *die Lage, -n; der Drehort, -e (film)*
lock *das Kombinationsschloss, ¨-er*
logical *logisch*
to log on/off *an/abmelden (computers)*
long *lang*
look *der Blick, -, der Ausblick, -e*
to look *gucken (So. German), blicken, aussehen*
    to look at *ansehen, anschauen, besichtigen*
    to look at one another *sich ansehen*
    to look at something *sich etwas anschauen*
    to look for *suchen*
    gut aussehen *to look good*
    Looks like it! *Es sieht so aus!*
to lose *verlieren*
lot (a) *eine Menge, viel*
loud *laut*
lounge *die Wartehalle, -n*
love *die Liebe*
luck *das Glück*
luggage *das Gepäck*
    luggage cart *der Gepäckwagen, -*
lunch *das Mittagessen, -*

M

magazine *die Zeitschrift, -en*
magnificent *großartig*
maid *das Zimmermädchen, -*
mail *die Post*
    air mail *die Luftpost*
    e-mail *die E-Mail, -s*
mailbox *der Briefkasten, ¨-*
main course *die Hauptspeise,-n*
major *bedeutend, der/die/das Haupt- . . .*
majority *der Hauptteil, -e, die Mehrheit, -en*
to make *machen, tun*
man *der Mann, ¨-er, der Mensch, -en, -en*
manager *der Geschäftsführer, -, der Manager, -*
manual *von Hand, manuell, nicht automatisch*
    manual dexterity *handwerkliches Geschick*
manufacturer *der Fabrikant, -en*
many *viele*
to march *aufziehen, marschieren*
mark *der Fleck, -en*
market *der Markt, ¨-e*

market analysis die Marktanalyse, -en
marmalade die Orangen-Marmelade, -n
married verheiratet
mass media die Massenmedia
massage die Massage, -n
master craftsman der Meister
material das Material, -ien
material materiell
matinee die Matinée, -n
mature reif
May der Mai
may (to be allowed to) dürfen
meadow die Wiese, -n
me mich, mir
meal das Essen, das Festessen
to mean meinen
    How do you mean (that)? Wie meinst du das? (infml.)
    Do you really mean that? Meinen Sie das wirklich? (fml.)
meat das Fleisch
    meatballs die Buletten, Fleischklößchen
medication das Medikament, -e, das Präparat, -e
medicine die Medizin, -en; das Mittel
medieval mittelalterlich
Mediterranean Sea das Mittelmeer
    Mediterranean island die Mittelmeerinsel, -n
to meet treffen
    to meet one another sich treffen
    to meet again (sich) wiedersehen
meeting die Verabredung, -en, das Treffen, die Zusammenkunft, ¨-e; die Besprechung, -en
member das Mitglied, -er (group); das Glied, -er (body)
membership die Mitgliedschaft, -en
memory die Erinnerung, -en
    in memory of zur Erinnerung an
menu die Speisekarte, -n
merchandise die Ware, -n
message die Nachricht, -en
messenger der Bote, -n
metal das Metall
middle die Mitte, -n
    in the middle of mitten auf/in (+ dat.)
Middle Ages das Mittelalter
midnight die Mitternacht, ¨-e
milk die Milch
million die Million, -en
    a million eine Million
millionaire der Millionär, -e

mine meiner, meine, meines
mineral water das Mineralwasser, -
minimal minimal, mindestens
minute die Minute, -n
miracle das Wunder, -e
to miss (train, appointment) verpassen
    to be missing fehlen
to misspell falsch schreiben
mistake der Fehler, -
Mister Herr (address)
mixed gemischt
to mix up durcheinander bringen
model das Modell, -e
molar der Backenzahn, ¨-e
mom die Mama, -s
moment der Moment, -e
    Just a moment! Einen Moment!, Augenblick, bitte!
Monday der Montag
money das Geld, -er
monstrous monströs
month der Monat, -e
moon der Mond, -e
more mehr
morning der Morgen, -e
    good morning guten Morgen
    in the morning morgens
mornings morgens
mortgage die Hypothek, -en
most meist, meistens, überwiegend
mostly überwiegend
mother die Mutter, ¨-
motorcycle das Motorrad, ¨-er
mountain der Berg, -e
    the mountains das Gebirge
    mountain railway die Bergbahn, -en
mouse die Maus, ¨-e
mouth der Mund, ¨-er
mouthwash das Mundwasser, -
to move bewegen, umziehen
move der Umzug, ¨-e
mover der Spediteur, -e
    moving company die Spedition, -en
movie der Film, -e
    movie fan der Filmenthusiast, -en,
much viel
    too much zu viel
mud der Lehm
    mud pack die Lehmpackung, -en
muggy schwül
mural die Wandmalerei, -en
museum das Museum, Museen
music die Musik
    classical music die klassische Musik

musician der Musiker, -
must (to have to) müssen
moustache der Schnurrbart, ¨-e
mustard der Senf
my mein
    for my sake (in regards to me) für mich, meinetwegen

N

name der Name, -n
to name nennen
    to name a beneficiary einen Nutznießer einsetzen
to narrate erzählen
narrow eng
near bei, nahe
neck der Nacken, -
necklace die Kette, -n
to need brauchen
negotiation die Verhandlung, -en
neighbor der Nachbar, -n
neighborhood die Nachbarschaft, -en; die Umgebung, -en, die Nähe
nephew der Neffe, -n
net das Netz, -e
new neu
    New Year Neujahr
    new year das neue Jahr
news die Nachricht(en)
    news broadcast die Nachrichten
newspaper die Zeitung, -en
newsstand der Kiosk, -e
never niemals, nie
next nächste, -r, -s, neben, der Nächste (the next), daneben (besides)
nice nett, schön
niece die Nichte, -n
night die Nacht, ¨-e
    at night nachts, in der Nacht
    Good night. Gute Nacht.
no nein
nobody niemand
noon der Mittag, -e
normally normalerweise
north der Norden, nördlich
North Sea die Nordsee
northerly, northern nördlich
nose die Nase, -n
not nicht
    not anymore nicht mehr
    Not at all! (Don't mention it!) Aber nicht doch!
    not at all gar nicht, überhaupt nicht
    not only . . . but also nicht nur . . . sondern auch
    not yet noch nicht
note die Notiz, -en

notebook
das Notizbuch, ¨-er
nothing nichts
notification die
Benachrichtigung, -en
to notify benachrichtigen (jmdn.),
ausrichten (jmdm.)
novel der Roman, -e
November der November
now jetzt
nowadays heutzutage
nowhere nirgendwo, nirgends
to numb betäuben
number die Nummer, -n, die
Zahl, -en;
    room number die
    Zimmernummer, -n
    wrong number falsch
    verbunden
numerous viele
nurse (female) die
Krankenschwester, -n
nurse (male) der Krankenpfleger

O

object der Artikel, -, der
Gegenstand, ¨-e
obvious offensichtlich
obviously offensichtlich, offenbar
ocean das Meer, -e
October der Oktober
odd seltsam
    odd number die ungerade
    Zahl
of von
    of course selbstverständlich
    in the course of während
offer das Angebot, -e
    special offer das
    Sonderangebot, -e
to offer anbieten
office das Büro, -s
    home office das
    Arbeitszimmer, -
    main post office die
    Hauptpost
    post office die Post, das
    Postamt, ¨-er
official der Beamte, -n, die
Beamtin, -nen
oil das Öl
ointment das Öl, -e,
die Salbe, -n
old alt
    old–fashioned altertümlich;
    unmodern, altmodisch
on an auf
    on top of auf (+ dat.)
    onto auf (+ acc.)
once einmal
    once more noch einmal
oneself selber, selbst

onion die Zwiebel, -n
only nur
open geöffnet
to open aufmachen, öffnen
    to open an account ein
    Konto einrichten/eröffnen
operator die Vermittlung
(telephone), der Bedienende
(usage)
to operate bedienen, betreiben
(machinery), operieren (medicine)
operation der Betrieb
(machinery), die Operation
(medicine)
    operation manual die
    Gebrauchsanweisung, die
    Bedienungsanleitung
opinion die Ansicht, -en; die
Meinung, -en
    opinion poll die
    Meinungsumfrage, -n
    in my opinion . . . meiner
    Meinung nach . . .
    matter of opinion die
    Meinungssache, die
    Ansichtssache
option die Option
or oder
orange die Apfelsine, -en, die
Orange, -n
orange juice
der Orangensaft, ¨-e
order der Auftrag, ¨-e, die
Ordnung
to order beauftragen, bestellen
    Would you like to order?
    Möchten Sie bestellen?
order confirmation die
Auftragsbestätigung
to orient oneself sich
orientieren
others andere
otherwise sonst
out hinaus/heraus
out of aus
    out of all (things)
    ausgerechnet
outside draußen, außerhalb (+
gen.)
over über
to oversleep verschlafen
overview der Überblick, -e
own eigen

P

to pack packen
package das Päckchen, - die
Verpackung, -en
pain die Schmerzen
to paint malen (art), streichen
(wall)
painter der Maler, -

painting das Gemälde, -, die
Malerei, -en
pair das Paar, -e
    a pair of socks ein Paar
    Socken
pale blass
panorama das Panorama, -s
pants die Hose, -n
paper (slip of) der Zettel, -
paprika der/das Paprika
parade der Umzug, ¨-e, die
Parade, -en
to parade aufziehen,
parents die Eltern
park der Park, -s
to park parken, parkieren (Swiss)
parking garage
das Parkhaus, ¨-er
parking lot der Parkplatz, ¨-e
part der/das Teil, -e
participant der Teilnehmer, der
Befragte, -n
to participate mitmachen,
teilnehmen(an)
particular besonders
partial(ly) anteilig, teilweise
partly teils, teilweise
party das Fest, -e
party (political) die Partei, -en
    splinter party die
    Splitterpartei, -en
to pass bestehen (exam),
überholen (traffic)
    to pass by vorbeigehen
    to pass one's time Zeit
    verbringen
passport der Pass, ¨-e, der
Reisepass, ¨-e
    passport control die
    Passkontrolle
pasta die Nudeln, die
Nudelspeisen
pastime die Freizeit
pastime activity die
Freizeitbeschäftigung, -en
pastry das Gebäck
path der Pfad, -e
pathological krankhaft
patience die Geduld
patient geduldig
patient (female) die Patientin,
-nen
patient (male) der Patient, -en
to pay bezahlen, begleichen
(Rechnung)
    to pay back zurückzahlen
    to pay out auszahlen
    down payment die
    Anzahlung, -en
pea die Erbse, -n
pear die Birne, -n
peculiar seltsam
pedestrian der Fußgänger, -

pedestrian zone *die Fußgängerzone, -n*
pedicure *die Fußpflege*
pedicurist (female) *die Fußpflegerin, -nen*
pedicurist (male) *der Fußpfleger, -*
Pentecost *Pfingsten*
people *die Leute*
pepper *der Pfeffer (spice), die Paprika schote, -n (bell pepper)*
performance *die Vorstellung, -en*
perhaps *vielleicht*
permanent wave *die Dauerwelle, -n*
to permit *gestatten, zulassen*
perseverance *die Ausdauer*
personal(ly) *persönlich*
pharmacist *der Apotheker, -, die Apothekerin, -nen*
pharmacy *die Apotheke, -n*
phone *das Telefon, -e*
phone booth *die Telefonzelle, -en*
phone number *die Rufnummer -n, die Telefonnummer, -n*
photo *die Aufnahme, -n, das Photo, -s, das Foto, -s*
photographer (male) *der Photograph, -en, der Fotograf, en*
photographer (female) *die Photographin, -nen, die Fotografin, -en*
to phrase *formulieren*
physician (female) *die Ärztin, -nen*
physician (male) *der Arzt, ¨-e*
to pick *aussuchen*
pickle *die Gurke*
picture *das Bild, -er*
piece *das Stück, -e*
pilot *der Pilot, -en*
pill *die Tablette, -n*
pillow *das Kissen, -*
pineapple *die Ananas*
pink *rosa*
place *der Platz, ¨-e*
to place *setzen, stellen*
plan *der Plan, ¨-e*
    seating plan *der Sitzplan, ¨-e*
to plan *planen*
planetarium *das Planetarium, -arien*
plaque *der Zahnbelag*
to plaster *verputzen, vergipsen*
plate *der Teller, -*
platform *der Bahnsteig, -e*
play *das Theaterstück, -e*
player (female) *die Spielerin, -nen*
player (male) *der Spieler, -*
to play *spielen*
playwright *der Dramatiker, -*

pleasant *angenehm*
please *bitte*
to please *gefallen*
    Pleased to meet you! *Freut mich!*
pleasure *die Lust, ¨-e, das Vergnügen, -*
    With pleasure! *Mit Vergnügen!*
plug (spark) *die Zündkerze, -n*
plum *die Pflaume, -n*
plumber *der Flaschner (So. German), -der Klempner, -*
point *der Punkt, -e*
    to get to the point *zur Sache kommen*
to point *zeigen*
to point out *hervorheben*
politically *politisch*
policeman *der Polizist, -en*
politician *der Politiker, -*
politics *die Politik*
poor *arm*
popular *beliebt*
population *die Bevölkerung, -en*
pork *das Schweinefleisch*
post office *die Post*
possibility *die Möglichkeit, -en*
postcard *die Ansichtskarte, -n*
postpone *verschieben*
pot *der Topf, ¨-e, der Kochtopf, ¨-e*
potato *die Kartoffel, -n*
    fried potatoes *die Bratkartoffeln*
    potato salad *der Kartoffelsalat*
    mashed potatoes *der Kartoffelbrei*
potential *potentiell*
potential (noun) *das Potential, die Möglichkeit, -en*
potter *der Töpfer, -*
pottery *die Töpferei*
pound *das Pfund, -e*
powder *der Körperpuder, -*
preferably *lieber*
pregnancy *die Schwangerschaft, -en*
pregnant *schwanger*
preparation *das Präparat, -e*
to prescribe *verschreiben, vorschreiben*
to preserve *erhalten*
to pretend *so tun als ob, vortäuschen*
president *der Präsident, -en*
press *die Presse*
pretty *hübsch*
price *der Preis, -e*
    price range *die Preislage, -n*
prize *der Preis, -e*
prize recipient *der Preisträger, -, die Preisträgerin, -nen*

probably *wahrscheinlich, wohl*
problem *das Problem, -e*
profession *der Beruf, -e*
    What's your profession? *Was sind Sie von Beruf? (fml.)*
professor (male) *der Professor, -en*
professor (female) *die Professorin, -nen*
program *das Programm, -e*
    cable program *das Kabelfernsehprogramm, -e*
to promenade *promenieren, spazieren gehen*
to promise *versprechen*
prospect (for a profession) *die Berufsaussicht, -en*
prune *die Backpflaume, -n*
pub *die Gaststätte, -n; das Lokal, -e*
public *öffentlich*
    public transportation *öffentliche Verkehrsmittel*
punctual *pünktlich*
purchase *der Einkauf, ¨-e*
purse *die Geldbörse, -n, die Tasche, -n*
to put *setzen, stecken, stellen, legen*
    to put on (clothes) *anziehen*
    not to put up with *sich (etwas) nicht gefallen lassen*

Q

quadruple *vierfach*
quality *die Qualität*
quantity *die Quantität, -en*
quarter *das Viertel, -*
query *die Anfrage, -en*
question *die Frage, -en*
    That's out of the question! *Das Kommt (überhaupt) nicht in Frage!*
    Without question!/Without a doubt! *Ohne Frage!*
to question *fragen*
quick *schnell*
quiet *ruhig, still*
    Be quiet! *Sei doch still!*
to quiet *beruhigen*
quite *ganz, ziemlich*
quiz (review) *die Wiederholungsprüfung, (die klassenarbeit, -en), -en*

R

radio *das Radio, -s*
railroad *die Bahn, -en, die Eisenbahn, -en*
rain *der Regen*
to rain *regnen*
raincoat *der Regenmantel, ¨-*

rapid *rapide, schnell*
rare *selten, rar*
rarety *die Rarität, -en*
rash *der Ausschlag, ¨-e*
rather *sondern; ziemlich*
razor *der Rasierapparat, -e*
reachable *erreichbar*
ready *fertig*
real *real, wirklich, echt*
reality *die Wirklichkeit, -en*
really *wirklich*
    Do you really mean that?
    Ist das ihr Ernst?
reasonable *preisgünstig;
vernünftig*
to rebuild *umbauen*
receipt *die Quittung, -en*
reception *der Empfang, ¨-e, die
Rezeption, -en*
reception clerk (male) *der
Empfangschef, -s*
reception clerk (female) *die
Empfangsdame, -n*
to receive *empfangen, erhalten,
bekommen*
receiver (telephone) *der Hörer, -*
receiver (of mail) *der
Empfänger, -*
recipe *das Rezept, -e*
recognition *die Anerkennung, -en*
to recognize *erkennen,
wiedererkennen*
to recommend *empfehlen*
    What do you recommend?
    Was empfehlen Sie?
    The chef recommends . . .
    der Küchenchef empfiehlt . . .
to recuperate *sich erholen*
red *rot*
reddish *rötlich*
red wine *der Rotwein, -e*
refreshing *erfrischend*
refrigerator *der Kühlschrank, ¨-e*
refund *die (Kosten)erstattung, -en,
die Rückerstattung, -en*
to refund *zurückzahlen*
to register *(sich) eintragen*
registrar's office *das
Standesamt, ¨-er*
regular(ly) *regelmäßig*
to reimburse *zurückzahlen*
relative *der/die Verwandte, -n, -n*
to relax *sich ausruhen, erholen,
sich entspannen*
relaxation *die Erholung, die
Entspannung*
reliable *zuverlässig*
religion *die Religion, -en*
to rely upon *sich verlassen auf*
remarkable *bemerkenswert*
remittance order *der
Überweisungsauftrag*

to remodel *umbauen*
to remove *entfernen*
to renovate *renovieren*
rent *die Miete, -n*
    rent with utilities included
    die Warmmiete
    rent without utilities *die
    Kaltmiete*
    rent deposit, security *die
    Kaution, -en*
to rent out *vermieten*
rental car *der Mietwagen, -*
to repair *reparieren*
to replace *ersetzen*
to report *berichten*
to represent *vertreten*
Republic (Federal) *die
Bundesrepublik*
reputation *der Ruf*
to request *bitten, anfordern*
request *die Bitte, -n,
die Anfrage, -n*
to require *benötigen*
to reserve *reservieren, bestellen*
reservation *die Reservierung, -en*
reserved *reserviert*
to reside *wohnen*
resident (local) *der/die
Einheimische, -n*
resistable *widerstehlich*
resort (health) *der Badeort, -e,
der Kurort, -e*
respect *die Achtung, der Respekt*
to respect *respektieren*
responsible *verantwortlich*
responsibility *die
Verantwortung, -en*
to rest *sich ausruhen, sich erholen*
rest *die Erholung*
rest room *die Toilette, das WC*
restaurant *das Restaurant, -s*
restless *unruhig*
to restore *restaurieren*
restoration *die Restaurierung, -en*
result *das Ergebnis, -se*
    election result *das
    Wahlergebnis, -se*
return *die Rückkehr*
to return *zurückkommen,
zurückkehren*
reunification *die
Wiedervereinigung*
to reward *belohnen*
rice *der Reis*
rich(ly) *reich*
to ride *fahren, (horse) reiten*
ridiculous *lächerlich*
right *rechts, richtig*
    the right thing *das Richtige*
    I have just the right thing!
    *Ich habe genau das Richtige.
    (store)*

    All right then! *Also gut! Na
    schön!*
right (n.) *das Recht, -e*
    to be right *Recht haben*
    basic rights *die Grundrechte*
    right to vote
    das Wahlrecht, -e
    right to assembly *das
    Versammlungsrecht, -e*
    right to possession *das
    Eigentumsrecht, -e*
right *rechts (direction)*
right away *sofort*
rightfully *rechtmäßig*
ring *der Ring, -e*
to ring *läuten*
ripe *reif*
river *der Fluss, ¨-e, der Strom, ¨-e*
roast *der Rostbraten, -, der
Braten, -*
rock *der Felsen, -, der Stein, -e*
role *die Rolle, -n*
roll *das Brötchen, -*
romantic *romantisch*
roof *das Dach, ¨-er*
roofer *der Dachdecker, -*
room *der Raum, ¨-e, das Zimmer, -*
    child's room *Kinderzimmer, -*
    double room *das
    Doppelzimmer, -*
    fitting room *die
    Umkleidekabine, -n*
    laundry room *die
    Waschküche, -n*
    living room *das
    Wohnzimmer, -*
    single room *das
    Einzelzimmer, -*
    room service *der
    Zimmerservice*
    waiting room *das
    Wartezimmer, -*
roomy *geräumig*
root *die Wurzel, -n*
    root canal *der Wurzelkanal, ¨-e*
Rose Monday *der Rosenmontag
(Monday before Lent)*
rough *stürmisch, rauh*
routine *die Routine, -n*
to rub *(ein)reiben*
rug *der Teppich, -e*
ruin *die Ruine, -n*
to run *laufen, rennen*
to run away *weglaufen*

S

safe *sicher*
safety *die Sicherheit, -en*
sailboat *das Segelboot, -e*
salad *der Salat, -e*
salami *die Salami, -s*

salary *das Gehalt, ¨-er*
sale *der Verkauf, ¨-e*
sales figures *die Verkaufszahlen*
salesman *der Verkäufer, -*
saleswoman *die Verkäuferin, -nen*
salt *das Salz, -e*
salve *die Salbe, -n*
sample *das Beispiel, -e, das Muster, -*
sand *der Sand*
sandwich *das Butterbrot, -e*
sandy *sandig*
Saturday *der Samstag, Sonnabend*
    Saturday edition (of the newspaper) *die Samstagsausgabe, -n*
sauerkraut *das Sauerkraut*
sausage *die Wurst, ¨-e*
to save *sparen (money), speichern (a computer file), retten (someone)*
to say *sagen*
scale *die Waage, -n*
scarf *der Schal, -s*
scene *die Szene, -n*
schedule *der Plan, ¨-e, der Fahrplan, ¨-e (bus, train)*
school *die Schule, -n*
    elementary school (up to 4th grade) *die Grundschule*
    junior high (5th to 9th grade) *die Hauptschule*
    middle school (5th to 10th grade) *die Realschule*
    inclusive school (1st to 10th grade) *die Gesamtschule*
    high school (10th to 13th grade) *das Gymnasium, Gymnasien*
    vocational school *die Berufsschule*
    special needs school *die Sonderschule, -n*
scientist *der Wissenschaftler, -*
scissors *die Schere, -n*
to scold *schimpfen mit*
score *das Ergebnis, -se*
scream *der Schrei, -e*
to scream *schreien*
screw *die Schraube, -n*
sculptor *der Bildhauer, -*
sculpture *die Bildhauerei, die Plastik -en, die Skulptur, -en*
sea *die See, das Meer, -e*
seaside *am Meer*
to search for *suchen*
season *die Jahreszeit, -en; die Spielzeit, -en (Sport)*
    vacation season *die Feriensaison*

seat *der Platz, ¨-e*
    backseat *der Rücksitz, -e*
    front seat *der Vordersitz, -e*
seaweed *der Seetang*
second *die Sekunde, -n*
secret *das Geheimnis, -se*
secretary (female) *die Sekretärin, -nen*
secretary (male) *der Sekretär, -e*
secure *sicher*
securities (stock exchange) *die Pfandbriefe*
security *die Sicherheit, -en, Geborgenheit (comfort)*
to see *sehen*
    See you later! *Bis später!*
seldom *selten*
self *selbst, selber*
to sell *verkaufen*
to send *schicken; senden*
    to send off *abschicken*
    to send to *schicken an (+ acc.)*
sender *der Absender, -*
sensitive *empfindlich*
sentence *der Satz, ¨-e*
to separate *teilen, trennen*
September *der September*
serious *ernst*
    Are you serious? *Ist das dein Ernst? (infml.)*
to take seriously *ernst nehmen*
seriousness *der Ernst*
to serve *servieren*
service *der Dienst, -e*
to set *setzen*
several *einige*
severe *streng, hart*
sexy (attractive) *sexy*
shall (to be supposed to) *sollen*
shampoo *das Shampoo, -s*
to share *teilen*
to shave *(sich) rasieren*
    to shave off *abrasieren*
    to shave the neck *ausrasieren*
shaving cream *die Rasiercreme, -s*
shelf *das Regal, -e*
shelter *der Schutz, das Heim*
shepherd (boy) *der Hirten(junge), -n*
to shine *scheinen*
ship *das Schiff, -e*
shipping department *der Versand*
shipping trade *die Schifffahrt (marine)*
shirt *das Hemd, -en*
shock *der Schreck, -en*
shoe *der Schuh, -e*

shop *das Geschäft, -e*
    coffee shop *das Café, -s*
    flower shop *das Blumengeschäft, -e*
    pizza shop *die Pizzeria, Pizzerien*
to shop *einkaufen*
shopping *Einkäufe machen*
    shopping list *die Einkaufsliste, -n*
    shopping center *das Einkaufszentrum, -zentren*
shore *die Küste, -n*
short *kurz*
    on short notice *kurzfristig*
short list *die engere Auswahl, -en*
shot *die Spritze, -n*
shoulder *die Schulter, -n*
to show *zeigen*
shower *die Dusche, -n*
to shower *duschen*
    to take a shower *sich duschen*
shrimp salad *der Krabbensalat, -e*
to shut *zumachen, schließen*
to shut down (computers) *beenden, abschließen, herunterfahren*
shy *schüchtern*
siblings *die Geschwister*
sick *krank*
side *die Seite, -n*
side dish *die Beilage, -n*
sight *die Sicht, der Ausblick, -e*
sights *die Sehenswürdigkeiten*
sightseeing tour *die Besichtigungstour, -en*
sign *das Schild, -er*
silence *die Ruhe*
silk *die Seide, -n*
silly *dumm, albern*
silver *das Silber*
silverware *das Besteck, -e*
similar *ähnlich*
simple *einfach*
to sin *sündigen*
since *seit*
sincerely *Mit freundlichen Grüßen*
singer *der Sänger*
single (not married) *ledig*
singly (piece by piece) *einzeln*
sink *der Ausguss, ¨-e*
sister *die Schwester, -n*
    sister-in-law *die Schwägerin, -nen*
to sit *sitzen*
    Sit down! *Setzen Sie sich! Setz dich! Setzt euch!*
size *die Größe, -n*
to ski *Ski laufen, Ski fahren*

skiing vacation *der Skiurlaub, -e*
skill *die Fähigkeit, -en, die Kenntnis, -se*
skirt *der Rock, ¨-e*
sky *der Himmel, -*
slacks *die Hose, -n*
to sleep *schlafen*
    sleepyhead *die Schlafmütze (coll.)*
slender *schlank*
sliced *geschnitten*
    not sliced *im/am Stück*
slight *wenig, nur, gering(fügig)*
small *klein*
to smile *lächeln, schmunzeln*
smoker *der Raucher, -*
smooth *glatt*
snow *der Schnee*
to snow *schneien*
snowfall *der Schneefall, ¨-e*
snuff *der Schnupftabak*
soap *die Seife, -n*
soap opera *die Seifenoper, -n*
soccer *der Fußball, ¨-e*
    soccer field *das Fußballfeld, -er*
    soccer team *die Fußballmannschaft, -en*
    soccer match *das Fußballspiel, -e*
    soccer stadium *das Fußballstadion, -stadien*
social sciences *die Sozialwissenschaft, -en*
sock *die Socke, -n*
socket (electric) *die Steckdose, -n*
sofa *das Sofa, -s*
soft *weich, leise (not loud)*
soft drink *das alkoholfreie Getränk, -e*
sold out *ausgebucht, ausverkauft*
solution *die Lösung, -en*
    solution suggestion *der Lösungsvorschlag, ¨-e*
to solve *lösen*
some *einige, ein paar, etwas*
somehow *irgendwie*
someone, somebody *jemand, irgendwer*
something *etwas, irgendetwas*
sometimes *manchmal*
somewhere *irgendwo*
son *der Sohn, ¨-e*
    son-in-law *der Schwiegersohn, ¨-e*
soon *bald*
    as soon as possible *baldmöglichst*
sorrow *die Sorge, -n*
Sorry! *Verzeihung! Entschuldigung! Es tut mir leid!*
to sound *klingen, lauten*

soup *die Suppe, -n*
sour *sauer*
southerly, southern *südlich*
souvenir *das Andenken, -*
spa *der Badeort, -e, der Kurort, -e*
spacious *geräumig*
Spain *Spanien*
to speak *reden, sprechen*
speaker *der Redner, -*
specialty *die Spezialität, -en*
spectator sport *der Zuschauersport*
speech *die Rede, -n*
to speed *rasen*
speed limit *die Geschwindigkeitsbegrenzung*
speedometer *der Tacho, -s, der Tachometer, -*
to spend *ausgeben (Geld), verbringen (Zeit)*
spinach *der Spinat*
splendid *glänzend*
splendor *die Pracht*
spoiled *verkorkst (coll.), verwöhnt (child)*
spoilsport *der Spielverderber, -*
spoon *der Löffel*
sport *der Sport*
    sports club *der Sportverein, -e*
    to engage in sports *Sport treiben*
    sports section (of the newspaper) *der Sportteil*
spot *der Fleck, -en*
sprain *die Zerrung, -en*
to sprain *zerren*
spring *der Frühling; die Quelle, -n*
    medicinal spring *die Heilquelle, -n*
to sprinkle *streuen*
square *der Platz, ¨-e*
stable *stabil*
stability *die Stabilität*
stack *der Stapel, -*
stadium *das Stadion, Stadien*
stage *die Bühne, -n*
stain *der Fleck, -en*
stairs *die Treppe, -n*
staircase *das Treppenhaus, ¨-er*
stamp *die Briefmarke, -en*
to stand *stehen*
to start *beginnen, anfangen, starten*
starter *der Anlasser, -*
state *der Staat, -en*
to state *angeben*
statement *der Kontoauszug, ¨-e (bank); die Angabe, -n (making a statement)*
station (train) *der Bahnhof, ¨-e*
station (radio or TV) *der*

Sender, -
stay *der Aufenthalt, -e*
to stay *bleiben*
to steam *dampfen*
steamboat *der Dampfer, -*
    steamboat trip *die Dampferfahrt, -en*
steel (stainless) *der (Edel)stahl*
steep *steil*
to stick to *stecken, kleben*
still *trotzdem, immer noch*
still water *stehendes Gewässer, -*
to stipulate *verordnen, festsetzen*
to stitch (a wound) *nähen*
stock exchange *die Börse, -n*
stock *die Aktie(n)*
stomach *der Bauch, ¨-e, der Magen, -*
stomachache *die Magenschmerzen, die Bauchschmerzen*
to stop *halten, stehenbleiben, aufhören*
storage (room/space) *der Abstellraum, ¨-e*
storm *der Sturm, ¨-e*
    storm warning *die Sturmwarnung, -en*
    violent storm *das Unwetter, -*
to storm *stürmen*
stormy *stürmisch*
stove *der Herd, -e*
straight *gerade*
    straight ahead *geradeaus*
strange *seltsam*
street *die Straße, -n*
    side street *die Nebenstraße, -n*
    main street *die Hauptstraße, -n*
street car *die Straßenbahn, -en*
strenuous *anstrengend*
strike *der Streik, -s*
striking *eindrucksvoll*
strong *stark, kräftig*
strudel *der Strudel, -*
to struggle *kämpfen*
student (male) *der Student, -en*
student (female) *die Studentin, -nen*
studies *das Studium, Studien*
to study *studieren*
to stumble *stolpern*
stupid *dumm*
style *der Stil*
subject *das Fach, ¨-er*
subordinate *untergeordnet*
to subsidize *fördern, unterstützen*
subsidy *die Förderung, -en*
subway *die U-Bahn, -en*
success *der Erfolg, -e*
successful *erfolgreich*

such *solche*
suddenly *plötzlich*
to suffer *leiden*
to suffer from *leiden an*
to suffice *genügen*
sufficient *genügend*
sugar *der Zucker*
to suggest *vorschlagen*
suggestion *der Vorschlag, ¨-e*
suit *der Anzug, ¨-e*
to suit *passen*
suitcase *der Koffer, -*
summer *der Sommer*
summit *der Gipfel, -*
sun *die Sonne, -n*
    sun protection oil *das Sonnenschutzöl, -e*
sunburn *der Sonnenbrand, ¨-e*
Sunday *der Sonntag*
sunny *sonnig*
sunscreen (lotion) *die Sonnenschutzcreme, -s*
sunshine *der Sonnenschein*
suntan *die Bräune*
superfluous *überflüssig*
to supervise *überwachen, beaufsichtigen*
supervisor (male) *der Vorgesetzte, -n*
supervisor (female) *die Vorgesetzte, -n*
supermarket *der Supermarkt, ¨-e*
supper *das Abendessen, -*
supplier *der Lieferant, -en*
to support *unterstützen*
support *die Unterstützung, -en*
supporting role *die Nebenrolle, -n*
surcharge *der Aufschlag, ¨-e, der Zuschlag, ¨-e*
    spa surcharge *die Kurtaxe, -n*
surface *die (Ober)Fläche, -n*
surplus *das Überangebot, der Überschuss*
surprise *die Überraschung, -en*
to surprise *überraschen*
suspense *die Spannung*
    crime (suspense) TV series *die Krimiserie, -n*
to swallow *einnehmen, schlucken*
to swamp *überschütten*
swamp *der Sumpf*
sweater *der Pullover, -*
sweet *süß, lieb*
    How sweet of you! *Wie lieb von dir! (infml.)*
sweets *die Süßwaren*
swelling *die Schwellung, -en*
swimming (to go) *schwimmen gehen*

to switch (channels) *umschalten*
Switzerland *die Schweiz*
syllable *die Silbe*
symptom *das Symptom, -e*

T

table *der Tisch, -e*
    The table is set! *Der Tisch ist gedeckt!*
table lamp *die Tischlampe, -n*
to take *bringen; einnehmen; nehmen*
    to take a picture *aufnehmen*
    to take a seat *sich setzen*
    to take advantage *zugreifen*
    to take off *ausziehen (clothing), starten (plane)*
    to take out (stains) *entfernen*
    to take place *stattfinden*
    to take an opportunity *eine gelegenheit ergreifen*
to talk *reden, sprechen*
    to talk about *sprechen über (+ acc.)*
    to be talked into *sich überreden lassen*
talk *das Gespräch, -e*
task *die Aufgabe, -n*
taste *der Geschmack, ¨-er*
to taste *schmecken*
tasteful *geschmackvoll*
tax *die Steuer, -n*
    tax cut *die Steuersenkung, -en*
    tax increase *die Steuererhöhung, -en*
taxi *das Taxi, -s*
Taxi stand *der Taxistand, ¨-e*
tea *der Tee, -s*
to teach *lehren, unterrichten*
teacher *der Lehrer, -*
team (sport) *die Mannschaft, -en, das Team, -s*
to tear *zerren*
teeth *die Zähne; das Gebiss, -e (set of)*
    brushing teeth *die Zähne putzen*
telephone *das Telefon, -e, der Apparat, -e*
by telephone *telefonisch*
    coin-operated telephone *der Münzfernsprecher, -*
    over the telephone *telefonisch*
    telephone book *das Telefonbuch, ¨-er*
    telephone conversation *das Telefongespräch, -e*
    telephone card *die Telefonkarte, -n*

telephone number *die Telefonnummer, -n*
to telephone *telefonieren*
    to reach by telephone *telefonisch erreichen*
television *das Fernsehen, -*
television set *der Fernsehapparat, -e*
to tell *erzählen*
    to tell about *erzählen von (+ dat.)*
    Tell me! *Sag mal!*
teller *der/die Bankangestellte, -n, -n*
temperature *die Temperatur, -en*
    highest average temperature *durchschnittliche Höchsttemperatur*
    lowest average temperature *durchschnittliche Tiefsttemperatur/ Niedrigsttemperatur*
tenant *der Mieter, -*
tendon *die Sehne, -n*
terrace *die Terrasse, -n*
terrible *furchtbar, schlimm*
to test *überprüfen*
than *als*
to thank *danken*
    Thank you! *Danke*
    Thank you from the heart! *Herzlichen Dank!*
    Many thanks! *Vielen Dank!*
    Thanks a million! *Tausend Dank!*
thanks *der Dank*
that *dass, das*
theater *das Theater, -*
    court theater *das Hoftheater, -*
    state theater *das Staatstheater, -*
    municipal theater *das Stadttheater, -*
    theater box office *die Theaterkasse, -n*
theatergoer *der Theaterbesucher, -*
theft *der Diebstahl, ¨-e*
then *dann*
there *da, dort*
    over there *dort drüben*
    (to) there *dorthin*
    up there *da oben*
thereafter *danach*
therefore *darum, deswegen, deshalb*
these *dieser*
thief (male) *der Dieb, -e*
thief (female) *die Diebin, -nen*
thing *die Sache, -n; das Ding, -e*
to think *denken*

to think of denken an (+ acc.)

to think about nachdenken, (sich) überlegen

thin dünn

this dieser, diese, dieses

thorough(ly) sorgfältig, genau, gründlich

those jene

thought der Gedanke, -n

thousand tausend

thread der Faden, ¨-

threatening bedrohlich

thrilling spannend

throat der Hals, ¨-e

sore throat die Halsschmerzen, das Halsweh

through durch

throughout überall, in ganz . . .

thunder der Donner

thunder and lightning, thunderstorm das Gewitter, -

Thuringia Thüringen

Thursday der Donnerstag

thus somit, so, auf diese Art

ticket die Fahrkarte, -n

tie die Krawatte, -n

tiler der Fliesenleger, -

time die Zeit

closing time (store) der Ladenschluss

halftime die Halbzeit, -en

many times x-mal

several times mehrmals

short time die Weile

three times a day dreimal täglich

in time rechtzeitig

Time is money. Zeit ist Geld.

What time is it? Wie spät ist es?

tip das Trinkgeld, -er

tire der Reifen, -

tired müde, erschöpft

tiredness die Müdigkeit

tiring ermüdend

title der Titel, -

to an, nach, zu

tone der Ton, ¨-e

speaking in such a tone einen (solchen) Ton anschlagen

I won't accept this kind of tone. Ich verbitte mir diesen Ton.

to tip over umstoßen

today heute

toe der Zeh, -en

toenail der Fußnagel, ¨-e, der Zehennagel

together zusammen, gemeinsam

to tolerate vertragen

toll die Straßenbenutzungsgebühr

tomato die Tomate, -n

tomorrow morgen

tomorrow morning morgen früh

toolbox der Werkzeugkasten, -

tooth der Zahn, ¨-e

front tooth der Vorderzahn, ¨-e

wisdom tooth der Weisheitszahn, ¨-e

toothache die Zahnschmerzen (pl.), das Zahnweh

toothbrush die Zahnbürste, -n

toothless zahnlos

toothpaste die Zahnpasta, Zahnpasten

top die Spitze, -n, der Gipfel, -

topical aktuell

torte die Torte, -n

tour (group) die Gruppentour, -en

tour (guided) die Führung, -en

tourism der Tourismus, der Fremdenverkehr

tourist der Tourist

tourist center das Touristenzentrum

to tow abschleppen

toward nach

towel (bath/beach) das Handtuch, ¨-er; das Badetuch, ¨-er

tower der Turm, ¨-e

town die Stadt, ¨-e

old town die Altstadt, ¨-e

small town die Kleinstadt, ¨-e

town hall das Rathaus, ¨-er

totally absolut, total

trace die Spur, -en

track (educational) der Bildungsweg; -e, das Gleis (train)

track and field die Leichtathletik

trade das Handwerk

traffic der Verkehr

traffic free zone die verkehrsfreie Zone

traffic jam der Verkehrsstau, -s

traffic rule die Verkehrsregel, -n

traffic sign das Verkehrsschild, -er

trail der Pfad, -e

trailer der Anhänger, -

train der Zug, ¨-e, die Bahn, -en

short distance train der Nahverkehrszug, ¨-e; der Personenzug, ¨-e

to train ausbilden (professionally), trainieren (sport)

trainee der Auszubildende, -n

training die Ausbildung, -en

to transfer (money) überweisen

transformer der Transformator, -en

transport der Transport, -e

transportation (means of) die Transportmöglichkeit, -en

travel die Reise, -n

travel agency das Reisebüro, -s

travel bag die Reisetasche, -n

travel guide der Reiseführer, - (book)

to travel reisen

traveler der/die Reisende, -n, -n

treasure der Schatz, ¨-e

to treat behandeln

treatment die Kur, -en

tree der Baum, ¨-e

trial (court) das Verfahren, -, die Verhandlung, -en

to trim stutzen

trip die Reise, -n

round-trip hin und zurück

triple dreifach

tropical tropisch, Tropen-

trouble der Ärger, -, das Problem, -e

truck der Lastwagen, -

true wahr

to be true stimmen

to try versuchen

to try on anprobieren

Tuesday der Dienstag

turkey die Pute, -n (female), der Truthahn, ¨-ne (male)

to turn (to make a turn) abbiegen

to turn on einschalten

twin der Zwilling, -e

U

umbrella der Schirm, -e

unacceptable nicht akzeptabel

unable unfähig

unbelievable unglaublich

uncertain unsicher

uncle der Onkel, -

unclear unklar

under unter

to underline unterstreichen

to understand verstehen

understanding das Verständnis, -se

to undress ausziehen

to get undressed sich ausziehen

unemployment die Arbeitslosigkeit

unforgettable unvergesslich

unfortunate bedauerlich, unglücklich, unselig

unfortunately leider, unglücklicherweise

unhappy *unglücklich*
unification *der Vereinigung, -en*
unimaginable *unvorstellbar*
uninteresting *uninteressant*
union *die Gewerkschaft, -en*
unit *die Einheit, -en*
united *vereint*
unity *die Einigkeit*
university *die Universität, -en, die Hochschule, -n*
to unload *ausladen, abladen*
unknown *unbekannt*
unpleasant *unangenehm*
unsafe *unsicher, gefährlich*
unsuccessful *erfolglos*
until *bis*
unique *einzigartig*
up *auf, her-/hinauf*
upholstery *die Polsterung*
upper *obere, -r, -s*
upstairs *oben*
urgent *dringend*
us *uns*
usage *der Gebrauch, ¨-e*
to use *benutzen, gebrauchen*
useful *nützlich*
useless *nutzlos*
user *der Benutzer, -, der Verbraucher, -*
user-friendly *benutzerfreundlich*
usual *normal, gewöhnlich, üblich*
utilities *die Nebenkosten, Strom-, Heiz- und Telefonkosten*
utmost *äußerst*

V

vacation *der Urlaub, -e; die Ferien (pl.)*
 seaside vacation *der Badeurlaub, -e*
 skiing vacation *der Skiurlaub*
 vacation spot *der Urlaubsort, -e*
 in need of a vacation *urlaubsreif*
vaccination *die Impfung, -en*
valid *gültig*
validity *die Gültigkeit, -en*
valley *das Tal, ¨-er*
value *der Wert, -e*
varied *unterschiedlich*
variety *die Vielfalt (no plural); die Vielzahl (no plural)*
various *verschieden, unterschiedlich*
vase *die Vase, -n*
VCR *das Videogerät, -e, der Videorekorder, -*
veal *das Kalbfleisch*
vegetarian *der Vegetarier, -*

vegetable *das Gemüse*
to verify *(auf seine Richtigkeit) prüfen, überprüfen*
versatile *vielseitig*
versatility *die Vielseitigkeit*
very *sehr*
victory *der Sieg, -e*
video *das Video, -s, die Videokassette*
to view *besichtigen, (sich) ansehen*
village *das Dorf, ¨-er*
vine *die Rebe, -n*
vineyard *das Weingut, ¨-er*
vintage *der Prädikatswein, -e, der Jahreswein, -e, Antik-; Jahrgang*
to visit *besuchen*
visit *der Besuch*
visitor *der Besucher, -*
visitor (spa) *der Kurgast, ¨-e*
vocable *die Vokabel, -n*
vocabulary *das Wörterverzeichnis, -se*
void *ungültig*
volt *das Volt, -*
vote *die Stimme, -n*
to vote *wählen*
 right to vote *das Wahlrecht*
 vote (to cast one's) *seine Stimme abgeben, zur Urne gehen, wählen*
voter (female) *die Wählerin, -nen*
voter (male) *der Wähler, -*
 voter turnout *die Wahlbeteiligung*

W

to wait *warten*
 to wait for *warten auf (+ acc.)*
waiter *der Kellner, -*
waitress *die Kellnerin, -nen*
to wake *wecken*
 to wake up *aufwachen*
to walk *gehen, spazieren gehen*
walk *der Spaziergang, ¨-e*
 walking speed *das Schritttempo*
wall *die Wand, ¨-e*
wallpaper *die Tapete, -n*
to wander *wandern*
to want to *wollen*
wardrobe *der Kleiderschrank, ¨-e*
warm *warm*
to warm up *aufwärmen*
warmth *die Wärme*
to warn *warnen*
warning *die Warnung, -en*
warranty *die Garantie, -n, der Garantieschein, -e*

to wash *waschen*
 to wash by hand *mit der Hand waschen*
 to wash (oneself) *sich waschen*
watch *die Armbanduhr, -en*
to watch *beobachten, (zu)sehen, zuschauen*
to watch TV *fernsehen*
water *das Wasser, ¨-*
water pipe *die Wasserleitung, en*
waterway *der Schifffahrtsweg, -e*
wave *die Welle, -n*
wavy *wellig*
way *der Weg, -e*
 one way *einfach*
 one-way street *die Einbahnstraße*
weak *schwach*
to wear *tragen*
 wearable *tragbar*
weather *das Wetter*
weather report *der Wetterbericht, -e*
weaver *der Weber, -*
weaving *das Weben, -, die Weberei, -*
web page *die Web-Seite, -n*
wedding *die Hochzeit, -en*
 wedding ceremony *die Trauung, -en*
 church wedding *die kirchliche Trauung*
 civil wedding *die standesamtliche Trauung*
 wedding anniversary *der Hochzeitstag, -e*
Wednesday *der Mittwoch*
week *die Woche, -n*
 day of the week *der Wochentag, -e*
to weigh *wiegen*
well *gut; die Quelle, -n*
westerly, western *westlich*
 farther west *weiter westlich*
wet *nass*
what *was*
when *als, wann, wenn*
whenever *wenn*
where *wo*
 from where *woher*
 where (to) *wohin*
whether *ob*
which *welche, -r, -s*
while *die Weile, während*
white *weiß*
white wine *der Weißwein, -e*
Whitsuntide *Pfingsten*
who *wer*
whom *wem (dat.), wen (acc.)*
why *warum*
wide *weit, breit*

widow *der Witwer, -,*
die Witwe, -n
wife *die Frau, -en, die Ehefrau,*
-en, die Gemahlin, -nen
will *der Wille*
Where there's a will,
there's a way. *Wo ein Wille*
ist, ist auch ein Weg.
willing *bereit*
willingly *gern*
to win *gewinnen*
wind *der Wind, -e*
window *das Fenster, -*
window *der Schalter, - (bank,*
post office)
wine *der Wein, -e, der Sekt*
(sparkling)
wine cooler (spritzer) *die*
Weinschorle, -n
winner *der Sieger, -*
winter *der Winter, -*
winter morning *der*
Wintermorgen
to wish *wünschen*
wit *die Schlagfertigkeit (no plural)*
witch *die Hexe, -n*
with *bei, mit*
without *ohne*
witness *der Zeuge, -n/-n, die*
Zeugin, -nen
to witness *bezeugen; miterleben*
witty *witzig*

woman *die Frau, -en*
women's size *die*
Frauengröße, -n (clothing)
to wonder *(sich) wundern; sich*
fragen
woods *der Wald, ¨-er*
word *das Wort, -e*
world *die Welt, -en*
worldwide *weltweit*
work *die Arbeit, -en*
flexible working hours *die*
Gleitzeit
non-flexible working time
die Kernarbeitszeit
to work *arbeiten*
worker (foreign) *der*
Gastarbeiter, -
to be worried *besorgt sein*
to worry *Sorgen haben*
to be worth *wert sein*
wound *die Wunde, -n*
wrapping *die Verpackung, -en*
to write *schreiben*
to write about *schreiben*
über (+ acc.)
to write to *schreiben an (+*
acc.)

X ray *die Röntgenaufnahme, -n,*
das Röntgenbild, -er

yacht *die Jacht, -en*
to yawn *gähnen*
year *das Jahr, -e*
yearly *jährlich*
yeast *die Hefe*
to yell *schreien*
yellow *gelb*
yes *ja*
yesterday *gestern*
yet *schon, noch*
not yet *noch nicht*
to yield *Vorfahrt gewähren*
Yield *Vorfahrt beachten!*
yield *die Rendite*
yogurt *das/der Jog(h)urt*
you *du, Sie, ihr*
young *jung*
your *dein, Ihr*
youth *die Jugend*

zero *null*
not feeling up to doing
anything *null Bock haben*
(coll.)
ZIP code *die Postleitzahl, -en*
zipper *der Reißverschluss, ¨-e*

GERMANY

SWITZERLAND

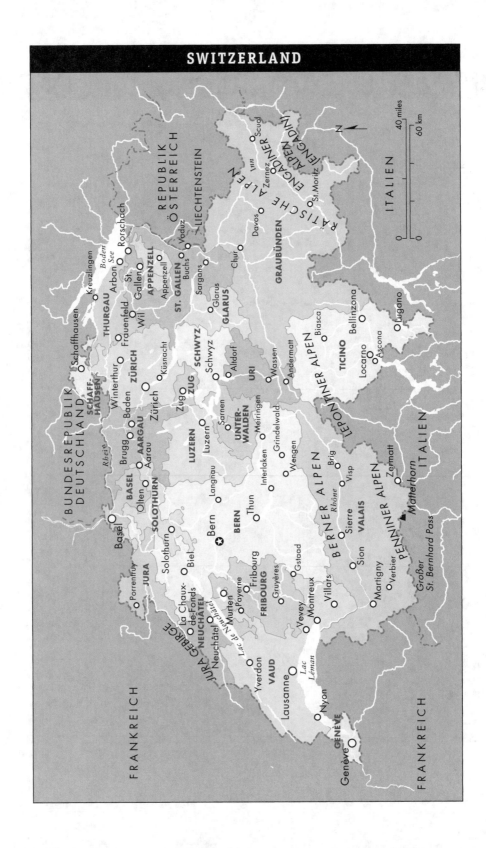

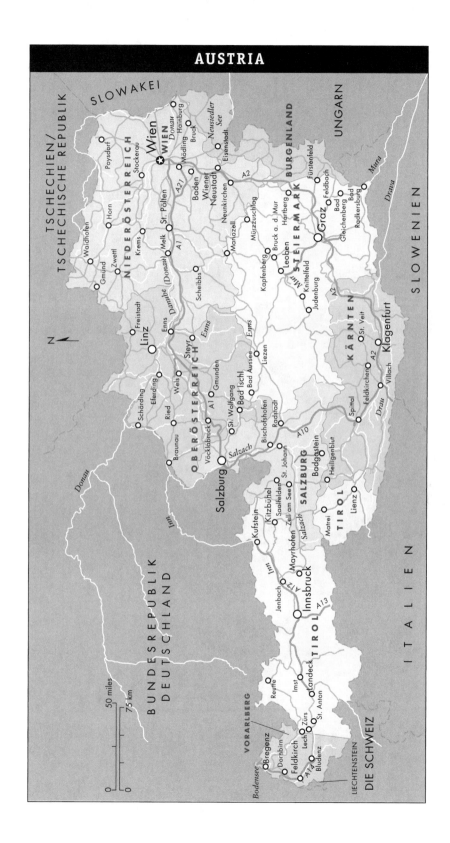

AUSTRIA

INDEX